BIBLE CHARACTERS

THE GREAT AND THE NOT SO GREAT

366 Daily Devotionals

By David Meengs

Bible Characters,
The Great and the Not So Great
By David Meengs
English

Copyright 2013
© Biblical Counseling Trust of India

All Scripture quotations are from the NIV unless otherwise mentioned.

ISBN - 978-0-9849619-1-7

Published and distributed by:
    Biblical Counselling Trust Of India,
    Plot No.1, Muthu Mari Amman Koil Street,
    Madhavaram, Chennai - 600 060.
    India.
    E-mail: bcworldwide@hotmail.com

Printed in the USA by Dickinson Press Inc.

Dedication

This book is dedicated to our dear grandchildren: Amber, Erika, Jacob, Sydney, Samuel, Shelby, Nathan, Josie, Emily, Abigail, and Ian. We thank God for placing you into our covenant family! You are precious to God and to us. May you grow into godly characters for the King of kings. May you learn from these Bible characters how to live as a child of God.

Grandpa and Grandma
David and Mary Meengs

"Therefore we also, since we are surrounded by so great a cloud of witnesses, let us lay aside every weight, and the sin which so easily ensnares us, and let us run with endurance the race that is set before us."
Hebrews 12:1 NKJV

Bible Characters

The Great and the Not So Great

366 Daily Devotionals

Thank You

First and foremost, thanks to our loving God for giving us a Bible full of great counseling examples to guide us in life's journey. We also thank God for opening our eyes to the truth that never changes! He is so gracious to us His children.

Thank you to my life partner, my dear wife Mary. She is a good example of what a believer in Christ should look like. Our 43 years of marriage have been wonderful. She has been patient in reading and rereading as she edited the devotions in this publication and in many others. She has corrected mistakes and has given good advice when something was not said as well as it could have been. There are so many helpful comments that are hers. Thanks also to daughter Becky who spent so much of her time looking at these devotions, checking references and helping to find mistakes before you do.

Thank you to the staff in India who have been a big blessing. They have taken care of so many day to day details, so that I could concentrate on writing devotionals like this one and also teach. Particular thanks to Sherine, the manager of The Biblical Counselling Trust of India. Thanks also to Jansy, our publication manager, who does so much to get publications out in various languages.

Again we want to thank our God who has written our names on His hand before the creation of the world. He is the One who calls us and equips us to serve Him and His church. He has blessed us, protected us and encouraged us every step of the way!

The Author,
David Meengs

January

Day	Text	Title of the Devotional
1.	Genesis 1:27	Adam, made in the image of God
2.	Genesis 2:22-23	Eve, the mother of all the living
3.	Genesis 3:1	Eve, the first to sin
4.	Genesis 3:21	Adam and Eve, the first to be restored
5.	Genesis 4:6-7	Cain's long-faced devotion
6.	Hebrews 11:4	Abel's righteous sacrifice
7.	Genesis 5:24	Enoch, God's walking friend
8.	Genesis 5:27	Methuselah, lived long, but *"he died"*!
9.	Genesis 6:20	Noah, a picture of God's grace
10.	Matthew 24:37	Noah, a picture of God's judgment
11.	Genesis 9:12-13	God's (and our) rainbow in the clouds
12.	Gen. 9:18a & 19b	Noah's sons, fathers of many nations
13.	Genesis 9:22	Ham's sin teaches us to honor our fathers!
14.	Genesis 11:4	*"Us,"* build a monument to self
15.	Genesis 13:8-11a	Lot lives by sight
16.	Gen. 13:4b & 18	Abram lives by faith
17.	Genesis 16:2	Hagar, Sarai's bad advice!
18.	Genesis 17:7	Abraham, father of many by covenant
19.	Luke 17:32	Lot's wife, missed the kingdom
20.	Luke 17:32	Lot's wife, one with many privileges
21.	1 Peter 3:5-6	Sarah, a beautiful woman of hope
22.	Genesis 17:19b	Isaac, the son of promise
23.	Genesis 19:30-32	Lot's daughters, poor choices, again!
24.	Genesis 20:2-3	Abimelech warned; Sarah protected
25.	Genesis 22:1a	Abraham's faith, tested again
26.	Genesis 23:19	Abraham buried his beloved Sarah
27.	Genesis 24:14a	Eliezer's prayer for a girl is answered
28.	Genesis 27:6	Rebekah, so beautiful yet so deceptive
29.	Genesis 25:18	Ishmael, the "hostile" son
30.	Gen. 25:21b-23	Jacob and Esau, the difference
31.	Genesis 26:6-7	Isaac's failure to trust in God

February

March

Day	Text	Title of the Devotional
1.	Exodus 35:30-31	Bezalel, a craftsman chosen by God
2.	Leviticus 10:1-2	Nadab's naughty worship
3.	Numbers 12:1-2	Moses, he also had family problems
4.	Numbers 12:1-3	Miriam, gifted, but so much self-importance!
5.	Numbers 13:1-2	Twelve spies go to investigate
6.	Numbers 16:8-9	Korah's occupy priesthood movement
7.	Numbers 23:25-26	Balaam cannot curse God's people!
8.	Numbers 35:6a	The Levites' city of refuge points to Jesus
9.	Deuteronomy 6:4-9	Israel's advice on raising children
10.	Joshua 1:9	Joshua, strong and courageous
11.	Joshua 2:10-11	Rahab's statement of faith
12.	Joshua 7:20-21a	Achan's suicidal greed
13.	Joshua 14:8b	Caleb follows God wholeheartedly
14.	Judges 1:6-7	Adoni-Bezek loses his thumbs and big toes
15.	Judges 3:17	King Eglon, a picture of Israel's fat sins
16.	Judges 5:5-7	Deborah, a mother in Israel
17.	Judges 6:14-16a	Gideon, a humble man of God
18.	Judges 9:4-5a	Abimelech, an abomination of a man
19.	Judges 11:30-31	Jephthah's vow, foolish or faith?
20.	Judges 11:36-37	Jephthah's daughter, sacrificed to God?
21.	Judges 13:8	Manoah, concerned about raising a child
22.	Judges 13:22-23	Manoah's wife, a trusting faith
23.	Judges 14:1-2	Samson, completely addicted!
24.	Judges 16:4	Delilah, Satan's star servant
25.	Judges 16:28a	Samson's spectacular finish
26.	Ruth 1:11a & 13b	Naomi, bitter to better by God's grace
27.	Ruth 1:16	Ruth, a gentle Gentile, Jesus' ancestor
28.	Ruth 4:9-10a	Boaz, shows us what a redeemer does
29.	1 Samuel 1:6-7	Peninnah's pathetic provocations
30.	1 Samuel 1:11b	Hanna's honorable humility
31.	1 Samuel 2:12	Hophni and Phineas, just plain corrupt

April

May

Day	Text	Title of the Devotional

June

Day   Text   Title of the Devotional

1. 2 Kings 6:16   Elisha's elegant ears and eyes
2. 2 Kings 8:16b-18   Jehoram, married evil and did evil
3. 2 Kings 9:20b   Jehu, a hard charging man
4. 2 Kings 11:12   Jehoiada the priest promotes King Joash
5. 2 Kings 15:32b-34   Jotham, made wise choices!
6. 2 Kings 16:7   Ahaz bows to a foreign, pagan king
7. 2 Kings 16:11   Uriah the priest, builds the devil an altar
8. 2 Kings 18:5-7a   Hezekiah, a man God gave more time to
9. 2 Kings 21:1-2   Manasseh, so evil, repented, was saved!
10. 2 Kings 22:1-2   Josiah, a child king who loved God
11. 1 Chron. 10:13-14   Saul, the people's choice, removed by God
12. 2 Chron. 17:3-4   Jehoshaphat *"sought the God of his father"*
13. 2 Chron. 25:9   Amaziah learns a big money principle!
14. 2 Chron. 26:3-5   Uzziah's life shows success is conditional
15. Ezra 1:1   Cyrus, a pagan king commissioned by God
16. Ezra 7:8-10   Ezra, faithful priest and teacher
17. Nehemiah 1:6b-9   Nehemiah, chosen to rebuild Jerusalem
18. Nehemiah 2:10   Sanballat, Satan's agent to stop missions
19. Esther 2:15   Esther, the girl who won a beauty contest
20. Esther 4:11a   King Ahasuerus, approach with caution!
21. Esther 7:3   Esther's protection is Haman's judgment
22. Esther 8:1-2a   Mordecai, doorkeeper then Prime Minister
23. Job 1:9-10   Satan, he knows what you are doing!
24. Job 1:20-22   Job, tested by God, tempted by Satan
25. Job 2:7b-9   Job's wife doesn't stand by her man!
26. Job 19:25   Job's faith grows, Satan's hope dims
27. Psalm 25:11   David's prayer of a sincere believer
28. Psalm 38:1-2   David's painful depression
29. Psalm 51:1-3   David's healing confession
30. Psalm 73:2-5   Asaph, from sinful envy to godly praise

July

August

September

Day	Text	Title of the Devotional
1.	Matthew 27:5	Judas' suicide - Part 2
2.	Matthew 28:5-6	Jesus' resurrection and ours
3.	Matt. 28:18-20	Jesus' command, our commission or omission?
4.	Mark 1:29-31	Simon Peter's mother-in-law
5.	Mark 1:40-42	A leper is made clean
6.	Mark 2:10-12	The paralytic, forgiven and healed
7.	Mark 3:34	Mary, a mother who learns to let go
8.	Mark 4:3	A farmer "went out"!
9.	Mark 4:3-8	A farmer's four types of soil
10.	Mark 4:37-38	The Teacher tames the tempest
11.	Mark 5:22-24a	Jairus, "Don't be afraid, just believe"
12.	Mark 6:17	Herodias, she "nursed a grudge"
13.	Mark 7:27-29	The begging woman of Canaan
14.	Mark 10:45	Mark, the one who learned to serve
15.	Mark 10:47b	Blind Bartimaeus, he cried for mercy
16.	Mark 12:41-42	The widow's mite shows her mighty heart
17.	Mark 15:21	Simon of Cyrene has a divine detour
18.	Mark 15:33-34 & 39	The Centurion sees Jesus die & believes
19.	Mark 15:40-41	Many women care about Jesus
20.	Luke 1:11-13	Zechariah, God remembers His covenant
21.	Luke 1:23-25	Elizabeth, a good wife and mother!
22.	Luke 1:38	Mary, the mother of my Lord
23.	Luke 2:1&3	Caesar Augustus, moves on God's schedule
24.	Luke 2:10b-11	Baby Jesus, born "Lord," for you!
25.	Luke 2:25	Grandpa Simeon blesses Jesus' family
26.	Luke 2:36-37	Grandma Anna, thankful, not bitter!
27.	Luke 2:40	Jesus' leadership training started young
28.	Luke 2:52	Jesus' leadership training "grew"
29.	Luke 3:2b-3	John's mission, prepare for the Messiah
30.	Luke 7:37-38	A woman who anointed the feet of Jesus

October

November

December

JANUARY

Adam in the Garden of Eden

"Now the LORD God had planted a garden in the east, in Eden; and there He put the man He had formed."
Genesis 2:8

January 1

"So God created man in His own image, in the image of God He created him; male and female He created them." Genesis 1:27

Adam, made in the image of God

God created man after He created the rest of the world, the fish, the birds and the animals. But now man is created differently. He has part of God's image in him. So how is this possible?

God the Father does not have a body. Yet Adam, was put into the world with a perfect body. Neither Adam nor Eve had any genetic or physical defects of any kind. And since God is eternal, man was designed to live forever. Luke even calls Adam, *"the son of God,"* in his genealogy in Luke 3:38 NKJV. However, sin changed Adam's eternal body from never dying to, *"You will surely die."*

"In His own image," mostly refers to the Spirit of God. Essentially, *"God is Spirit,"* John 4:24a. He put His Spirit not only into Adam, but into every person that has ever lived. Whether we live 100 years or just for a few seconds, each and every life has an eternal spirit. In this sense, we are far more spiritual than we are physical. Our spirits live forever! God gave Adam and all of us a conscience, a moral compass if you will. We are created, able to know right from wrong.

God also made us *"in His own image,"* as social people. From the very beginning, God existed socially in Trinity. God the Father, the Son and the Spirit relate perfectly to one another. We were created in the image of God, to know God socially! Adam and Eve knew God socially before they sinned, but sin ruined that close relationship!

In salvation, God restores a sinner back into *"His own image."* God first promised a Savior to Adam and Eve and to us also in Genesis 3:15. Then in Genesis 3:21, God killed an innocent animal, the first death of any kind in the world. God shed innocent blood to pay for Adam's guilty blood. God covered Adam's sin completely by Himself. That is what grace is. Just as God restored Adam and Eve, so also when we believe in the perfect blood of Jesus, we are restored, holy and without sin!

Prayer: Dear Lord, we see the Gospel message here! You restored Adam and Eve back into Your image through innocent blood that was shed, all pointing to Jesus who would shed His perfect blood. We thank You for Your mercy to us sinners. In Jesus' name we pray. Amen.

January 2

"Then the Lord God made a woman from the rib He had taken out of the man, and He brought her to the man. The man said, 'This is now bone of my bones and flesh of my flesh; she shall be called 'woman' for she was taken out of man.'" Genesis 2:22-23

Eve, the mother of all the living

Life for Eve is divided into two parts. She had a much different life before she and Adam fell into sin, than after they fell. We can hardly imagine Eve's life at first. Her relationship to God and to her husband was perfect. Even all the birds and animals were loving and kind. A tiger was a harmless, big "house cat."

The meaning of the name given to the first woman describes who she is. Eve means, "the mother of all the living." Eve was made. She was not created like everything else. In the beginning, the animals and birds all had a mate, a partner to live with. Then we read, *"But for Adam no suitable helper was found,"* Genesis 2:20b. Then God put Adam *"into a deep sleep."* While Adam was sleeping, God made a woman from one of his rib bones. Why did God not just speak Eve into existence like the other things He created? God made Adam sleep to show us that Adam had nothing to do with the making of Eve.

But why a rib bone? Why was Eve not made from a bone from another part of Adam's body? God is giving us an important picture. Eve was not made out of Adam's head bone to rule over him. Nor was she made from a foot bone to be stepped on by Adam. Eve was made out of Adam's side bone, to be equal with him, from under his arm to be protected by him. Eve was made from the bone the closest to Adam's heart to be loved by him, to be one with him!

Yes, God made Eve to be loved! How sad and sinful it is that so many women are abused and not loved today. We need to follow God's pattern and love one another. That must start in marriage and in our homes. We need to be what God designed us to be!

Prayer: Lord, how wonderful it is to see that we did not come from a monkey, but that our great-grandmother was actually made by You! You made a perfect man and a perfect woman, created in Your image to act like You do. May You bless our relationships today. In Jesus' name we pray. Amen.

"Now the serpent was more crafty than any of the wild animals the Lord God had made. He said to the woman, 'Did God really say, 'You must not eat from any tree in the garden'?'" Genesis 3:1

Eve, the first to sin

There was a day when all of human history was forever changed. Satan came to visit Eve in the form of a snake. Since it was only Adam and Eve in the Garden of Eden, they probably talked to the animals quite a bit. At this time, the animals were all tame and they did not eat each other either. There was no death, because there was no sin of any kind.

Satan did not want Adam and Eve to be holy! So he gave Eve bad advice. Satan lied to Eve three different ways. First, he got Eve to <u>doubt</u> the wisdom of God, who had told her and Adam not to eat from that one tree. Second, he convinced her that she <u>would not die</u> if she ate that fruit. Then, Satan told Eve she would be just <u>like God</u> if she ate from the tree. Well, Eve listened to Satan. She did what God forbid her to do! That is what sin is. The one simple command that was so easy to keep, she did not keep! To break such a simple command made the offense against God, all the greater!

Not only did Eve eat, she gave some of the fruit to her husband. Instead of glorifying God by being obedient, Eve glorified Satan by being disobedient! Eve was also tricked into glorifying herself. And this is our big problem yet today!

The result of Eve's and then Adam's sin is they were immediately separated from God who is holy. Eve suddenly had relationship problems with her husband Adam. Far more than that, because Eve and her husband sinned, every child, grandchild and those of us who are alive today are born sinners. Now that Eve and Adam are sinners, they must die. *"For the wages of sin is death."* Eve and Adam were lovingly warned by God that they would die if they ate from that one tree. Their death was both a spiritual and physical death.

Satan was also cursed! He came to Eve walking, but left crawling on his belly in the dust. Do we walk with God or crawl with Satan?

Prayer: Lord, we see the results of the disobedience of Eve yet today. We are born disobedient and need Your forgiveness to be one with You again. Lord forgive us our sins. In Jesus' name we pray. Amen.

January 4

"The Lord God made garments of skin for Adam and his wife and clothed them." Genesis 3:21

Adam and Eve, the first to be restored

Justice would have been served if God allowed Adam and Eve to die as unforgiven sinners! But He did not do that! God immediately showed His concern for the lost souls of both Adam and Eve. He came to them, even while they were still with that serpent Satan! Why? Because as sinners, they were already enslaved to Satan and could not possibly come back to God on their own! God's coming to them clearly demonstrated His love and is a picture of God's grace to us all.

God also made a promise to the evil Satan, in the hearing of both Adam and Eve. God said, *"And I will put enmity between you and the woman, (Eve) and between your seed and her Seed (Jesus); He shall bruise your head, and you shall bruise His heel,"* Genesis 3:15 NKJV. I used the NKJV because *"Seed"* is capitalized. The NIV uses the word *"offspring"* which is not capitalized and is not so clear that the *"Seed"* is Jesus. So God promises that Jesus will fight Satan, and Jesus will win! This *"Seed"* will reconcile Adam and Eve to God once again. This *"Seed"* also reconciles Adam and Eve to each other again, for their marriage relationship was already strained from their sin.

The proof to us that God restored Adam and Eve, comes right after Adam and Eve failed to cover their own sin by picking fig leaves. *"The Lord God made garments of skin for Adam and his wife and clothed them,"* Genesis 3:21. This is a picture of God's forgiving grace because Adam and Eve did nothing to cover their sin. God provided the innocent blood. God killed the animal. God even put the "skin clothes" on Adam and Eve! This was the first death of any living being, the first blood that was ever shed, the first sacrifice of the Old Testament. And it all points to the *"Seed,"* Jesus, that would come some day!

Why did God kill an animal to forgive Adam's sin? *"For the life of a creature is in the blood, and I have given it to you to make atonement for yourselves on the altar; it is the blood that makes atonement for one's life,"* Leviticus 17:11. The shed blood points to Jesus!

Prayer: Lord, what a beautiful Savior You are! Your grace is so amazing in restoring us to You! We praise You. In Jesus' name we pray. Amen.

January 5

"Then the Lord said to Cain, 'Why are you angry? Why is your face downcast? If you do what is right, will you not be accepted? But if you do not do what is right, sin is crouching at your door; it desires to have you, but you must master it.'" Genesis 4:6-7

Cain's long-faced devotion

What would Cain look like in a Christian family today? That is a fair question, because the life of Cain is a big warning to us! Cain was not devoted to God or to his family! Cain did not worship in a pleasing way! Something was wrong with Cain's heart. He was incredibly self-centered instead of God-centered and other-centered. Cain did not really love God or his brother Abel! *"If anyone says, 'I love God,' yet hates his brother, he is a liar. For anyone who does not love his brother, whom he has seen, cannot love God, whom he has not seen,"* 1 John 4:20. Cain's words, *"Am I my brother's keeper,"* clearly showed his angry, selfish heart that was evil. If Cain had come confessing his sin, God would have forgiven him. Then Cain's long face would have been replaced with a joyful smile! His lack of love for God showed up on his *"downcast"* face! Today there are faces in church that say, "I am here under protest." There are mouths that do not sing. There are minds that are elsewhere.

Cain came to worship with a completely wrong attitude! Because Cain didn't respect God, God didn't respect Cain! We must know, *"If anyone turns a deaf ear to the law, even his prayers are <u>detestable</u>,"* Proverbs 28:9. Cain hated the law of God that teaches us to love. How can Cain bring an offering to God when he didn't even want to be in God's presence? Cain worshiped without character and his prayers didn't make it past the tree tops! God is always aware of the condition of our hearts!

Cain's offering itself, was inferior to Abel's. Cain's offering said, "Thanks for the nice produce." Abel's offering of a piece of lamb, looked to God for atonement for his sin. Abel came humbly to worship. Cain came proudly. Abel's offering was accepted. Cain's was rejected. Whose shoes do we worship in, Abel's or Cain's?

Prayer: Lord, we are too often just like Cain! We come to worship You in body but not with our mind. Forgive us Lord. May we worship in spirit and in truth. And truthfully, we too need our sins forgiven and a closer walk with You and others. Lord, forgive us! In Jesus' name we pray. Amen.

January 6

"By faith Abel offered God a better sacrifice than Cain did. By faith he was commended as a righteous man, when God spoke well of his offerings. And by faith he still speaks, even though he is dead."
Hebrews 11:4

Abel's righteous sacrifice

Abel's name is mentioned first in the heroes of the faith chapter. Yet in Genesis, Abel's name is in just a few verses. We know that *"Abel brought fat portions from some of the firstborn of his flock. The Lord looked with favor on Abel and his offering,"* Genesis 4:4. Yet what is so noteworthy here in Hebrews is not what Abel brought as an offering! God was not as interested in the rituals, the ceremonies and the sacrifices, as He is with the heart of the one bringing these things! Notice that it is his *"faith"* that is being held up here in Hebrews, to encourage us! After all, these men and women were able to endure much suffering for God because they had a solid faith! The loud point is, our *"faith,"* must be made of the same substance as their *"faith"*!

It was *"by faith,"* that Abel brought *"a better sacrifice."* By faith, Abel brought a lamb, knowing that someday Jesus the Lamb of God, would provide atonement for sins. Abel's significant *"faith,"* along with the others listed in Hebrews, saw that God's eternal kingdom was far more important than the comforts of this age! They were able to bear extreme difficulties because they knew that the here and now is not all there is! Because a strong faith is so important, Hebrews 11 begins with a definition of faith. *"Now faith is being sure of what we hope for and certain of what we do not see,"* Hebrews 11:1. Abel was sure of what he hoped for! None of us can live wisely in the light of eternity unless we are also *"sure,"* absolutely *"sure,"* just like Abel was. May God help us!

Prayer: Lord, Your kingdom is worth living for! You are worth living for! Lord, expose our idols that esteem other things more than You! May the unseen world be as real to us as it was to the saints that are listed in Hebrews 11. Lord help us because faith is a gift from You! And by it, we know that Your Word is true. Increase our faith, so that Your kingdom may be advanced. Make us trophies of Your grace for Your glory! In Jesus' name we pray. Amen.

January 7

"Enoch walked with God; then he was no more, because God took him away." Genesis 5:24

Enoch, God's walking friend

Enoch here is the seventh generation from Adam through Seth. The generations are: 1. Adam; 2. Seth; 3. Enosh; 4. Kenan; 5. Mahalalel; 6. Jared; 7. Enoch. As we piece together what is written about Enoch, we see a big contrast. We see the godly life of prophet Enoch, as compared to the ungodly lives of false teachers and others.

We read the simple but powerful truth; *"Enoch walked with God."* Enoch loved God and God loved him. Enoch trusted in God. Our problem is we still have idols that we love more than God, and we spend too much time walking and talking to and about them! Enoch did not do this. He truly enjoyed God more than anything else!

Enoch had to be in step with God to walk with Him! He loved what God loved. He hated what God hated. In Jude, we see Enoch hated evil. *"Enoch, the seventh from Adam, prophesied about these men: (evil men) 'See, the Lord is coming with thousands upon thousands of His holy ones to judge everyone, and to convict all the <u>ungodly</u> of all the <u>ungodly</u> acts they have done in the <u>ungodly</u> way, and of all the harsh words <u>ungodly</u> sinners have spoken against Him.' These men are grumblers and faultfinders; they follow their own evil desires; they boast about themselves and flatter others for their own advantage,"* Jude 14-16. The *"ungodly"* are those who had no reverence for God in thought, word or deed! Enoch's life shows us the ungodly will be severely judged!

See the contrast of Enoch and all those who walk with God like he did. *"By faith Enoch was taken from this life, so that he did not experience death; he could not be found, because God had taken him away. For before he was taken, he was commended as one who pleased God. And without faith it is impossible to please God, because <u>anyone who comes to Him must believe that He exists and that He rewards those who earnestly seek Him</u>,"* Hebrews 11:5-6. This truth is for us today!

Prayer: Lord, through Enoch, we see that You judge evil and evil men severely. We also see that those who walk with You by faith are rewarded greatly. We thank You for teaching us these things so that we will keep our eyes on You. In Jesus' name we pray. Amen.

January 8

"Altogether, Methuselah lived 969 years, and then he died."
Genesis 5:27

Methuselah lived long, but *"he died"*!

The historical record in Genesis shows us that Methuselah lived longer than anyone else had ever lived. Our text says he lived 969 years. To put this into perspective, this earth is about 6000 years old. My New King James Bible has a timeline before each chapter in the Bible. The Genesis record of creation is listed as beginning in 4004 B.C. (Before Christ). That means the world began about 6017 years ago. Science will never tell you that, but God who was there does, and God doesn't lie! The scientists who say the earth is older were not there. So Methuselah lived roughly 1/6 of the time this Earth has existed! Wow! He spent almost 1000 years on this earth! Methuselah died the year the flood came. Some say that Noah and Shem buried him in a cave.

But guess what? *"He died"*! Methuselah died. We must not focus so much on the number 969 in our text, that we don't see the last two words, *"he died."* Beyond that, Methuselah's life of 969 years are not even a single grain of sand on all the sea shores of the world when compared to eternity! Methuselah was not immortal! *"He died."*

Like Methuselah, we are not immortal either. We may not give much thought to eternity but that does not change the reality of it. We may even be thinking, "I wish I could live 969 years." Like Methuselah, we will die! If he had a tombstone, it would read something like this: "Methuselah, Born 3000 B.C. - Died 2031 B.C. The one who waited the longest to die!"

But why would we want to live for only 969 years, when we can live for eternity? The years in eternity are a zillion times more than 969 years. Be sure of this fact! *"Man is destined to die once, and after that to face judgment,"* Hebrews 9:27b. Therein lies the big test of every life. Are we ready to face the judgment that is coming after our death? We are only ready, if we flee to Christ! Then we will live forever!

Prayer: Lord, may the words *"he died,"* move us to seek Your mercy and forgiveness for our sin. Put Your Spirit in us Lord, so that we may be ready to die. In Christ's name we pray. Amen.

January 9

"Two of every kind of bird, of every kind of animal and of every kind of creature that moves along the ground will come to you to be kept alive." Genesis 6:20

Noah, a picture of God's grace

In our text, God told Noah these exact words of grace: *"will come."* We need to see them also, as this is really important theology! I say that because hardly a week goes by that I do not hear someone say how man has a free will to choose God in the salvation process. If only they would see the truth of God's grace in the events surrounding the ark and the flood.

Noah is commanded to make an ark, which is a picture of Heaven. Noah himself, is a picture of Jesus. In our text, the *"bird,"* *"animal,"* and *"creature,"* that *"will come to you,"* is a picture of God calling Christians into Heaven. By God's grace alone, not every animal and bird was doomed to the destruction that was soon coming. Why did these animals come to the ark? Did any one of them come of their own "free will"? No way! And neither do we! God made them willing to come! Same with us! Was there any good in the selected birds or animals that caused them to come? No, God worked through His Spirit to move them. Same with us! Did Noah keep the animals safe the whole journey? Yes, and so too God keeps us so safe that no one can snatch us out of His hand. God has many ways to show us that His grace is all of Him, and nothing of us.

Picture the procession that God is calling to Heaven! They are coming from every tribe and nation. All who are called, come! Do we understand our privileged position if God has called us? And if God is currently calling us, we *"will come"* because God will make us come! Notice also, there is just one door to get into the ark, and there is one Door into Heaven. Jesus said, *"I am the gate; whoever enters through Me will be saved,"* John 10:9a.

Prayer: Lord, the truth of the ark is even more amazing when we understand the picture! Truly *"Blessed is the man whom You choose, and cause to approach You, that he may dwell in Your courts,"* Psalm 65:4a NKJV. In Christ Jesus' name we pray. Amen.

January 10

"As it was in the days of Noah, so will it be at the coming of the Son of Man." Matthew 24:37

Noah, a picture of God's judgment

The worldwide flood that God sent in Noah's time was not just His saving of His own people. It was also His judgment against the wickedness that was increasing on the earth. In our text, Jesus is talking about the Judgment at the end of the world by comparing it to the flood in Noah's time. Jesus also tells us that the conditions in the world in Noah's time, are important to understand the coming Last Judgment.

In Noah's time, people thought they were secure. But they were actually careless as far as eternity was concerned. *"For in the days before the flood, people were eating and drinking, marrying and giving in marriage, up to the day Noah entered the ark,"* Matthew 24:38. It was life as usual! They were clueless and careless about their personal coming judgment! *"They knew nothing about what would happen until the flood came and took them all away. That is how it will be at the coming of the Son of Man,"* Matthew 28:39.

The end of the world will be so sudden that, *"Two men will be in the field; one will be taken and the other left. Two women will be grinding with a hand mill; one will be taken and the other left,"* Matthew 24:40-41. If we are waiting to "get right" with God and are thinking we have lots of time, we will most likely run out of time! The reason is, *"No one knows about that day or hour, not even the angels in Heaven, nor the Son, but only the Father,"* Matthew 24:36.

We also need to know what the "moral" climate was like in the time of Noah. *"The earth was <u>corrupt</u> in God's sight and was <u>full of violence</u>,"* Genesis 6:11. What do we see in our world today but *"violence"* and *"corruption"* increasing more and more! So many people are unconcerned about the eternity that awaits them! If they only knew, putting off seeking God until tomorrow is Satan's plan! Tomorrow is Satan's favorite day! Today is the day of salvation!

Prayer: Dear Lord, You told us to be ready. You tell us to seek You while You may be found. You so lovingly warn us to be ready, to flee to You today, while there is still time. May many flee to You this day! In Christ's name we pray. Amen.

January 11

"And God said, 'This is the sign of the covenant I am making between Me and you and every living creature with you, a covenant for all generations to come. I have set My rainbow in the clouds, and it will be the sign of the covenant between Me and the earth.'" Genesis 9:12-13

God's (and our) rainbow in the clouds

What do we think of when we see a rainbow in the clouds? We may think it is beautiful and it is. But far more than that, a rainbow is a sign and a seal from the finger of God. He is pointing to a specific promise that He is giving to us and to all the earth! With the flood over, God is giving a covenant, a holy agreement, a solemn oath to Noah, to the animals and to us. See how many times in the span of ten verses we read the words, *"I now establish,"* or *"I am making."* I count seven times, God's perfect number.

"I now establish My covenant with you and with your descendants after you and with every living creature that was with you-the birds, the livestock and all the wild animals, all those that came out of the ark with you-every living creature on the earth," Genesis 9:9-10.

The rainbow is not just for us to see and remember God's promises! Far more amazing, the rainbow is a sign for God to see and remember His promises to us! God's eye is on us! *"Whenever I bring clouds over the earth and the rainbow appears in the clouds, I will remember My covenant between Me and you and all living creatures of every kind. Never again will the waters become a flood to destroy all life. Whenever the rainbow appears in the clouds, I will see it and remember the everlasting covenant between God and all living creatures of every kind on the earth,"* Genesis 9:14-16.

Since God's eye is upon us, remembering us, then we too must look to Him! We must remember that we are here on this earth to find God, as Acts 17:27 teaches. It is our responsibility to *"seek Him and perhaps reach out to Him and find Him."* What are we reaching for?

Prayer: Lord, how amazing, You put a sign in the sky to remember us, and to show Yourself to us. How Your creation points to You so that all men are without excuse! Open our eyes Lord to see who You are! In Jesus' name we pray. Amen.

January 12

"The sons of Noah who came out of the ark were Shem, Ham and Japheth... from them came the people who were scattered over the earth." Genesis 9:18a &19b

Noah's sons, fathers of many nations

Only Noah and his wife, and his three sons and their wives were left on the earth. It is not recorded anywhere that Noah and his wife had any more children after this. For this reason we read in our text that from Shem, Ham and Japheth came every race of people who would inhabit the whole earth.

We notice that Shem is listed first. Yet in Genesis 10:21, Japheth is clearly called the older brother. Shem is likely listed before Japheth, because Abram and Christ are from his lineage. Shem is the great grandfather of Eber, who is considered to be the father of the Hebrew people. Then, five generations later, Abram comes. Through Abram, Shem is the father of both the Jewish and Islamic faiths. Shem may also be listed first because he received a greater blessing from Noah, his father. Interestingly, Noah said, *"Blessed be the Lord, the God of Shem!"* Genesis 9:26b. Shem's descendants grew to be many in Egypt but then God moved them to Canaan and later to parts of Asia.

Japheth is believed to be the father of those who settled in Europe and the Americas and also parts of Asia. Japheth's descendants settled the farthest from the new nation of Israel. Japheth was more of a philosopher than his brothers. Thus, it is believed that his descendants formed the belief system of the Hindus and Confucius.

Ham is the father of African people and of those with a darker skin color. His sons were involved in making many tools for getting work done easier. We will read more about Ham tomorrow.

Prayer: Lord, it is interesting how the three sons of Noah became the fathers of all the people on the earth. You moved them where You wanted them to be and blessed them there. You worked through them to bring a Savior into the world for us. We praise You for making people from every nation to be Your children. In Jesus' name we pray. Amen.

January 13

"Ham, the father of Canaan, saw his father's nakedness and told his two brothers outside." Genesis 9:22

Ham's sin teaches us to honor our fathers!

After the flood, Noah returned to farming. This was likely his work before he became a carpenter and built the ark. He now grows a vineyard among other things and sampled the wine he made. He obviously drank too much of that wine and got himself drunk. We can be quite certain that drinking too much wine was not a regular habit of Noah. For we read that *"Noah was a righteous man, blameless among the people of his time, and he walked with God,"* Genesis 6:9b. However, righteous people do sin and there are consequences when they do!

Ham happened to find father Noah drunk and uncovered in his tent. Ham immediately went and told his brothers. By doing this, Ham was broadcasting the sin of his father and was not showing respect! In fact, Ham was mocking his father. We know from the fifth commandment that it will go well for us if we honor our fathers.

It did not go well for Ham when he mocked his father! His mistake cost him and his descendants a life of misery. Noah, immediately the next day, put a curse on Canaan, one of Ham's four sons. Why Canaan? We are not told. But perhaps Canaan also found out about Noah's sin and mocked him. Anyway, the very next day, Noah gave these very words of prophesy: *"Cursed be Canaan! The lowest of slaves will he be to his brothers,"* Genesis 9:25.

Over the years, many people have misused this verse to say the black race is supposed to be slaves to the white and brown races. But that is not true! Canaan is just one of the four sons of Ham. Noah's curse on Canaan came true when the Israelites entered Canaan, defeated them, and then made them slaves.

Prayer: Lord, we can see that after the flood, normal life returns. Noah goes back to farming. But he sinned and his sons sinned. How they and we also need Your forgiveness! May we learn from this that one quick sin can have devastating effects on our children for many generations! Lord, strengthen us for the sake of Your kingdom. Give us hearts to be a blessing to others. In Jesus' name we pray. Amen.

"Then they said, 'Come, let us build ourselves a city, with a tower that reaches to the Heavens, so that we may make a name for ourselves and not be scattered over the face of the whole earth.'" Genesis 11:4

"Us," build a monument to self

Two thousand years have now passed since Adam. The Old Testament is half over. The building of the Tower of Babel is also after the flood, just 4000 years ago. Man is still wicked. Selfishness has been the ruin of man since Adam. Eve was selfish when she ate the fruit. Cain was selfish when he killed Abel. By Genesis 6:5, we read that, *"The Lord saw how great man's wickedness on the earth had become, and that every inclination of the thoughts of his heart was only evil all the time."* Do not believe the world's lies that your big problem in life is that you hate yourself, and that you need to love yourself more to have a happy life.

We are just like *"us,"* in our text. In fact this is us. We also want to *"make a name for ourselves"*! That is our problem! God put us in the world to bring glory to His name. The Creator determines how we the creature must act.

We might think that since there was just one language in the world, the people could worship God together and bear one another's burdens. But that is not the case with the soul sickness of selfishness. God responding quickly to stop *"us"* who want to build a monument to self is our warning! God said, *"Come, let Us go down and confuse their language so they will not understand each other,"* Genesis 11:7. This *"Us"* is God in Trinity. The big *"Us,"* corrects the small *"us"*!

God let these people build for a short time, but then He confused their language. Once they could no longer understand each other, they stopped building. The little that was built of their planned tower, now became a monument to the foolishness of elevating self! You would think that we would have learned our lesson by now. But no, we still love *"us,"* too much which is to our own ruin.

Prayer: Lord, in Your grace, You have given *"us"* a clear warning here! Two thousand years later, You sent Your own Son who clearly told *"us"* again that we need to deny self and follow His humble example of loving You and reaching out to others. Help us Lord for we are weak. In Jesus' name we pray. Amen.

January 15

"So Abram said to Lot, 'Let's not have any quarreling... for we are brothers. Is not the whole land before you? Let's part company. If you go to the left, I'll go to the right...' Lot looked up and saw that the whole plain of the Jordan was well watered, like the garden of the Lord, like the land of Egypt, toward Zoar... So Lot chose for himself the whole plain of the Jordan and set out towards the east."
Genesis 13:8-11a

Lot lives by sight

To lead us into a closer walk with Him, God shows us the lives of two kinds of Christians living side by side. Abram, a strong believer, lived by faith. Lot, a much weaker Christian, lived by sight. We examine their lives to see how to live by faith. See how there are three kinds of people in every church. There are unbelievers. There are the righteous who are mostly indifferent and unproductive, (the Lots). Then there are the righteous who are serious, productive, and want to please God, (the Abrams).

When Abram said for Lot to choose first, Lot looked up. He saw green, and he drooled over the possible riches. He lived by sight. So first of all, Lot looked to Sodom. Secondly, Lot moved towards Sodom and pitched his tent outside the city gates, verse 12. Third, Lot moved into Sodom. We read in Genesis 14:12, *"he was living in Sodom."* Fourth, He was a leader in Sodom. *"Lot was sitting in the gateway of the city"* in Genesis 19:1b. Do you see the progression of this man, Lot, and his family. Lot was, *"a righteous man,"* according to 2 Peter 2:7a. Yes, but he was indifferent and unproductive for the Lord.

Lot went for the blessings. He went for prosperity and lost everything! Abram went for faithfulness and received prosperity! Abram valued relationships over "his rights." He had the right to go to Sodom but it was not good for his relationship to God or for his family's relationships! Abram valued godliness over greed! And, Abram valued God's eternal promises over his own immediate pleasures.

Prayer: Dear Lord, You have invested much in us. You shed Your Son's blood to purchase our salvation. We pray that our pilgrimage will please You and promote Your eternal kingdom. In Jesus' name we pray. Amen.

January 16

"There Abram called on the name of the Lord." "So Abram moved his tents and went to live near the great trees of Mamre at Hebron, where he built an altar to the Lord." Genesis 13:4b & 18

Abram lives by faith

Chapter 13 begins with Abram returning to the first altar he built in Canaan. Then he *"moved."* At the end of the chapter our text shows he again, *"built an altar."* Faithful Abram *"moved his tents"* but built altars! How this must shout to us about what is important. We are far more likely to build our tents and pay little attention to God's Altar, Jesus Christ! See how by faith Abram lived out his faith.

1. Abram worked for reconciliation. Abram and Lot's men were fighting. The rest of the world was watching. Abram faithfully took the initiative to fix this broken relationship. Do we? Jesus said, *"leave your gift there in front of the altar. First go and be reconciled to your brother; then come and offer your gift,"* Matthew 5:24. Abram put this verse into practice and then went to build another altar.

2. Abram pleaded for the fighting to stop. Abram kindly said, *"Let's not have any quarreling between you and me, or between your herdsmen and mine, for we are brothers,"* Genesis 13:8. Abram didn't go to others and complain about his troubles; he went to Lot. *"If your brother sins against you, go and show him his fault, just between the two of you,"* Matthew 18:15a. What a faithful response to fix a close relationship. May we learn from it!

3. Abram by faith knew God would bless him, no matter what Lot did! Abram had the right to choose which way he went! But he gave up his "rights" and waited for God to make His way plain! That is Christian maturity, patience and waiting on God. We have way too many "rights" that we insist on, pointing to our lack of faith! We must learn to wait for God like faithful Abram did!

Prayer: Lord, humanly speaking, Lot had a piece of paradise on earth. But Abram got the promise and Your presence! How much better to have more of You! Lord, help us to say by faith, *"I would rather be a doorkeeper in the house of my God than dwell in the tents of the wicked,"* Psalm 84:10b. In Jesus' name we pray. Amen.

January 17

"She said to Abram, 'The Lord has kept me from having children. Go, sleep with my maidservant; perhaps I can build a family through her.' Abram agreed to what Sarai said." Genesis 16:2

Hagar, Sarai's bad advice!

God promised Abram and Sarai that He would bless them with descendents. But by age 75, Sarai's patience ran out! Her physical ability to bear children was way over. So even though she was a Christian, she now takes matters into her own hands. She tells her husband, "Take my servant Hagar and give me a child through her." *"Abram agreed,"* way too easily! We still suffer with the results of that sinful, sexual union. For Hagar bore Ishmael, the enemy of Isaac and his descendants until this very day!

God was noticeably silent for a time, after speaking definite promises to Abram and Sarai. God's silence was testing them! This was a time to listen, to wait on God and to be obedient! Take note that "culture" permitted Sarai to do what she did. But it was not God's way, or according to His promise. When God gives us a clear vision for what He has called us to do, and then a period of darkness comes, may we be still and faithful! God will surely bring His promises to pass! This 13 years of silence was part of God's discipleship program for Abram and Sarai. Their self-sufficiency was totally destroyed. God's name was lifted up! It is always the Bible and God that are wise, not culture!

To try fix things, Sarai then sent Hagar away. For all practical purposes, that was murder. Hagar could not live without protection, food and shelter! That was rather demonic on Sarai's part, and Abram went along with it. But there's a lesson from Hagar here too!

"The angel of the Lord (Jesus Christ) found Hagar near a spring in the desert," Genesis 16:7a. *"Then the angel of the Lord told her, 'Go back to your mistress and submit to her,'"* Genesis 16:9. Here we see God's <u>benevolent love</u> to Hagar. But how different is God's <u>gracious love</u> to Abram and Sarai, for Hagar never became a believer!

Prayer: Lord, we see Sarah a mother of faith, yet she made mistakes. Lord, how often we can't see past the end of our noses! Teach us to patiently wait on You and not do things our own way. Lord, like a tender shepherd, lead and guide us! In Jesus' name we pray. Amen.

January 18

"I will establish My covenant as an everlasting covenant between Me and you and your descendants after you for the generations to come, to be your God and the God of your descendants after you."
Genesis 17:7

Abraham, father of many by covenant

At age 99, God changed Abram's name to Abraham. God tells us why He did this. *"Your name will be Abraham, for I have made you a father of many nations,"* Genesis 17:5b. But why did God do this at age 99? God wanted to show Abraham, and us who are alive today, that this blessing of a covenantal promise is God driven, yet we do have responsibilities. God was literally putting His mark on Abraham! He commanded Abraham, *"You are to undergo circumcision, and it will be the sign of the covenant between Me and you,"* Genesis 17:11. This act by God, and man's response to it, is important! It is the beginning of the first sacrament that God gave to His church.

God told Abraham, *"For the generations to come every male among you who is eight days old must be circumcised,"* Genesis 17:12a. Years later, in Exodus 4:24-26, when Moses didn't do this to his son, God almost killed him. Why? God wanted His mark on His people!

A sacrament is both a sign and a seal of God's covenantal agreement with His people. In it, God promises to bless them. In the Old Testament, blood was shed to forgive sins. Just as we could see the blood flowing from the sacrifices, we could know, that blood was for the forgiveness of our personal sin. In the New Testament, the blood sacrifices were done away with after Christ shed His blood once and for all. Now in the New Testament, we see water baptism as a sign of the covenant. Just as we can see water wash the filth from our body, we can know in baptism that Christ washes the filth of sin from us! Thus baptism is a sign and a seal yet today of what God is doing in us! And it all started with God giving this covenant to Abraham, the father of many nations!

Prayer: Lord, we are so amazed at Your grace in selecting Abraham to be Your child for all the world to see! And then we understand that You love us covenantally also. We worship You for teaching us about Your grace to us! In Jesus' name we pray. Amen.

January 19

"Remember Lot's wife!" Luke 17:32

Lot's wife, missed the kingdom

In the context of our text, Jesus surprises His disciples by telling them that the kingdom of God is not <u>coming</u>, but that <u>it is here already</u>! Jesus was pointing to how God's kingdom is even now, in the hearts of men! He then reminded His disciples how suddenly the flood came in Noah's time! Instantly, most of people missed the opportunity of catching the kingdom of God! They were totally unconcerned. They were completely unprepared. Jesus is telling His disciples and us to make sure we are prepared! *"Remember Lot's wife!"* It can happen to us!

Just three words. Such a short verse. Such a big warning! Serious words, because Lot's wife professed to know religion! Her husband was a *"righteous man,"* 2 Peter 2:8. She even left Sodom with him the day Sodom was being destroyed! But she disobeyed and looked back towards the city! She was in love with the world that was passing away! She was quickly struck dead! She became a pillar of salt, a monument of unbelief to us who are alive today! The Lord Jesus Christ uses her up as an example to His Church! *"Remember Lot's wife!"* It can happen to us!

Jesus does not ask us to remember Abraham, Isaac, Jacob, Sarah, Hannah, or Ruth. He singles out the one whose soul was so close to the truth, yet so completely lost forever! Jesus is describing the awful state of unreadiness in which many are currently in. Consider also that it is Jesus Himself giving us this warning! The Lord Jesus, the One who is full of love, mercy, and compassion, warns us. He who wept over unbelieving Jerusalem, warns us. He who prayed for the men that crucified Him, pleads with us. He warns us here to take care of our precious and eternal souls! *"Remember Lot's wife!"* It can happen to us!

Prayer: Dear Lord, we are so grateful for Your loving concern for our souls! We see that in our text You are not addressing people who hated You. You are talking to Peter, James and John, those whom You loved! To them You cautioned, *"Remember Lot's wife!"* *"Remember,"* because we are all in danger of forgetting the seriousness of the kingdom of God in us! Help us remember Lord! Mold and make us after Your will! In Jesus' name we pray. Amen.

January 20

"Remember Lot's wife!" Luke 17:32

Lot's wife, one with many privileges
In the days of Abraham and Lot, there were only a few Christian families. Lot's wife had that great privilege! She had a godly husband! Abraham was her uncle! The faith, knowledge, and the prayers of these two righteous men were hers to see and hear! Yet what good did these privileges have on her heart? None it seems! Even with all her opportunities and special warnings, she lived and died graceless, godless, and unbelieving. Her eyes of understanding were never opened. Her conscience was never really awakened. Her will was never really brought into a state of obedience to God. Her heart was never really set on things above! How many in the church are just like Lot's wife? How much more terrible will be their fate in The Judgment!

When the Gentile centurion came to Jesus and believed, Jesus pronounced a more serious judgment on those in Israel who did not believe. He said, *"The sons of the kingdom will be cast into outer darkness. There will be weeping and gnashing of teeth,"* Matthew 8:12 NKJV. Not just darkness, *"outer darkness"*! A more horrible Hell will be theirs! Why? Because those of us who lived in Christian families have heard the truth, yet we have rejected it!

We may be thinking, "I am not what I should be today!" Or, "I have so many more years to get serious with God!" If we think like that, then these words, *"Remember Lot's wife,"* are for us! How can we even say, "I will get serious with God later"? How do we know that? Later or tomorrow are Satan's words! He knows that day will never come! Plus, we could die suddenly! The world could end. But more than that, we are forgetting something. It is God who calls us and convicts our spirit to come to Him. What if God stops calling our number?

Prayer: Lord, Judas surely heard You say, *"Remember Lot's wife!"* Yet Judas did not *"Remember"*! Lord, we do not want to be like Judas, so close to the truth, yet so lost! Lord, we know that after Judas betrayed You, he *"was remorseful and brought back the thirty pieces of silver to the chief priest and elders, saying, 'I have sinned.'"* Yet he did not come to You, and he was lost for all eternity! Help us *"remember"* Lord! That is our fervent prayer! In Jesus' name we pray. Amen.

January 21

"For this is the way the holy women of the past who put their hope in God used to make themselves beautiful. They were submissive to their own husbands, like Sarah, who obeyed Abraham and called him her master. You are her daughters if you do what is right and do not give way to fear." 1 Peter 3:5-6

Sarah, a beautiful woman of hope

God did not give up on Sarah when she sinned! God helped her to learn from her mistakes as He still does with us. Peter tells us how Sarah became a beautiful spiritual mother to us, as well as a physical mother. See how she is such a good example!

Peter tells us what the world will never tell us. Sarah was submissive! She was humble and easy to live with. She greatly respected God and her husband. Purity and reverence defined her. Sarah was a beautiful woman to look at. There are many references to that. But more importantly, she had a personality that wouldn't quit. Peter didn't write about her beautiful face, but about her beautiful heart! Her face became wrinkled with age, while her gentle heart shines still today and forever! She is alive in Heaven today and this is what her life speaks to us:

"Your beauty should not come from outward adornment, such as braided hair and the wearing of gold jewelry and fine clothes. Instead, it should be that of your inner self, <u>the unfading beauty</u> of a gentle and quiet spirit, which is of great worth in God's sight," 1 Peter 3:3-4.

Jewelry and nice clothes are not wrong! But the real issue is, "What are we like on the inside?" Sarah's hope was in God. <u>Sarah won over her husband with her godly behavior, not with her "good looks."</u> Sarah's life-style of submissiveness to God and to her husband are shown here as how to win over anyone who is difficult. She did not retaliate in any way. Sarah trusted in God to see and act, while she waited patiently.

Prayer: Lord, our harsh words and bitter attitudes to those who hurt us make us so ugly! Help us to become like Sarah, one who learned to trust in You and committed herself to Your good providence. May our submissive actions also speak louder than words can ever express! In Jesus' name we pray. Amen.

January 22

"Your wife Sarah will bear you a son, and you will call him Isaac. I will establish My covenant with him as an everlasting covenant for his descendants after him." Genesis 17:19b

Isaac, the son of promise

The life of Isaac points to the life of Christ. See how some of the ways Isaac was like Jesus. First of all, Isaac was a miracle child, born way past the age when it was possible for parents to bear children. Abraham, his father, was 100 years old, and his mother, Sarah, was 90 when he was born. Isaac's name means "laughter." Both Abraham and Sarah laughed for joy, mixed with some unbelief, when they heard about the miracle that they were going to have a baby. The promised child to Abraham was born by the power of God alone, just like the birth of Jesus!

The life of Isaac, as the promised seed, gave life to many just as God promised Abraham. The life of Jesus, as the promised Seed, gives life to many just as God promised. Isaac was placed on the altar as a sacrifice. Jesus was placed on the Cross as our sacrifice. Isaac had to carry the wood to the site of the sacrifice. Jesus had to carry the Cross to Calvary. Isaac was placed on the altar and was bound to it. Jesus was placed on the Cross and bound to it. Isaac was spared when God provided a substitute ram. We were spared when God provided His substitute Lamb. Jesus became the Lamb of God, the sacrifice that would take away the sin of every believer!

It seems that Isaac had a more, laid back personality than his wife Rebekah, or his two sons, Jacob and Esau. Remember he was kind of a mama's boy growing up, and it was hard for him to move on after his mother died. It seems that Isaac's trials in life were not as severe as Abraham's or Jacob's! Why is this? Is it because he lacked the strength of faith to endure them, like they did? Probably, and how true that is today still. God gives us trials according to our spiritual strength, as well as the additional spiritual strength for every trial!

Prayer: Lord, we see Your faithfulness to Your promises in Isaac's life. How You use his life to point us to Christ, to whom every knee shall bow. May our lives also point to Christ! In Jesus' name we pray. Amen.

January 23

"Lot and his two daughters left Zoar... and... lived in a cave. One day the older daughter said to the younger, 'Our father is old, and there is no man around here to lie with us, as is the custom all over the earth. Let's get our father to drink wine and then lie with him and preserve our family line through our father.'" Genesis 19:30-32

Lot's daughters, poor choices, again!

Father Lot chose Sodom because it "looked" better. It turned out to be a poor choice. Everything he worked for burned up, along with the rest of the city. Lot's wife died and became a monument to poor choices as they fled the city! Lot and his two daughters survived. Refugees, they are now in survival mode in a mountain cave. How this family has been plagued by their own poor choices!

Lot's two daughters were unnamed perhaps because God wants us to think about what they did wrong, not who they were! They each wanted a child, but had no husband. Their solution was another poor choice. They got their father drunk to have children though him. Both had a baby boy. One became the father of the Moabites, the other the father of the Ammonites. Both became Israel's enemies!

How does one family make so many foolish choices? They barely escaped Sodom's flames! The wicked practices of Sodom followed them! Lot's daughters doubted God's ability to care for them! They worried their opportunity to bear a child was gone! Jesus calls worry *"little faith."* They could have prayed and sought out their great uncle Abraham for advice. But no, they took matters into their own hands!

Lot was not innocent either. He kept himself sober and pure in wicked Sodom! But in the mountains, he dropped his guard. Getting drunk is not only sin, it welcomes in other sins! Lot *"was not aware"* of what his daughters did when he was drunk! When tempted to sin, *"Flee the evil desires of youth, and pursue righteousness, faith, love and peace, along with those who call on the Lord out of a pure heart,"* 2 Timothy 2:22.

Prayer: Lord, You show us that Lot and his daughters did *"flee"* the sin in Sodom! But they did not *"pursue righteousness"* and sin caught up with them. Lord, make us chase after righteousness which comes out of a pure heart! In Jesus' name we pray. Amen.

January 24

"Abraham said of his wife Sarah, 'She is my sister.' Then Abimelech king of Gerar sent for Sarah and took her. But God came to Abimelech in a dream one night and said to him, 'You are as good as dead because of the woman you have taken; she is a married woman.'"
Genesis 20:2-3

Abimelech warned; Sarah protected

Abimelech is a Philistine king, not a believer. Abraham is now going into his territory. As Abraham and Sarah travel to this pagan place, think of what has happened before this. Abraham and Sarah were visited by an angel in Chapter 18. They were promised a child who would be the heir of many people in years to come. But now Abraham has a big faith test. Can God protect him and Sarah? Can he trust God to keep His end of the covenant agreement? Abraham surely has some doubt, for this is why he lies to Abimelech! He tells Abimelech, Sarah "is my sister." This is a half truth, for Sarah is his half sister. But giving half of the truth is still a lie when it is presented as the whole truth. And, this is the second time Abraham and Sarah told this same lie! They did it in Egypt, years before this! How often we repeat our sins! God's kingdom was not protected with this lie and neither was Sarah! She was at great risk! Like Abraham, we often trust God at times, then at other times, we have our faith fail miserably as we give in to fear. Perfect love casts out fear and Abraham's love was not yet so perfect!

Abimelech takes Sarah who is most likely pregnant with Isaac. In spite Abraham's sin, God protects them anyway! God warns Abimelech that he is "*as good as dead because of the woman you have taken.*" How true for anyone who even contemplates adultery, for Abimelech had not yet touched Sarah. That too, was an act of God! Often sin is thought of, but not carried out because of God's intervention! We would be far more wicked if we were left to our own evil inclinations! How mercifully the Good Shepherd protects His sheep and their lambs!

Prayer: Lord, so much goes on concerning Your preserving graces to believers, but also to all people. Lord without Your hand of protection, we are all "*as good as dead.*" We praise You for all Your divine attributes that are constantly at work in this world! In Jesus' name we pray. Amen.

January 25

"Some time later God tested Abraham." Genesis 22:1a

Abraham's faith, tested again

Faith must be tested, often! It is good to look at how God tested Abraham, because God tests us for the very same reasons! Earlier in Genesis 15, God made a covenant agreement with Abraham. God promised Abraham that He would bless him. However, all covenants come with conditions! Abraham needed to be faithful to God by obeying Him. In the same way, God makes a covenantal agreement with each of us, in giving us salvation! Very soon after this, God allows and even designs tests, specifically tailored for us, so we can prove our faithfulness to His covenant, and also He proves His faithfulness to us!

So God told Abraham, *"Take your son, your only son, Isaac, whom you love, and go to the region of Moriah. Sacrifice him there as a burnt offering on one of the mountains I will tell you about,"* Genesis 22:2. Now Abraham was well aware that Isaac was the son of promise! Abraham did not argue with God, plead with God, or delay in his obedience to God's test! *"Early the next morning Abraham got up and saddled his donkey. He took with him two of his servants and his son Isaac. When he had cut enough wood for the burnt offering, he set out for the place God had told him about,"* Genesis 22:3.

Abraham had complete faith that God would either raise his son from the dead or somehow bless his act of obedience. Faith does not doubt or question why, but true faith believes and acts according to the commands of God. *"When they reached the place God had told him about, Abraham built an altar there and arranged the wood on it. He bound his son Isaac and laid him on the altar, on top of the wood,"* Genesis 22:9. Do we trust and obey God like this? Or, do we make excuses for not being obedient? The faith of Abraham is a clear picture of what God later did with His own Son when Christ was sacrificed for our sins!

Prayer: Lord, we can see that Abraham's time of testing was a blessing. You were not being cruel to him. So too, You tell us that our faith is tested like gold in the fire. Our impurities, our sins are burned off, and we shine much brighter for all eternity. And through it all, You are glorified. We worship You for how You "refine" us! In Jesus' name we pray. Amen.

January 26

"Abraham buried His wife Sarah in the cave in the field of Machpelah near Mamre (which is at Hebron) in the land of Canaan."
Genesis 23:19

Abraham buried his beloved Sarah

A whole chapter is devoted to burying Sarah! Before this, nothing is said about burial. Abraham may have started a practice of burying a body at death, instead of burning it. Since Abraham is considered to be the father of the Jews and Gentile believers, this is an important precedent. The fact that Abraham bought a family burial plot in Canaan itself, is significant. It is the only property Abraham ever owned! This says something about Abraham's hope in the future promises of God!

After Abraham buried Sarah, there are many references of God's people who died and *"were buried."* It seems burial is the respectful way to say good-by to the dead. We do not discard a body like it is rubbish. We bury it with a solemn ceremony. Jacob said, *"There Abraham and his wife Sarah were buried, there Isaac and his wife Rebekah were buried, and there I buried Leah,"* Genesis 49:31.

A human body returns to what it was made from, dust. But we are not burying dust! We view the body. We take the body to the cemetery. We meditate on how that body will someday be raised. We lower a body into the ground. We respectfully say good-by to a body and thank God for what that somebody meant to us!

The Bible rejects the pagan idea that a person is merely a soul that exists in the body for a little while. They don't know that a body is coming back out of that grave! In fact, *"the dead in Christ will rise first,"* 1 Thessalonians 4:16b. This rising is a dead body! The Bible teaches about body-sleep, not soul-sleep! A sleeping body needs to be put to bed, thus burial. Jesus' body was put in a grave and then came out! A Christian's body must be put in a grave and it too will come out again. Those who burn a body lack the hope of the resurrection. The few references to bodies being burned after death are ones of judgment, as in Leviticus 21:9.

Prayer: Lord, thank You for burying Sarah and Your Son. Thank You that in Christ, our bodies will come out of the grave again and forever be with You! What hope we have! In Jesus' name we pray. Amen.

January 27

"May it be that when I say to a girl, 'Please let down your jar that I may have a drink,' and she says, 'Drink, and I'll water your camels too' - let her be the one You have chosen for Your servant Isaac."
Genesis 24:14a

Eliezer's prayer for a girl is answered

Genesis 24 tells how Eliezer went back to Abraham's relatives to get a wife for Isaac. He was instructed not to get Isaac a wife from the land of Canaan. You may remember that God made a covenant promise to Abraham that He would make a great nation of him and his children. God promised to give the land of Canaan to Abraham some day. If Isaac were to marry a girl from the land of Canaan, his children would be Canaanites. Isaac could not marry a girl outside of God's covenant plan! This has huge implications for marriages today! When you seek a wife or husband, do not even think of going outside the Christian covenant community! You must marry a Christian to be faithful to the covenant promises you have to God! If you are faithful, God's kingdom advances and He can openly bless you!

Eliezer prayerfully travels to the town of Nahor. God directs him to go to the well where the people gather to get water. As Eliezer stood by the well at the watering time, he specifically prayed the prayer in our text. He pleads with God to select the right girl. Our text says, *"let her be the one You have chosen."* The word *"chosen"* means "appointed" in the original. How beautiful is God's immediate answer! *"Before he finished praying, Rebekah came out with her jar on her shoulder,"* Genesis 24:15a. How wonderful when we are completely in the will of God, walking and praying to Him! Eliezer's mission was quickly accomplished.

Think on Ephesians 2:10; *"We are God's workmanship, created in Christ Jesus to do good works, which God prepared in advance for us to do."* God knows whom He wants us to marry, to accomplish the work He has prepared for us to do! Marriage is a prayerful matter!

Prayer: Lord, we are in awe of how You move in our lives, making wise choices for us! May we lean on You in true faith like Abraham and Eliezer did. In Jesus' name we pray. Amen.

January 28

"Rebekah said to her son Jacob, 'Look, I overheard your father say to your brother Esau, "Bring me some game and prepare me some tasty food to eat, so that I may give you my blessing in the presence of the Lord before I die."'" Genesis 27:6

Rebekah, so beautiful yet so deceptive

Rebekah was one "good looking" girl! Genesis 24:16 says, *"The girl was very beautiful."* Like Abraham's Sarah, she was easy to look at, and people took notice of her. Rebekah was also a "good worker," quick to grasp what needed to be done and quick to do it! She went to get water for ten camels. That's a lot of water! And she did not stop till she had the job done. This was no easy task, yet she did it willingly. She even ran home after that! She was definitely a woman on the move! These character traits were already seen by Eliezer, when he was looking for Isaac's wife. He noticed that she was quite a woman! He did not smooth talk her to win her over, but he waited on the Lord and prayed! How instructive for us!

Rebekah quickly agrees to marry Isaac and go to him. She even agreed to go the very next day, trusting this was God's will for her life. We see obedience and boldness in the character of Rebekah. Bold, because she would travel about 550 miles, and would likely never see her family again. We see boldness of character forty years later in her marriage. Some of it was for good. Yet some of her boldness is negative, for Rebekah was greatly responsible for the breakup of her family. She and Isaac both played favorites. Isaac loved Esau. Rebekah loved Jacob. She boldly moves to steal the blessing for her favorite, Jacob. Truly, God knew this would happen, but Rebekah was still wrong in what she did. She deceived her husband. Esau now hates Jacob all the more. Fearing Esau, Jacob leaves for a distant land. The family is never together again, and Rebekah is much at fault for all of this.

Prayer: Lord, we see a lovely wife in Rebekah who began her life so well! She followed Your will. She respected her husband. But then she became quite selfish and her manipulation broke up her family. May we learn from her mistakes to be faithful and considerate. Forgive us for our "family mistakes"! In Jesus' name we pray. Amen.

January 29

"His descendants settled in the area from Havilah to Shur, near the border of Egypt, as you go toward Asshur. And they lived in hostility toward all their brothers." Genesis 25:18

Ishmael, the "hostile" son

Ishmael was the first son of Abraham. Isaac was the second. But Ishmael was not the promised son. Yet still, God said to Abraham, *"I will make the son of the maidservant (Hagar) into a nation also, because he is your offspring,"* Genesis 21:13. According to the command of God, Abraham sent Ishmael and his mother Hagar out. The mother thought they would die in the desert. But once again, God speaks to her and said, *"Lift the boy up and take him by the hand, for I will make him into a great nation,"* Genesis 21:18.

Ishmael grew up, *"in the Desert of Paran, his mother got a wife for him from Egypt,"* Genesis 21:21b. His father, *"Abraham left everything he owned to Isaac. But while he was still living, he gave gifts to the sons of his concubines and sent them away from his son Isaac to the land of the east,"* Genesis 25:5-6. Ishmael had twelve sons who became *"tribal rulers according to their settlements and camps,"* Genesis 25:16b. God is making Ishmael into a great nation.

We cannot understand the main difference between Isaac and Ishmael apart from Genesis 3:15, which explains the antitheses. This is a big word to explain the God-ordained hostility between the seed of the woman (Jesus and his children) and the seed of those who are against God. Interestingly, good and evil came from the same father! Sarah calls Ishmael the son of Hagar, and Hagar herself, *"the Egyptian"* in Genesis 21:9. Egypt was a symbol of evil and sin in the Bible. In time, Ishmael does far worse than mock Isaac! *"His descendants settled in the area from Havilah to Shur, near the border of Egypt, as you go toward Asshur. And they lived in hostility toward all their brothers,"* Genesis 25:18.

Prayer: Lord, You show us the history of people and nations and how they are enemies of Your people to this day. Lord help us to understand Your God-ordained hostility that exists in the world. May we be grateful for our spiritual blessings! In Jesus' name we pray. Amen.

"Rebekah became pregnant. The babies jostled each other within her, and she said, 'Why is this happening to me?' So she went to inquire of the Lord. The Lord said to her, 'Two nations are in your womb, and two people from within you will be separated; one people will be stronger than the other, and the older will serve the younger.'" Genesis 25:21b-23

Jacob and Esau, the difference

Our text helps us understand more about the differences between Jacob and Esau. Before the twins were even born, God's sovereignty was already at work in their lives. Paul explained the doctrine of election by using Jacob and Esau as an example of a wider truth! God said, *"Jacob I loved, but Esau I hated,"* Romans 9:13b. Why? God tells us. *"Before the twins were born or had done anything good or bad-in order that God's purpose in election might stand: not by works but by him who calls–she was told, 'The older will serve the younger,'"* Romans 9:11-12.

There is more to Esau's life than God's sovereignty. He also failed in his <u>personal responsibility</u> to love God and be faithful! The book of Hebrews warns us, *"See that no one is sexually immoral, or is godless like Esau, who for a single meal sold his inheritance rights as the oldest son. Afterward, as you know, when he wanted to inherit this blessing, he was rejected. He could bring about no change of mind, though he sought the blessing with tears,"* Hebrews 12:16-17.

Esau despised his birthright by selling it for a bowl of stew. Normally, the birthright of the oldest gave two thirds of his father's estate to him. But more importantly, the birthright gave spiritual blessings. These Jacob wisely wanted, while Esau had no use for them. So Esau sold his eternal soul for a very short, physical pleasure. This is why Hebrews calls him foolish! The warning for us is this: We must not give up our spiritual life for physical pleasures of any kind! If we say to God, "I do not value a relationship with You and Your rules for living," then we too have sold our birthright just like Esau!

Prayer: Lord, we have a spiritual birthright that You in covenant gave to us! May we not despise our Christian heritage like Esau did by embracing sin and worldly pleasures! Lord, make us repent of our foolish choices and turn to You. In Jesus' name we pray. Amen.

January 31

"So Isaac stayed in Gerar. When the men of that place asked him about his wife, he said, 'She is my sister,' because he was afraid to say, 'She is my wife.' He thought, 'The men of this place might kill me on account of Rebekah, because she is beautiful.'" Genesis 26:6-7

Isaac's failure to trust in God

There is a famine and Isaac needs to go to where there is food. God warns Isaac, don't leave Canaan and go to Egypt. Why? If God is going to give this land to Isaac, he needs to be there to accept it! So Isaac moves near Gerar, a Canaanite town where Abimelech is king. *"When the men of that place asked him about his wife, he said, 'She is my sister,' because he was afraid to say, 'She is my wife.'"* Isaac thought these people would kill him to steal his beautiful Rebekah. Isaac thought his lying could protect him, where as he thought God could not! Isaac fails a big test! His great sin here is often our sin also! This difficult time should have caused Isaac to pray to God, not lie to God and others! Do we in our trials trust that God, our Good Shepherd, will protect us? What a lack of faith in God's almighty and powerful attributes when we act like Isaac did here! Does God ever need our help in protecting us?

If God has promised to give Isaac the land of Canaan, (and give us Heaven which Canaan is a symbol of) then He has to protect us! After all, we belong to him! We are His prized possession! Jesus even said about His sheep, *"I give them eternal life, and they shall never perish; no one can snatch them out of My hand,"* John 10:28.

Know this about Isaac's faith and ours! Faith will be tested! Isaac miserably failed this particular exam! After Isaac fails, God moves a pagan king to shame him, rebuke him, and then bless him! Is God good or not? *"Abimelech king of the Philistines looked down from a window and saw Isaac caressing his wife Rebekah,"* Genesis 26:8b. Even though Isaac's faith was weak, God had mercy on Isaac. So great is the grace and love of our God for us, His children!

Prayer: Lord, what important lessons You teach us in the Bible. We learn from Isaac's failure that You want to prove Your great power and protection in life's serious trials. Lord, make us trust in You when we are tempted to lie and be fearful. In Jesus' name we pray. Amen.

FEBRUARY

Pharoah's daughter finds Baby Moses in a basket

"Then Pharaoh's daughter went down to the Nile to bathe, and her attendants were walking along the river bank. She saw the basket among the reeds and sent her slave girl to get it. She opened it and saw the baby." Exodus 2:5-6a

February 1

"When Esau was forty years old, he married Judith daughter of Beeri the Hittite, and also Basemath daughter of Elon the Hittite. They were a source of grief to Isaac and Rebekah." Genesis 26:34-35

Esau's foolish marriages

To instruct us and our covenant youth, God gives us clear facts about twin boys. Jacob married right and was blessed. Esau married wrong and was cursed. Sad to say, many young people follow the way of Esau. Years later they find out that God's way was the wise way!

Think of how Esau and Jacob were born of the same mother and father. They were part of the same covenant God established with their grandfather Abraham. Yet they were so different in the choices they made in life. The foolish life of Esau shouts to us not to repeat his mistakes! We need God's warning, for it is still so common to have a son or daughter who is brought up right, but then foolishly marries wrong. Then the last part of their life is a slow slide away from God.

Esau did not make wise decisions because he went with his feelings instead of doing what was right! He was a very selfish young man. He was intent on following the ways of the world, instead of the ways of God. It was his persistence in not following the ways of God and his parents that led to his poor choices concerning marriage!

It grieved God and Esau's parents that he did not even consult them for their advice or consent in marriage. It also grieved God and his parents that he married out of the covenant, to unbelievers, to people who walked to the beat of a different drum. In doing so, Esau called down curses upon himself and his family for generations to come. God still promises He will give covenant breakers the curses listed in Deuteronomy 28:15-68. Please do not test God in this!

Prayer: Lord, we do not want to end up like Esau with a bad marriage and with poor relationships! We thank You for showing us how important it is to marry with eternity in mind. So we pray and plead, fill us with a wise and obedient spirit! Mold us into families that love and serve You and each other! Thank You for Your guidance and protection in our wicked and self-seeking world. In Christ Jesus' name we pray. Amen.

February 2

"'You know that I've worked for your father with all my strength, yet your father has cheated me by changing my wages ten times. However, God has not allowed him to harm me." Genesis 31:6-7

Laban, cheating was his life

Laban is the brother of Rebekah. We first see him when Eliezer, the servant of Abraham went to get a wife for Isaac. When Eliezer gave gold gifts to Rebekah, the then young Laban runs to welcome Eliezer! Laban's first words to Eliezer are: *"Come, you who are blessed by the Lord,"* Genesis 24:31a. He already had his eyes on the blessings!

A generation later, Jacob goes to Laban to find a wife. Jacob sees Rachel and is in love! A month later Jacob agrees to work seven years to get Rachel's hand in marriage. But Laban cheats him by giving him Leah, the older sister. Jacob marries Rachel a week later, but he still had to work seven more years for her.

Laban used Jacob to accumulate wealth for himself. After 14 years of this, Jacob wants to leave. Laban agrees to give Jacob all the streaked or colored goats. Years later, there are many streaked and colored goats, but few white ones. And Laban despises Jacob more. Jacob wants to go home to Canaan, sick of Laban's attitude and cheating! He says to Rachel and Leah, *"You know that I've worked for your father with all my strength, yet your father has cheated me by changing my wages ten times. However, God has not allowed him to harm me,"* Genesis 31:6-7. Laban's cheating did not harm Jacob. Laban's cheating only harmed himself! May this teach us to be honest in everything! Cheaters never prosper! God will not be mocked!

God saw *"all"* of Laban's cheating, everything big and small! God said to Jacob, *"I have seen all that Laban has been doing to you. I am the God of Bethel, where you anointed a pillar and where you made a vow to Me. Now leave this land at once and go back to your native land,"* Genesis 31:12b-13. As Christians, our *"native"* land is Heaven and no one can cheat us out of it!

Prayer: Lord, You saw it *"all."* May this be both a warning and a comfort to us. You held Laban accountable! You protected Jacob! You are such a beautiful and just God! We worship You. In Jesus' name we pray. Amen.

February 3

"He (Jacob) struggled with the angel and overcame Him; he wept and begged for His favor. He found Him at Bethel and talked with Him there-the Lord God Almighty, the Lord is His name of renown!" Hosea 12:4-5

Jacob, he wrestled with God

Jacob is in the process of leaving Uncle Laban, also his father-in-law. He is on his way to Canaan. He knows he's going to meet up with his brother Esau, and he is terrified! Keep in mind that Jacob was a very deceitful man! Already in the womb, *"He grasped his brother's heel."* He deceived his father Isaac! He deceived his brother Esau and stole his birthright. Jacob deceived his Uncle Laban whom he was just leaving. In fact, Jacob's name means deceiver! So quite naturally, there is a fear factor going on in Jacob's heart that is very well deserved! After all, *"fear has to do with punishment,"* 1 John 4:18b. And Jacob deserves every bit of it. Ah, but this Jacob is so much like us! And now we see the grace of God to Jacob, and to us!

Jacob's family moves ahead of him to meet Esau. Jacob stays behind to pray. We read, *"a man (God) wrestled with him till daybreak,"* Genesis 32:24b. Jacob refused to let Him go, and God put Jacob's hip out of joint with a mere touch of a finger. He could have killed him! Still Jacob would not let go until God blessed him! And here we see the grace of God! *"Then the man (God) said, 'Your name will no longer be Jacob, but Israel, because you have struggled with God and with men and have overcome,"* Genesis 32:28. God blessed Jacob by changing his name to Israel. That same name is given to every true Christian!

We have the beginning of a new day. We have a new nation. We have a new people! All a gift of God because no deceiver merits salvation! It is the grace of God! *"As a man he struggled with God. He struggled with the angel and overcame him; <u>he wept and begged for His favor</u>. He found Him at Bethel and talked with Him there-the Lord God Almighty, the Lord is His name of renown!"* Hosea 12:3b-5.

Prayer: Lord, like Jacob so many years ago, we too seek You! Take our hearts of deceit and make us act like Your precious children. How amazing! Jacob's gracious pardon, is also freely given to us in Jesus Christ! In His name we pray. Amen.

February 4

"He loved Rachel more than Leah." Genesis 29:30b

Leah, knew the loneliness of favoritism

Laban had two daughters, and Jacob had eyes for Rachel the younger one. He agreed to work for seven years to get Rachel as his wife. But then, daddy Laban cheats Jacob and gives him Leah instead. A week later Rachel also became his wife. *"Leah had weak eyes, but Rachel was lovely in form, and beautiful. Jacob was in love with Rachel,"* Genesis 29:17-18a. From Jacob's eyes, Rachel was "hot" and Leah was "not." From God's eyes, Leah was more beautiful spiritually speaking.

Jacob was married to both. He had a marriage contract to love both! But he played favorites. He loved Rachel more. His favoritism, tempted (but not caused) Rachel to become proud and Leah to become down and depressed. God saw what was going on. He saw the pain and the loneliness of Leah. Even though Jacob thought much of Rachel and little of Leah, God saw things differently, and did something about it! He blessed Leah more and gave her children.

To better understand Leah's lonely pain, look at what she said after the birth of each son. Child one, she named Reuben. *"Because the Lord has seen my misery. Surely my husband will love me now,"* Genesis 29:32b. Child two, she named Simeon, *"It is because the Lord heard that I am not loved, He gave me this one too,"* Genesis 29:33b. Child three, she named Levi, *"Now at last my husband will become attached to me, because I have borne him three sons,"* Genesis 29:34b. Jacob was wrong, but so was the bitterness in Leah! But she repents! See her words.

Child four, Judah is born. *"This time I will praise the Lord,"* Genesis 29:35b. Ah, Leah finally has a right response to Jacob's favoritism! Her eyes wisely switch from seeing herself as a victim, to one who was blessed by God! What an important lesson for us. Leah was abused, but her wrong response to that abuse hurt her even more! She changed her attitude, and so can we. From Judah's line came Jesus! Yes, Leah was blessed more by God who saw her difficult situation!

Prayer: Lord, what important lessons You teach us through Leah. Forgive us if we've played favorites. Forgive us if we've held on to bitterness because of favoritism to others! In Jesus' name we pray. Amen.

February 5

"When Rachel saw that she was not bearing Jacob any children, she became jealous of her sister. So she said to Jacob, 'Give me children, or I'll die!'" Genesis 30:1

Rachel's sinful *"jealousy"*

Rachel and Hanna were both childless. Yet their responses were completely different. Their responses are our responses. May we learn from them! Rachel's response to not having children was so bad. She was mad that her sister had children, mad at her husband and mad at God! Her sin of *"jealousy,"* is called *"envy"* in the NKJV. *"Jealousy,"* not only strongly desires what others have, but soon wants to deprive them of it also! Later in the same chapter it is recorded that Rachel gave her servant girl to her husband to have children through her. Bad move! When her servant Bilhah bore a second son to Jacob she said, *"I have had a great struggle with my sister, and I have won."* Winning was more important than acting right. Rachel was that jealous!

Rachel's evil eye toward her sister was like Cain's *"envy"* that killed Abel. This bitter spirit in Rachel, is the same *"bitter envy"* that James calls *"demonic"* in James 3:14-15 NKJV. Basically, forgiveness and bitterness are two opposite reactions to the same problem. One is God's way of living and one is Satan's way of living.

Think of why *"envy"* and *"jealousy"* are so offensive to God. It accuses Him of not being fair to us! It is a big dissatisfaction with God's providence, which is His ability to provide for us! Notice how Rachel did not demand one child, but said, *"give me children or I'll die."* God gave her children but then she died on the birth of the second child. It seems that God graciously gave Rachel children not for her own purpose, but for His. It is not recorded that Rachel ever went to God in prayer to seek His help! And, God is the One who opens and shuts the womb according to Psalm 127. Rachel may have been beautiful on the outside but she was demanding and manipulative on the inside.

Prayer: Lord, forgive us for acting like Rachel. We too have been envious of others. Our jealous hearts have accused You of not being fair. Lord, perfect us, for You are the Author and Perfector of our faith. In Jesus' name we pray. Amen.

February 6

"Now Dinah, the daughter Leah had borne to Jacob, went out to visit the women of the land. When Shechem son of Hamor the Hivite, the ruler of that area, saw her, he took her and violated her." Genesis 34:1-2

Dinah, she should have stayed home!

Dinah's life warns us about the danger that exists out "in the world." Dinah is now about 15 years old, the only daughter of Jacob. As such, she was surely the darling of the family. Her twelve brothers watched over her, likely giving her whatever she wanted.

Dinah *"went out to visit the women of the land,"* are the only words we are given. She wanted to see more closely how the young pagan girls her age lived. We can only imagine that these young girls of the land were the more popular and influential ones. *"The women of the land,"* obviously took Dinah to a party or to a gathering where young men were present. She meets "Mr. Prince Charming," she thinks. He is Shechem, the son of *"the ruler of that area."* Shechem also was used to getting what he wanted! When he saw the beautiful Dinah, he thought his burning lust for this new girl was really love. He really wanted Dinah's body and he took it, most likely against her will. Suddenly Dinah is shamed for life, spoiled!

Dinah needed to learn something! A young man does not need a relationship to get physical quickly! Just the sight of beautiful Dinah was enough to excite him. Since this boy is used to getting what he wants, Dinah's "no," does not stop him! She foolishly thought she was safe! This Biblical event teaches us that even girls from upright families need to protect themselves from the "world's" ways!

You could call this event "recreational dating" or dating for fun. The danger is, you can fall in love quickly! God's process of finding a spouse is not first <u>love,</u> and then <u>consider if they are the right one for you</u>! God's way is first <u>consider the godly qualifications,</u> and then love. Listen to God. Respect your parents. You will never regret it!

Prayer: Dear Lord, forgive us for seeing how close we can get to how the world lives! Help us appreciate our families and not run from them like Dinah did. Help the church to do a better job with social, supervised, group encounters. In Christ's name we pray. Amen.

February 7

"At that time Judah left his brothers and went down to stay with a man of Adullam named Hirah. There Judah met the daughter of a Canaanite man." Genesis 38:1-2a

Judah's wandering eyes

Judah and his brothers sold Joseph to Midianite slave traders, thinking they would have peace in their life. Well, they quickly found out that their jealousy, their cheating and lying, did not bring any peace at all! In fact, no sin ever brings peace. So Judah now leaves his brothers to try put some excitement in his life. He goes to live with a unbelieving man, where he quickly meets an unbelieving woman. He thinks he will now have peace and comfort. Judah marries this woman, whose name we don't even know! Judah was not a very good man at this point! Yet still, he may have been the best of his bad brothers. At least Judah did not want to kill Joseph!

As Genesis 38 continues, Judah cheats Tamar, the wife of his sons. Then Judah goes to what he thought was a prostitute, who ends up being Tamar, the former wife of his two dead sons. Through Judah, she gives birth to twins. One of them is Perez, who ends up being in the line of King David and eventually Jesus. What can we learn from all of these character flaws of Judah, Jesus ancestor?

Jesus was born from a line of sinners, to associate with sinners, to save sinners! No person has ever been born into the family of God based on their own merit! It is purely the grace of God that anyone is His child! Judah had a believing father in Jacob, a believing grandfather in Isaac, and a believing great grandfather in Abraham. Still, he was not concerned about a relationship with God. He did not pay attention to God's rules for living. What about us? Do we have a covenantal upbringing? Are we ignoring what we were taught? Are we living as the world does? Is there any peace in living without knowing Christ?

Prayer: Lord, we are much like Judah! How kind and loving You are to have mercy on us sinners. Lord, how the life of Judah highlights the depths of Your love to us in Christ! We thank You for it. In Jesus' name we pray. Amen.

February 8

"From the time he (Potiphar) put him (Joseph) in charge of his household and of all that he owned, the Lord blessed the household of the Egyptian because of Joseph. The blessing of the Lord was on everything Potiphar had, both in the house and in the field." Genesis 39:5

Potiphar, an official used to train Joseph

Genesis 39 begins as God quickly transfers young Joseph away from the Ishmaelite slave traders. He is now in the employment of Potiphar, who was *"one of Pharoah's officials, the captain of the guard,"* Genesis 39:1b. When we look at the life of Potiphar, we see God blessing the life of an unbelieving government official through a faithful Christian worker like Joseph. It is a good business decision to hire Christians!

Verse two is so wonderfully clear! *"The Lord was with Joseph and he prospered,"* Genesis 39:2a. Potiphar noticed something different about Joseph. He not only saw that Joseph was blessed, but he knew that it was the hand of God that was giving the blessing!

We are so privileged to see how the godly Joseph, unlike his ungodly brother Judah, lived God's way in a wicked culture! By doing this, God shows us the bankruptcy of a pagan system. Even an unbelieving, corrupt food-lover like Potiphar could see that Joseph would not lie, cheat or steal. In fact, never before had Potiphar seen such loyalty in a person. Potiphar was so impressed with Joseph, that he quickly put Joseph, *"in charge of his household, and all that he owned."* Next we read that Potiphar prospered in *"everything"* that Joseph was in charge of!

But the real hero here is God! He uses an ungodly government official to disciple young Joseph in the ways of officials, rulers and kings. God is training Joseph to become a great leader. And guess what? God still completely equips those He chooses to use for His purposes! And God's ways of training are always right and effective!

Prayer: Lord, we see here and also later on how You, in Your own way, equipped normal people like Joseph, Moses and Daniel to be Your bright lights in dark places. Lord equip us also to sparkle for You! Use us to show a dark world that You are Almighty God. Lord, we have but one life to give; we want to give it in service for Your kingdom. In Jesus' name we pray. Amen.

February 9

"Now Joseph was well-built and handsome, and after a while his master's wife took notice of Joseph and said, 'Come to bed with me!' But he refused." Genesis 39:6b-8a

Potiphar's wife tries to pollute Joseph

Slaves were the possession of their masters to be used any way the master wanted. And no one would interfere! So when Potiphar's wife tries to catch Joseph, she was in the right according to the Egyptian way of living. But by this time, Potiphar's wife knows that Joseph is a decent man with a moral compass. But Potiphar's wife was used to getting what she wanted. Her desire for Joseph had nothing to do with love and everything to do with lust and power.

Potiphar's wife probably does not realize it, but Satan wants to use her to tempt Joseph. At the very same time, God uses this trial as a test for Joseph to prove the reality of his faith! Joseph does not waver, but replies with the now famous quote: *"How then could I do such a wicked thing and sin against God?"* Genesis 39:9b.

If only we could keep this conviction of Joseph in the forefront of our minds! We know our sin hurts us, but so often we still sin! We know our sin hurts others, and we still sin! But when we are finally convicted that our sin is against God, we may finally stop sinning! The fear of the Lord is truly the beginning of wisdom!

One of the secrets to Joseph being able to resist the advances of Potiphar's wife is that he refused to even be in the same room with her! But she did not give up on trying to catch him! Day after day she stayed after him. And when she did reach out for him, he fled. After this, God tests Joseph in other ways. Then, He blesses Joseph greatly! We never hear of Potiphar's wife again! It was safe for God to bless Joseph, because Joseph remained humble and obedient to God! Would God have blessed Joseph if he had given in to the evil demands of Potiphar's wife? It's not likely! Is it safe for God to bless us?

Prayer: Lord, we have much to learn about temptation! May we have the mind of Joseph! May we flee temptation of all kinds and be faithful! And where we have sinned, may we confess it and receive Your forgiveness, and be restored. In Jesus' name we pray. Amen.

February 10

"And Pharaoh was angry with his two officers, the chief butler and the chief baker. So he put them in custody in the house of the captain of the guard, in the prison, the place where Joseph was confined."
Genesis 40:2-3 NKJV

Mr. Butler & Mr. Baker, placed by God

The "Chief Butler" and "Chief Baker," are out of favor with King Pharaoh. They are thrown into prison with the forgotten Joseph, who has not been forgotten by the King of the Universe. This *"captain of the guard,"* in our text is Potiphar, Joseph's former boss. Potiphar now has Joseph in charge of the prison. The well-being of the prisoners is in Joseph's hands. See how the life of Joseph points to Christ! Joseph's humble beginnings are like Christ's humble beginning! And our well-being is totally in Jesus' hands, just as the Butler and Baker are now in Joseph's hands!

God is up to something big here! Mr. Butler and Mr. Baker have very unusual dreams, on the same night! God has 100% access to the spirits of all people! How this must cause us to pray more! God reveals the meaning of the dreams to Joseph and they come true, exactly! God shows us His complete control in seemingly impossible situations! God is teaching us to trust, love and respect Him more. What shouts to us is: *"Our struggle is not against flesh and blood, but against the rulers, against the authorities, against the powers of this dark world and against the spiritual forces of evil in the heavenly realms,"* Ephesians 6:12. Believe it and pray accordingly! The battle is far bigger than us!

Witness the heart of Joseph concerning the two men. *"He saw that they were dejected,"* Genesis 40:6b. Notice he cared that they were hurting. He knew their pain! Jesus knows our pain! These two big men were without the counsel of the pagan magicians and sorcerers that were the wisdom of the land. But God has His servant in place to help them. Are we in place to help hurting people who have a relationship problem with the King of kings?

Prayer: Lord, Your ways are so far superior to the ways of man. We need You. We need Your wisdom and knowledge. Open our eyes so that we might see more clearly how great You are! Teach us to trust in You more and more. In Jesus' name we pray. Amen.

February 11

"Then he gave them these instructions: 'I am about to be gathered to my people. Bury me with my fathers in the cave in the field of Ephron the Hittite, the cave in the field of Machpelah, near Mamre in Canaan... There Abraham and his wife Sarah were buried, there Isaac and his wife Rebekah were buried, and there I buried Leah.'" Genesis 49:29-31

Jacob and Joseph's bones are in Canaan!

Death bed instructions are one of the most serious discussions that ever take place! Perhaps this is where the term "dead serious" comes from. In most cases it is now about family and faith! Both Jacob and Joseph left detailed instructions concerning their bodies after death. Why did Jacob and Joseph both say about the same words in our text? Jacob here is specific that his body is to be buried in Canaan, the promised land! This is where his family, <u>who believed</u>, were buried! See the faith words of Jacob as he says, *"I am about to be gathered to my people."*

"Joseph said to his brothers, 'I am about to die. But God will surely come to your aid and take you up out of this land to the land He promised on oath to Abraham, Isaac and Jacob.' And Joseph made the sons of Israel swear an oath and said, 'God will surely come to your aid, and then you must carry my bones up from this place,'" Genesis 50:24-25. Joseph was commended in the faith chapter, Hebrews 11:22, as having the eyes of faith when he said this!

Both Jacob and Joseph believed God's promises about His people entering the promised land some day! They would both tell you, it matters little how long you live on this earth! <u>But where you spend eternity is what's important!</u> Will your bones be in Canaan, in the new Heavens and Earth that is to come? Will you be forever with the family of God and the good angels?

Prayer: Dear Lord, two words describe the hope and prayer of every true Christian. Two words we want our children, grandchildren, family and friends to take to heart. Those words are, "Be There." Live with Heaven in mind, so that when it is our time to meet our Maker, we can peacefully fold up our legs in bed like Jacob did, waiting for God to take us to the Promised Land! Praise God for His mercy and grace to all who believe. In Jesus' name we pray. Amen.

February 12

"You intended to harm me, but God intended it for good to accomplish what is now being done, the saving of many lives." Genesis 50:20

Joseph's attitude to his suffering

You know Joseph's story. His brothers sold him. He was a slave for seven years, in prison for seven more. He was separated from his family. He was totally out of his comfort zone! He suffered so much! In all of this time, it is never recorded that Joseph did anything wrong! So why did Joseph need to go through all these difficult trials and tribulations? Our text tells us, for *"the saving of many lives."* Joseph's sufferings were for God's glory first. Secondly, his sufferings were for the benefit of others. And thirdly, they were also for Joseph's *"good"*! And Joseph knew it! More than that, he accepted it! That is why Joseph had such a great attitude! <u>And many were saved because of it!</u>

Joseph's life points to Jesus who was a perfect man, the God-Man. God also allowed people to mistreat Jesus. He suffered more than Joseph, more than any person ever has or ever will suffer! What is the reason? Like Joseph, He suffered for, *"the saving of many lives"*!

Now, we are suffering! We have problems! At times people treat us like slaves. At times we feel like we're in jail! We are forsaken by brothers and sisters in Christ that should be loving us! People say nasty things about us! What do we make of it all? How is our attitude? Are we aware that our sufferings are for the very same reasons as Jesus' and Joseph's? Do we yet know, God wants to use us too, *"for the saving of many lives"*?

God wants us to know that He didn't save us just to take us to Heaven; He also saved us to use us as His servant, *"for the saving of many lives."*! Our problem is, when we became Christians we didn't look much like Christ yet! So God in His wisdom, through sufferings of various kinds, conforms us to the image of Christ! Why? So that He can use us *"for the saving of many lives"*! May we bring our attitude to suffering in line with God's design for our lives!!

Prayer: Lord, You are an awesome God! Forgive us for wanting to get out of our trials instead of appreciating what You are doing through them! Lord, use us for Your purposes! In Jesus' name we pray. Amen.

February 13

"Now a man of the house of Levi married a Levite woman, and she became pregnant and gave birth to a son. When she saw that he was a fine child, she hid him for three months." Exodus 2:1-2

Jochebed, the precious mother of Moses

It is now, 400 years after Joseph. There are two million people in Israel. Formerly the Israelites were welcome in Egypt. Now they are seen as a threat. The Egyptian government makes them slaves to control them, to use them for their own gain. God's people are in bondage and <u>need a deliverer</u>! See how God raises one up!

Both of Moses' parents were Levites, the tribe that priests came from. Later, in Numbers, we find their names. *"The name of Amram's wife was Jochebed… To Amram she bore Aaron, Moses and their sister Miriam,"* Numbers 26:59. Just before Moses' birth, Pharoah commanded that all the boy babies be put into the sea and killed. Jochebed would not do this. After hiding baby Moses for three months, she put him in a little boat basket. Jochebed entrusted the life of Moses to God's mercy!

God "arranges" Pharoah's daughter to take a bath in the Nile river. God "makes" her see the little boat. God "moves" her to have compassion for little Moses. Older sister, Miriam, "happens" to be watching. She asks the princess, *"Shall I go and get one of the Hebrew women to nurse the baby for you?"* Exodus 2:7b. Now God "makes" Pharoah's daughter answer, *"'Yes, go,' she answered. And the girl went and got the baby's <u>mother</u>,"* Exodus 2:8. Pharoah's daughter now "pays" Jochebed to care for her own son. By God's provision, Moses is now the protected son of Pharoah's daughter. What better way to learn how the country runs, to prepare him for his future work as a deliverer from Pharoah's oppressive government. Moses is 100% God's deliverer, trained God's way.

Jochebed took care of little Moses until he was weaned, about four years old or so. How she prayed and taught him, knowing he would soon be living in a wicked and godless world! May we pray and prepare our children just like Jochebed did!

Prayer: Lord, what a comfort this chapter is about how Your eye is on Your people. May this move us to praise and to trust in Your total control of world events yet today. In Jesus' name we pray. Amen.

February 14

"Now a priest of Midian had seven daughters, and they came to draw water and fill the troughs to water their father's flock. Some shepherds came along and drove them away, but Moses got up and came to their rescue and watered their flock." Exodus 2:16-17

Moses, a man who cared about justice

When Moses grew up, we see that he was a man with an acute sense of justice. He stepped in when an Egyptian was beating a Hebrew. He stepped in when two Hebrews were fighting. In our text, he moves in to help seven young ladies who were being mistreated by other shepherds. Moses cared about and protected those who were unable to protect themselves. Moses knew he was spared from injustice as a baby when other boy babies were killed. Moses understood mercy firsthand. Does the same mercy of God move us to be merciful to others?

God put a sense of justice in Moses, because God cares about injustice! His perfect justice flows out of His holy and just character. Much later, when the Israelites were fasting and praying, but were not concerned about injustice, God rebuked them! He told them, and us, *"Is not this the kind of fasting I have chosen: to loose the chains of injustice and untie the cords of the yoke, to set the oppressed free and break every yoke?"* Isaiah 58:6.

God was specific about who needed justice. *"If you spend yourselves in behalf of the hungry and satisfy the needs of the oppressed, then your light will rise in the darkness, and your night will become like the noonday,"* Isaiah 58:10. There are "oppressed" orphans and widows. Who will cry out for them and be their mouthpiece to seek justice? There are those in families who face so much abuse. Who will bring them a word of comfort and a hand of help in God's name? Yesterday a pastor said, "My salary is for me and my family, not for the hurting!" What is our salary for?

Prayer: Lord, we have heard the quote: "All it takes for injustice and evil to triumph is for good people to do nothing." Lord, too often we have done nothing. Forgive us and move us with Your sense of justice in our hearts. Give us every resource we need to help others, and protect us as we do! In Jesus' name we pray. Amen.

"Who am I, that I should go to Pharaoh and bring the Israelites out of Egypt?" "What if they do not believe me or listen to me and say, 'The Lord did not appear to you'?" "O Lord, I have never been eloquent, neither in the past nor since You have spoken to Your servant. I am slow of speech and tongue." "O Lord, please send someone else to do it."
Exodus 3:11b, 4:1b, 10b & 13b

Moses' four excuses not to do ministry

Moses was called by God to deliver people from sin. This is also our calling as Christians! The following excuses of Moses, not to do God's work, are also our worthless excuses not to serve God!

1. *"Who am I, that I should go...?"* - I have just ordinary abilities. I lack what it takes to deliver anyone from bondage. God answers Moses, *"I will be with you,"* Exodus 3:12b. God promises His presence! God even promises results! *"You will worship God on this mountain,"* Exodus 3:12c. Jesus promised both His presence in the Great Commission and results that His Word would not return void. We must go in faith and obedience.

2. *"What if they do not believe me or listen to me...?"* - God told Moses to throw the stick he was holding on the ground. It became a snake. If God can use a stick in your hand to convince them, how much more can He use His Word to pierce their hearts?

3. *"I have never been eloquent."* - *"The Lord said to him, 'Who gave man his mouth?"* Exodus 4:11. *"Now go; I will help you speak and will teach you what to say,"* Exodus 4:12. When will we depend on God's resources? We are not competent in ourselves! *"Our competence comes from God,"* 2 Corinthians 3:5b. We are dependent on God's eloquence!

4. *"O Lord, please send someone else to do it."* - Like Moses, we try every excuse we can think of to get away from our God-given responsibility to witness to others who are in bondage to sin. God blocks our every excuse and commands us to go!

Prayer: Lord, like Moses, You commissioned us! Jesus' final words in Acts 1:8b are: *"You will be My witnesses in Jerusalem, and in all Judea and Samaria, and to the ends of the earth."* Lord, we are grateful for Your direction, presence, protection and commission! Make us effective for You! In Jesus' name we pray. Amen.

February 16

"At a lodging place on the way, the Lord met [Moses] and was about to kill him. But Zipporah took a flint knife, cut off her son's foreskin and touched [Moses'] feet with it. 'Surely you are a bridegroom of blood to me,' she said. So the Lord let him alone." Exodus 4:24-26a

Zipporah didn't understand the sacraments

Moses is going to Egypt to free Israel from slavery! Suddenly, God interrupts his journey to vividly point to his serious sin of omission. He failed to circumcise his second son! It appears from the context, that his wife Zipporah, was strongly opposed to God's bloody initiation rite into the covenant. Starting with Abraham, God commanded His people, *"Every male among you who is eight days old must be circumcised,"* Genesis 17:1b. In fact, God repeats the words *"must be,"* many times in just five verses. Then God warns, *"Any uncircumcised male, who has not been circumcised in the flesh, will be cut off from his people; he has broken My covenant,"* Genesis 17:14.

Our text in the NIV, is not very clear. The original Hebrew reads "him" instead of "[Moses]". The context makes the word "him," Gershom, the uncircumcised son of Moses. Zipporah did the cutting, it appears in frustration. For her words accuse God and Moses of being bloodthirsty! But Zipporah did not understand something! Blood had to be shed to rescue us from sin! Moses had to be faithful to the covenant to be a deliverer. After all, he is a picture of Jesus! There is no salvation without the precious blood of Christ being shed!

Zipporah's actions could better be described as "swiping" instead of "touching" the feet of Gershom with the bloody skin. For it is the very same word used for putting the blood on the doorpost of the houses on that first Passover. Again, it all points to Jesus' blood! It also points to baptism which replaced circumcision. The bloody rite became bloodless with the shedding of Christ's blood. The water of baptism symbolizes that Christ alone cleanses us from our sin. Zipporah didn't understand God's sacrament of holy baptism. Do we?

Prayer: Lord, You show us how sacraments point to Christ alone, cleansing us from our sin. May we preach and teach that message of the Cross, that Jesus alone saves! In Jesus' name we pray. Amen.

February 17

"I am the Lord, and I will bring you <u>out from</u> under the yoke of the Egyptians. I will free you from being slaves to them, and I will redeem you with an outstretched arm and with mighty acts of judgment."
Exodus 6:6b

Moses, God's "out of, across & into" plan

Our title is a basic summary of life, and the mission God has called us to. This is a good evangelism lesson from the life of Moses. We must see the big picture of what is happening to infant Israel. God's plan for them, and for us also, is to be delivered <u>out of</u> sin, brought <u>across</u> the wilderness of life, and led <u>into</u> the Promised Land!

Joseph has been gone for 400 years, but God did not forget His promise to Abraham to make a great nation from him. About 2 million Israelite people are now alive, but they are slaves! <u>Slaves cannot free themselves</u>! So God acts to deliver His people from Egypt. This is also a picture of our slavery to sin. Let us see both Israel's and our, out of-across-and into-plan of God.

Out of — Moses as a type of Jesus was sent by God to deliver His people out of slavery. Paul wrote, *"For we know that our old self was crucified with Him so that the body of sin might be done away with, that we should no longer be slaves to sin — because anyone who has died has been freed from sin,"* Romans 6:6-7. Many people ask, "What is this or that person's problem? They just don't seem able to live for God." The answer is: most likely, they are still, *"slaves to sin."* They need to be delivered "out of" bondage by Jesus! Slaves cannot deliver themselves.

Across — Just as Moses led the people through the wilderness, we too must go through ours! Peter wrote, *"Dear friends, do not be surprised at the painful trial you are suffering, as though something strange were happening to you,"* 1 Peter 4:12. All Christians must go "across" the wilderness on their spiritual journey.

Into — The Christian's final step is going "into" Heaven!

Prayer: Lord, Your grace alone delivered us "out of" sin. It is Your grace and power that brings us "across" the wilderness of life. Your great mercy leads us "into" Heaven. We glorify Your name. In Jesus' name we pray. Amen.

February 18

"Therefore, say to the Israelites: 'I am the Lord, and I will bring you out from under the yoke of the Egyptians. I will free you from being slaves to them, and I will redeem you with an outstretched arm and with mighty acts of judgment. I will take you as My own people, and I will be your God. Then you will know that I am the Lord your God, who brought you out from under the yoke of the Egyptians."

Exodus 6:6-7

The gods of Egypt, defeated by God

Some of the plagues on Egypt seem strange. Why turn a river into blood? Why send frogs, gnats and flies in such great numbers? God had good reasons! The Egyptians served many gods, and in 400 years the children of Israel worshiped these same gods. We will look at the gods of Egypt that were defeated and try to understand how this impacts our world today. May we see that God is all powerful; and that the gods of this world are powerless!

First, God turned the Nile River into blood in Exodus 7:14-25. The Nile gave its life-giving water in a desert place. Man, animals and the crops couldn't live without it! The river was considered to be the blood of the underworld god "Orisis." A main god of the Egyptians, "Khnum," was believed to protect the Nile; he failed. Even the crocodile god "Hapi," had to run for his life to live! On the first plague, already God showed His almighty power, and the Egyptian gods powerless.

Second, God caused frogs to overrun the land in Exodus 8:1-15. "Heget" was a goddess, considered to be the wife of the creator god. She was also thought to be the goddess of birth and fertility, and had the head of a frog. How fitting that God told Pharaoh that the frogs *"will come up into your palace and your bedroom and onto your bed,"* Exodus 8:3b. If you killed a frog you could be killed! And now there were dead frogs all over Egypt! Instead of giving life, the frogs were a rotten pile of death!

Prayer: Dear Father in Heaven, thank You for giving Your Son's blood to give life to us all. Also, it is You alone, not any idol god, who gives children to parents. How great You are! How the idols of the land are worthless! We worship You! In Jesus' name we pray. Amen.

February 19

*"I will deal differently with the land of Goshen, where My people live;
no swarms of flies will be there, so that you will know that I, the Lord,
am in this land. I will make a distinction between My people and your
people. This miraculous sign will occur tomorrow."*
Exodus 8:22b-23

Egypt gets judgment; Israel gets mercy
Third, God made the dust to become gnats, Exodus 8:16-19. "Set"
was the god of the desert and of storms. The gnats, including fleas and
lice, came from the desert dust in a storm. Gnats infested man and beast
alike. Gnats were on their skin, in their skin, under their skin. The Egyptian
priests shaved their body hair daily, to be "clean" to do sacrifices. But
they couldn't shave due to the gnats, thus they could not do any sacrifices.
Our God is so incredible. Even a flea is subject to His will! In Exodus
8:19a, *"the magicians said to Pharaoh, 'This is the finger of God.'"* Exactly!
That's what they were supposed to learn!

Fourth, God sent swarms of flies, Exodus 8:20-32. "Amon Ra" was
thought to be the creator god. He had the head of a beetle which is
likely what these "swarms" were. Our text is clear that this particular
plague was not on the children of Israel. Whereas the first was
"everywhere in Egypt." The second was in the *"whole country"* The third
was *"throughout the land of Egypt."* The reason for this: God's children
also had to be convinced that the Lord, their God, could protect them,
and the gods of Egypt, could protect no one! God now makes "a
distinction" between His covenant people and pagan unbelievers. The
use of the word *"tomorrow"* and the fact that it happened the next day,
shows that God keeps His judgment promises. Yet, in the very same day,
His people experience God's abundant grace! The prophet said, *"And
you will again see the distinction between the righteous and the wicked,
between those who serve God and those who do not,"* Malachi 3:18.

Prayer: Dear Merciful Father, how amazing is Your abundant grace to
Your people yet today. We do not deserve Your distinctive blessings
but we sure are thankful for them! Thank You for giving us what we
need, not what we deserve! In Jesus' name we pray. Amen.

February 20

"The hand of the Lord will bring a terrible plague on your livestock in the field – on your horses and donkeys and camels and on your cattle and sheep and goats." Exodus 9:3

Egyptians' possessions and health taken

Fifth, God plagues the Egyptians' livestock, Exodus 9:1-7. Animals were sacred in Egypt. There were many animal-headed deities. "Hathor" was a goddess with a cow's head. "Apis" was the bull god. Many bull calves were sacrificed. But practically speaking, the cattle provided food, milk and transportation for the people. When the best bull of the land died, he was embalmed and a new one was sought. The bull was believed to have the gift of prophesy. Later when the Israelites made a golden calf, they were looking for a prophetic message, to see what was going to happen to them. In this plague God attacks the prized possessions of the Egyptians! Once again, He protects the cattle of His chosen people. Even in the wilderness, the Israelites' shoes and clothing did not wear out for 40 years. God protected their possessions as He still protects His people yet today!

Sixth, the Lord sends boils, Exodus 9:8-12. "Sekmet," was the Egyptian goddess they believed kept their diseases away. "Imholep," was the god of medicine. "Sunu," was the god of pestilence. None of these gods were able to protect the Egyptians from the plague of boils. The boils were even on their animals. Now we see that their personal bodies are more seriously afflicted. The gods of Egypt are shown for what they are: no power, nothing and nonsense. They were given to the people by Satan himself to keep them from the real God who made them and all things.

Prayer: Lord, how powerful You are. You know our thoughts and stubborn hearts. You saw all of the gods of the Egyptians and You see our gods today. May we not harden our hearts to You, for we are not innocent. Like Pharaoh and his people, we have "things," gods really, that we have served more than You! Lord bring revival in our hearts! In Jesus' name we pray. Amen.

February 21

"This time I will send the full force of My plagues against you and against your officials and your people, so you may know that there is no one like Me in all the earth." Exodus 9:14

The Egyptians' crops fail by God's hand

Seventh, God sends hail, Exodus 9:13-35. The biggest hail storm ever falls on Egypt. Their crop failure is completely by the hand of God, not by "mother nature." "Set," the Egyptian god of the storms was without power to stop it. "Nut," the goddess of the sky controlled nothing! God shows Egypt and us that He is the One in control of not just this hail storm, but every storm, big or small. *"Throughout Egypt hail struck everything in the fields – both men and animals; it beat down everything growing in the fields and stripped every tree,"* Exodus 9:25.

Eighth, God sends the locust, Exodus 10:1-20. What the hail missed, the locust ate. This was complete devastation! "Thermuths" the goddess of the harvest was asleep. "Nepri" the god of the grain crops was silenced. "Seth" the god of all growing crops was absent. To make sure the people completely noticed, God sent the locust in from the east. They normally came from the south. God is so in control! He alone gives a harvest to all people everywhere!

Ninth, darkness is over the whole land, Exodus 10:21-29. "Hathor" was the Egyptian god of the sky. "Ra or Re" was their sun god, who they believed was born every morning. All the Pharaoh kings, were considered to be direct sons of "Ra." With darkness for three days, their sun god could not show his face! Darkness was also a sign of God's judgment. This is exactly why it was dark for three hours when Jesus died. God was judging our sin just like He judged the sins of Egypt!

Prayer: Lord, Your providence, Your power and Your grace to those You are saving is so amazing. What a complete picture of how narrow Your road of grace is to Your people. How wide Your road of wrath is to those who harden their hearts! May we flee to You today in true repentance. You alone are God and You alone can save us. We thank You for teaching us through words and pictures. In Jesus' name we pray. Amen.

February 22

"On the same night I will pass through Egypt and strike down every firstborn — both men and animals — and I will bring judgment on all the gods of Egypt. I am the Lord." Exodus 12:12

The gods of Egypt, defeated by God!
Tenth, the death of the firstborn, Exodus 11:1 — 12:30. "Min" was a god of reproduction. "Isis" was the god who protected children. Besides that, Pharaoh was a main god. Even before the plagues began, God told Moses, He would harden Pharaoh's heart and Pharaoh would not let the children of Israel go. When that happens, *"Say to Pharaoh 'This is what the Lord says: Israel is My firstborn son, and I told you, "Let My son go, so he may worship Me." But you refused to let him go; so I will kill your firstborn son,'"* Exodus 4:22-23. God warned Pharaoh 9 times, *"Let My people go."* Now God will deliver His people, showing everyone He is stronger than Pharaoh also!

So in the first nine plagues, God told Moses, *"stretch out your hand,"* and the plagues happened. This tenth and final plague of death is God's responsibility. God says, *"I will go throughout Egypt."* Judgment day came on God's schedule to Pharaoh and all of Egypt! And so it will come again someday soon!

For 80 years, Pharaoh killed so many boy babies and later on girl babies too. Is God paying back Pharaoh for taking so many innocent lives? God did say, *"It is Mine to avenge; I will repay. In due time their foot will slip; their day of disaster is near and their doom rushes upon them,"* Deuteronomy 32:35. May we today repent of our great sin of abortion! We also deserve the harsh judgment of God!

Don't miss the obvious: The children of Israel were spared. The wrath of God passed over them because of the innocent blood of the lamb on their doorpost. When Christ's shed blood is on the doorpost of our hearts, we too are spared from eternal death! It will pass over us, just as the killing angel passed over all Israel! God gave His firstborn to spare us from His wrath! No god can save us. They are all powerless!

Prayer: Lord, we see Your mercy and judgment on the same day, a sign of Your coming judgment that the whole world will soon see. May we be ready for that day. In Jesus' name we pray. Amen.

February 23

"I will harden the hearts of the Egyptians so that they will go in after them. And I will gain glory through Pharaoh and all his army, through his chariots and his horsemen. The Egyptians will know that I am the Lord when I gain glory through Pharaoh." Exodus 14:17-18a

Pharaoh's life, for the glory of God!

Egypt is a symbol of evil or sin. Pharaoh is a picture of the ruler of evil. Moses is a deliverer, pointing to Jesus who is coming. The crossing of the Red Sea is a picture of our baptism, a sign of the covenant God has with us and we have with God! Canaan is a picture of Heaven. The desert is a picture of our trials on the way to Heaven.

Pharaoh's life teaches us that God is glorified when He defeats evil. Twice God points this out in our text so we don't miss it! We often don't like the doctrine of election. We say it's not fair of God! But the truth is, God did bring Pharaoh into the world to bring glory to His holy name. God also defeated Pharaoh's gods in Egypt!

Why do we think it is unfair of God, to raise up a Pharaoh, just to destroy him? Is it because we believe a loving God would not do that? Is it because we think all people somehow deserve salvation? But is not the opposite what is really true? *"The wages of sin is death,"* Romans 6:23a. That is exactly what we deserve! Pharaoh got what he deserved. If we, through God's grace, have salvation, it is we who did not get what we deserved!

Paul teaches basically the same truth. *"For the Scripture says to Pharaoh: 'I raised you up for this very purpose, that I might display My power in you and that My name might be proclaimed in all the earth. Therefore God has mercy on whom He wants to have mercy, and He hardens whom He wants to harden,"* Romans 9:17-18.

If we still think God is unfair, then God through Paul asks us a very good question, *"Does not the potter* (God) *have the right to make out of the same lump of clay* (all people) *some pottery for noble purposes* (Christians) *and some for common use?"* Romans 9:21.

Prayer: Lord, we are humbled. The main difference between Pharaoh and us is Your electing grace. We do not deserve it but how we thank You for it. In Jesus' name we pray. Amen.

February 24

"In the desert the whole community grumbled against Moses and Aaron. The Israelites said to them, 'If only we had died by the Lord's hand in Egypt! There we sat around pots of meat and ate all the food we wanted, but You have brought us out into this desert to starve this entire assembly to death.'" Exodus 16:2-3

The Israelites grumble and stumble!

The Israelites are 45 days out of Egypt. Their salvation is complete. They have been delivered from slavery. But now their bread from Egypt is gone. So they cry for the comforts of their old life! They accuse Moses and Aaron of wanting to kill them. Filled with self-pity, they say, *"If only we had died by the Lord's hand in Egypt!"* Self-pity kills yet today! It kills physically, spiritually, mentally, socially, even financially. Israel's grumbling is recorded here for us to see the foolishness of it!

Grumbling is a very serious offense to God and to the family of God! Did God make some mistake in bringing those He saves out of bondage to sin and Satan? What is God's purpose for Israel's wilderness trials and for ours? Is it to kill us? If so, God could have done that at or before the crossing of the Red Sea!

Believe, O Israel! Believe, O Christian! The God who spared us is completely able to care for us! Don't we see it? God our teacher is testing our faith. Our grumbling is failing the test miserably! James said, *"Count it all joy when you fall into various trials!"* The right attitude is gratitude and joy, not grumbling!

God put us here to love Him first and others second. It is a summary of the Law and the whole Bible. God tests us with trials to see if we have learned life's lessons! Are we still impatient? Do we lack gratitude for what God has already done and continues to do? Let us not selfishly stumble and grumble, accusing God of not caring for us!

Prayer: Lord, how our faults are like Old Testament Israel's. And we also have the New Testament to help us! We know that, *"He who began a good work in you will complete it."* We know Jesus said, *"No one can snatch us out of His hand."* Paul even wrote, *"Nothing can separate us from the love of God."* Yet still, we grumble. Lord, forgive us for our selfish ways of living! In Jesus' name we pray. Amen.

February 25

"The Israelites ate manna forty years, until they came to a land that was settled; they ate manna until they reached the border of Canaan."
Exodus 16:35

The Israelites' manna, and yours

This 40 year "Manna" event is not recorded just for the benefit of Old Testament Israel. It is also recorded for us! Christians are the present day Israel, also God's chosen people promised to Abraham. What does this mean for us that God provided manna for forty years? We must see two important truths. <u>God's sovereignty gave the manna</u> and <u>it's our responsibility to pick it up</u>!

The Israelites were delivered from bondage. We were delivered from bondage to sin. Forty years they were in a wilderness, same as our adult lifetime! Suddenly they have trials. So do we. Will they trust God to care for them? Will we? The enemy was after them, but God protected them. He protects us from Satan also! They were baptized in the sea. We were most likely baptized! Then the children of Israel needed water in a desert. God provided it. Next they were hungry, in a desert with no food! If they had not been fed by God, they would have surely died! Could God provide for them? He gladly did! *"The Lord said to Moses, 'I will rain down bread from Heaven for you,'"* Exodus 16:4a.

The Old Testament manna points to Jesus in the New Testament. God sent our Manna (Jesus) from Heaven! *"The Bread of God is He who comes down from Heaven and gives life to the world,"* John 6:33. Jesus said to the people and to us, *"I am the Bread of life. He who comes to Me will never go hungry,"* John 6:35a. If we do not eat physically and spiritually, we die. God gives us bread that never spoils, which is Jesus Himself. Will we pick Him up? Will we accept Him? <u>The Israelites had to go out to get the manna</u>! Jesus said, *"Ask and it will be given to you; seek and you will find; knock and the door will be open to you,"* Luke 11:9. We have the gracious invitation to have Manna in our wilderness, for all our years, and for all eternity!

Prayer: Lord, we see here both Your amazing grace and the personal responsibility of each of us to seek and find You. Open our eyes and our hearts to You. Fill us with Jesus! In His name we pray. Amen.

"Moses father-in-law replied, 'What you are doing is not good. You and these people who come to you will only wear yourselves out. The work is too heavy for you; you cannot handle it alone.'" Exodus 18:17-18

Jethro, he understood discipleship

We have before us one of the most important truths in the Bible! It is mostly a rebuke to Moses for not doing discipleship God's way. Moses was working from sunup to sundown. Day after day, Moses worked without taking a break. Moses was exhausted, burned out, stressed out! And Moses was not the only one getting worn out! The people were not getting answers or help for their problems. Their difficult issues remained. Yet, the biggest problem Moses had was his "go it alone attitude." God was not being glorified in the best way! So God sent Moses' *"father-in-law"* to rebuke him for not using His "discipleship process" to train others to help lead God's people to the Promised Land!

Part of Moses' problem was he was gifted, he could do things better than anyone else! Yet still, he was not using his gifts to train others. When we are not willing to take the time to train others, discipleship stops! What happens if a mother or father does not train/disciple their children? What happens when a teacher displays to the students how great he or she is but does not train/disciple the students to think? What happens when a manager in the workplace fails to train others? What happens when the pastor does not teach others to do the work of the Lord? The answer is: not much!

Jesus commanded us, *"go and make disciples."* Train, communicate, discipline, praise and rebuke are all Bible themes and part of the discipleship process. These words from Moses' father-in-law are for us today. *"What you are doing is not good. You and these people who come to you will only wear yourselves out. The work is too heavy for you; you cannot handle it alone,"* Exodus 18:17-18.

Prayer: Lord, forgive us for not taking more seriously the command and responsibility to disciple and train others. Thank You for helping us see that discipleship at every level is important to You, to advance Your kingdom. Lord, move us to take the time to be more faithful in discipleship! In Jesus' name we pray. Amen.

February 27

"Moses went up to God, and the Lord called to him from the mountain and said, 'This is what you are to say to the house of Jacob and what you are to tell the people of Israel: "You yourselves have seen what I did to Egypt, and how I carried you on eagles' wings and brought you to Myself. Now if you obey Me fully and keep My covenant, then out of all nations you will be My treasured possession. Although the whole earth is Mine, you will be for Me a kingdom of priests and a holy nation.'" Exodus 19:3-6a

Moses and the covenants from God

The Mosaic Covenant, is this covenant God gave to Moses in our text. But, how is this different than the Abrahamic Covenant given to Abraham? God gave Abraham a <u>Promise</u>, a <u>Seed</u>, that is Christ. Through Him all the nations of the world would be blessed! *"The Scriptures foresaw that God would justify the Gentiles by faith, and announced the Gospel in advance to Abraham,"* Galatians 3:8a. God promised Abraham a <u>land</u>, Canaan. By faith, Abraham believed this covenant promise!

The Mosaic Covenant was a <u>picture</u> of Christ coming. It shows us more completely how obedience and faith are required. Obedience, because the Law or Ten Commandments are now given. *"If you obey me fully,"* makes the covenant conditional. The covenant is by faith also, because the tabernacle was central with all of its ceremonies and sacrifices. All, a <u>picture</u> of Christ and His church. Moses is the mediator of the covenant, a <u>picture</u> of the coming Mediator, Jesus Christ.

Later, in the New Testament, we have the <u>provision</u> of a New Covenant. Jesus, the Messiah has arrived. New, because the many animal sacrifices have been replaced with Christ's one sacrifice. New, because He <u>provided</u> the way for us to come close to God. New, because we have been <u>provided</u> His Spirit in fuller measure. New, because believers are <u>provided</u> with a new power to stop sinning.

Prayer: Lord, after we were separated from You by Adam's sin, we needed You to seek us out and establish a saving covenant with us. We worship You for <u>promising</u> Christ, for giving us a <u>picture</u> of His coming and then <u>providing</u> us forgiveness in Him. You are so gracious! We thank You! In Jesus' name we pray. Amen.

"Now take Aaron your brother, and his sons with him, from among the children of Israel, that he may minister to Me as priest, Aaron and Aaron's sons: Nadab, Abihu, Eleazar, and Ithamar." Exodus 28:1 NKJV

Aaron, and the office of priest

In Exodus 20, the Law of God is given in the form of the Ten Commandments. Then, rules for justice and the religious feasts were set up. God covenantally pledged Himself to His people in Exodus 24. The first temple called the Ark of the Covenant was given. Now priests were needed to carry out the duties. Since leaving Egypt, Moses acted as priest, but he also held the office of prophet. In our text, God now directs Moses to *"take Aaron your brother, and his sons with him, from among the children of Israel, that he may minister to Me as priest."* From now on, the priest would be from the tribe of Levi, descendants of Aaron. There were many priests that served in the temple system, but there was one main High Priest. The first was Aaron.

The duty of the High Priest was to see that the various priests were doing their job properly. There was that one big day of the year, the Day of Atonement. On that day, once a year, the High Priest alone entered the Holy of Holies. He first made a sacrifice for his own sins, then he sacrificed for the sins of the people. This was the practice of God's people until the death of Jesus on the Cross. At that time, God ripped the veil of the temple in half to show that the office of priest was replaced by His Son. Jesus told the Samaritan woman, the place for worship was no longer on any mountain, but was He Himself. The old temple was destroyed about 70 A.D.

Do you see the picture of how Jesus replaced the priest and sacrificial system? Jesus is now our place of worship. Jesus is now our eternal High Priest. Jesus is, once and for all, the sacrifice for our sins! The whole Old Testament system pointed to Jesus coming into the world!

Prayer: Lord, how privileged we are to have Jesus as our High Priest! Anytime we can go to Him and have our sins forgiven. How graciously You restore us to the condition of Adam before he sinned. We are now perfect in Your sight because Jesus took our sin! We worship You. In Jesus' name we pray. Amen.

February 29

"So all the people broke off the golden earrings which were in their ears, and brought them to Aaron. And he received the gold from their hand, and he fashioned it with an engraving tool, and made a molded calf. Then they said, 'This is your god, O Israel, that brought you out of the land of Egypt!'" Exodus 32:3-4 NKJV

The people want an idol, not God

The Israelites heard the law given by God in Exodus 20, and trembled! Then God called Moses to the mountain top to give him the commandments, carved in stone by His own finger. The introduction and first commandment the people heard just days before they built a calf was this: *"I am the Lord your God, who brought you out of the land of Egypt, out of the house of bondage. You shall have no other gods before Me. You shall not make for yourself any carved image, or any likeness of anything that is in Heaven above, or that is in the earth beneath, or that is in the water under the earth; you shall not bow down to them nor serve them. For I, the Lord your God, am a jealous God,"* Exodus 20:2-5a NKJV. And they made the calf anyway!

While God was giving a "hard copy" of the Law to Moses, the people and Aaron, made a golden calf. They bowed down to it, claiming this god brought them out of Egypt! How quickly we sinful people forget God!

Do we still have idols? Do we have other gods? Do we bow down to them? Yes, we not only serve idols, we do exactly what the Bible warns us not to do! *"They (and we) exchanged the truth of God for a lie, and worshiped and served created things rather than the Creator—who is forever praised. Amen,"* Romans 1:25. Anything that is more important to us than God, is an idol. For us, our golden calf is being a slave to getting more money, sex, drugs, alcohol, food, T.V., sports and much more! Examining our hearts to see what idols we have is so important that John even ended his book to believers saying, *"Dear children, keep yourselves from idols,"* 1 John 5:21.

Prayer: Lord, help us to search our hearts for the idols we still have. Convict us of those things in our lives that are more important to us than a close relationship with You. Help us to love You more than anything else. In Jesus' name we pray. Amen.

MARCH

The spies returning from Canaan with fruit from the land

"When they reached the Valley of Eshcol, they cut off a branch bearing a single cluster of grapes. Two of them carried it on a pole between them, along with some pomegranates and figs." Numbers 13:23

March 1

"Then Moses said to the Israelites, 'See, the Lord has chosen Bezalel son of Uri, the son of Hur, of the tribe of Judah, and He has filled him with the Spirit of God, with skill, ability and knowledge in all kinds of crafts.'" Exodus 35:30-31

Bezalel, a craftsman chosen by God

What a meaningful verse! The words, *"the Lord has chosen,"* are so very precious. Here we have a God-fearing common man who is good with his hands. He can make things, all kinds of things, excellent things! He is not some second class person just because he may not have a college degree! *"The Lord has chosen,"* this particular man, to make a lasting difference with his hands! This construction worker is 100% God's ministry worker to do good!

The beautiful words, *"the Lord has chosen,"* must inspire every construction worker to have a right attitude as they go to work every day. God is sending you! Construction workers can be rough as well as tough. Their language is generally more crude and sometimes more vulgar than the "office person." Mr. and Mrs. Construction Worker, you need to remember that God is sending you as a Christian to do His work. You need to act like His employee! Since actions speak louder than words, let your labor speak well of you. Be a leader in the wolf pack, but be a lamb. Show that God's craftsmen are the very best workers! Be a godly example. After all, Jesus was a Carpenter!

These instructive words, *"the Lord has chosen"* must also inspire every wife or family member to think well of your construction worker. He or she is not merely going to work, God is sending them to do His work! Are you giving your blessing to them and praying for them just like the church does when they send a missionary? Your construction worker is on God's mission!

Prayer: Lord, we see that a Christian working man is not only sent by You, but You *"fill him with the Spirit of God."* We see Jesus had more "working men" as His disciples than any other kind. Like their Master before them, they took rough and tough people like themselves and shaped them into jewels for King Jesus. Lord help every Christian worker to make a difference for You! In Jesus' name we pray. Amen.

March 2

"Aaron's sons Nadab and Abihu took their censers, put fire in them and added incense; and they offered unauthorized fire before the Lord, contrary to His command. So fire came out from the presence of the Lord and consumed them, and they died before the Lord."
Leviticus 10:1-2

Nadab's naughty worship

God gave Aaron and his four sons the responsibility of the office of priesthood. The very next day, two of Aaron's sons are killed by God. They did not worship God as He commanded them to. What did Nadab and Abihu do that was so displeasing to God? We should know so that we do not repeat their mistakes!

In Exodus 30:1-5, God gave specific instructions for the building of the altar of incense. Then God described in verse six exactly where the altar must be! *"Put the altar in front of the curtain that is before the ark of the Testimony – before the atonement cover that is over the Testimony – where I will meet with you."* Every morning and evening, the priest offered specific incense to God. The sweet smoke rising was symbolic of Jesus prayerfully interceding for us in Heaven. The people prayed as the priest offered incense. So what was wrong?

<u>Moses had the only supply of incense</u>! Moses was a type of Jesus. And Jesus' prayers of intercession are the only way to God for us. Nadab and Abihu found their own source. They got "censor fire" from the wrong place! Were Nadab and Abihu too proud of their new office? Were they still high from the feast the day before? Maybe. But we do know that two new priests are instantly dead for doing things their own way concerning the worship of God!

We must approach God reverently in worship! We must not change God's message! God's message must change us! Our prayers must lift up God's name, not our own! Our worship must be meaningful, not mindless!

Prayer: Lord, so often the tone of our worship shouts that we are big and You are small. We are too proud, much like Nadab and Abihu! Forgive us and make us more mindful and sincere in our worship. In Jesus' name we pray. Amen.

March 3

"Then Miriam and Aaron spoke against Moses because of the Ethiopian woman whom he had married; for he had married an Ethiopian woman. And they said, 'Has the Lord indeed spoken only through Moses? Has He not spoken through us also?' And the Lord heard it." Numbers 12:1-2 NKJV

Moses, he also had family problems

There are two important matters in our text. First, Moses married into a Gentile race of people and Miriam and Aaron had a problem with it. However, God didn't and He severely disciplined brother Aaron and sister Miriam for speaking out against it. Think about other examples of "mixed" marriages in the Bible. In Genesis 16:1, Abraham married into another race; so did Joseph in Genesis 41:45. Ruth and Boaz were from different races, as well as Salmon and Rahab. David married into another race. But far more than that, Jesus put His holy hands on lepers. He ate with prostitutes and sinners. He touched the blind and the lame. As Bridegroom to the Church, His bride, Christ married *"from every tribe and language and people and nation,"* Revelation 5:9b. What matters is that every Christian must marry another sincere believer.

A second and just as important issue is in verse two. Miriam and Aaron were extremely jealous of Moses. They were bitter that God chose to speak through Moses. Even the Israelite people spoke evil of Moses many times. We learn from this that those God chooses to honor, will be rebuked by men and women, <u>even by Christians who should know better</u>! And so it will happen to us. We should not think this kind of trial to be so strange! If we are jealous for God, a great many people will think we are a religious nut!

Consider what Jesus went through and be encouraged! Jesus too had His family problems, and He was a perfect man! We read that, *"even His own brothers did not believe in Him,"* John 7:5.

Prayer: Lord, give us a good attitude when others are against us, especially when it's family and our Christian community. You told us that what happened to You, will also happen to us. May we not be sidetracked by these difficult issues but keep our eyes on You, the Author and Perfector of our faith. In Jesus' name we pray. Amen.

"Miriam and Aaron began to talk against Moses because of his Cushite wife, for he had married a Cushite. 'Has the Lord spoken only through Moses?' they asked. 'Hasn't He also spoken through us?' And the Lord heard this. (Now Moses was a very humble man, more humble than anyone else on the face of the earth.)" Numbers 12:1-3

Miriam, gifted, but so much self-importance!

As a little girl, Miriam protected her baby brother. She even arranged to have her mother care for him when Pharaoh's daughter found him in his little basket boat. Much later, when the Israelites safely crossed the sea to flee from Pharaoh, Miriam led the women in song about how God protected His people. But soon after this, Miriam became filled with too much self-importance. Our text explains how Miriam and Aaron jealously thought they were equal with Moses. The Lord heard and responded quickly! In verses 6-8, God pointed out to Miriam and Aaron that He spoke to prophets through visions, but He spoke face to face with Moses. God asks them, *"Why then were you not afraid to speak against My servant Moses?"* Immediately, *"The anger of the Lord, burned against them and... there stood Miriam-leprous, like snow. Aaron turned toward her and saw that she had leprosy,"* Numbers 12:9-10.

As a prophetess, Miriam should have been more concerned for the people! Instead, she cared more about herself! Moses was a type of Christ, a mediator to God for the people, and also from God to the people. To reject Moses, was to reject Christ! Thinking they were equal is like us claiming to be equal to our Mediator, Jesus Christ!

How quickly, Aaron's attitude changed after he saw the leprosy of Miriam! *"He said to Moses, 'Please, my lord, do not hold against us the sin we have so foolishly committed,'"* Numbers 12:11. Now Aaron calls Moses, *"my lord."* He also saw his sin and was sorry! It is Moses who now intercedes with God to heal Miriam! God heard his prayer and healed Miriam after seven days. Yet still, think of how Israel's journey to the promised land was delayed as they waited a week for Miriam to heal!

Prayer: Lord, You teach us much through this event. Your kingdom is hindered because of our self-importance. Forgive us Lord! Make us humble like Moses was. In Jesus' name we pray. Amen.

March 5

"And the Lord spoke to Moses saying, 'Send men to spy out the land of Canaan, which I am giving to the children of Israel; from each tribe of their fathers you shall send a man, every one a leader among them.'"
Numbers 13:1-2 NKJV

Twelve spies go to investigate

The Israelites are close to Canaan. Are they ready to enter it? We are close to Heaven! Are we ready to enter it? So God tests their faith, (and ours) to see if it's true faith! God tells Moses to send a representative from each tribe to see what is in the new land. When the twelve returned, *"They gave Moses this account: 'We went into the land to which you sent us, and it does flow with milk and honey! Here is its fruit. But the people who live there are powerful, and the cities are fortified and very large. We even saw descendants of Anak there,'"* Numbers 13:27-28.

Caleb said, *"We should go up and take possession of the land, for we can certainly do it,"* Numbers 13:30b. But the ten men did not agree! Their lack of faith shows in their words, *"We can't attack those people; they are stronger than we are,"* Numbers 13:31b. They had no faith in God! They did not yet believe God, even after all His miracles! They didn't believe God was bigger than any problem that was in front of them! We should learn from this that miracles alone don't make believers! For they would not go in and take the land God was giving them as a gift! For this unbelief, for this not trusting in God, they wandered for forty years in the desert. In the end, they died in the wilderness, missing Heaven, because of their unbelief! They wandered forty years, one year for every day they spied out the land of Canaan!

What about us and our spiritual journey? How big is our faith in God? Do we know that trusting in Christ is meant for us who are weak? Do we yet know that His strength perfectly compensates for our weakness? Have we yet experienced that He is trustworthy and true? Or, does God still need to send us more difficult trials, to teach us that His grace and power are sufficient for us! He is still teaching me!

Prayer: Lord, we would never learn to trust in You if You did not build our faith one trial at a time. We praise You for showing us Your great strength and salvation. In Jesus' name we pray. Amen.

March 6

"Moses also said to Korah, 'Now listen, you Levites! Isn't it enough for you that the God of Israel has separated you from the rest of the Israelite community and brought you near Himself to do the work at the Lord's tabernacle and to stand before the community and minister to them?'" Numbers 16:8-9

Korah's occupy priesthood movement

Korah was a Levite with a giant itch to be more than he presently was. His two friends, Dathan and Abiram, were from the tribe of Reuben. There were also 250 other men. These were "well-known community leaders," not your average common man! These were current leaders in ministry who wanted more power and control over the people than they presently had! Knock! Knock! This fits us also.

Moses here talks mostly to Korah as he is the ringleader and he represents what the other "community leaders" are thinking. Notice that Korah and his associates want a better <u>position</u>. They already had a <u>job</u>, and an important one! Moses points that out! But <u>they were not content to serve</u>. In their arrogance, they thought that they could do a better job than Moses and Aaron. They saw this wandering in the desert as a waste of time and openly said so. They did not have the faith that God would lead them <u>through</u> the desert and bring them <u>to</u> the Promised Land!

"Mr. Korah, God does not need our proud advice! He wants our humble service. Why don't we all just report for duty with a thankful heart? We will never find peace, joy and fulfillment in a bigger position. More respect is not our greatest need! Sincere service is what we are lacking. God's sheep need food! If we feed them, then we too will be satisfied!"

But Korah and company did not want to serve. Rather than lift up their hands to God in worship, they pointed to themselves. Moses told the 250 men to separate from Korah, Dathan and Abiram. Then God opened the earth and swallowed them up. Gone! They are witnesses to us about how important it is to love and serve God and His people.

Prayer: Lord, what graphic scenes You give to move us out of our selfishness and into Your service. Lord, use us for Your glory. In Jesus' name we pray. Amen.

March 7

"Then Balak said to Balaam, 'Neither curse them at all nor bless them at all!' Balaam answered, 'Did I not tell you I must do whatever the Lord says?'" Numbers 23:25-26

Balaam cannot curse God's people!

In Numbers 22, Moabite King Balak, a descendent of Lot, was afraid of Israel. So he hired the evil prophet Balaam to practice divination and put a curse on Israel. But God appears to the evil Balaam and tells him not to curse His people! King Balak continues calling Balaam, even promising him a big gift! God finally allows this wicked prophet to go, but told him *"do only what I tell you,"* Numbers 22:20b.

Balaam went the next morning and the *"angel of the Lord,"* blocked his path three times. Balaam's donkey saw the angel, but Balaam did not. So Balaam beat his donkey for stopping. God put words in the donkey's mouth, complaining about the beating. God then opens Balaam's eyes and he sees the angel of the Lord in the road, with a sword in his hand. The angel tells Balaam he would have killed him, not the donkey, if he tried to get pass. Finally, wicked Balaam performs a sacrifice and God tells him to bless Israel with His words in Numbers 23:7-10. He does, and now the wicked King Balak is really upset!

A second time King Balak hires Balaam to perform another sacrifice to curse the people of God! Again Balaam blesses God's people in Numbers 23:18-24. A third time, Balak hires Balaam to sacrifice another 7 bulls and 7 rams on 7 altars. The result is the same. God's people are blessed! And then we read the words concerning Israel, *"May those who bless you be blessed and those who curse you be cursed,"* Numbers 24:9b. No one can curse God's people without God's permission! If they try, they will be cursed. With this in mind, will wicked leaders today prosper if they try to harm Christians? *"If God is for us, who can be against us?"* Romans 8:31b.

Prayer: Lord, how great and awesome a protector You are! We also see that You can use a man in Your service even if he is not holy or well pleasing to You. Even a donkey can be used to speak Your message! How much more then must we Your children speak and sing praises to You. In Jesus' name we pray. Amen.

March 8

"Six of the towns you give the Levites will be cities of refuge, to which a person who has killed someone may flee." Numbers 35:6a

The Levites' city of refuge points to Jesus

The implications of the verse before us is simply amazing! It is a beautiful display of law, grace and our salvation in Jesus Christ, who is our City of Refuge! Let us see how!

The people are now entering a new land. God gives His people good laws to set up an orderly society. God now provides legal protection for anyone who has killed someone. Six cities, governed by six priests, are set up. All are within a half day's journey from anywhere in the country. In these *"cities of refuge," "a person who has killed someone"* accidentally or intentionally, could flee to it. He would be safe, until his trial date came up. If the trial determines the killing was not intentional, he would be guilty of manslaughter. Then he could stay in that city of refuge until the priest in charge of that city died. After which he would be set free, as if the crime never happened. Christ, our High Priest, set us free when He died.

With a pre-planned murder, the murderer was sentenced to death. Then he was handed over to the avenger, to be put to death. The avenger is the closest family member of the one who was killed! The Hebrew word for *"avenger"* is *"gaal,"* also the word used for "kinsman-redeemer." Boaz and Jesus are "kinsman-redeemers"! This now applies to us.

We are murderers under the law of God, for anger is considered murder. Lust is considered adultery, another capital crime! We must flee immediately to our *"city of refuge,"* to the Cross of Christ! We have intentional sins of commission and unintentional sins of omission! We are guilty! Our court date comes on Judgment Day. We are found guilty! The Avenger, our "Kinsman-Redeemer," or Jesus, the One we have harmed the most, comes for us and stands in our place! We are set free. Our crime is completely avenged! We are fully restored to the Father! *"How shall we escape if we neglect so great a salvation?"* Hebrews 2:3a NKJV.

Prayer: Lord, we are guilty! May we flee to Christ our High Priest, before we are condemned! May Your Spirit convict us and push us to that only Priest today! In Jesus' name we pray. Amen.

March 9

"Hear, O Israel: The Lord our God, the Lord is one. Love the Lord your God with all your heart and with all your soul and with all your strength. These commandments that I give you today are to be upon your hearts. Impress them on your children. Talk about them when you sit at home and when you walk along the road, when you lie down and when you get up. Tie them as symbols on your hands and bind them on your foreheads. Write them on the doorframes of your houses and on your gates." Deuteronomy 6:4-9

Israel's advice on raising children

The first two lines of our text is called the Shema in Hebrew. From earliest childhood the Jewish children memorized this. The reason is: these few verses are a good summary of the Christian religion. Since there were no Bibles then, the fathers would do as God commanded, *"write them on the doorframes of your houses and on your gates."*

"The Lord our God, the Lord is one." Children, there is no other real God! Our one God always existed. No one made Him! Our "one God" made everything, and He made us too. In fact children, when we look around in the world, we will see people who make gods out of wood and stone, but there is only one real God.

Children, even though we are called to <u>look to</u> "one God," know that He is always <u>looking at us also</u>! The "gods" that people make, who are really not gods, can't look at us. They are never aware of how we are living. Their "gods" cannot see us or care about us! Our God is not like that. He made us for Himself! He wants us to be holy like He is. That is why He cares so much about how we live! We cannot see our God because He is a Spirit. He wants to live in our heart!

God created us to love Him. If we do not love Him, we will never listen to how He wants us to live. But we all have a serious problem, we are born selfish. We want to love self the most. God gave us Ten Commandments to teach us to love Him and others. We need God living in our hearts to do this! Let's ask Him to live in us.

Prayer: Lord, You are the one true God! Live in us. Make us love You. Make us holy. Make us to be a blessing in Your world, for Your name's sake. In Jesus' name we pray. Amen.

March 10

"Have I not commanded you? Be strong and courageous. Do not be terrified; do not be discouraged, for the Lord your God will be with you wherever you go." Joshua 1:9

Joshua, strong and courageous

These words of God were comforting and inspiring to Joshua as he faced many obstacles in his service to God. This same verse has been a big comfort to me. God reminds us all, *"Be strong and courageous."* Why? What good is armor on a soldier if there is no courage in the heart? The battle is the Lord's, not ours. As we go forward in faith, the hand of God <u>protects</u> and <u>directs</u> us!

Young person, listen carefully to God here! This promise is for you too! God told Joshua He would bless him. All Joshua had to do was *"be careful to obey all the law,"* in verse 7. You also need to be concerned about being faithful; God will take care of the blessings! You must go to school, to work, and/or spend much time in your home. It is easy to forget these words of God soon after you hear them. More than you will ever know, it matters how you live! God knows the Ten Commandments are critical to direct you! God not only wants you to be faithful, but courageously faithful! The point is, *"Be strong and courageous,"* in how much you love God and how you serve Him!

The opposite of courage is fear. Satan wants us to fear! When we fear, we are useless, not moving, doing nothing for the kingdom of God. Disciple John tells us in 1 John 4:18 NKJV, *"There is no fear in love, but perfect love casts out fear."* That is exactly why God tells Joshua and us, *"Do not be terrified; do not be discouraged, for the Lord your God will be <u>with you</u> wherever you go,"* Joshua 1:9. These words of encouragement from God are even more for us today than for Joshua! God wants these words to ring in our ears so that we will faithfully move for Him. *"Be strong and courageous"*! We will never ever regret it!

Prayer: Lord, what beautiful promises You give! When Jesus left this earth He too said *"Go,"* and then promised, *"Surely I am <u>with you always</u>, to the very end of the age."* Lord, thank You for selecting, protecting and directing us! Forgive us when we fearfully fail to trust and obey You. In Jesus' name we pray. Amen.

March 11

"We have heard how the Lord dried up the water of the Red Sea for you when you came out of Egypt, and what you did to Sihon and Og, the two kings of the Amorites east of the Jordan, whom you completely destroyed. When we heard of it, our hearts melted and everyone's courage failed because of you, for the Lord your God is God in Heaven above and on the earth below." Joshua 2:10-11

Rahab's statement of faith

God's miracles are evangelistic in nature as His children march to Canaan. Rahab's testimony is proof of that! Romans one tells us that all people are without excuse. We can know who God is, just by observing His creation. Rahab heard how God dried up the Jordan River, at flood stage even! Millions of people crossed over. Apply Rahab's knowledge to that horrible tsunami in Japan, and before that, one in Indonesia and India. God uses drastic measures to help us see who He is!

Rahab was a former prostitute, but God changed her! God arranged for two spies to be sheltered in her house. God can use anyone to accomplish His purposes. No one can stop Him. The spies promised Rahab that she and her family would be saved when Jericho was destroyed. All she had to do was leave that scarlet cord hanging outside the same window the spies escaped from. That scarlet rope that saved the spies, saved Rahab! That scarlet rope of redemption will save us too! It points to the redeeming blood of Jesus Christ!

Jericho was the Titanic of cities, two days journey from the Jordan. The walls were so thick that Rahab's house was part of the wall. No one thought these walls could come down! But God did it, by the breath of His mouth. In fact, Rahab's name means, "breath of God." This world will be destroyed some day by the breath of God. Only the scarlet red blood of Christ will save anyone. No one apart from that blood can be saved. No one can hide!

Prayer: Lord, You show us total destruction and total salvation in one Bible character! Your saving of Rahab stands as a testimony of Your grace and power! This Gentile prostitute was an ancestor of Jesus, proof that Jesus welcomes all kinds of people into Your family. Move us and our families to Jesus! In His name we pray. Amen.

March 12

"Achan replied, 'It is true! I have sinned against the Lord, the God of Israel. This is what I have done. When I saw in the plunder a beautiful robe from Babylonia, two hundred shekels of silver and a wedge of gold weighing fifty shekels, I coveted them and took them.'"
Joshua 7:20-21a

Achan's suicidal greed

The fifth chapter of Joshua begins with the Israelites entering Canaan. All males are given the sign of the covenant, circumcision. The Passover is celebrated. Here are the only two sacraments Jesus later gave us, Baptism and the Lord's Supper. Both are signs of the covenantal relationship we have with God!

The first battle in Canaan now happens. Jericho falls without the people lifting a finger. God only tells His people, *"Keep away from the devoted things, so that you will not bring about your own destruction by taking any of them. Otherwise you will make the camp of Israel liable to destruction and bring trouble on it. All the silver and gold and the articles of bronze and iron are sacred to the Lord and must go into His treasury,"* Joshua 6:18-19. The first fruits of victory must go to God! But, this is also a test of the Israelites' faithfulness.

Achan alone, took some of the valuables as God watched. God delays His punishment until Israel goes into battle against a small city and gets beaten. National sins are a responsibility of all people! Defeated, the children of Israel are shocked and cry to God. He points out Achan's sin of covetousness, calling it, *"stealing"* and *"lying."* Stealing because the things belonged to God. Lying, because Achan tried to cover it up. Notice that it is <u>Achan's lack of faith that leads him to steal</u>! Those who steal think God cannot care for them! *"A greedy man brings trouble to his family, but he who hates bribes will live,"* Proverbs 15:27. Achan would be the first to tell us, greed is spiritual suicide!

Prayer: Lord, help us to clearly understand that in The Judgment, You will not ask us how much money we made, but You will ask us if we compromised our character to get it. You will not ask how many clothes we have in our tent (homes), but how many people did we help to clothe! Lord build our faith. In Jesus' name we pray. Amen.

March 13

"I, however, followed the Lord my God wholeheartedly."
Joshua 14:8b

Caleb follows God wholeheartedly

Caleb was a man from the tribe of Judah who loved God. He followed *"God wholeheartedly."* His life long desire was to follow God! Caleb is first mentioned as one of the twelve spies that Moses sent out into the land of Canaan. All twelve saw a beautiful land. All twelve *"saw descendants of Anak,"* the giants and the *"fortified cities."* Ten said "It's too difficult." Caleb said, *"We should go up and take possession of the land, for we can certainly do it,"* Numbers 13:30b.

Contrast the willingness of Caleb and Joshua to the unwillingness of the other ten who said, *"We can't attack those people; they are stronger than we are,"* Plus, the ten went among the people of Israel discouraging them! They said, *"We seemed like grasshoppers in our own eyes, and we looked the same to them,"* Numbers 13:33b. The ten did not understand, giants are grasshoppers to God!

The ten cowards and those who listened to them, didn't make it to the Promised Land! In Revelation 21:8b NKJV, *"the cowardly"* are listed first of those who *"shall have their part in the lake which burns with fire and brimstone."* This is an eternal Hell. Being a coward is not profitable for this life or for the next!

Jesus said, *"He who is not with Me is against Me,"* Matthew 12:30a. Our life is either for Christ, or it is against Christ. Life has no "neutral" like a transmission in a car does. The ten spies were in reverse gear, against God! Caleb was in overdrive for God! What gear are we in? Are we willing to go forward for God *"wholeheartedly"*?

Forty-five years later, at the age of 85, Caleb returned to the land of the giants. He said to Joshua, *"I am still as strong today as the day Moses sent me out,"* Joshua 14:11a. Caleb fought the giants and took the land! Caleb fought knowing the size of his God! Faith fights giants for God. Faith settles us into The Promised Land!

Prayer: Lord, we thank You for sharing the life of Caleb with us. We pray that we will be faithful, just like him. Strengthen us to serve You *"wholeheartedly."* In Jesus' name we pray. Amen.

"Adoni-Bezek fled, but they chased him and caught him, and cut off his thumbs and big toes. Then Adoni-Bezek said, 'Seventy kings with their thumbs and big toes cut off have picked up scraps under my table. Now God has paid me back for what I did to them.' They brought him to Jerusalem and he died there." Judges 1:6-7

Adoni-Bezek loses his thumbs and big toes

King Adoni-Bezek was cruel! If he had a nick name, King Bully would have fit him! When he defeated seventy different kings, he had their thumbs and big toes cut off. Without thumbs, a soldier could not throw a spear. Without toes, they could not run. Adoni-Bezek further humiliated these men by making them eat under his table, just like a pack of dogs. The seventy didn't get real food, they got the garbage. Pigs had better food. Adoni-Bezek had such a high opinion of himself, that he counted the seventy men he conquered, trophies of his greatness. Adoni-Bezek's problem was, he mocked God's concern for justice.

What do we do to try to be great? Do we cut people with our words and actions to humiliate them? Along with Adoni-Bezek, we must learn something! *"God cannot be mocked. A man reaps what he sows. The one who sows to please his sinful nature, from that nature, will reap destruction; the one who sows to please the Spirit, from the Spirit will reap eternal life,"* Galatians 6:7b-8.

Adoni-Bezek was captured. God gave the proud king his wages for his dirty deeds. His thumbs and big toes were cut off. He now knew, *"The Lord detests all the proud of heart. Be sure of this: They will not go unpunished,"* Proverbs 16:5. He was forced to admit: *"God has paid me back for what I did."* He now understands, God loves justice. *"Better a little with righteousness than much gain with injustice,"* Proverbs 16:8.

As Christians, God holds us to an even higher standard. We have His softening grace in us. God demands that we show it. May the world see that we are Christians by our love. May we live to further His kingdom and not our own like King Adoni-Bezek!

Prayer: Lord, we see again that You hate injustice and bullying of all kinds, at all levels. Forgive us for when we have bullied other people to show off. In Jesus' name we pray. Amen.

March 15

"He (Ehud) presented the tribute (tax) to Eglon king of Moab, who was a very fat man." Judges 3:17

King Eglon, a picture of Israel's fat sins

Eglon was *"king of Moab for eighteen years,"* Judges 3:14b. Moab was a pagan country, totally sold out to wicked living. And Israel worshiped the gods and practices of these heathen people. Eglon's name means "fattened calf," and he was a big fat man! Israel cried out for deliverance after 18 years of slavery to Eglon. God sends Ehud, a deliverer and a judge that points to Christ, our Deliverer!

Ehud was *"a left-handed man,"* Judges 3:15b. His right hand was useless. With limited <u>ability</u>, his <u>availability</u> to God was his strength! Christian, this availability is our strength too! Ehud had a plan. Jesus gave us a commission! Ehud makes an 18 inch sword. We have a double-edged sword, God's Word!

Ehud goes to the fat king! His sword is hidden on his right side. No one suspects Ehud is carrying a weapon. Ehud pays Israel's tax to the king. We too pay heavy tax for our deeds of the flesh! Ehud tells the king that he has a secret for him. Jesus has a secret for us, His Word! Eglon invites Ehud into the palace, hoping he will get a bribe. How the wicked always lust for more! They are never satisfied!

King Eglon relaxes. Our fat flesh is not on guard either! *"He was sitting alone in the upper room of his summer palace,"* Judges 3:20b. How we love our comforts! The king stands. Ehud uses his left hand around his back to get his sword and *"plunged it into the king's belly. Even the handle sank in after the blade... and the fat closed in over it,"* Judges 3:21b-22b. How too, the Word of God completely penetrates our wicked hearts! Ehud *"did not draw the dagger out of his belly and his entrails came out,"* Judges 3:22b NKJV. The NIV completely omits this *"entrails"* part which is really poop or dung. It stunk bad in that wicked palace! Our sins stink bad to God! Ehud, *"shut the doors."* Jesus shuts the doors to our sin! The fat deeds of the flesh are butchered! Jesus forgives! The Israelites are delivered. We are set free, to worship God!

Prayer: Lord, the imagery You give us in the Bible convicts us! Deliver us, so that we may live for You! In Jesus' name we pray. Amen.

March 16

"The mountains quaked before the Lord, the One of Sinai, before the Lord, the God of Israel. In the days of Shamgar son of Anath, in the days of Jael, the roads were abandoned; travelers took to winding paths. Village life in Israel ceased, ceased until I, Deborah, arose, arose a mother in Israel." Judges 5:5-7

Deborah, a mother in Israel

After the 3rd judge Shamgar, Israel again forsook God. Then God forsook them, again handing Israel over to their enemies. For 20 years, Israel cries again for God's mercy and in God's time, He raises up Deborah, to be His deliverer. She was the 4th judge of Israel, about 200 years after Rahab, 100 years before Ruth. Deborah is the only woman judge and there are a full two chapters devoted to her rule. Some of the male judges are mentioned in just one or two verses. So, why Deborah? What do we make of all of this?

First of all, Deborah was a prophetess. There were others. Miriam, the sister of Moses and Aaron, was a prophetess. Huldah in the time of Jeremiah, and Anna when Jesus was born, were also. Some say that Deborah was raised up because there were no qualified men. If that is true, then what do we say about Miriam and Huldah? Moses and Jeremiah were definitely qualified!

A prophetess taught, encouraged and warned the people just like a prophet did. But Deborah is also a judge. As such, she was the highest, ruling authority and judicial figure in the land of Israel. She decided innocence or guilt, life or death, mercy or penalty. There were "lower courts," but Deborah was the lone, supreme court justice.

Deborah is also the head of the military. She sent or ordered Barak to fight against Sisera, Israel's enemy. In Judges 5, Deborah composed and sang a song in worship to the Lord. Perhaps most importantly, Deborah was, as our text describes, *"a mother in Israel."* She cared! She was devoted to God, and God chose to use her great mothering skills!

Prayer: Lord, we are humbled that You used Deborah to be Your judge to once again bring many to repentance and faith. May we never think we are too small or insignificant to be used by You to make a difference in our world. In Jesus' name we pray. Amen.

"The Lord turned to him and said, 'Go in the strength you have and save Israel out of Midian's hand. Am I not sending you?' 'But Lord,' Gideon asked, 'how can I save Israel? My clan is the weakest in Manasseh, and I am the least in my family.' The Lord answered, 'I will be with you.'" Judges 6:14-16a

Gideon, a humble man of God

Again, Israel is not faithful, so God let the Midianites invade and plunder them. Again they cry to God. He hears them and sends an uneducated, simple but obedient man to rescue His people. Gideon, also called Jerubbaal, was not from a prominent family. God went to a common man whose family was dirt poor and the least famous. After choosing Gideon, 32,000 men came to help him fight. Yet only 300 were accepted by God, one out of a 100! God wanted to make sure we all know that our victory over evil is because of God's ability to save, not because of man's doing! Throughout history, there has always been a remnant God has used to stand for Him. God seeks out His own kind of people, He equips them and then He uses them. God does this <u>for His own glory</u>.

We must not listen when others say we are too small or don't have the qualifications to make a difference for God. Gideon tried that line on God, saying, *"How can I save Israel? My clan is the weakest in Manasseh, and I am the least in my family."* God qualified Gideon. God made him qualified. Don't forget this, for it is still a big problem today! Many who think they are gifted to be God's mouthpiece, aren't! There was only one person that Jesus could not train, it was the religious elite in His day. They were too full of themselves. It is not possible to pour water into a full vessel!

Gideon was jealous for God's kingdom, not for his own kingdom! Gideon saw God going before him, opening the way to serve Him and His people! We need to get going and bring honor to God's holy name. And if we are not willing to give God the glory, He will not bless our work for Him!

Prayer: Lord, Your ways are so much wiser than our ways. Lord, the Kingdom is Yours. The glory is Yours. We are Yours. Use us for Your purposes. In Jesus' name we pray. Amen.

March 18

"They gave him seventy shekels of silver from the temple of Baal-Berith, and Abimelech used it to hire reckless adventurers, who became his followers. He went to his father's house in Ophrah and on one stone murdered his seventy brothers." Judges 9:4-5a

Abimelech, an abomination of a man

What a warning this "*Abimelech,*" this 71st son of Gideon, is to us! Gideon, "*had seventy sons of his own, for he had many wives. His concubine, who lived in Shechem, also bore him a son, whom he named Abimelech,*" Judges 8:30-31. Gideon made a big mistake in taking many wives. Then he fathered a son by a slave girl. This son would become a real monster to the children of Israel! Affairs have consequences!

Now Gideon dies. "*No sooner had Gideon died than the Israelites again prostituted themselves to the Baals,*" Judges 8:33a. They quickly forget God and Gideon. The people of Israel are not thankful for their deliverance! <u>When God is forgotten, He is replaced!</u> Abimelech, the half brother, plots his way into leadership! And the Shechem city fathers accept Abimelech, even though he has not displayed any talent as a leader! They gave Abimelech 70 pieces of silver, Baal's offerings, to set up his new government. Abimelech hires "*reckless adventurers*" to advise him. These lawless, bully buddies now help to change the direction of the country! History has a way of repeating itself.

Abimelech murders Gideon's 70 sons, and the people crown him king. But cheaters never prosper; God always has the last word! Three years later, God sends an evil spirit to ruin the alliance that Abimelech has with the people of Shechem. Abimelech kills most of the people in this Israelite city and the rest flee to a pagan temple which he burns down. So much for Abimelech's pretended love! Then Abimelech goes to burn down a neighbor city and God has a woman drop a stone on his head, killing him! God is the One in charge!

Prayer: Lord, we see the consequences of forsaking You in favor of other gods. We see that when we do not honor You, You dishonor us. How quickly You can raise up an abomination like Abimelech to even eliminate a whole city of people who reject You. Lord turn our hearts to You in true devotion. In Jesus' name we pray. Amen.

March 19

"And Jephthah made a vow to the Lord: 'If You give the Ammonites into my hand, whatever comes out of the door of my house to meet me when I return in triumph from the Ammonites will be the Lord's, and I will sacrifice it as a burnt offering.'" Judges 11:30-31

Jephthah's vow, foolish or faith?

"Jephthah the Gileadite was a mighty warrior. His father was Gilead; his mother was a prostitute," Judges 11:1. God again uses the weak, to shame the "wise." God here uses the illegitimate son of a Gentile prostitute to deliver His people who are selling themselves to other gods. Jephthah is a deliverer for God where 50 years before, another illegitimate son, Abimelech is a deliverer for Satan!

Jephthah is zealous to try prove three things: his loyalty to God, his legitimacy as a good son of his father, and that he is a true Israelite! So he makes a vow. *"If You give the Ammonites into my hand, whatever comes out of the door of my house to meet me when I return in triumph from the Ammonites will be the Lord's, and I will sacrifice it as a burnt offering."* Jephthah wins the battle over the Ammonites! He returns home, happy and celebrating! And, out of his house first to greet him dancing, comes his only child, a young, marriage age daughter! Jephthah cries out! *"Oh! My daughter. You have made me miserable and wretched, because I have made a vow to the Lord that I cannot break."* Judges 11:35b. We will see her response tomorrow.

If Jephthah keeps his vow, he breaks the sixth commandment, *"You shall not murder,"* Deuteronomy 5:17. If he does not keep the vow, that too is serious! *"When you make a vow to God, do not delay in fulfilling it. He has no pleasure in fools; fulfill your vow. It is better not to vow than to make a vow and not fulfill it,"* Ecclesiastes 5:4-5. We must be careful here. Jephthah is listed in the hall of faith in Hebrews 11:32. His vow was foolish, but it was also an act of faith looking to please God.

Prayer: Lord, we can feel the pain of Jephthah. Even our best works for You are tainted with sin! Jephthah's foolishness cost him his only child. Lord, Your wisdom cost You Your only Son! Lord, help us to make wise vows to love You more, to celebrate Your gift of Jesus to us. In Jesus' name we pray. Amen.

"'My father,' she replied, 'you have given your word to the Lord. Do to me just as you promised, now that the Lord has avenged you of your enemies, the Ammonites. But grant me this one request,' she said. 'Give me two months to roam the hills and weep with my friends, because I will never marry." Judges 11:36-37

Jephthah's daughter, sacrificed to God?

Jephthah has one daughter, no sons. He loved her much. You know about his vow from yesterday. Now we see his daughter's request. Jephthah *"let her go for two months. She and the girls went into the hills and wept because she would never marry. After the two months, she returned to her father and he did to her as he had vowed. And she was a virgin,"* Judges11:38b-39a.

There is debate as to whether Jephthah really sacrificed her on an altar to God. I believe he did, for it says, *"he did to her as he vowed."* Also, the next verse says her mountain trip started a new custom. *"Each year the young women of Israel go out for four days to commemorate the daughter of Jephthah the Gileadite,"* Judges 11:40. A memorial event is held to remember someone! It seems she gave her life willingly for her father, for her God, and for her country. And she did not have a two month wild party of sinning! She was a very good and pure girl. The Bible points out, *"and she was a virgin."*

Why did Jephthah do it? He was surely aware of how Abraham by faith went to sacrifice Isaac on the altar. He knew that God in His mercy stopped Abraham. Why didn't God stop Jephthah? Maybe this is a good place to apply Deuteronomy 29:29. *"The secret things belong to the Lord our God, but the things revealed belong to us and to our children forever, that we may follow all the words of this law."*

Prayer: Lord, we do know from Your Word and from experience that vows do work to correct a weakness in our faith and obedience to You. We also know that vows should not be used to try purchase a favor from You. So Lord, help us to make and keep wise vows, as a means of showing our thanksgiving to You! Lord increase our faith and understanding of Your Word. In Jesus' name we pray. Amen.

March 21

"Then Manoah prayed to the Lord: 'O Lord, I beg You, let the man of God You sent to us come again to teach us how to bring up the boy who is to be born.'" Judges 13:8

Manoah, concerned about raising a child

Samson had great parents. Father Manoah is pleading for the angel who came to see his wife, to reappear and teach them. If God was miraculously going to give them a baby, they wanted to know how to care for God's child. Two other sets of elderly parents had this same kind of visit. Abram and Sarai had an angel visit them. Zechariah and Elizabeth had this happen also. Why? God gave them a baby when it was literally impossible for them to conceive. The angel came so that they clearly knew this child was God's, for a specific purpose. But then, is this not basically true for every child?

Manoah and his wife were praying; they were concerned parents! Samson, as we will soon see, was a rather wild boy, with some very bad habits. These things happen even in the best of families. But, the parents are praying, and never quit praying. They knew for sure this was a child of God and they never stopped praying! God answers the prayers of His faithful believers. Samson's life ended well even though it did not start well! We may not have begun so well ourselves. Do not think this so strange! It is true for most of us. But the question is: If we are a parent will we continue to pray for our "wild child," or give up on them? And if we are that wild Samson kind of child, will we finish well as Samson did, or will we continue in our wickedness?

Samson was taught the right things even though he did not always do the right things. Later on he realized he was wasting his life on his very selfish activities. May we get to this point while we are still young! It is the main job of every parent to be concerned about the selfishness that is in the heart of every child!

Prayer: Lord, may we follow the example of Manoah and his wife and be concerned that our children live godly lives. Because Lord, all children belong to You and are merely on loan for us to bring up Your way. Bless them Lord, and use them for Your glory as You did in the life of Samson. In Jesus' name we pray. Amen.

March 22

"'We are doomed to die!' he said to his wife. 'We have seen God!' But his wife answered, 'If the Lord had meant to kill us, He would not have accepted a burnt offering and grain offering from our hands, nor shown us all these things or now told us this.'" Judges 13:22-23

Manoah's wife, a trusting faith

We cannot fully understand the life of Samson without looking at the faith of his mother also. Samson's mother is simply called Manoah's wife. Her real name is not given to us. Yet what is given is a glimpse into a woman with a trusting faith. Perhaps we do not have her name because God in His wisdom wants us to take notice of how true faith in a common believer responds to events that God places before them.

An angel of God visits Manoah's wife with a message. She who was barren now has a divine appointment to bear a special Nazirite child. A Nazirite is a person especially consecrated to God. They were not permitted to drink wine, cut their hair, touch a dead body, or eat anything unclean. Her child Samson would *"begin the deliverance of Israel from the hands of the Philistines,"* Judges 13:5b. Samuel, John the Baptist, and Jesus were also Nazirites.

Manoah's wife told her husband she had been visited by a man of God who, *"looked like an angel of God, very awesome."* Manoah was afraid. He greatly suspected she had seen God, and no one could see God and live. This is why he said, *"We are doomed to die!"* She wisely reasoned, <u>if God had designed for them to perish under His wrath, He surely would not have given them such a huge measure of His grace</u>! O how we need this kind of trusting faith in the character of God!

Manoah's wife has a serious responsibility! She must believe in her divine appointment, and be obedient in preparation for it! She must avoid wine, strong drink and not touch anything unclean. She must protect her child before and after he is born! How we need millions of mothers today who think and act like Manoah's wife!

Prayer: Lord, give us a trusting faith like Manoah's wife. What great protection that would be even for our unborn babies! For what should be the safest place on earth has become a war zone. Lord, move us to love life like You do. In Jesus' name we pray. Amen.

"Samson went down to Timnah and saw there a Philistine woman. When he returned, he said to his father and mother, 'I have seen a Philistine woman in Timnah; now get her for me as my wife.'" Judges 14:1-2

Samson, completely addicted!

These are uncomfortable subjects, but God includes them to warn us of one of the greatest dangers we will ever face. Samson had a sexual addiction. Sex was his idol! It is what he thought about. It is what he pursued with a mad vengeance. Notice Samson's demanding words, *"get her for me."* Uncontrolled lust does not have a logical brain! It is not that Samson did not love God at this point! But the problem was, he loved his idol more! We pursue what we love the most!

Just think! He who was born to be pure, was impure! The very first words we read about Samson growing up are: *"Samson went down to Timnah and saw there a young Philistine woman. When he returned, he said to his father and mother, 'I have seen a Philistine woman in Timnah; now get her for me as my wife,'"* Judges 14:1-2. Do not think this is Delilah. She comes later, in tomorrow's devotion. This is another woman. Samson did not care what this woman's heart was like! He saw her cute body and wanted it for himself. The world says, "This was love at first sight." God says that it is lust at first sight. This "lust marriage" lasted just one week. Then her father gave her to another man. Lust is that temporary! Soon after that, the village people burned her and her father. Here we see God's sure judgment of immoral sin!

However, Samson's lust still controls him! *"One day Samson went to Gaza, where he saw a prostitute. He went in to spend the night with her,"* Judges 16:1. This is now woman number two. But it does not end here either! Lust, unlike love, is never satisfied! Like a fire, it only wants more fuel to consume! Next on the list is Delilah! All these women were pagan, and Samson didn't care! Serving his idol god of lust was more important than serving his God in Heaven! But God has the last say! After Delilah, God mercifully tore Samson's eyes of lust from him!

Prayer: Lord, Samson's problem is our problem today. Internet porn and loose living has become so common and it is killing us. Turn us Lord, from these wicked sins. In Jesus' name we pray. Amen.

March 24

"Some time later, he fell in love with a woman in the valley of Sorek whose name was Delilah." Judges 16:4

Delilah, Satan's star servant

Outwardly, Delilah was a beauty! Inwardly, she was ugly, hard and sold herself to whoever would pay her the most for her beauty. She believed, that because of her extraordinary beauty, she deserved the best things money could buy! Filled with this evil pride, Delilah pretends to love Samson. She deceives him and delivers his body and mind to the enemy! Her seductive manipulation works on Samson like a snake charmer. Delilah knows exactly what she is doing as she struts her stuff! Samson is bewitched, intoxicated and mesmerized.

Delilah is so in love with her power. Like many movie stars, she acts the part of a demonic mediator to bring Samson to Satan! The pagan Philistine rulers and God know something! A woman like Delilah will, *"cast down many wounded, and all who were slain by her were strong men,"* Proverbs 7:26b NKJV. <u>Dainty Delilah does, what the strong soldiers could not do</u>! *"The lords of the Philistines came up to her and said to her, 'Entice him, and find out where his great strength lies, and by what means we may overpower him, that we may bind him to afflict him; and every one of us will give you 1,100 pieces of silver,'"* Judges 16:5 NKJV. Her pimps have spoken!

Delilah finally gets to Samson's heart. She says to him, *"<u>How can you say, 'I love you,</u>' when you won't confide in me?"* Judges 16:15a. Smooth talking Delilah questions Samson's devotion to her! Someone, will say these words to us! "How can you say, I love you, when you will not do this or that sin with me?" <u>Are we willing to be disloyal to God to prove our loyalty to some person?</u> Samson did, and he lost his eyes! He compromised the values of his Christian upbringing! God allowed the enemy to afflict Samson. Uncontrolled lust burns our spiritual eyes!

Prayer: Lord, open our eyes to the spiritual battle for our bodies and souls. Samson willingly gave up his relationship with You for power and pleasure, only to become powerless and pleasureless! Lord, You alone are our strength, our joy and our salvation! In Jesus' name we pray. Amen.

March 25

"Then Samson prayed to the Lord, 'O Sovereign Lord, remember me. O God, please strengthen me just once more." Judges 16:28a

Samson's spectacular finish

"Then Samson prayed." These words show us our responsibility to seek God, to know Him and to love Him. Samson finally changes. But we also see God's sovereignty and His grace here. It is God's Spirit who convicted Samson of his selfish and wayward ways. Samson now has a clear vision in his heart on how he has wasted his life chasing after things that have no eternal value! Like the "Prodigal Son" in Luke 15, Samson now comes to his spiritual senses!

"O Sovereign Lord, remember me." This sincere prayer of just five words is one that God hears! God is already at work in Samson. *"For it is God who works in you to will and to act according to His good purpose,"* Philippians 2:13. God graciously gave Samson the desire to finish his life well, for the honor of God and His Kingdom. *"Please strengthen me just once more"*! This beautiful short prayer must also be ours! God graciously answered Samson's prayer. God gave Samson the strength to pull down the temple of Dagon and all of its idolatrous worship. In Samson's death, *"all the lords of the Philistines"* were killed. In death, Samson defeated more of God's enemies than he ever did in his life! This is exactly what Jesus did!

The story of Samson teaches us that addicted people can change! *"And that is what some of you <u>were</u>. But you <u>were</u> washed, you <u>were</u> sanctified, you <u>were</u> justified in the name of the Lord Jesus Christ and by the Spirit of our God,"* 1 Corinthians 6:11. *"Were,"* is past tense. Samson is no longer addicted! Samson lost his great strength by sinning. He regained his strength by prayer and repentance! His pattern of living is changed! Samson prays to God to give him strength one more time to defeat God's enemies. God does, and Samson is listed in the hall of faith in Hebrews 11. He finished well. Will we?

Prayer: Lord, through Your Word, we see that the ability to change comes through You, not a program! It is a miracle really! We are born slaves to sin and Your mercy changes us to be slaves of righteousness. We thank You Lord! In Christ's name we pray. Amen.

March 26

"But Naomi said, 'Return home, my daughters. Why would you come with me?" "It is more bitter for me than for you, because the Lord's hand has gone out against me!" Ruth 1:11a & 13b

Naomi, bitter to better by God's grace

To understand God's message in the book of Ruth, we need to understand how Naomi's family fits into it. Naomi and her husband leave Bethlehem bankrupt, materially and spiritually. They left God, meaning they broke covenant with Him and went to Moab, a pagan county. Their two boys married pagan wives, Orpah and Ruth. This shows more covenant unfaithfulness. Naomi's husband and two sons now die in this foreign land, a picture of how they lived and died as unbelievers. They were apart from God and lost for all eternity.

With these facts in mind, examine what Naomi says to her two daughters-in-law? "'Don't call me Naomi,' she told them. 'Call me Mara, because <u>the Almighty has made my life very bitter</u>, I went away full, but <u>the Lord has brought me back empty</u>. Why call me Naomi? The Lord has afflicted me; <u>the Almighty has brought misfortune upon me</u>,'" Ruth 1:20-21. These are Naomi's bitter and backward thoughts! The opposite is what's really true. It was Naomi's family who turned their backs on God and their family heritage. They left home "spiritually" empty, not full. They left Bethlehem to try a radically different life-style, one which never works out! Naomi is the prodigal daughter coming back home!

God had to empty Naomi of her spiritual folly, so He could begin to bless her. Naomi didn't deserve one crumb of blessing from God, and neither do we! What a picture of God's grace in the life of Naomi! How great our salvation is also! God's irresistible grace draws her and Ruth to Himself! Did God do this all, just because He loved Naomi and Ruth? No, God did this first of all for His own name's sake! He is preparing for His Son to be born in Bethlehem about 1,200 years later.

Prayer: Lord, what a stern warning this is for us who willingly break covenant with You. At the same time, what a beautiful demonstration of Your grace. You bring the remnants of Naomi's family back into fellowship with You and Your people. You take our brokenness and give us Your completeness. We thank You. In Jesus' name we pray. Amen.

"But Ruth replied, 'Don't urge me to leave you or to return back from you. Where you go I will go, and where you stay I will stay. Your people will be my people and your God my God.'" Ruth 1:16

Ruth, a gentle Gentile, Jesus' ancestor

Ruth was born a pagan. Believing Naomi was used to bring Ruth to a life of faith in God. Ruth was transformed. Now her life is one of loyalty, faith, and dependence on God. Her life is a good lesson for us as we face uncertainty. Ruth learned that she could depend on God. She now knows by faith that God did not rescue her from paganism and bondage to sin, just to kill her off. Her situation was difficult! She had no husband or money, but see her response. Ruth did not lock herself in her house or cry because things were tough. She went out, and in her going and in her doing, God directed her steps, for His glory and for her good! God is willing to do this for us also!

The life of Ruth shows us God's eternal plan for all believers! God promised Abraham he would be the father of many nations, not just the Jewish people. Jesus came to reach out to every nation, tribe and language. Ruth's life and our Christian life are also examples of the diversity that exists in Jesus' royal family. See how this is so!

The grace of God not only selected and rescued the unlikely Ruth, His grace still selects unlikely people like us! Her dead husband's father left Bethlehem, bankrupt physically and spiritually, mostly spiritually! Her husband's father had two sons who also left Bethlehem, that name which means, "the house of bread." The sons were completely unfaithful! They married pagan wives in a pagan land. Ruth's pagan husband dies and now she is really bankrupt! Ruth stays with Naomi and became a Christian through her witness. Naomi urges her to leave, but Ruth refuses to go back to a pointless life! Ruth's life is but one example of broken people made whole and being a part of God's family! Through Ruth, Jesus was born in Bethlehem, a descendent of both Jews and Gentiles, those He came to save!

Prayer: Lord, what beautiful, real people You show us, clearly displaying how You are our complete Savior. We praise and worship You. In Jesus' name we pray. Amen.

March 28

"Then Boaz announced to the elders and all the people, 'Today you are witnesses that I have bought from Naomi all the property of Elimelech, Kilion and Mahlons. I have also acquired Ruth the Moabitess, Mahlon's widow, as my wife, in order to maintain the name of the dead with his property, so that his name will not disappear from among his family or from the town records.'" Ruth 4:9-10a

Boaz, shows us what a redeemer does

It is the responsibility of the nearest relative to redeem the life of a person in Ruth's situation. Her husband's father, Elimelech, sold all his property to stay alive, then died. Mahlon, her husband, dies without them having a child. There is no heir! The nearest relative, by law must redeem Ruth! This means he must marry Ruth and give her a child to continue the family name, and protect her from others taking advantage of her in any way. See here a picture of our salvation!

Mother-in-law Naomi, tells Ruth to go to the foot of the bed where Boaz will sleep, (the Holy Spirit sends us to the foot of the Cross). Ruth privately asks Boaz to protect and care for her, (we ask Jesus to be our Saviour). Boaz is a respectable, good man, (Jesus is perfect Man). Ruth asks Boaz, *"Spread the corner of your garment over me, since you are a kinsman-redeemer,"* Ruth 3:9b, (we ask Jesus, "You are the perfect Son of God, cover my sin with Your perfect robes of righteousness!").

Boaz says, *"The Lord bless you, my daughter, ... You have not run after the younger men, whether rich or poor. And now, my daughter, don't be afraid. I will do for you all you ask,"* Ruth 3:10-11a. (This is a picture of God's covenant love to us! God blesses us when we do not run after other gods for help!) Boaz redeems Ruth, paying all the family debts, (Jesus pays for all our sins, our past sins, our present sins and even our future sins!). From Boaz and Ruth's marriage came Obed, the father of Jesse, the father of David, Christ's ancestors. From our marriage to Christ and a Christian spouse, comes believing children who have believing children!

Prayer: Lord, how privileged we are to have a Redeemer in Jesus. We are restored, Your adopted child, co-heirs with Jesus Christ, eternally Yours. We worship You! In Jesus' name we pray. Amen.

"And because the Lord had closed her (Hannah's) womb, her rival (Peninnah) kept provoking her in order to irritate her. This went on year after year. Whenever Hannah went up to the house of the Lord, her rival provoked her till she wept and would not eat." 1 Samuel 1:6-7

Peninnah's pathetic provocations

Peninnah was the second wife of Elkanah, a prosperous man from a good family. He took Peninnah as a second wife because the first wife, Hannah, did not give him any children. This made Peninnah very proud of her esteemed position as she bore his children. Peninnah mocked, looked down on, and purposely rubbed in Hannah's face that she was blessed by God, and Hannah was not! She pushed Hannah so hard that Hannah wept! *"In bitterness of soul Hannah wept much and prayed to the Lord,"* 1 Samuel 1:10. Hannah's response must be our response to those who greatly trouble us! She did not berate her husband for taking a second wife. She did not yell back at Peninnah for all of the cruelty. She did not accuse God of being unfair! She humbled herself before the one true God, to whom Peter said, *"Cast all your anxiety on Him because He cares for you,"* 1 Peter 5:7.

But what about Peninnah's sin? Is it ours? Have we been very successful in business and people look up to us, and we are proud of it? Has God really blessed us? Do we have a good number of children and plenty to live on? Has any of this made us proud? Do we think that we have these blessings mostly because we have worked hard while others have not? Do we know that prosperity is perhaps the most difficult test that God could ever send our way? One reason is: we do not dread such blessings; we welcome them. We fail to trust God for our needs!

Actually Hannah was the one loved by God! And Peninnah's life is presented to us as a warning! Don't be like her! Do not let the blessings and prosperity that we have, make us proud and cause us to look down on those who seem less fortunate!

Prayer: Lord, we are so much like Peninnah! We do not deserve Your blessings! If we have them, then surely You are testing us, just like You did to Peninnah. Lord, help us to remain humble when You shine Your face upon us! In Jesus' name we pray. Amen.

Hannah prayed: *"O Lord Almighty, if you will only look upon Your servant's misery and remember me and not forget Your servant but give her a son, then I will give him to the Lord for all the days of his life, and no razor will ever be used on his head."* 1 Samuel 1:11b

Hannah's honorable humility

We now see Hannah's most honorable humility. Hannah was the first wife of Elkanah, his first love. We have already seen how Peninnah the second wife of Elkanah, was a big headache to Hannah. She *"kept provoking her in order to irritate her. This went on year after year. Whenever Hannah went up to the house of the Lord, her rival provoked her till she wept and would not eat,"* 1 Samuel 1:6b-7.

Even though Peninnah pushed Hannah to tears, she did not retaliate like Rachel did to Leah! Hannah knew, even though others tempted her sorely, God was her help surely! <u>Hannah did not look to God to beat others down, but for Him to bless her for the sake of His own name.</u> That is the kind of humility in prayer we need!

Eli, the old priest accused Hannah of being drunk when she was in the temple praying. Interestingly, Eli questions Hannah who was a godly woman, yet never confronted his own sons who were godless! Hannah quietly told Eli, *"I am a woman who is deeply troubled. I have not been drinking wine or beer; I was pouring out my soul to the Lord. Do not take your servant for a wicked woman; I have been praying here out of my great anguish and grief,"* 1 Samuel 1:15b-16. What a gracious, godly response to an evil accusation! Hannah knew God!

After praying in the temple, Hannah's *"face was no longer downcast."* Her sadness was over! Are we sad about something? Take it to God in prayer like Hannah did! We must not stare at our problem, but look to God! Hannah went home and then we read the great words, *"<u>The Lord remembered her,</u>"* 1 Samuel 1:19b. Hanna's prayer is recorded in 1 Samuel 2:1-10. Hannah dedicated baby Samuel to God.

Prayer: Lord, You are still all powerful, have all wisdom, and see everything! Your mercy and grace is still so beautiful and You are ready to give it. *"Remember"* us as You *"remembered her."* And may we then *"remember"* and honor You! In Jesus' name we pray. Amen.

March 31

"Now the sons of Eli were corrupt; they did not know the Lord."
1 Samuel 2:12 NKJV

Hophni and Phineas, just plain corrupt

Corrupt priests and pastors are not a new thing. Hophni and Phineas were corrupt. They acted like sons of Satan, doing evil instead of good. They took from God and from the people. Instead of serving God and others, they served themselves. They had way too much self-esteem and far too little God-esteem! They were flat out selfish! The reason or cause of their wickedness was not a minor character flaw.

Hophni and Phineas were corrupt because, *"they did not know the Lord"*! They knew about the Lord, but were not Christian. Their hearts were not changed by the Spirit of God. Their sins were not forgiven by Jesus. They were as Romans 6:6 teaches, *"slaves to sin."* They were never set free. They were unable to do good because they were godless. A heart that is not right cannot do right! After all, *"it is God who works in you both to will and to do for His good pleasure,"* Philippians 2:13 NKJV. God did not know them. Therefore, *"they did not know the Lord."*

Hophni and Phineas were taught and had the knowledge of what a priest must do. But they lived in hatred of the law of God! The proof is, they tempted others to sin instead of encouraging them to be holy! A priest was to help the people to have their sin covered but they did what they could to heap more sin on the people!

The sacrifices the people brought were for God, but Hophni and Phineas wanted even the best of that for themselves! They were in the ministry for what they could get out of it! They thought they could make more money by cheating God and the people. And they did, temporarily. But God always has the last word. He ended their wickedness. They died hostile to God. They will forever fully experience God's wrath in an eternity that lasts forever.

Prayer: Lord, how sad it is that some of those who are in office to be a blessing to Your kingdom, are the cause of so much evil. We pray for them to repent. We pray for those who have a Hophni and Phineas for a pastor or priest. Lord come to their rescue for Your name's sake. In Jesus' name we pray. Amen.

APRIL

David playing his harp for King Saul

"Saul's attendants said to him, 'See, an evil spirit from God is tormenting you. Let our lord command his servants here to search for someone who can play the harp. He will play when the evil spirit from God comes upon you, and you will feel better.'" 1 Samuel 16:15-16

April 1

"Why do you scorn My sacrifice and offering that I prescribed for My dwelling? Why do you <u>honor your sons more than Me</u> by fattening yourselves on the choice parts of every offering made by My people Israel?" 1 Samuel 2:29

Eli's evil errors

The life of Eli and his evil errors scream out a warning to every parent and church leader. Eli's sinful leadership habits brought God's holy judgment. 1 Samuel begins with God contrasting the bitter attitude of Eli's family, to the loving sweet service of Samuel's. We must know Eli's errors, but choose Samuel's humble style!

1. <u>Father Eli</u> did not live to honor God. When God summed up Eli's lifetime of bad choices regarding his parenting habits, He said, *"<u>You honor your sons more than Me</u>."* Whatever Eli's sons wanted, they got. Permissiveness ruled Eli's home! What God wanted didn't matter! God's law did not guide Eli's home at all! God's perfect standard of the parent's need to correct a child bent on doing wrong, was ignored! Like all children, Eli's children were selfish! <u>They</u> wanted to be in charge and were! They did what they wanted to do and were never disciplined. Eli's failure to discipline his boys, resulted in their never learning to love and respect their Heavenly Father or their earthly father! <u>Eli gave his children privileges, without requiring responsibility</u>! That ruins a child! God said in judgment of Eli; *"I told him that I would judge his family forever because of the sin he knew about; his sons made themselves contemptible, and he failed to restrain them,"* 1 Samuel 3:13.

2. <u>Priest Eli</u> was more a thief than a chief. His priestly family demanded and took *"by force,"* the best of what was offered to God! Money, food, pleasure, and immoral behavior were their real gods! That is what they lived for! Eli's family did more to separate the people from God, than draw them to God! Eli was blind to the spiritual needs of the people because his real mission was a life of privilege and comfort.

Prayer: Lord, to our shame, we copy Eli! We ask You for Your forgiveness. You have said: *"Those who honor Me I will honor, but those who despise Me will be disdained."* Lord, help us to honor You in all that we do. In Jesus' name we pray. Amen.

April 2

"The Lord came and stood there, calling as at other times, 'Samuel! Samuel!' Then Samuel said, 'Speak, for Your servant is listening.'"
1 Samuel 3:10

Samuel's sweet surrender

At first I called this 'Samuel's Sweet Service.' But he only had "sweet service" because he was surrendered to God. How beautiful Samuel's words were to God's ears, especially because Eli, his sons and Israel were not listening to Him, not surrendered to Him! This must shout to us what salvation and a pleasing life to God is all about!

We live in a wicked world; even the church is corrupt like it was in Samuel's day. Notice who God in His wisdom selects to do His work, to be His mouthpiece to all this wickedness! A little boy who is weak by the world's standards, without education, without much spiritual training, but "surrendered" to God! We must learn from Samuel's life of devotion!

1. <u>We need to be called by God to have a life of dedicated surrendered service</u>. Those God calls, He equips to serve Him! We often think that if we get equipped, if we get the education, then God will call. That's not how God normally worked in the history of the Bible. Again and again, *"God chose the foolish things of the world to shame the wise; God chose the weak things of the world to shame the strong,"* 1 Corinthians 1:27.

2. <u>Samuel was pure in the midst of wickedness</u>. If ever a godly attribute in ministry is needed today, it is this. A minister of God who is not interested in living a pure life is already disqualified, regardless of any degrees! Eli and his sons thought they were, "the qualified," but they were surrendered to Satan, not God. They mocked God and had profane worship. They lived for their own pleasure. Samuel lived a pure life for God in the midst of evil filth!

Prayer: Lord, Samuel heard Your voice while he was sleeping! When we are awake, we do not hear Your voice as we should! Lord, if we were more surrendered to You, we could be more useful for You. May Samuel's sweet words of devotion be ours! *"Speak, for Your servant is listening"*! In Jesus' name we pray. Amen.

April 3

"'What shall we do with the ark of the Lord? Tell us how we should send it back to its place.' They answered, 'If you return the ark of the God of Israel, do not send it away empty, but by all means send a guilt offering to Him. Then you will be healed, and you will know why His hand has not been lifted from you." 1 Samuel 6:2b-3

The Philistines recognize their guilt

The ark was a symbol of God's presence and it held the original stone copy of the Ten Commandments. God allowed the ark of the covenant to be captured by the wicked, pagan Philistines. For seven months the Philistines were punished for keeping the ark. For seven months the Israelites were punished for not having the ark. But God is working everything to show His Almighty power.

The Philistines were afflicted with tumors wherever the ark went. They finally moved the ark into a farm field and then the mice in the fields destroyed the crops. God is teaching pagans, without the help of any man. God shows them His power. God refuses to shower them with His blessings because their hearts are not right! Instead, God curses them so much, that they clearly know it is from God alone.

The Philistines learned they were guilty in taking the ark. The Israelites were guilty in neglecting the ark. They consulted their pagan priests asking, "What shall we do?" Our text is their answer; *"Do not send it away empty, but by all means send a guilt offering to Him. Then you will be healed."* Pagans are confessing their sin! Was Israel confessing theirs? No, even Eli's sons were drinking and fornicating in the presence of God! Are we confessing our sins?

God uses pagan Philistines to shame us into seeing what is obvious: We sin! A pagan priest knows the land will be healed if they confess their sin and offer a guilt offering. What is our excuse? We know Jesus, the One who takes away sin, and we can go to Him anytime. Are we going? Are we confessing? *"If we confess our sins, He is faithful and just and will forgive us our sins and purify us from all unrighteousness"*!

Prayer: Lord, we too sin against Your holy presence. We are more likely to confess other people's sin than we are to confess our own. Lord, put us on our knees where we belong. In Jesus' name we pray. Amen.

April 4

"And Samuel said to the whole house of Israel, 'If you are returning to the Lord with all your hearts, then rid yourselves of the foreign gods and the Ashtoreths and commit yourselves to the Lord and serve Him only, and He will deliver you out of the hand of the Philistines.'"

1 Samuel 7:3

Samuel preaches repentance

Samuel was in a real war for the souls of men, and he knew it! He makes a big point on what Biblical repentance looks like. We came to worship God, but wedo not let go of our other gods. Real repentance is <u>putting off the old</u>, <u>replacing it</u>, and <u>putting on the new</u>. Those are three major points. Many of us are miserable and failing because true repentance is lacking!

Think of Rachel, the wife of Jacob. She sat on her old idol gods as she made her spiritual and physical journey in life. She did not put them off! She did not replace them. Therefore she could not cling to God alone! Now, in our text, we have *"the whole house of Israel"* sitting on idols! The people cannot return to God until they dump their idols. Don't think that we do not have idols that keep us from serving God!

Do we hold a deck of cards more than the Bible. Do we play or watch sports more than we spend time with God? Do we find shopping more enjoyable than time alone with God or in corporate worship? Whatever keeps us from serving and loving God more, we must put that idol off! Anything more important than God and a relationship with Him is the *"foreign gods"* in our text. God made us for Himself! He is a jealous God. He cannot stand to be in second place!

God allowed the wicked Philistines to conquer Israel, to turn their cold hearts back to Himself! So many times in history God allowed His people to lose their privileged status because of the idols they failed to put off! They loved the wicked ways of the land more than the ways of God! Samuel is teaching us not to follow the way of the wicked!

Prayer: Lord, convict us by Your Holy Spirit what we need to put off. Give us the power to change more and more for Your honor and for our good. In Jesus' name we pray. Amen.

April 5

"When Samuel grew old, he appointed his sons as judges for Israel. The name of his firstborn was Joel and the name of his second son was Abijah, and they served at Beersheba. But his sons did not walk in his ways. They turned aside after dishonest gain and accepted bribes and perverted justice." 1 Samuel 8:1-3

Joel and Abijah, not allowed in ministry

Joel and Abijah, the two sons of Samuel, were appointed to the ministry by their father. For a good reason, the *"elders of Israel"* did not want them. They were wrong in wanting a king like the rest of the countries. But they were right in not wanting Samuel's two wicked sons. The common practice today of handing down a ministry to a son is very questionable. What if that son is like Samuel's sons?

Once a group of pastors said that another minister of a church nearby was dying and there was no one to pass the leadership to. He had no sons or daughters! I asked if he had trained up anyone in all of his years of discipleship? Yes, but the property is in this pastor's name. It's his church. How can that be? The church belongs to the Lord Jesus Christ! He owns the believers! It is one thing if a piece of property and a building is in a pastor's name. But in this particular church, the "believers" were not willing to accept another pastor or go to another church either! Jesus had many believers, no land, no church building and He passed the leadership on to His disciples. We in turn too often pass on a church building, but there is no qualified leadership! This is close to what Israel's problem was!

What happened to the inner call of God for His work? God puts His Spirit in those He calls, everytime! Joel and Abijah may have shown some signs of promise growing up, but when they started "ministry" they took bribes. They were bought, hired by whoever would pay the most for their decision. Their habits pointed to the fact that they were unbelievers, not qualified. The blind cannot lead the blind!

Prayer: Lord, help us! We have run Your church like a corrupt business. Then we wonder what's wrong! Lord correct us. Call good workers for Your kingdom, and give us the wisdom to recognize them. In Jesus' name we pray. Amen.

April 6

"So all the elders of Israel gathered together and came to Samuel at Ramah. They said to him, 'You are old, and your sons do not walk in your ways; now appoint a king to lead us, such as all the other nations have.'" 1 Samuel 8:4-5

Israel wants a king, not God

Our text is a huge turning point in the history of Israel. Joshua led the people of Israel into the new land of Canaan 350 years before this. Then the various judges took over, ending with Samuel. The spiritual condition was bad. Rather than driving out the pagan nations and their idolatry, the people mixed their beliefs with what God taught them about His rules for living. As a result, God sent conflict and chaos to His chosen people. The people rebelled. God rebuked them. They repented and God restored them. There were seven major periods in this 350 year cycle. Finally, when the last judge and prophet Samuel was about to die, the wicked sons of Samuel started to govern Israel. The people said, "No, we want a king, like the other nations!" Samuel hears their request for a king and cries to God. The Lord comforts Samuel and tells him that the people did not reject Samuel's leadership as much as that of God Himself! The people wanted a king, *"like the other nations."* They wanted idols too!

Israel rejecting God is a warning to every nation on earth. What kind of leader we want is so important. God demands to be served and worshiped. We must learn from history. *"Everything that was written in the past was written to teach us, so... we might have hope,"* Romans 15:4. The Biblical principle is this: Any people or nation that rejects God does not want His presence, wisdom, power, providence, goodness, love and grace! *"Blessed is the nation whose God is the Lord,"* Psalm 33:12a. May the imprint of God be all over our land more and more!

Prayer: Lord, we want You! We want Your holy laws to lead and guide us. We want Your abundant grace to govern us. We want Your Spirit to live in us. Lord, we know from Your Word that no nation or people has long survived who have rejected You. Forgive our waywardness! Lead on, O King eternal! In Jesus' name we pray. Amen.

April 7

"But Samuel said to Saul, 'I will not return with you, for you have rejected the Word of the Lord, and the Lord has rejected you from being king over Israel.' And as Samuel turned around to go away, Saul seized the edge of his robe, and it tore. So Samuel said to him, 'The Lord has torn the kingdom of Israel from you today, and has given it to a neighbor of yours, who is better than you.'" 1 Samuel 15:26-28 NKJV

Saul, the kingdom is ripped from him!

King Saul is a good example of God's <u>sovereignty</u> in putting him on the throne. We also see Saul's personal <u>responsibility</u> to God, to govern righteously. These two points are true for each of us, but are especially for leaders!

Saul starts to do things his way instead of God's way. Samuel warns Saul to repent, but Saul does not. Shortly after this, God gives a clear command to Saul! *"This is what the Lord almighty says: 'I will punish the Amalekites for what they did to Israel when they waylaid them as they came up from Egypt. Now go, attack the Amalekites and totally destroy everything that belongs to them. Do not spare them,"* 1 Samuel 15:2b-3a. The command is clear but Saul again does as he wants to do!

Saul decides to keep the best of the sheep and does not kill the Amalekite king. Saul reasoned that the best sheep could be sacrificed to God! But God wanted their obedience far more than their sacrifices! What are sacrifices to God if we do not love Him?

Then we read the famous verse, *"Has the Lord as great delight in burnt offerings and sacrifices, as in obeying the voice of the Lord? Behold, to obey is better than sacrifice, and to heed than the fat of rams. For rebellion is as the sin of witchcraft, and stubbornness is as iniquity and idolatry. Because you have rejected the Word of the Lord, He also has rejected you from being king,"* 1 Samuel 15:22-23 NKJV.

Saul had his chance to repent but he refused and God ripped the kingdom from Saul physically and spiritually! What will we do?

Prayer: Lord, we can see that Saul is a lot like us, partially obedient, and You are not pleased! Lord, You call us to repentance, to live Your way, not ours. Help us to do the responsible thing and obey You in all things! In Jesus' name we pray. Amen.

April 8

"Then Samuel said, 'Bring Agag king of the Amalekites here to me.'...
'As your sword has made women childless, so shall your mother be
childless among women.' And Samuel hacked Agag in pieces before
the Lord in Gilgal." 1 Samuel 15:32a & 33b NKJV

King Agag, paid back for killing children

The Amalekites were unmerciful cowards, nomadic descendants of Esau. God, with His acute and holy sense of justice hated them. See why: *"Remember what the Amalekites did to you along the way when you came out of Egypt. When you were weary and worn out, they met you on your journey and cut off all who were lagging behind; they had no fear of God... You shall blot out the memory of Amalek from under Heaven. Do not forget!"* Deuteronomy 25:17-19. They attacked from the rear, cutting down the weak, the lame, the children, and the pregnant mothers. They had zero compassion!

Now God tells Saul to eliminate the Amalekites, but Saul spares the king, the worst offender of them all! Like Agag, Saul killed the most innocent and spared the most guilty! How does this speak to us? Who do the Amalekites look like today? Hitler was an Agag. But he too is gone. Now who resembles an Agag or an Amalekite?

The abortion industry is filled with ruthless cowards! In the USA alone 50 million helpless babies have been butchered in the womb. We may know this is happening with our minds, but is it real to us? Google "partial birth abortion" or "abortion." If the pictures do not make us sick, then we are just as spiritually dead as the Amalekites were!

Everyone Agag killed bore the image of God! All were fearfully and wonderfully made by Him! To destroy what God has made is worse than wicked. God will not stand for it! *"He will deliver the needy who cry out, the afflicted who have no one to help. He will take pity on the weak and needy and save the needy from death. He will rescue them from oppression and violence, for precious is their blood in His sight,"* Psalm 72:12-14. Will you pray and help?

Prayer: Lord, You tell us in Isaiah, *"Learn to do right! Seek justice, encourage the oppressed. Defend the cause of the fatherless."* Lord, forgive us for not doing this. In Jesus' name we pray. Amen.

April 9

"When Eliab, David's older brother, heard him speaking (about Goliath) with the men, he burned with anger at him and asked, 'Why have you come down here? And with whom did you leave those few sheep in the desert? I know how conceited you are and how wicked your heart is; you came down only to watch the battle.'" 1 Samuel 17:28

Eliab, David's angry and jealous brother

Think about what David's older brother Eliab saw. The prophet Samuel came to their house and selected David, the youngest of eight boys. *"Samuel took the horn of oil and anointed him <u>in the presence of his brothers</u>, and from that day on the Spirit of the Lord came upon David in power,"* 1 Samuel 16:13a. David's brothers were fully aware of Samuel's mission and David's commission!

Much later we read, *"David came to Saul and entered into his service. Saul liked him very much, and David became one of his armor-bearers,"* 1 Samuel 16:21. Plus, David played the harp for Saul. Eliab was aware of all of these things. Now David is asking, *"Who is this uncircumcised Philistine that he should defy the armies of the living God?"* 1 Samuel 17:26b. Eliab hears David talking and blows up in anger. He is thinking, "Little hot shot, who do you think you are?"

Eliab was guilty of everything he was accusing David of. When Samuel came to anoint a son of Jesse, God said of Eliab, *"Man looks at the outward appearance, but the Lord looks at the heart,"* 1 Samuel 16:7b. God saw Eliab was not very righteous. Eliab was angry and *"man's anger does not bring about the righteous life that God desires,"* James 1:20. An angry heart is selfish, fearful, proud and jealous. Eliab was much like King Saul as we shall see. Filled with pride, Eliab would not accept that God honored and gifted David.

Prayer: Lord, we are much like Eliab! We say to You and others "Why is this person gifted and honored above me?" Lord, if You pour Your Spirit out on others, we should expect fruit from that and rejoice. Our own hearts are the problem, not actions of others! Every Christian is Your *"workmanship, created in Christ Jesus to do good works, which God prepared in advance for us to do."* Lord, may we rejoice in what You are doing in others. In Jesus' name we pray. Amen.

April 10

"Your servant has killed both the lion and the bear; this uncircumcised Philistine will be like one of them, because he has defied the armies of the living God. The Lord who has delivered me from the paw of the lion and the paw of the bear will deliver me from the hand of this Philistine." 1 Samuel 17:36-37

David's giant victory

Goliath the Philistine directly challenged the God of Israel when he said in 1 Samuel 17:10b, *"This day I defy the ranks of Israel."* He is saying that God cannot protect His people. Anyone who is so against God's believers, thinks little of how big God is in defense of them! Goliath is a picture of evil. God is beginning to show how He delivers His people from evil. David heard Goliath's big bad mouth mock Israel and God. David was shocked that no one was willing to fight for God's name! So David volunteers, and is brought to King Saul. See our text for what David then said to King Saul.

Already at a young age, David experienced the hand of God delivering him out of seemingly impossible situations! Our own amazing deliverances by God must encourage us to be bold for God! Being bold is not "risky" but is instead an act of faith based on the sure knowledge that the battle is the Lord's. God wants us in the battle for the glory of His name.

David was offered armor, but he refused. It was not comfortable. The world's weapons in a spiritual battle are not useful! He went with his shepherd's tools. (Our main "shepherd's tool" is the Bible!) Surely everyone but God, thought David was quite the fool. But David believed clearly what he *"said to the Philistine, 'You come against me with sword and spear and javelin, but I come against you in the name of the Lord Almighty, the God of the armies of Israel, whom you have defied,'"* 1 Samuel 17:45. With a sling and a stone, David killed the giant. Devotion to God is the best preparation for our giant victory!

Prayer: Lord, what beautiful words You moved David to speak, *"may the whole world know that there is a God in Israel."* Yes, and You are our God, and You still move giants today so that Your name may be made known! We praise You. In Jesus' name we pray. Amen.

April 11

"David said to the Philistine, 'You come against me with sword and spear and javelin, but I come against you in the name of the Lord Almighty, the God of the armies of Israel, whom you have defied.'"
1 Samuel 17:45

Goliath loses his big head

Physically, Goliath was a giant; *"he was over nine feet tall,"* 1 Samuel 17:4b. He was the champion warrior of the wicked Philistines, an enemy of God and His people. But spiritually speaking, Goliath was a mouse. His great, physical ability and his little, spiritual concern, are big warnings to us! This huge giant thought he was totally invincible. He thought no one could ever defeat him. He was about to learn about life the hard way! To defy God is to lose your head!

It is God with His giant attributes, that controls everyone and everything. God made Goliath appear on the world's stage to teach a big object lesson. God's people still have fear problems. Evil is "out there" and it is always big! But God is bigger and stronger!

To teach us about His power, God makes Goliath appear big and strong, a nasty bully! God made Goliath look unstoppable with his huge size, his thick armor and his big spear. He even gave Goliath a big mouth! God made Goliath for the same reason He makes everyone, for His own glory and praise! By defeating the strong Goliath, God shows who is really weak. No matter how big we are in our own eyes, if we do not fear God, we will fall as hard as Goliath did!

One principle here is that God will cut down every big mouth that blasphemes His holy name. If we defy God we are eternally dead. Also, God uses the weak things, like a shepherd boy who is surrendered to Him, to be stronger than any giant! Goliath also represents our problems that seem too big for us. God does not even need a small stone do smash our problems, a single word from Him and all creation must obey.

Prayer: Lord, what great lengths You went through in designing characters, just to teach us. Knowledge of Your grace to us gets bigger every day. We praise You for it. In Jesus' name we pray. Amen.

April 12

"As they danced they sang: 'Saul has slain his thousands, and David his tens of thousands.' Saul was very angry; this refrain galled him. 'They have credited David with tens of thousands,' he thought, 'but me with only thousands. What more can he get but the kingdom?' And from that time on Saul kept a jealous eye on David." 1 Samuel 18:7-9

Saul's jealously defined and defiled him!

King Saul's kingdom was going nowhere. Israel's enemy was right in their face every day and Saul and his whole army could do nothing about it. Saul was basically a coward at heart. He was not motivated by a love for God, thus God was not motivated to bless him. Saul was the people's choice, but not God's! So God raises up a real man, one after His own heart, David the shepherd.

After David kills the giant, the people took notice of his courage and sang the praises to David in our text. Well, Saul couldn't take it! If anyone got more attention and praise than he did, a grinding bitterness formed in his heart. The reason is: Saul ruled for his own glory. David was concerned about God's glory! This difference is what life is all about! <u>Saul was so intensely jealous of David that just one day after David killed the giant, Saul throws a spear at David to kill him!</u> Can you imagine that? God, through David, kills Saul's real enemy, and Saul thinks David is the enemy! The logic of jealousy is that twisted and demonic!

Saul was insecure and fearful! This quickly led to his instant anger. Over time, Saul became hard and bitter. His selfish sin shows us the real problem with jealousy. The evil thoughts in Saul's heart quickly moves his mouth, hands and feet into action! <u>Saul tries to remove David because he sees him as a threat to his own greatness!</u> That is exactly how selfish a jealous heart really is! The murderous spear that Saul hurled at David, was directed at God also. He thought, "God is not fair to me!" Do we have any of Saul's spiritual sickness in us? We do! And we need to repent of it!

Prayer: Lord, You tell us (Hebrews 12:15) that bitterness will cause us much trouble and will eventually defile us. May we never miss Your grace because of it. Lord, we thank You for warning us again and again! In Jesus' name we pray. Amen.

April 13

"Jonathan said to David, 'Go in peace, for we have sworn friendship with each other in the name of the Lord, saying, 'The Lord is witness between you and me, and between your descendants and my descendants forever.'" 1 Samuel 20:42a

Jonathan, what it means to be a friend

We can learn much about what it means to be a true friend from the relationship of Jonathan and David. Jonathan was born into a life of privilege, the eldest son of King Saul. According to the rules of the land, Jonathan would be the next king. He had what most of the world strives for. He had power, prestige, money and any comfort he wanted. Yet it seems that from the moment David killed the giant Goliath, Jonathan not only loved David for his courage and zeal for the Lord, but he loved him as a person also.

It is recorded that young David was ushered into King Saul's presence while still holding the head of the giant. What a gory sight that must have been! Then, *"after David had finished talking with Saul, Jonathan became one in spirit with David, and he loved him as himself,"* 1 Samuel 18:1. What stands out, are two opposite responses to David coming on the scene. Father Saul already had a wary eye on David. Jonathan immediately wanted to be a close friend. There was no jealousy in him, nor was David ever jealous of Jonathan. Love is not jealous! How protective it is when leaders cooperate in the service of God!

"Jonathan made a covenant with David because he loved him as himself," 1 Samuel 18:3. A covenant is a commitment to love someone, no matter what! Love does not create or cause commitment! It is commitment or covenant that is the very cause of love! True friends are committed to each other, in the name of the Lord, for the cause is ultimately the Lord's. When Jonathan made a covenant, he said to David, *"Show me unfailing kindness like that of the Lord as long as I live, so that I may not be killed, and do not ever cut off your kindness from my family,"* 1 Samuel 20:14-15a.

Prayer: Lord, we have much to learn about the commitment in a friendship! Help us to model that jealous-free relationship of Jonathan and David. In Jesus' name we pray. Amen.

April 14

"He said to Saul, 'Why do you listen when men say, "David is bent on harming you"? This day you have seen with your own eyes how the Lord delivered you into my hands in the cave. Some urged me to kill you, but I spared you; I said, "I will not lift my hands against my master, because he is the Lord's anointed." See my father...'"
1 Samuel 24:9-11a

David's enemy blesses his spiritual life!

You have seen Saul's intense hatred of David. How will David respond? How will we respond to those who try to hurt us? This is one of life's most important tests, a big exam! Our response will greatly determine our spiritual, physical, mental, even our social well-being. The truth is, our enemies can be used by Satan to make us more ugly! Or, our enemies can be used by God to make us more beautiful. David's right response protected him! So will ours! Let's see what David did.

In response to Saul's trying to eliminate him, David did not retaliate! He did not take matters into his own hands. He calls Saul, *"my master,"* *"the Lord's anointed"'* and *"my father."* From a cave, David wrote: *"In my distress I called to the Lord; I cried to my God for help. From His temple He heard my voice; my cry came before Him, into His ears." "He reached down from on high and took hold of me; He drew me out of deep waters. He rescued me from my powerful enemy; from my foes, who were too strong for me,"* Psalm 18:6 & 16-17. God's faithful mercy built up David's faith. Through it all, David learned to be gracious instead of vengeful, forgiving instead of bitter, loving instead of angry!

David had another choice! Satan would have him try to eliminate Saul! Satan wanted him to keep bitterness in his heart towards Saul. But God protected David's attitude, his heart! God knows there is no peace in a bitter response to evil! David's "cave experiences," taught him to look to God. As he did, his faith grew. He learned from his difficult experiences to totally trust in God. And so must we!

Prayer: Lord, we do not like our "cave experiences," but they sure are profitable as You teach us to trust in You. Your protection of our body and soul is so complete! We praise You for maturing us! In Jesus, our blessed Redeemer's name we pray. Amen.

April 15

"His name was Nabal and his wife's name was Abigail. She was an intelligent and beautiful woman, but her husband, a Calebite, was surly and mean in his dealings." 1 Samuel 25:3

Nabal, a surly and mean drunk

Nabal is first introduced like this: "*A certain man in Maon, who had property there at Carmel, was very wealthy. He had a thousand goats and three thousand sheep, which he was shearing in Carmel,*" 1 Samuel 25:2. When it came to this world's goods, Nabal had a truck load. But when it came to spiritual goods, Nabal had an empty basket.

Nabal had at least two houses, one was in the desert and one was in the mountains. Sheep-shearing time in the mountains was a holiday festival, a time of thanksgiving. David and his small band protected Nabal's sheep from pirates and panthers. David now needs food for his men. So naturally David asks Nabal for a gift to feed his men. It was a most reasonable request. Nabal's foolish response was, "*Why should I take my bread and water, and meat that I have slaughtered for my shearers, and give it to men coming from who knows where?*" 1 Samuel 25:11.

Nabal didn't get it. He did not understand how his wealth, which was a gift from God, carried with it responsibilities to be a blessing to God's kingdom. Instead of being thankful to God for what he had, he was bitter towards everyone! He was a nasty, arrogant, obstinate man with an "attitude." He regularly used and abused people for his own gain. He ruled by fear and threat, not by love. There was nothing decent about him. His selfish life stands out as a warning to us!

Nabal's servants were far wiser than he was. They said, "*Disaster is hanging over our master and his whole household. He is such a wicked man that no one can talk to him,*" 1 Samuel 25:17b. What kind of personality do others see in us? What does God see? Do we share the blessings God has given us? The Bible is telling us, "*disaster is hanging*" if we live like Nabal did.

Prayer: Lord, we can see that Nabal was extremely self-centered. He was uncaring and unrepentant until the day he died. Moments after death he surely realized his big mistake. May we realize ours now and be a blessing to many. In Jesus' name we pray. Amen.

April 16

"His name was Nabal and his wife's name was Abigail. She was an intelligent and beautiful woman, but her husband, a Calebite, was surly and mean in his dealings." 1 Samuel 25:3

Abigail, beauty married to a beast!

Abigail was definitely the better half of her marriage to Nabal. She was everything he was not. Our text says, *"she was an intelligent and beautiful woman."* When she heard how her *"surly and mean"* husband responded to David's servants, she moved quickly to keep the peace. David in the meantime is on his way to kill every male in Nabal's employment. David here is overacting, about as much as the beast Nabal was!

"Abigail lost no time." Immediately, she works to bring a royal banquet to David and his men! Nabal would not give a drop of water to David, but Abigail brings a feast! *"When Abigail saw David, she quickly got off her donkey and bowed down before David with her face to the ground,"* 1 Samuel 25:23. We see her humility, reverence and even submission to David. She personally pleads with David to put the blame for Nabal's rude selfish sin on herself. Is this also not a picture of what Christ does for us before His Father?

Abigail wisely points out to David how the Lord is working through her to keep David from avenging himself concerning Nabal's insult. David appreciates Abigail's wisdom and how she is an ambassador for good! She also respectfully reminds David that he is appointed by God as *"leader over Israel."* How different from the foolish Nabal who said, *"Who is this David? Who is this son of Jesse?"*

Abigail returned home and finds the beast Nabal drunk. When she tells him the next day how close he came to bringing death on himself and all the males in his household, he had a heart attack. God took his life, totally avenging David! *"Vengeance is mine sayeth the Lord"* was just as true in the Old Testament as it is in the New.

Prayer: Lord, we see once again how important it is to be equally yoked. What a good wife Abigail was to Nabal even though he was a most difficult husband. May we learn to be wise and faithful just as Abigail was. In Jesus' name we pray. Amen.

April 17

"Saul said... 'Find me a woman who is a medium, so I may go and inquire of her.' 'There is one in Endor,' they said." 1 Samuel 28:7

The witch of Endor, an enemy of God

The life of Saul is in a downward spiral away from God. Unbelievers are like that! One of the last things Saul did, was go to the witch of Endor for advice. He wanted her to contact the spirit of the dead prophet Samuel to see if he should go to war? Saul has already, *"inquired of the Lord, but the Lord did not answer him,"* 1 Samuel 28:6a. God did tell us in Psalm 66:18 that if sin is safe in our hearts, He will not listen. So Saul goes to a witch, who is a medium. She is a mediator to access spirits that are not holy. When she tries to contact the dead through a séance (an evil worship service), she takes the place of Christ, our Mediator. God was clear about witches! *"The person who turns after mediums and familiar spirits, to prostitute himself with them, I will set My face against that person and cut him off from his people. Sanctify yourselves therefore, and be holy, for I am the Lord your God,"* Leviticus 20:6-7 NKJV.

Today the practice of witchcraft is called Wicca. They try to get us connected to spiritual forces. They cast spells to control goddess, gods and other people. There are rites and rituals. Young people are especially attracted to Wicca, because there are no rules of right or wrong. They then basically create their own rules. They create their own goddess and gods. They accept a god who will justify whatever they want to do! Wicca is a selfish religion! It's interesting how many who are into witchcraft and magic are against the bad habits of others, yet they have no real standard of right and wrong for themselves.

When someone we care about is interested in Wicca, we should gently ask them why. We must be like Paul on Mars Hill and minister to them about the hope that we have in Christ! Plus we must not fear someone involved with Wicca. Greater is He (God), who is in us!

Prayer: Lord, You are a jealous God for good reasons! You made us for Your own glory and praise. Jesus is the only Mediator You allow into Your holy presence. Your Spirit is the only One who sanctifies us. We praise You for who You are. In Christ's name we pray. Amen.

April 18

"David was greatly distressed because the men were talking of stoning him; each one was bitter in spirit because of his sons and daughters. But David found strength in the Lord his God... and David inquired of the Lord." 1 Samuel 30:6 & 8a

David gave God his difficult decisions

Amalekite raiders attacked the place where the families of David and his men were staying. As a result, David's men were talking of stoning him. He was afraid, yet he knew the Lord was his help and strength. David's response to this and other difficult times must be ours! *"He inquired of the Lord."* Do we do that? Yes, we have even more resources than David! We have the whole Bible. We have the Holy Spirit in greater measure. We have a sympathetic High Priest Jesus, who is ready and willing to help us in our time of need!

A concern I hear often is this: "I don't know how to make a difficult decision." Go to God as David did! Go to the Bible, to that revealed will of God that holds the answer to almost every question. We have the information for both big and small decisions. However, we need to approach the Bible reverently, repeatedly, and prayerfully, then look for God's answer. The Bible is not like other books! We need to prayerfully seek and search out the Bible, not just simply read it! We also need to be prepared for God to speak to us!

If we do not go to God or to His Word, we will find a god who is in line with our sinful nature! But if God determines where He is to be found, then there, at that place, our sinful natures will be exposed! Go to that Cross of Jesus Christ! The message of the Bible, in both the Old and New Testament, is God's revealed and holy will for our life!

David not only respected God and His wisdom, he loved Him! He knew the heart of God and wanted to learn more about it. He knew God would tell him the truth even if the truth hurt!

Prayer: Dear Lord, Your loving presence is so wonderful, so comforting and so directive. We are so thankful that we can cast all of our cares on You because You care for us! Guide us into Your truth! In Jesus' name we pray. Amen.

April 19

"Joab stabbed him in the stomach, and he died. Later, when David heard about this, he said, 'I and my kingdom are forever innocent before the Lord concerning the blood of Abner son of Ner. May his blood fall upon the head of Joab and upon all his father's house!'"
2 Samuel 3:27b-29a

Joab, jealous of the competition

Joab was David's army commander. He was also David's nephew. Even though he was related to David, he was not related to David's God. Joab won many important battles for David. He was a skilled soldier who David had confidence in, at first anyway. Joab's pride teaches us that we may be brilliant, but we also need a redeemed personality to be in that great hall of fame, in Heaven!

Abner was King Saul's commander. When Saul fell and died, Abner went to David for mercy and to peacefully help him. This is a good picture of us sinners going to Christ for mercy and pardon. David graciously welcomed him and sent him on a mission. We have a mission from Jesus too. But Joab went after Abner and murdered him.

Amasa was the commander of Absalom's insurgency. Amasa had killed Joab's brother, but that was an act in war. Amasa, like Abner, was pardoned by David, commissioned, then stabbed! Joab's pattern of jealousy in eliminating the competition was evil! Who do we stab with our words and actions to build up ourselves?

David said, *"I and my kingdom are forever innocent before the Lord concerning the blood of Abner son of Ner. May his blood fall upon the head of Joab and upon all his father's house! May Joab's house never be without someone who has a running sore or leprosy or who leans on a crutch or who falls by the sword or who lacks food,"* 2 Samuel 3:28b-29. David and Israel wept with Abner's death. David rejected Joab. Jesus is not impressed with our efforts to elevate ourselves by eliminating others! Joab's evil ways did not help his family, instead it cursed them!

Prayer: Lord, You graciously give us a home with Abner who was saved! You give us a warning with Joab who was lost! The wise Solomon killed him. So too, Your wise Son judges all evildoers. Forgive us by Your grace so Your justice does not kill us. In Jesus' name we pray. Amen.

April 20

"And Mephibosheth lived in Jerusalem, because he always ate at the King's table, and he was crippled in both feet." 2 Samuel 9:13

Mephibosheth, by grace, just like me!

The crippled Mephibosheth is one of the most descriptive characters in the Bible. In picture form, we see the amazing love and grace of God to us undeserving sinners.

It was normal for a new king to kill all the family members of the former king, lest they rise up against him. But David had a covenant with Jonathan (and God has one with us) to show kindness to his family after he was dead. David remembers that covenant and searches to see if there were any descendants of Jonathan. There was one son left who was five when his father was killed. His nurse dropped him as they ran for their lives, crippling him in both feet. The fact that he was crippled, is mentioned many times for a good reason. <u>King David, sought out the lame one who could not come or approach the king on his own!</u> King Jesus also seeks out us who are unable to come to Him! Plus He makes us walk in this world and the next.

"'Don't be afraid,' David said to him (Mephibosheth), *'for I will surely show you kindness for the sake of your father Jonathan. I will restore to you all the land that belonged to your grandfather Saul, and you will always eat at my table,'"* 2 Samuel 9:7. The lame man's response: *"Mephibosheth bowed down and said, 'What is your servant, that you should notice a dead dog like me?'"* 2 Samuel 9:8.

King David gave the lame one the privileges his sons had! Our Father in Heaven also invites us to come and eat at the King's table! *"Come, all you who are thirsty, come to the waters; and you who have no money, come, buy and eat!"* Isaiah 55:1. God even makes us joint heirs with Jesus Christ! Mephibosheth knew he was lame and did not deserve to eat at the king's table! Do we know how lame we really are? Do we realize we do not deserve to eat at God's table? May we never forget Mephibosheth! He is a picture of our depravity and our salvation!

Prayer: Lord, how much You love us in Christ! We know that we will sing praises in eternity of Your love and grace shown to us lame sinners. May we begin to praise You now! In Jesus' name we pray. Amen.

April 21

"One evening David got up from his bed and walked around on the roof of the palace. From the roof he saw a woman bathing. The woman was very beautiful, and David sent someone to find out about her. The man said. 'Isn't this Bathsheba, the daughter of Eliam and the wife of Uriah the Hittite?'" 2 Samuel 11:2-3

Bathsheba, a sinner and ancestor of Jesus

David's sin is obvious. With Bathsheba part, we have questions. David should have been busy with kingly duties or even at war with his men. Instead his telescope eyes are on the neighbor's house. He watches Bathsheba bathe. Did she know he was watching? Quite likely she did, as it was not dark out yet! David looked, then acted. He knew Bathsheba was married! He knew her grandfather Ahithophel, (David's trusted advisor). He knew her father Eliam, (he was one of David's 30 'mighty men' as was Bathsheba's husband Uriah).

In verse four we read that David sent messengers to get her and then, *"she came to him."* The words seem to suggest that she was a willing participant. Perhaps she thought she could do better than Uriah who was a Hittite foreigner. In later years, Bathsheba was very manipulative and aggressive in the way she got her son on the throne.

But what about us? Women need to protect their modesty. Men need to guard the windows to their hearts, which is their eyes. Today, we have "Bathshebas" by the thousands on the Internet and men who are looking down to see them! What are the ladies doing to attract the male eyes? Ladies, if showing your body off is more important than keeping your heart pure, then you are not innocent! For then you too are compromising that which is meant for marriage alone! Desire what God wants for you: be pure in the midst of wickedness! If you think an affair will get you a marriage, it will also get you a divorce later!

Jesus is from the line of Bathsheba. If we have sinned like Bathsheba, seek Jesus. He will forgive and purify us. Live for Him. We will never regret it!

Prayer: Lord, You tell us the truth about improper relationships to clearly warn us. You do this because You love us so much. May we love You in return! In Jesus' name we pray. Amen.

April 22

"Uriah said to David, 'The ark and Israel and Judah are staying in tents, and my master Joab and my lord's men are camped in the open fields. How could I go to my house to eat and drink and lie with my wife? As surely as you live, I will not do such a thing!'" 2 Samuel 11:11

Uriah, a faithful soldier of the Cross

Uriah is first introduced to us as the husband of Bathsheba. She is the woman David had an affair with and became pregnant from it. Upon hearing the news of her conceiving a child, David calls for Uriah her husband to come home from the battle. David wants Uriah to take some time off, to be with his wife. David is doing everything he can to make it seem like Uriah is the father of the child growing in Bathsheba. But the faithful Uriah does not go home and his reasons are in our text.

Uriah gives good reasons to show that he is a man of noble character. Uriah rightly places duty over pleasure! His concern to be faithful to God and country are the complete reverse of David's recent concern. David had just put the pleasures of the flesh before his sense of duty to God and country. How often do we do the same thing? How often do "pleasures" of many kinds prevent us from being a faithful soldier of the Cross?

"My master Joab and my lord's men are camped in the open fields." These words of Uriah, not only accuse David, they accuse us all! Did not our Lord and Master Jesus, commonly sleep in the fields with a stone for a pillow! Are we more like David who had a greater desire to be "comfortable"? Or, are we more like Uriah who put duty before pleasure? Does duty or pleasure speak the loudest when it comes to our normal daily schedule?

The prophet Nathan used Uriah's faithfulness and sense of duty to help David to see his selfish unfaithfulness. Convicted of his sin, David now teaches us in Psalm 51, how important it is to confess our sin and serve the Lord as the faithful Uriah did.

Prayer: Lord, we thank You for showing us the life of Uriah. May we embrace our duty to be soldiers of the Cross for You, and be against the pleasures of this world that Satan wants us to seek after! Lord forgive our unfaithfulness and make us faithful! In Jesus' name we pray. Amen.

April 23

"Then Nathan said to David, 'You are the man! This is what the Lord, the God of Israel, says: 'I anointed you king over Israel, and I delivered you from the hand of Saul. I gave your master's house to you, and your master's wives into your arms! I gave you the house of Israel and Judah. And if all of this had been too little, I would have given you even more. Why did you despise the Word of the Lord by doing what is evil in His eyes?'" 2 Samuel 12:7-9a

Nathan, tells God's truth with love

Nathan was God's prophet. A prophet is to speak the words of God. He must say what God wants him to say, that is to speak the truth. But more than that, he must speak the truth in the right way, which is with love. One of the greatest needs today is for Christians to be God's mouthpiece to those who have lost their moral compass.

King David sinned against the Lord. To make matters worse, David did not confess his sin. Instead he tried to cover it up. David tried to live as if nothing was wrong. God in His mercy to David, (and to His church) went after David to convict him. Today God still goes after us when we sin. He does this through His Word and by His Spirit.

God sent Nathan to confront David. The words of our text are the exact words God wanted Nathan to say. We see Nathan's faithfulness in speaking God's words that work powerfully to bring conviction. The question is: Are we willing to bring words that God can use to bring conviction in someone's life? To do that, we must first agree with God about what He says is sinful. Then when we agree with God about sin, we go against a world that considers nothing sin! The world considers it progressive and liberating to believe and do whatever one wants to do. But the truth is, they are blind to the real truth! They are not liberated but are in bondage to sin. No one changes to go God's way until they are first convicted of their sin. May God give us the boldness and grace to confront sin and sinners, just like the prophet Nathan did!

Prayer: Lord, You tell us, *"there is a way that seems right to a man, but in the end it leads to death,"* (Proverbs 14:12). Lord, send a Nathan to us when we need it. Make us a Nathan to others when they need it. In Jesus' name we pray. Amen.

April 24

"The Lord struck the child that Uriah's wife had borne to David, and he became ill." 2 Samuel 12:15b

David repents, but consequences remain

After Nathan the prophet confronted David with his sin of murder and adultery, David repented and admitted his sin in verse 13. If we have committed these sins we too can be forgiven! And do not think that we have not done what David did! We too commit these sins! We lust after others and Jesus called lust, adultery. We are angry at others and anger is the first stage of murder. But even though David was forgiven, serious consequences still remained. He felt God's loving discipline through affliction. Through these two great offenses by David, we learn much about <u>how</u> God afflicts us, and <u>why</u> He does so.

First, the baby became sick and died. *"The Lord struck the child that Uriah's wife had borne to David, and he became ill,"* 2 Samuel 12:15b. Note that God calls Bathsheba here, *"Uriah's wife."* God still saw this baby as a child of Uriah's wife! Plus, *"The sword will never depart from your house,"* 2 Samuel 12:10a. Just as David used the sword on Uriah, now God afflicts David with the sword. David *"despised"* God when he took *"Uriah's wife."* What David did in secret with *"Uriah's wife,"* God openly allowed David's family to do. Sin has consequences! God's reason for afflicting David, *"You have made the enemies of the Lord show utter contempt,"* 2 Samuel 12:14b.

God is not a cruel Judge here! He is a merciful Judge and a loving Father! God says to His children, to every single one, *"My son, (daughters too) do not make light of the Lord's discipline, and do not lose heart when He rebukes you, because <u>the Lord disciplines those He loves</u>, and He punishes everyone He accepts as a son,"* Hebrews 12:5b-6. Read more in Hebrews and see how God disciplines us so, *"that we may share in His holiness,"* Hebrews 12:10b.

Prayer: Lord, we see that David's sin had consequences. We also see a pattern of sin continuing to the next generation, to his children. May that fact push us to repent for the good of our families. We do not want our sins repeated. Turn us away from sin and back to You! In Christ's name we pray. Amen.

April 25

"In the course of time, Amnon son of David fell in love with Tamar, the beautiful sister of Absalom son of David." 2 Samuel 13:1

Amnon, privileged, immoral and dead

It is hard to talk about what happens here, but we must! The Bible openly lays out the faults of young men so we can learn from their sin. In our text we have Amnon, the king's son. He had a huge desire to be physically involved with his own half-sister! It says Amnon *"fell in love."* But this *"love"* is really lust that is burning him up! To be intimate with an immediate family member is called incest. It is the grossest of sins, described in Leviticus 18, and is punishable by death! Amnon's selfish desire overruled his brain! That is what lust does! *"Amnon was so distressed over his sister Tamar that he became sick,"* 2 Samuel 13:2a NKJV. He then plotted and schemed how he could get at his sister. Doing the unthinkable, he then abused his own sister.

Godly parents can have wicked children as is the case here. Grace does not always run in the family bloodlines, but corruption surely does! It is true that David committed adultery, but he still had a tender heart! An unclean spirit from Satan had a solid hold on Amnon who then acted accordingly. A man who is so given into lust imagines that the other person will like what he has to offer. But his sister is rightly shocked and repulsed by the idea. She pleads with him not to *"be like one of the wicked fools in Israel."* Besides not wanting to be defiled, Tamar tries to reason with Amnon for his own good. But he would not listen! Lust is not only <u>blind</u> to the truth, it does not want to <u>hear</u> the truth!

Then after the act we read, *"Then Amnon hated her with intense hatred. In fact, he hated her more than he had loved her. Amnon said to her, 'Get up and get out!'"* 2 Samuel 13:15. Tamar became, *"a desolate woman"*! Two years later, the immoral Amnon is dead!

Prayer: Lord, how unloving and selfish is a heart that is filled with lust! How harmful lustful thoughts, words and actions are to Your kingdom and to others also. In the end, lust is death for the one who does not repent of this wicked way of living! Lord put Your Spirit in us so that we have the will to act and to do for Your good pleasure! In Jesus' name we pray. Amen.

April 26

"Tamar put ashes on her head and tore the ornamented robe she was wearing. She put her hand on her head and went away, weeping aloud as she went." 2 Samuel 13:19

Tamar, King David's beautiful daughter

Tamar is described to us as beautiful. She was also a humble girl with a servant heart, even though she was a daughter of a king! She baked some bread to serve her half-brother because he was supposedly sick. But he grabbed her and did the unthinkable.

What can we learn from Tamar that we did not see yesterday in the life of Amnon? We can see that Tamar is wise. She reasoned with Amnon not to do this wicked thing when she was assaulted by him. She said that he should respect her as a woman and as a sister. She pointed out that wicked Canaanites do these things, but we are God's people! Tamar finally pleads with her brother that their father David could allow them to be married! For even though it was against the law, she knew that Abraham married his half-sister years before! Perhaps she was trying to get Amnon to think, but his evil lust would not listen to reason! Lust is like that!

After Amnon abused her, Tamar again pleads with her brother not to send her out, perhaps implying they could still be married and both of them could retain some honor. But Amnon refused. He only wanted her body, but not her as a person! So Amnon had his servant remove Tamar from his house like she was garbage. *"Tamar put ashes on her head and tore the ornamented robe she was wearing. She put her hand on her head and went away, weeping aloud as she went,"* 2 Samuel 13:19. Defiled and scorned through no fault of her own, *"Tamar remained desolate in her brother Absalom's house,"* 2 Samuel 13:20b NKJV. Her life was basically ruined! No one would come forward to marry her now!

Prayer: Lord, we cry out for Tamar and those like her. The only comfort we see is that Tamar was a woman of faith and virtue, yet she saw so little compassion from her family. <u>But,</u> we know that she is Your daughter for all eternity. We know that You wipe away every tear and sorrow! Help us to understand and love those who are abused. In Jesus' name we pray. Amen.

April 27

"Tamar remained desolate in her brother Absalom's house."
2 Samuel 13:20b NKJV

Tamar, responding to her horrible abuse

Father David was *"very angry"* about what happened to Tamar. But we do not read he did anything about it! It is not written that David comforted Tamar, nor is it written that David confronted his son Amnon. *"Tamar remained desolate."* Do we feel her pain? She was a decent, young woman. It is not recorded that anyone ever ministered to her or comforted her. Her brother Absalom took her in, but our text gives the picture of a life of shame, without hope and without affection. How are we to minister to the "Tamars" of this world? The church needs to speak up! There are many who have been hurt. They carry this pain in their hearts. So many still have emotional scars, even after years.

Perhaps Tamar did have one fault. If she kept bitterness in her heart, it would serve to keep her in a *"desolate"* condition. Some time ago, I was speaking on the topic of forgiveness to a group who were abused in various ways. One woman angrily shouted, "If you knew all the things my husband did to me you would not tell me I needed to forgive him." I kindly suggested to her that if her husband died, she would still hate him, and he would still control her, even ten years after his death. Her own bitterness towards him for what he had done, was actually hurting her even more than what he did to her! Was this part of Tamar's problem? We do not know.

We do need to put our arms of support around those who have been hurt. We need to use acts of compassion and words of hope. But don't say as Absalom did, *"Don't take this to heart."* Abuse is very personal and it is very much a heart issue!

Prayer: Lord, we have so much to learn! We know abuse hurts. We also know that Your Son, Jesus, was abused more than anyone else ever was! By Your grace we are devoted to Him. May we show our concern to others who have been abused. Jesus' ministry was especially about reaching out to those who have been hurt by others. May we do the same. They need the comfort that only Christ can bring. In Jesus' name we pray. Amen.

April 28

"In all Israel there was not a man so highly praised for his handsome appearance as Absalom. From the top of his head to the sole of his foot there was no blemish in him." 2 Samuel 14:25

Absalom, good looking and proud of it

Absalom was the best looking guy in the land. People did not just notice that Absalom was "hot," they told him he was. Absalom's response was one of pride and arrogance! Absalom did not realize that his outward beauty was just skin deep. He did not see that his heart was ugly! The fact that he had no blemish from head to toe, became a curse instead of a blessing! His life ended up a big waste. God specifically shows us these things so we can learn, and not respond like Absalom did.

Absalom was so full of himself, that he tried to kill his own father and replace him. Absalom's extreme self-love prevented him from loving anyone except himself! God in His mercy gives us a tragic picture of how Absalom failed. Think of what Absalom threw away! He tossed aside his life of privilege. He scorned his covenant upbringing. He lived for more self-esteem! And we have people telling us we need more self-esteem to get through life! Such foolish people need to examine the life of Absalom! He had a whole nation of people adoring him and he still wanted more attention! It is Christ-esteem and esteeming others that makes a person beautiful. Absalom's life of pride shouts to us that real beauty is in the heart, not on the outside!

God even teaches us with Absalom's death! First, 20,000 men died who followed this foolish guy! Then Absalom tries to escape death, but he can't escape his God-given appointment. Riding on his royal mule, (the best luxury vehicle available) he gets his gorgeous head of hair caught in a tree. He's hanging between Heaven and earth. No good on earth, not fit for Heaven. He dies. His greatest pride, his hair, hangs him! How we need to learn that pride kills!

Prayer: Lord, Absalom is not the only one that tried to steal the throne that belongs to You alone. In pride, we also have a great desire to be noticed just like Absalom. Yet Lord, You put us here in this world to notice You and to love others. Help us in our weakness. In Jesus' name we pray. Amen.

"Now David had been told, 'Ahithophel is among the conspirators with Absalom.' So David prayed, 'O Lord, turn Ahithophel's counsel into foolishness.'" 2 Samuel 15:31

Ahithophel, from wise to foolish in a day

God presents us the life of Ahithophel. He shows us how He wonderfully protects his beloved child, King David. Ahithophel began as one of David's most trusted advisors. David also considered him a close friend! But when Absalom tried to take over the throne, Ahithophel quickly went with him. It seems that Ahithophel was a slick talking opportunist.

In the context of our text, David is fleeing for his life. He is in the process of going, *"up the Mount of Olives, weeping as he went,"* 2 Samuel 15:30b. As he climbs the mountain, David is told, *"'Ahithophel is among the conspirators with Absalom.' So David prayed, 'O Lord, turn Ahithophel's counsel into foolishness,'"* 2 Samuel 15:31b. God quickly and completely protected His servant David! God is like that! For when David got to the top of the mountain, God had a trusted old friend named Hushai, waiting for him. God made Hushai willing to go to Jerusalem to help secure the throne for His child, David.

Ahithophel gives Absalom good advice, 'Strike David quickly.' But then Absalom also asked Hushai for his advice. *"Absalom and all the men of Israel said, 'The advice of Hushai the Arkite is better than that of Ahithophel.' For the Lord had determined to frustrate the good advice of Ahithophel in order to bring disaster on Absalom,"* 2 Samuel 17:14. Through Hushai then, God allows time for David to get away. God also allows time for Hushai to tell David of Absalom's plans.

Ahithophel is accustomed to getting his own way and does not take rejection well! He runs away to his house. *"He put his house in order and then hanged himself,"* 2 Samuel 17:23b. How amazing the sovereignty of God is! He quickly protects David. He removes the proud Ahithophel from the scene. And through it all, God protects His own name!

Prayer: Lord, You are beyond amazing as You work all things for the good of every believer. At the same time, You work all things to bring glory and honor to Your most holy name. We worship You! In Jesus' name we pray. Amen.

"When David had gone a short distance beyond the summit, there was Ziba, the steward of Mephibosheth, waiting to meet him. He had a string of donkeys saddled and loaded with two hundred loaves of bread, a hundred cakes of raisins, a hundred cakes of figs and a skin of wine." 2 Samuel 16:1

Ziba blesses the king, bows, then lies

David is on the run from his son Absalom. He climbs the Mount of Olives. As he gets to the peak, he learns that his friend and advisor Ahithophel, has also deserted him. Now as David looks over the top of the mountain, there is Ziba. He has a whole storehouse of goods for the tired and hungry company. What a welcome sight!

David asks Ziba, "Where is Mephibosheth, (Jonathan's son) your master's grandson?" Ziba tells David that Mephibosheth decided to stay in Jerusalem thinking, *"Today the house of Israel will give me back my grandfather's kingdom,"* 2 Samuel 16:3b. In other words, Mephibosheth has turned his back on David and now looks to Absalom to give <u>all</u> of King Saul's property back to him. This, after David had given all of Jonathan's (Saul's son) property to Mephibosheth! Ziba was managing this property for Mephibosheth, but Ziba wants the property for himself, and he lies to get it. David buys the lie and says, *"all that belonged to Mephibosheth is now yours."* Ziba's response to David is, *"I humbly bow."*

But there is nothing humble about Ziba! Later in 2 Samuel 19, when David returns victorious to Jerusalem, Mephibosheth is one of the first to meet him and sincerely welcomes him back. Mephibosheth is a dirty unkept mess! (Aren't we all?) David asks him, "'*Why didn't you go with me?"* Now we learn, Ziba prevented him from doing so, then lied to David about it!

David is crushed. His promise to his good friend Jonathan to care for his surviving children is broken. David offers other property to Mephibosheth, but <u>the humble Mephibosheth only wants to eat at the king's table and be in the king's presence</u>! What a testimony of a true believer. What is the most important thing to us?

Prayer: Lord, how privileged we are that You put together events in history, just to teach us. Lord forgive us when we are manipulative like Ziba. Make us like Mephibosheth! In Jesus' name we pray. Amen.

MAY

Elisha watching Elijah taking up to Heaven

"As they were walking along and talking together, suddenly a chariot of fire and horses of fire appeared and separated the two of them, and Elijah went up to Heaven in a whirlwind." 2 Kings 2:11

May 1

"As King David approached Bahurim, a man from the same clan as Saul's family came out from there. His name was Shimei son of Gera, and he cursed as he came out. He pelted David and all the king's officials with stones." 2 Samuel 16:5-6a

Shimei, curses the king then begs for mercy

Shimei hates King David with a passion! A volcano has been brewing in his heart for many years! When Shimei sees the king running for his life, his mouth erupts with curses. He even throws stones at David! A servant of David says, *"Why should this dead dog curse my lord the king? Let me go over and cut off his head."* David says, *"Leave him alone; let him curse, for the Lord has told him to. It may be that the Lord will see my distress and repay me with good for the cursing I am receiving today,"* 2 Samuel 16:11b-12. What great spiritual insight on David's part!

We see the foolishness of Shimei's bitter anger, and the wisdom of David's gracious response! God notices David's heart is humbled from Absalom's rebellion and Ahithophel's betrayal. David's response points to Jesus' response! When the people tried to kill Jesus, and when Judas betrayed Him, Jesus said, *"Father, forgive them"*!

David is back on Mount Zion, ascending the throne again! Shimei now fears the king and trembles. He knows that he is guilty and deserves death for all the curses and stones he threw at the king! Shimei fully understands that the wages of sin is death! His heavy guilt moves him to his knees before the reigning king! *"When Shimei son of Gera crossed the Jordan, he fell prostrate before the king and said to him, 'May my lord not hold me guilty. Do not remember how your servant did wrong,"* 2 Samuel 19:19a. David promised with an oath that Shimei would not die!

Shimei's problem is exactly ours! We are guilty of throwing stones at King Jesus and cursing Him. Have we crossed the Jordan to fall on our knees and beg for His mercy? We will also obtain mercy if we seek it! We will receive the same oath from King Jesus, *"You will not die"*!

Prayer: Lord, we have seen earlier how Ziba's blessing, ended up being a curse. Now we see Shimei's curses end up being blessings. Like David, how often we respond to people's curses better than to their blessings! Help us to understand these things. In Jesus' name we pray. Amen.

May 2

"Barzillai the Gileadite from Rogelim brought bedding and bowls and articles of pottery. They also brought wheat and barley, flour and roasted grain, beans and lentils, honey and curds, sheep, and cheese from cows' milk for David and his people to eat. For they said, 'The people have become hungry and tired and thirsty in the desert.'"
2 Samuel 17:27b-29

Barzillai, the king's encouraging servant

Barzillai name means iron, which is perhaps the most practical metal to serve the needs of man. Barzillai was a hard working common man who God blessed and was wealthy in many ways. He is a good example of how we must simply serve our King Jesus.

Barzillai mercifully provided for David and his men when he was fleeing for his life from Absalom. Barzillai brought David the necessary and practical things he needed to survive in the desert. Barzillai was the kind of man who saw a need and quickly moved to meet that need. Barzillai unselfishly encouraged and helped in meaningful ways. Barzillai lived out the verse, *"Therefore, as we have opportunity, let us do good to all people, especially to those who belong to the family of believers,"* Gal. 6:10. Praise God for the Barzillais He provides to build His church!

No one can do God's work without the aid of helpful people like Barzillai! See David in his distress! Sure, he needed the food and clothing, but David also needed encouragement and hope! God provided Barzillai to do both! Praise God for His practical grace and mercy!

After David's enemies were defeated, *"Barzillai the Gileadite also came down from Rogelim to cross the Jordan with the king and to send him on his way from there. Now Barzillai was a very old man, eighty years of age. He had provided for the king during his stay in Mahanaim, for he was a very wealthy man,"* 2 Samuel 19:31-32.

Prayer: Jesus said to the "Barzillais of our world; "Come, you who are blessed by My Father; take your inheritance prepared for you... For I was hungry and you gave me something to eat, I was thirsty and you gave me something to drink, I was a stranger and you invited Me in, I needed clothes and you clothed me." Lord, move us to be helpful like Barzillai was. In Jesus' name we pray. Amen.

May 3

"And say to Amasa, 'Are you not my own flesh and blood? May God deal with me, be it ever so severely, if from now on you are not the commander of my army in place of Joab.'" 2 Samuel 19:13

Amasa pardoned, commissioned, then stabbed

Amasa was the commander of Absalom's insurgency against King David. Absalom failed to take the kingdom from his father David and was killed. It was David's commander Joab who killed Absalom, even after David told Joab to take his son alive. Now David is back in Jerusalem in full power. One of the first things David does is send a note to Amasa. Our text records some of this information. See here how David's life points to the life of Jesus. David <u>called</u> Amasa and <u>pardoned</u> him for his tyranny. Amasa was then <u>commissioned</u> by David to replace Joab as the commander. Then David sent Amasa on a mission. Besides all that, Amasa was a <u>relative</u> of David.

Joab follows after Amasa, and when he sees Amasa coming towards him, he calls him brother. Joab then purposely lets his own sword fall from his scabbard. Joab pretends to pick it up to put it back, as he kisses Amasa in greeting. Holding Amasa in a friendly embrace, Joab takes his sword and kills him with one death blow. Judas betrayed Jesus in almost the same manner. Judas also pretended to love Jesus. He kissed Him in greeting, all while he was betraying Him to end Jesus' life.

How many people have we stabbed with our words and actions, that in their presence we pretended to love? Think of how God has <u>called</u> many people into a relationship with Him and has <u>pardoned</u> them! All had committed tyranny against Him. God has even <u>commissioned</u> each Christian to be a commander in His army. We are all brothers and sisters in Christ. And then in jealousy, we stab them with our words and actions. We are no better than the wicked Joab and Judas!

Prayer: Lord, we sometimes act like the warrior Joab who shed innocent blood in peacetime, as well as in war! Like him, we are so concerned about our own reputation that we stab others with our words and actions. Forgive us Lord. We want to be more like Jesus who worked to build others up. Strengthen us, we pray, to build Your kingdom! In Jesus' name we pray. Amen.

May 4

"A wise woman called from the city, 'Listen! Listen! Tell Joab to come here so I can speak to him.' He went toward her, and she asked, 'Are you Joab?' 'I am,' he answered. She said, 'Listen to what your servant has to say.' 'I'm listening' he said. She continued, 'Long ago they used to say, "Get your answer at Abel," and that settled it. We are the peaceful and faithful in Israel. You are trying to destroy a city that is a mother in Israel. Why do you want to swallow up the Lord's inheritance?'" 2 Samuel 20:16-19

A "wise woman" saves a city

The government is chasing Sheba, the most wanted criminal in the country. He locks himself in the city of Abel. The army commander, Joab, comes and starts to break down the walls to get the rebel Sheba. The people in the city, for whatever reason, do nothing at first! Then, an unnamed *"wise woman"* discusses the situation with Joab and realizes they would stop attacking if they could get the criminal Sheba.

The *"wise woman"* goes to work to bring peace. She convinces the "city fathers" to offer up this wanted criminal. Sheba's head flies over the wall and the attack stops. The *"wise woman"* wins the day, and the lives of many are spared.

Why were the government officials in Abel unconcerned about the safety of their city? Why didn't even one of them meet with Joab to discuss the situation? Or, did they admire this rebel Sheba? We are not told. But obviously they did not care much about the good of the city! They might have been big in power but they were small in the wisdom department. This unnamed lady won the day!

We see the value of acting wisely where God has placed us. The *"wise woman"* surely had a good reputation, otherwise the city council would not have listened. One woman did what she could and a whole city was saved. What can we do to save our city? What is tearing down our city walls? We must act wisely! The fear of the Lord is the beginning of wisdom! Let us ask God to help us make a difference in our city!

Prayer: Lord, like the wise woman, our names don't matter! What matters is that we live wisely. Spare our cities. Give us the wisdom and courage to act to save them. In Jesus' name we pray. Amen.

May 5

"Benaiah son of Jehoiada was a valiant fighter from Kabzeel, who performed great exploits. He struck down two of Moab's best men. He also went down into a pit on a snowy day and killed a lion."
2 Samuel 23:20

Benaiah, a courageous fighter!

Benaiah was one of David's 30 mighty men. His name means, "God has built." *"He was held in greater honor than any of the thirty,"* 2 Samuel 23:23a! Benaiah is a picture of a most honored believer! King David is a picture of King Jesus. Benaiah's life shouts to us what William Carey said, "Attempt great things for God; expect great things from God!"

Benaiah *"went down into a pit on a snowy day and killed a lion."* Benaiah was super courageous! He met the enemy head on! He chased that lion into a pit and then went and killed it. This event is on the pages of Scripture to teach us! *"Your enemy the devil prowls around like a roaring lion looking for someone to devour,"* 1 Peter 5:8b. Will we wait for that *"lion"* to attack us, or will we attack him first? The courage to fight Satan is not the absence of fear! Courage is moving ahead in God's strength in the very face of fear! Benaiah met the enemy. He overcame many obstacles and triumphed! We must remember that!

Lions in the Bible were usually tests from God. Samson and Daniel also met them and overcame them. God then moved them on to greater honor! There were others who did not pass the "lion" test and that was the end of them! Think of how right after Jesus' baptism in Matthew 3, the Holy Spirit led Jesus to Satan and Jesus overcame him! Greater is He who is in us, than he who is in the world!

Benaiah was promoted over David's guard, with 24,000 men. Benaiah stayed with David when he had to leave Jerusalem, shamed by Absalom. Benaiah stayed loyal to David to the end of his life! Benaiah was honored for his commitment to the king. And so are we honored when we are faithful to the King!

Prayer: Lord, what a beautiful example for us as we follow King Jesus! May we courageously face the lion tests You give us to strengthen our faith. Fill us with Your Spirit to battle Your enemies. Lord, You are worthy of our loyalty! In Jesus' name we pray. Amen.

May 6

"Now Adonijah, whose mother was Haggith, put himself forward and said, 'I will be king.' So he got chariots and horses ready, with fifty men to run ahead of him." 1 Kings 1:5

Adonijah, a man who wanted to be king

Adonijah was the second son of King David. Absalom was the first. Earlier Absalom died trying to take the throne from David. Now Adonijah proudly says he wants to be king, even though he knew that his father David was passing on the throne to Solomon, his third son.

Adonijah was wrong in demanding to be number one. But are we really any different? Are we not just like him! It is so easy to justify our own pride and lifting up ourselves! After all, the world tells us we need more self-esteem! The T.V. tells us we deserve to be number one. The psychologist tells us we need to love ourselves more to overcome our problems. But deep down, we know that God's will for us is to deny self, as Jesus taught us in Luke 9:23. We even admire people like Mother Theresa who loved God and others more than self!

Adonijah has a pride problem and it seems that his father David did nothing to help him overcome it. Scripture charges dad David with some of the blame for his sons super selfish behavior! It simply says, *"His father had never interfered with him by asking, 'Why do you behave as you do?'"* 1 Kings 1:6a. Growing up Adonijah did as he pleased just like his brother Absalom before him. Dad did not discipline him. Nor did his dad discipline son Amnon, and he ended up abusing his stepsister to get what he wanted! It is a parent's main job to stop the selfishness in a child. And it works best if the parents model just that!

Solomon, the wise son of David, saw firsthand how a selfish child who is unrestrained, stays selfish. In Proverbs 22:6, Solomon said: *"Train a child in the way he should go, and when he is old he will not turn from it."* This means, if a child is allowed to go his own selfish way, doing whatever he or she wants, they will continue in their selfishness, even when they are older.

Prayer: Lord, convict us of our own selfishness! We know that we can't really follow You and love others until we do! Help us to deny self just like Jesus said and did. In His name we pray. Amen.

May 7

"When the time drew near for David to die, he gave a charge to Solomon his son. 'I am about to go the way of all the earth,' he said. 'So be strong, show yourself a man, and observe what the Lord your God requires: Walk in His ways, and keep His decrees and commands, His laws and requirements, as written in the Law of Moses, so that you may prosper in all you do and wherever you go.'" 1 Kings 2:1-3

David's dying desire for his son's success

David knows he is about to die and he openly speaks about it. He gets right to the point in giving his final words of advice to his son Solomon. David's first words are, *"be strong."* Don't be a coward Solomon! Father David from his own experience, clearly saw the importance of being bold. David wanted Solomon to resolve to be bold for God also. David also knew by experience that God is faithful. And if we are bold for Him, He will act boldly for us in return.

"Walk in His ways." David knew by God's covenant promise, that his heirs ability to stay on the throne was conditional to their faithfulness in keeping covenant with God. This same covenant relationship responsibilities are true for us! If we want God's covenantal blessings we need to be faithful to His covenant. Deuteronomy 28 is very clear about the blessings for obedience and the curses for disobedience.

"Keep His decrees and commands." David knew that God's laws needed to guide his son, Solomon. The Ten Commandments are God's perfect rule of law for every nation. It is an orderly society that loves God's laws and obeys them. But be careful! God's grace needs to govern a home and nation also. Laying the law down without showing grace, promotes rebellion nationally, as well as in personal relationships. This is such a big point and one we will look at more in the John 1:14 devotion.

David was very aware that someday Jesus would come from his lineage. For this reason also, David was concerned that Solomon was faithful. But then, we are joint heirs with Jesus! We too need to walk as a child of God!

Prayer: Lord, may we all heed David's dying words to be bold and to walk in Your ways. May this never be far from our minds. Impress it upon us! In Jesus' name we pray. Amen.

May 8

"God said, 'Ask for whatever you want Me to give you.' Solomon answered... 'I am only a little child and do not know how to carry out my duties... So give your servant a discerning heart to govern Your people and to distinguish between right and wrong. For who is able to govern this great people of Yours?'" 1 Kings 3:5b-9

Solomon, the man who asked for wisdom

As we study the life of Solomon, I wondered, how can he be so wise if he had 1000 wives? Surely, he had to learn that was foolish! In the end, Solomon wrote three of the books in the Bible. And we know that, *"For prophecy never had its origin in the will of man, but men spoke from God as they were <u>carried along by the Holy Spirit</u>,"* 2 Peter 1:21. Only God can give wisdom to any person.

Solomon struggled some as he learned some of life's hard lessons. But he finished wiser and was able to give us wise writings. Solomon tried <u>everything</u>, and he found that it all was *"utterly meaningless!"* <u>Why?</u> <u>So we don't have to try everything!</u> Solomon's great wisdom meant little to him in the end! Pleasures of all kind were meaningless. A thousand wives, more gold than anyone, and the biggest house, did not satisfy! His work was meaningful in life, but at death, that too became meaningless!

Solomon's wisdom in Ecclesiastes teaches us many things! Godless learning leads to cynicism (1:7-8). Godless pride brings sorrow (1:16-18). Godless pleasure ends in disappointment. Godless labor leads to a hatred of life (2:17). Godless philosophy ends in emptiness. A godless life brings depression (4:2-3). Godless religion brings dread (5:4-7). Godless wealth is trouble (5:12). A Godless existence is frustrating (6:12). And finally, godless wisdom ends in despair (11:1-8).

Solomon shouts to us, have meaning in life! *"Fear God and keep His commandments, for this is the whole duty of man. For God will bring every deed into judgment, including every hidden thing, whether it is good or evil,"* Ecclesiastes 12:13b-14. God let Solomon try everything, to teach us what is important in life!

Prayer: Lord, have mercy on us! Help us to have a meaningful relationship with You and others. In Jesus' name we pray. Amen.

May 9

"When the queen of Sheba heard about the fame of Solomon and his relation to the name of the Lord, she came to test him with hard questions." 1 Kings 10:1

The Queen of Sheba searches for the truth

The Queen of Sheba was a wise and wealthy leader. When the news of Solomon's brilliant mind and many riches reached her, she journeyed far to see him. She was impressed! She recognized where this wisdom came from and said, *"Praise be to the Lord your God, who has delighted in you and placed you on the throne of Israel. Because of the Lord's eternal love for Israel, He has made you king, to maintain justice and righteousness,"* 1 Kings 10:9. That, is quite a statement!

The Queen of Sheba knew well the pagan style of leadership, not God's kind of leadership based on His Holy Law. She saw from Solomon that there is no better way to rule a country than by the Ten Commandments of God. She saw true liberty for the people within the framework of God's law, instead of a might-makes-right mentality! She saw the people loved their king because he cared about justice for all!

Jesus placed the Queen of Sheba, a pagan ruler, on better spiritual footing than the people of Israel and many who call themselves Christian today. Jesus said, *"The Queen of the South will rise at The Judgment with this generation and condemn it; for she came from the ends of the earth to listen to Solomon's wisdom, and now One greater than Solomon is here,"* Matthew 12:42.

The Queen of Sheba said to Solomon, *"The report I heard about you in my own country about your achievements and your wisdom is true... in wisdom and in wealth you have far exceeded the report I heard,"* 1 Kings10:6b-7. The Queen recognized that the God of Israel put Solomon where he was. She knew, God the giver of great gifts is greater even than the gifts! May we see God's greatness also!

Prayer: Lord, You made the queen say to Solomon, *"Praise be to the Lord your God, who has delighted in you and placed you on the throne of Israel. Because of the Lord's eternal love for Israel, He has made you a king, to maintain justice and righteousness."* How true this is for all leaders! May we believe it! In Jesus' name we pray. Amen.

May 10

"King Solomon, however, loved many foreign women besides Pharoah's daughter – Moabites, Ammonites, Edomites, Sidonians and Hittites. They were from nations about which the Lord had told the Israelites, 'You must not intermarry with them, because they will surely turn your hearts after their gods.' Nevertheless, Solomon held fast to them in love." 1 Kings 11:1-2

Solomon's foolish marriages led him astray

Solomon first married Pharoah's daughter, yet this was far more a business transaction than a God-honoring marriage. Solomon thought that marrying the daughters of powerful kings would win their favor and loyalty to his kingdom. God warned him and all Israel not to do this, not to be unequally yoked, not to intermarry with the enemies of God's people. But Solomon did it anyway! In the end, *"He had 700 wives of royal birth and 300 concubines, and his wives led him astray,"* 1 Kings 11:3. Solomon was very wise in other things, but when it came marriage, Solomon was a very foolish man. Exactly what God said would happen, did! *"His wives led him astray."* What a sad consequence for the nation of Israel and for Solomon personally! What a slap in the face to his awesome God!

The error of Solomon in marrying 700 times plus concubines, must teach every man and woman that one is God's number when it comes to marriage. One is God's number when it comes to worshiping Him is an even bigger point! More in both cases is not better, because it turns our hearts *"astray."* At the end of Solomon's life he wisely advised us, *"Remember your Creator in the days of your youth, before the days of trouble come and the years approach when you will say, 'I find no pleasure in them,'"* Ecclesiastes 12:1. Was he in part, thinking of his foolish marriages? I think so, because a good marriage to God and to a godly spouse gets better and better and leaves no regrets! We must learn wisdom from Solomon's mistakes!

Prayer: Lord, we can plainly see from Solomon's foolish marriages that we do not need the help of man to protect us! You show us that we just need to be faithful and You will protect us. In Jesus' name we pray. Amen.

May 11

"Then the Lord raised up against Solomon an adversary, Hadad the Edomite, from the royal line of Edom." 1 Kings 11:14

Hadad, a wicked man raised by God

Solomon needed to repent and fully turn to the Lord. We already learned from the life of King Saul that partial obedience is still disobedience. But we do see a difference between Saul and Solomon. A partially obedient unbeliever like Saul gets more wicked. A partially obedient believer like Solomon will grow in godliness. Both are responsible to repent. The difference is God who grants repentance!

In the last devotional we saw in the beginning of 1 Kings 11 Solomon's foolish sin in marrying many women, and most of them pagan. Now, see how a wise, holy and just God <u>deals</u> with a partially committed believer like Solomon. God in His boundless grace <u>makes</u> Solomon turn back to Him! In our text here and in the next two devotions, we see that *"the Lord raised up... an adversary."*

Twice God appeared to warn Solomon about his going after other gods, to please and worship them. We read in 1 Kings 11:9-10 that Solomon broke covenant with God. He broke a holy agreement. That is the main issue with God. He blessed Solomon but Solomon did not bless God back. He blessed other gods. Know this about God: He is jealous for us; He made us for Himself!

God raised up Hadad, (a descendent of Esau) to be a thorn to Solomon! Hadad was just a small boy when his people were destroyed by Israel. He fled to Egypt. There God strengthened him. God raised him up in Pharaoh's court and caused Hadad to be so in favor with Pharaoh that he was given Pharaoh's sister-in-law to marry! Do we see it?

Solomon's very first pagan wife was Pharoah's daughter! He thought a marriage to Pharoah's family would strengthen him but <u>God with a stroke of His little finger overrules Solomon's sinful logic</u>. God's holy justice had already raised up Pharoah's sister-in-law to marry wicked Hadad, causing Solomon to turn back to God.

Prayer: Lord, once again we are warned about the seriousness of keeping covenant with You! Help us to see our wayward ways. Make us return to You! In Jesus' name we pray. Amen.

May 12

*"And God raised up against Solomon another adversary,
Rezon son of Eliada."* 1 Kings 11:23a

Rezon, a 2nd wicked man raised by God

God is still not finished in getting Solomon's and our attention! He raises up yet another adversary to bring Solomon to repentance. What is so sad is that today, many would be Christians only see the devil's hand in Hadad and Rezon here! They do not see God's hand in the matter. They do not see that Satan's corrupting of these wicked men is but a tool of discipline by the hand of God as He works all things for His glory!

"Rezon was Israel's adversary as long as Solomon lived, adding to the trouble caused by Hadad. So Rezon ruled in Aram and was hostile toward Israel," 1 Kings 11:25. When we see a verse like this, think about what the antithesis is all about. The antithesis is that <u>God-ordained hostility</u> spoken of in Genesis 3:15. God spoke to the serpent, the devil, and said, *"<u>I will put enmity</u> between you and the woman, and between your offspring and hers, He will crush your head, and you will strike His heel."* This is a sharp division between the forces of evil and the forces of good. So then, God arranged, *"God raised up against Solomon,"* this evil man. God actually ordained him to do what he did! Solomon's sin had consequences. This *"adversary"* is a consequence of Solomon's lack of repentance concerning his serving pagan gods!

We can see from the life of Solomon a very common problem in the lives of so many of us. We see that prosperity breeds complacency. Solomon got lazy in his spiritual life, because he basically, "had it made." He had every kind of pleasure a sinful man seeks, except a close relationship with God. How his life warns us to let nothing move us away from God! If our spiritual life is cold to God, then we must pray about it. Seek God and speak openly to Him about how we want a closer walk with Him. It is not recorded that Solomon did this.

Prayer: Lord, we see that to protect Your holy name, You allowed a wicked man like Rezon to defeat Your King Solomon. You wanted him to come to his senses. As hard as it is to say Lord, we must say it, "Correct us in Your mercy for our eternal good and for Your glory." In Jesus' name we pray. Amen.

May 13

"Also, Jeroboam son of Nebat rebelled against the king. He was one of Solomon's officials." 1 Kings 11:26a

Jeroboam, he led the people astray

The first word of our text, *"also,"* shows that God is not finished with His judgment against Solomon. This time, one of Solomon's trusted officials rebels against him, one from inside the palace!

Ahijah the prophet rips his robe into ten pieces. He gives them to Jeroboam, signifying the ten tribes God would rip from Solomon and give to Jeroboam. God's reason: *"I will do this because they have forsaken Me and worshiped Ashtoreth the goddess of the Sidonians, Chemosh the god of the Moabites, and Molech the god of the Ammonites, and have not walked in My ways,"* 1 Kings 11:33a. These gods were connected to doing anything sexually, even in the temples. In fact, shrine prostitutes were part of the worship.

Solomon introduced these evil, religious practices to the people of Israel through his pagan wives! Later, Jezebel really promoted this wickedness. But do not think we are so far removed from this kind of thing ourselves! The worship of the Baals included child sacrifices to Molech. We do have these same kinds of issues today. And we see God ripping the kingdom away from Solomon for introducing it!

God now graciously gives a promise to Jeroboam; *"If you do whatever I command you and walk in My ways and do what is right in My eyes by keeping My statues and commands, as David My servant did, I will be with you. I will build you a dynasty as enduring as the one I built for David and will give Israel to you,"* 1 Kings 11:38. Later, Jeroboam did not do what God commanded! He did what he felt like doing. Jeroboam was like Humpty Dumpty, he had a great fall and he caused Israel to fall with him!

Prayer: Lord, how sinful we are! The sin and guilt of Solomon and Jeroboam is so great. But perhaps the greatest sin of all for them, and for us too, is that we can so flippantly turn to You and confess our sin, but we aren't serious about changing! Dear God grant us repentance. Move us to Yourself and heal us and our land. In Jesus' name we pray. Amen.

May 14

"By the word of the Lord a man of God came from Judah to Bethel, as Jeroboam was standing by the altar to make an offering. He cried out against the altar by the word of the Lord: 'O altar, altar! This is what the Lord says: "A son named Josiah will be born to the house of David. On you he will sacrifice the priests of the high places who now make offerings here, and human bones will be burned on you."'"

1 Kings 13:1-2

A man of God silences a king, then disobeys God

One day God impressed this chapter on me, to warn me! Then immediately, a man showed up at my place in Madras. He said God spoke to him, telling him that God wanted me to get involved in his ministry again. I did not go back. Years later I found out he was like the lying false prophet in this story.

Jeroboam dedicated a heathen altar at Bethel, the place that means "House of God." There, Jacob had his "ladder vision." There, Jacob wrestled with God. Now, God sends a *"man of God"* from Judah, to boldly confront Jeroboam of his sin. Jeroboam tries to stop the *"man of God"* and his arm is paralyzed. The *"man of God"* heals him. Jeroboam offers him a reward. But God had already cautioned the *"man of God,"* to immediately go home a different way, and without eating.

Another Israelite prophet from Bethel, hears how this bold *"man of God"* confronted Jeroboam. He hurries after him and finds him sitting under a tree. He lies to the *"man of God,"* (here was my warning) saying an angel appeared to him to get the *"man of God"* and feed him. The *"man of God"* goes back and eats (I didn't go). The man of God continues his journey, and a lion kills him. God judges sin, sometimes immediately!

We must listen to God's voice alone! And why was the *"man of God"* sitting under a tree when God told him to go home immediately? Why did he eat, when God said not to eat? Why did this "ministry worker" think he could do what he wanted? God used this *"man of God"* mightily to warn Jeroboam, but then he himself was disobedient.

Prayer: Lord, we see You severely judge the sin in wicked rulers, and in Your own children too. Lord, thank You for warning us often! In Jesus' name we pray. Amen.

May 15

"Ahab son of Omri did more evil in the eyes of the Lord than any of those before him." 1 Kings 16:30

Ahab, a king who sold himself to do evil

Ahab was one evil man. A few chapters after our text it says, *"There was never a man like Ahab, who sold himself to do evil in the eyes of the Lord, urged on by Jezebel his wife. He behaved in the vilest manner by going after idols,"* 1 Kings 21:25-26a. What was so evil in his life? *"He not only considered it trivial to commit the sins of Jeroboam son of Nebat, but he also married Jezebel daughter of Ethbaal king of the Sidonians, and began to serve Baal and worship him,"* 1 Kings 16:31.

God shows us the serious sins of Ahab, how he tried to fit into the culture of the land! Ahab had no fear of God. He did what he wanted to do. He married a woman who could have been called, "Mrs. Wicked." She hated God with a passion! Together, Ahab and his wife brought the worship of Baal into the mainstream of society! Baal was probably the most wicked of all the gods of Canaan! The worship of this idol required human sacrifice. In the spring of each year the women would bring their first born sons who were under one year old, to the priest of Baal. The priest would stand before a big idol of Baal that had a hot fire in its belly. Then the mother would hand her baby to the priest. He would slide the baby screaming onto Baal's fire red outstretched arms, right into its burning stomach. Why would anyone do such a thing? They selfishly believed that by sacrificing this little baby, their lives would be more blessed and more enjoyable! Such is the height of self-love!

A few years ago a magazine called "Biblical Archeology Review," told about a newly discovered baby cemetery spread over an area of 65,000 square feet. This cemetery held the remains of precious babies nine levels deep, covering 600 years of abuse! And it was not just pagans who did this! God's people followed. They would do "anything," just to fit in with the values of the culture, to be "more happy and blessed!"

Prayer: Lord, You lovingly warn us so many times. You created us for Yourself to be holy. May we love You as You want us too. Forgive our sins of selfishness and copying the world instead following Your holy ways. May Your truth and justice fill us. In Jesus' name we pray. Amen.

May 16

"He (Ahab) also married Jezebel daughter of Ethbaal king of the Sidonians, and began to serve Baal and worship him." 1 Kings 16:31b

Jezebel, one wicked queen

It is quite clear from the whole Bible that Jezebel was the queen mother of sexual immorality. Jezebel was the daughter of a Sidonian king named Ethbaal. She was an evil chip off the old block. As such, Jezebel hated God with a passion that is almost unmatched in the pages of the Bible. She not only led her husband Ahab astray, but all of Israel also. She promoted the thinking that anything concerning a physical relationship is okay. Jezebel was so zealous in her evil ways that she tried to stamp out God's righteous rules for what is most precious in a marriage relationship. See what a devotee of Baal believed.

Baal had a mistress called Ashtoreth. And the way you got that god to bless you, was to perform religious sex as a ritual in the temple itself! Why? So that the people and their animals would produce abundantly. All so that the people could be "happy, comfortable and blessed." Pagan kings encouraged the people to practice this life-style openly. Miss Evil Jezebel led Ahab to buy into this value system that insulted and mocked God's created order.

Right here is one warning, especially for the young people! Ahab's weak brand of "Christianity," if we can even call it that, did nothing to get Jezebel to become Christian. Instead, her wickedness did everything to bring Ahab into her Baal worship. Young men out there, learn from the lives of Ahab and Jezebel. If you want to marry a wild woman, she will surely corrupt you! And girls this works the other way too.

Jezebel was not content to just destroy her husband and the people of his country! *"Jezebel was killing off the Lord's prophets,"* 1 Kings 18:4a. Beyond that, she had *"four hundred and fifty prophets of Baal and the four hundred prophets of Asherah who eat at Jezebel's table!"* 1 Kings 18:19. Then, she also tried to kill Elijah. Jezebel was one wicked woman!

Prayer: Lord, we see here that You mercifully give us details about how an immoral life-style is so evil. We thank You for the loving warning. May we worship You and live holy lives that are pleasing to you. In Jesus' name we pray. Amen.

May 17

"In Ahab's time, Hiel of Bethel rebuilt Jericho. He laid its foundations at the cost of his firstborn son Abiram, and he set up its gates at the cost of his youngest son Segub, in accordance with the word of the Lord spoken by Joshua son of Nun." 1 Kings 16:34

Hiel, the one who built his own kingdom

God tore down the walls of Jericho for His chosen leader Joshua. God did this to eliminate evil, to make way for righteousness to prevail. Jericho was like a first-fruit offering that God gave to His new nation of Israel. After God demolished this city, *"Joshua pronounced this solemn oath: 'Cursed before the Lord is the man who undertakes to rebuild this city, Jericho: "At the cost of his firstborn son will he lay its foundations; at the cost of his youngest will he set up its gates,"'"* Joshua 6:26b.

Now in 1 Kings 16, we see that Ahab, the most wicked king ever is on the throne. Thus, we have two opposing kingdoms and principals contrasted! Jericho, the kingdom of man, is taken down. God's Kingdom is put into place. Now, at this time in Israel's history, wickedness is back in power. Wicked Hiel is intent on building <u>his</u> own kingdom also. And who is Hiel building his little kingdom for? It is for his family and for his own name to endure and be famous! <u>But,</u> *"He laid its foundations at the cost of his firstborn son Abiram."* And then when he finished building his Jericho, *"he set up its gates at the cost of his youngest son Segub."*

<u>Hiel spent his life building his own kingdom and it cost him his family!</u> It is possible there was no family left to give his estate to! Hiel stands out as a testimony to a life wasted on selfish gain to the scorn of the Word and the will of God. Man's ways of living tear apart families!

How many "Hiels" are still in the world today? How many are striving so hard to get money and possessions, that they sacrifice their family and their physical, spiritual and mental health? Then at the end of their lives they spend their money to try get their health and family back! Let us not be foolish by copying Hiel!

Prayer: Lord, You show us the foolishness of building our own kingdom when it is Your kingdom that will endure! Lord put our hearts on that as You commanded us to. In Jesus' name we pray. Amen.

"Then the Word of the Lord came to him: (Elijah) 'Go at once to Zarephath of Sidon and stay there. I have commanded a widow in that place to supply you with food.'" 1 Kings 17:8-9

Elijah's Zarephath pension plan

There is a severe famine in the land by the word of Elijah. God is in the process of teaching wicked King Ahab and backsliding Israel. Everyone is suffering; some are dying. Yet God's providence to Elijah remains incredible. "*I have <u>ordered the</u> ravens to feed you,*" 1 Kings 17:4b. God <u>commanded</u> birds to feed Elijah! Then God <u>commanded</u> Elijah! "*Go at once to Zarephath of Sidon and stay there. I have <u>commanded</u> a widow in that place to supply you with food,*" 1 Kings 17:9b.

A widow in good times, has next to nothing! But this is not just a widow! This is a poor widow from a pagan country during a time of famine. This woman is God's chosen vessel to rebuke wayward Israel and to bless Elijah. Surely there was a godly widow in the land of Israel. But, God wants to demonstrate to Elijah, to this widow and to us, that He can give a spiritual and a physical life to anyone He pleases!

Do we think our resources will not be sufficient to provide for our needs in retirement? Then look to God. He is far more reliable than the bank, the stock market, or any government! So we see the grace of God to Elijah. We also see Elijah listening and going where and when God tells him to go!

Notice also, the obedient faith of a poor woman who most likely has never heard of the God of Israel. The faith of this widow of Zarephath points us to the fact that everyone has a personal responsibility to believe as this woman did. But may we never lose sight of what is equally true! It is God who implants faith in all who do believe. We praise Him for His amazing grace! May we do so now as we come to Him in prayer.

Prayer: Lord, You are so amazing and so worthy of our worship! How wonderfully You provided for a widow, for Your servant Elijah and for us yet today! Peter was right. "*Cast all your anxiety on Him because He cares for you*"! Lord turn our temptation for anxious and fearful thoughts into opportunities to trust You! In Jesus' name we pray. Amen.

May 19

"And Ahab had summoned Obadiah, who was in charge of his palace. (Obadiah was a devout believer in the Lord. While Jezebel was killing off the Lord's prophets, Obadiah had taken a hundred prophets and hidden them in two caves, fifty in each, and had supplied them with food and water.)" 1 Kings 18:3-4

Obadiah, God's answer to an evil queen

By grace God has His remnant in every generation, in every country, in famine or in time of plenty. No one can stop God from spreading His Gospel. Many have tried; all have failed. The life of Obadiah is a testimony of the faithfulness of God. It is also a testimony of a faithful man in times of severe persecution! God <u>arranged</u> for a *"devout believer"* to be in charge of the palace of Ahab and Jezebel. <u>God fed 100 prophets from Jezebel's own table, while she was trying to eliminate them!</u> Don't expect that this is any different today!

Jezebel in her evil rampage, tried her best to wipe out the name of God and eliminate His prophets! Jezebel killed to try strengthen her hand. Surely she heard others speak about her evil ways. Quite simply, Jezebel hated God! When one hates God they also hate His people, especially those who teach His message! Jezebel was insecure, as many of the wicked in power are. And she should be, because anyone with such a wicked agenda is on a self-destructive suicide mission!

God always has the last word! See how 1 Kings 18 ends. There is the famous showdown on Mount Carmel. There are 850 pagan prophets who ate at Jezebel's table who are against God's prophet Elijah. Which God or god can send the fire to light the sacrifice? Jehovah God sends fire from Heaven! *"When all the people saw this, they fell prostrate and cried, 'The Lord – He is God! The Lord – He is God!'"* 1 Kings 18:39.

"Then Elijah commanded them, 'Seize the prophets of Baal. Don't let anyone get away!' They seized them, and Elijah had them brought down to the Kishon Valley and slaughtered them there," 1 Kings 18:40. How foolish it is not to trust in God!

Prayer: Lord, You are incredible. You move people and events to bring glory to Your name. You completely save and You completely destroy. May we trust You fully! In Jesus' name we pray. Amen.

May 20

"At the time of sacrifice, the prophet Elijah stepped forward and prayed: 'O Lord, God of Abraham, Isaac and Israel, let it be known today that You are God in Israel and that I am Your servant and have done all these things at Your command. Answer me, O Lord, answer me, so these people will know that You, O Lord, are God, and that You are turning their hearts back again.'" 1 Kings 18:36-37

Elijah, on the mountain of hope

Ahab had not seen Elijah for a *"few years"*! Not since the day Elijah told Ahab, *"As the Lord, the God of Israel, lives, whom I serve, there will be neither dew nor rain in the next few years except at my word,"* 1 Kings 17:1b. Everyone had suffered! God now has their attention! The time of God teaching the people humility is at its peak. God brings Elijah out of hiding to confront Ahab and the wicked prophets of Baal. We are looking at two radically different belief systems. What a tense situation this is! Something big is up and everyone knows it! But Elijah himself is not tense! Why, what is keeping Elijah so calm and focused? Look to see where Elijah's eyes are! Follow his eyes, because tomorrow we will see that Elijah is defeated and depressed when his eyes shift.

In prayer, Elijah is looking at God first and he is looking at the people who need to *"know that You, O Lord, are God, and that You are turning their hearts back again."* But before God can restore the people and send rain and more blessings, He makes them repent from their idolatry! God does this by asking a question. Which God or god can send the fire for the sacrifice? Fire, because atonement is needed to be pardoned from sin. No fire. No atonement. No pardon. However, the priest of Baal can't get their god to light the sacrifice.

Elijah steps in; he prays. God sends the fire, so powerful that even water, stones, wood and the sacrifice are all burned up completely. The people believe and shout, *"The Lord, He is God"*! And now at Elijah's command, the false prophets of Baal are all killed. The victory is God's, but it also belongs to Elijah and the people.

Prayer: Lord, what a huge display of Your power! You are so in control of this world and everything in it. You are God! May we acknowledge it and keep our eyes on You! In Jesus' name we pray. Amen.

May 21

"Elijah was afraid and ran for his life. When he came to Beersheba in Judah, he left his servant there, while he himself went a day's journey into the desert. He came to a broom tree, sat down under it and prayed that he might die. 'I have had enough, Lord,' he said. 'Take my life; I am no better than my ancestors.' Then he lay down under the tree and fell asleep." 1 Kings 19:3-5a

Elijah, in the valley of despair

Elijah was not always on the "mountain" in his walk with God. Yet God was always with Elijah. In 1 Kings 18, Elijah was victorious over 850 wicked prophets and he had hope! Yet now, he is suddenly defeated. He's tormented and even depressed. Why?

"Ahab told Jezebel everything Elijah had done and how he had killed all the prophets with the sword," 1 Kings 19:1. The wicked queen quickly sends a note to Elijah that she is going to kill him. Elijah's response in our text is too often our own response, and it is not good. Elijah wants to quit and says, *"I have had enough."*

How completely Elijah trusted God in a bigger trial the day before! Now a smaller threat to his safety and well-being comes and he panics. He fears so much that it turns into despair, all because he took his eyes off from God and His powerful attributes. God writes to us about Elijah's failure, so we will not fail in our trials!

Elijah runs to hide! Formerly, God hid Elijah! God kept Elijah safe in order to use him to expose pagan idolatry. But now Elijah retreats into the same wilderness that held Israel captive for 40 years. Truly, wherever God's children go, He is with them! God provided His angels to guard Elijah when he was sleeping and to feed him when he was awake! Our God does this for us also! We must not take our eyes off from God and doubt Him. He who is faithful will never leave or forsake us!

Prayer: Dear Lord, how we, like Elijah, lose sight of You and fall into self-pity and despair! Yet You never lose sight of us; You care for us even when we cannot care for ourselves! How comforting it is that You will never remove Your Almighty protecting hand from our lives! We worship You! In Jesus' name we pray. Amen.

"His officials said to him, (Ben-Hadad) 'Look, we have heard that the kings of the house of Israel are merciful. Let us go to the king of Israel with sackcloth around our waists and ropes around our heads. Perhaps he will spare your life...' They went to the king of Israel and said, 'Your servant Ben-Hadad says; 'Please let me live.'" 1 Kings 20:31-32a

Ben-Hadad, a wicked man needing mercy

What a turn of events in just a few days! The powerful, ruthless and wicked Ben-Hadad begins the chapter with bullying Ahab into giving him his gold, his wives and his children. In verse four, the weak Ahab gives in saying, "*I and all I have are yours!*" But Ahab's wiser advisers tell him not to bow to the insolent demands of Ben-Hadad. So now Ahab tells the boasting Hadad, "*One who puts on his armor should not boast like one who takes it off,*" 1 Kings 20:11b.

Ahab asks for God's help. Even though Ahab was also wicked, God acted because Ben-Hadad made the mistake of saying that God could not defend Israel. Beyond that, Ben-Hadad and his generals were drinking and partying, expecting a big victory. For the sake of His own name, God thoroughly defeats Ben-Hadad. God even made a wall fall on 27,000 of his men. Suddenly, Ben-Hadad is in hiding. Afraid for his life, he now begs King Ahab for mercy! He who once had not one ounce of mercy, begs for mercy to spare his own life!

We see so clearly here, what our position is before King Jesus. We have arrogantly offended Him. Yet there abounds more mercy for us than Ben-Hadad ever hoped for! Jesus will give mercy now and forever! God's storehouse of mercy is for those who like Ben-Hadad beg for it! Listen to Jesus, He says to us: "*Come to me, all you who are weary and burdened, and I will give you rest,*" Matthew 11:28.

Prayer: Lord, we are so much like Ben-Hadad! We are wicked, proud and not very merciful to others. Lord, we can only say to You the very words Ben-Hadad used, "*Please let me live.*" For Lord, Your mercy is greater than all our sin. Give us the mercy we need, not Your wrath that we deserve! Then, surely goodness and mercy shall follow us all the days of our lives! In Jesus' name we pray. Amen.

May 23

"They proclaimed a fast and seated Naboth in a prominent place among the people. Then two scoundrels came and sat opposite him and brought charges against Naboth before the people, saying, 'Naboth has cursed both God and the king.' So they took him outside the city and stoned him to death." 1 Kings 21:12-13

Naboth, a martyr for God

The faithful Naboth became one of the early martyrs for standing up for what he believed. In the whole process, God teaches us four important points about His sovereignty and sure justice.

First, King Ahab pouts. He acts like a spoiled child who wants another toy. When he could not have Naboth's choice vineyard he pouts. *"He lay on his bed sulking and refused to eat,"* 1 Kings 21:4b.

Second, Queen Jezebel plots. She tells Ahab, *"Get up and eat! Cheer up. I'll get you the vineyard of Naboth the Jezreelite,"* 1 Kings 21:7b. Mrs. Bully gets moving and arranges to have two people falsely accuse Naboth of cursing God and the king.

Third, Naboth perishes. He is martyred. He is a great example of faithfulness in the midst of wickedness! Martyrdom continues to this day! There have been more people martyred in the last century than in all the centuries combined since time began. Will it continue? Yes! The reason is: God loves His people too much to leave us in the state of complacency we are presently in. The blood of the martyrs has always been the seed of the Church! What we need today is revival, which never comes through prosperity! God allows martyrs because He has a plan to restore many to Himself through the death of His own Son.

Fourth, God prevails! God warned rulers that *"The prince must not take any of the inheritance of the people, driving them off their property,"* Ezekiel 46:18a. But Jezebel and Ahab went one step further; they murdered Naboth! In this event of Naboth's death, God tells Ahab and Jezebel that He will kill them in this very same vineyard and dogs will lick up their blood. And no one will care that they perished!

Prayer: Lord, You move in mysterious ways, Your wonders to perform! You are so in control. What comfort we have in the fact that, "This is my Father's world!" In Jesus' name we pray. Amen.

"But Jehoshaphat asked, 'Is there not a prophet of the Lord here whom we can inquire of?' The king of Israel answered Jehoshaphat, 'There is still one man through whom we can inquire of the Lord, but I hate him because he never prophesies anything good about me, but always bad. He is Micaiah son of Imlah.'" 1 Kings 22:7-8a

Micaiah, bold to speak God's truth!

Ahab asked Jehoshaphat to help him fight a battle. But Jehoshaphat wisely asks the king of Israel, *"Is there not a prophet of the Lord here whom we can inquire of?"* Ahab's answer reveals the spiritual condition of Israel. Ahab admits, *"There is the prophet Micaiah, but he doesn't tell me what I want to hear, so I don't like him!"*

Ahab had 400 of his own "prophets"! They were not prophets of God, but men who simply, "held the office." They told the king what he wanted to hear! In reality, they were sold out to Satan. With these "prophets" in his back pocket, Ahab could do whatever he wanted, and then claim the church was with him! A prophet, priest or pastor who will do what a wicked king wants, and not what God wants, is a false prophet.

Micaiah was truly a servant of God! Micaiah boldly said, *"As surely as the Lord lives, I can tell him only what the Lord tells me,"* 1 Kings 22:14. Micaiah tells the king the truth, that Israel will be without a shepherd if Ahab goes to war. Micaiah has his face slapped. The king yells out, *"'Put this fellow in prison, and give him nothing but bread and water until I return safely.' Micaiah declared, 'If you ever return safely, the Lord has not spoken through me,' Then he added, 'Mark my words, all you people!'"* 1 Kings 22:27b-28.

Would we tell the truth if it put us in prison? Would we be willing to go against 400 high ranking advisors who are all telling the king a lie? Do we open our mouth when it is not "politically correct" to do so? The day is coming and has already come, when we will need to make a choice, lie or tell the truth and be put in prison for it! If we will lie today to get a piece of chocolate, we will lie on bigger things tomorrow!

Prayer: Lord, we have no strength in ourselves to stand for You. The strength and courage comes from You and Your Holy Spirit. Make us strong for Your kingdom! In Jesus' name we pray. Amen.

"And the Lord said, 'Who will entice Ahab into attacking Ramoth Gilead and going to his death there?' One suggested this, and another that. Finally a spirit came forward, stood before the Lord and said, 'I will entice him.' 'By what means?' the Lord asked. "I will go out and be a lying spirit in the mouths of all of his prophets,' he said. 'You will succeed in enticing him,' said the Lord. 'Go and do it.'" 1 Kings 22:20-22

A lying spirit works for God

What a text we have before us! Yesterday we saw that God's prophet Micaiah told King Ahab that he would die if he went to war. Ahab's 400 prophets told the king that he would be victorious. These 400 so called "prophets," were convinced that Ahab would win. How were they so sure that Ahab would win, yet be literally, so "dead wrong."

Our text tells us a little about the goings on in Heaven concerning the spirit world. A spirit tells God he is willing to go to all of Ahab's prophets to deceive them about what would happen in battle. So then, with God's permission, a spirit lies to four hundred of Ahab's prophets for the purpose of eliminating Ahab. Spirits do God's will, which in this case, is to end the reign of Ahab. God is not limited to what resource He wants to use. He will achieve His predetermined purposes.

God as the King of the universe is greater than even the greatest ruler here on earth. That is the reason we have this unusual glimpse into the inner workings in Heaven. Micaiah told the king of Israel and the king of Judah, two of the greatest kings on this earth: *"I saw the Lord sitting on His throne with all the host of Heaven standing around Him on His right and on His left,"* 1 Kings 22:19b.

Do we see the King of kings? Do we see how every knee will bow to Him whether in Heaven or on earth? In all of our concerns both great and small, which king do we serve?

Prayer: Lord, we praise and worship You for using Your prophet Micaiah, a man just like us, to help us see the need to be more heavenly-minded! Lord we have so much to learn and so little time to learn it. Teach us Lord. In Jesus' name we pray. Amen.

"Jehoshaphat asked, 'Is there no prophet of the Lord here, that we may inquire of the Lord through him?' An officer of the king of Israel answered, 'Elisha son of Shaphat is here. <u>He used to pour water on the hands of Elijah</u>.'" 2 Kings 3:11

Elisha, educated to be a servant

Elisha was a holy, dedicated, servant leader! A big question that the life of Elisha sends to us is: Do we really desire to be a servant? Do we really want to <u>serve</u> God's people? A huge question is: What is the best way to train someone to be a servant leader? How did God go about it? We are shown in the life of Elisha! And this example does not stand alone. If we listed the names of Bible characters who were truly servant leaders like Elisha, it would fill this page. Even Jesus was described as the carpenter's son. We see servants, in training to be servants!

Notice the qualification listed here for Elisha's ministry: *"He used to pour water on the hands of Elijah."* And Elisha would not object to this introduction! It described his training and his deepest desire! Would we object to this kind of introduction? Or are we more comfortable with listing our degrees and accomplishments? What do we put on our business card or on our ministry home page? What kind of introduction did Jesus give for His ministry? He told us that He, *"did not come to be served but to serve,"* Matthew 20:28.

What happens in ministry when we do not have a servant heart? We will not have a sincere desire to make God and all of His holy attributes known! We will not have a real desire to be a blessing to others! Instead our ambition will be for greatness, for our name to be known! What is one test for a servant leader? If others are noticed more than us, what is our response? If there is anger and bitterness, we have some serious changing to do! Real servants, those with real servant hearts, do not mind being treated as servants! God help us!

Prayer: Lord, even though You were God in the flesh, You made yourself nothing, *"Taking the very nature of a servant."* Lord, we read of it, but don't quite get it! Lord take our pride, make us willing servants, useful for Your glory alone! In Jesus' name we pray. Amen.

"The wife of a man from the company of the prophets cried out to Elisha, 'Your servant my husband is dead, and you know that he revered the Lord. But now his creditor is coming to take my two boys as his slaves.' Elisha replied to her, 'How can I help you? Tell me, what do you have in your house?' 'Your servant has nothing there at all,' she said, 'except a little oil.'" 2 Kings 4:1-2

A widow and God's justice on display

Theologian Carl Henry once asked, "Is God both the God of justification and the God of justice?" Our text shows that God is! A prophet died, leaving a debt his widow couldn't pay. To settle the debt, his widow is forced to hand over her sons to a creditor. God steps in and miraculously multiplies her oil so she can pay the bills. We must not be so focused on the miracle, that we don't see our responsibility to do as God did in exercising just compassion.

Here in India, a family debt of less than 5000 rupees ($100.00) can place a child into being a "child laborer." The interest on the loan is so high that it is almost impossible to pay the loan off. So young children from the ages of 8 to 14 basically remain slaves, instead of being in school! Some parents even willingly put their child into this condition, just to receive the money the child can earn. It's amazing, other parents kill a child in the womb because they do not love them. Others, hire their children out because they do not love them!

Our God of love, speaks to us about these abuses! Why us? Because in so many places the local authorities cannot be trusted or relied on to be just! They are part of the problem! God tells us: "*Learn to do right! Seek justice, encourage the oppressed. Defend the cause of the fatherless, plead the case of the widow,*" Isaiah 1:17. We must pray and ask God to open our eyes to abuses of all kinds. For He is a God of justice, and we are His arms and legs to do good!

Prayer: Lord, we see that Elisha did not just say some kind words, wishing this widow woman well! He helped her well-being! Lord, we have among us those who need justice in a world that is uncaring. Surely You test us as Christians to see if we will reach out in love. May we be wise and obedient in these things. In Jesus' name we pray. Amen.

May 28

"She said to her husband, "I know that this man who often comes our way is a holy man of God. Let's make a small room on the roof and put in ita bed and a table, a chair and a lamp for him."
2 Kings 4:9-10a

The Shunammite gave and received mercy

The Bible is very clear about who this Shunammite woman was. She was a great woman who was rich, was married to an older man, yet was childless. This woman was very outgoing and perceptive. She saw a need for mercy in her community and then moved with haste to meet that need. She saw Elijah passing by and knew that he needed food. So she fed him. Then one day she spoke to her husband the words of our text. She had noticed that Elijah was *"a holy man of God."* This brings up a good point. What is it, that people notice about us? What are we coming and going from? What do we spend our time doing? May it be noticeable that we are working for God!

Secondly, she knew Elijah was walking great distances to do the work of the Lord and she wanted to ease his burden. So she said, *"Let's make a small room on the roof and put in it a bed and a table, a chair and a lamp for him."* This is exactly what Elijah and missionaries today need! How many other families, for the glory of God, have copied her wonderful act of mercy over the years?

In gratitude, Elijah wanted to do something for this kind woman. He told her, *"'About this time next year' Elijah said, 'you will hold a son in your arms.'"* Next year she did have a son. But then, her only son died at about the age of four. She laid her dead, little boy on Elijah's bed. Then she went to find Elijah with a sincere faith that Elijah could restore her son. And so it happened, Elijah prayed to God and He mercifully answered. Twice God was merciful to this Shunammite woman. Twice He gave life to her son! She who was merciful for the kingdom of God, received God's mercy in a most timely way! What a contrast to the wicked Jezebel who was eaten by dogs!

Prayer: Dear Lord, Jesus told us much later in Matthew 5:7: *"Blessed are the merciful, for they will be shown mercy."* Lord You are so merciful, and we praise You for it! In Jesus' name we pray. Amen.

May 29

"Now bands from Aram had gone out and had taken captive a young girl from Israel, and she served Naaman's wife. She said to her mistress, 'If only my master would see the prophet who is in Samaria! He would cure him of his leprosy.'" 2 Kings 5:2-3

A servant girl, a real missionary

What a beautiful example of a strong faith in a young girl. We do not know the age of this little "servant girl" from Israel. We do not know her name either. But since she is called a *"young girl"* she may have been as young as ten. God specifically chose this little girl to show that He wants to use little children to be a witness for Him.

There are many "Naamans" in this world." For Naaman is a picture of a person who has a great job, lots of money, loads of respect and is admired in society. But he is spiritually and physically unclean! Even the best physicians in Samaria cannot heal Naaman. He is doomed to a slow death as all who are without the cleansing blood of the Lord Jesus Christ! But this little girl knows that Elisha can heal Naaman. Now that is faith. We do not know if Elisha ever healed a leper before. But this little girl from Israel knew how Elisha had healed others. She knew by faith that leprosy was no different!

The fact that this little girl openly tells her master how he can be healed also shows us that she did not have a bitter attitude towards him. She had compassion for others, even in the midst of hardship! She had a forgiving spirit in spite of being taken from her family and loved ones. She had every reason to be bitter, but she chose to live and act in a gracious way. So many need to learn this truth!

This servant girl loved God and by faith knew that He was in total control of her life. Granted the deep faith of this little girl was a gift from God, but she also acted faithfully! "Little girl" served two masters well. She served her Master in Heaven and her master on earth. May God give us a mature faith like this, *"young girl."*

Prayer: Dear Lord, You humble and instructed us through the life of this *"young girl."* How You want us to point sinners to the greater Elisha, Jesus Christ, where unclean people can become as white as snow. Lord, use us for Your glory. In Jesus' name we pray. Amen.

"When Elisha the man of God heard that the king of Israel had torn his robes, he sent him this message: 'Why have you torn your robes? Have the man come to me and he will know that there is a prophet in Israel.' So Naaman went with his horses and chariots and stopped at the door of Elisha's house." 2 Kings 5:8-9

Naaman, from proud sinner to humble believer

Naaman was, *"commander of the army of the king of Aram... but he had leprosy."* 2 Kings 5:1. A letter was written to the king of Israel to arrange for a meeting with Elisha, all for the purpose of being healed. The king of Israel is shocked, fearful and angered that Naaman was coming to Israel for healing! He who was "God's king" had no faith in God or in God's prophets!

And what about Naaman? He comes to Elisha riding in luxury. Today it would be an armor-plated, air-conditioned luxury car! He expected Elisha to come to him, bow down, and magically heal him! He even brought tons of money to give for his healing. But Elisha would not even come out of his house!

"Elisha sent a messenger to say to him, 'Go, wash yourself seven times in the Jordan, and your flesh will be restored and you will be cleansed,'" 2 Kings 5:10. Naaman is very upset but his servants wisely tell him that he would have done any great thing to be healed. Please do what the prophet says! The rest is history; Naaman is completely, 100% healed!

Notice some important points. Cleansing for Naaman and for all of us is, by the command of the Great Prophet, Jesus Christ. Elisha is a picture of that! Naaman had to humble himself to be healed! He had to get out of his pretty chariot and obey! Naaman could not do any great work or pay a great sum of money to be healed! And *"there were many in Israel with leprosy in the time of Elijah the prophet, yet not one of them was cleansed — only Naaman the Syrian,"* Luke 4:27. God healed a Gentile, to shame faithless Israel!

Prayer: Lord, what a great picture of Your healing power. Naaman came a diseased, proud leper; he left a healed, humble believer! He came as a pagan; he left as Your child! He bears testimony of who You are! May we copy his faith and obedience! In Jesus' name we pray. Amen.

"Gehazi, the servant of Elisha the man of God, said to himself, 'My master was too easy on Naaman, this Armean, by not accepting from him what he brought. As surely as the Lord lives, I will run after him and get something from him.'" 2 Kings 5:20

Gehazi, so close to the truth, so far from God!

Gehazi runs after the rich Naaman. He lies to him to get some money that he does not deserve! Immediately Gehazi is judged severely as God gives him the leprosy that Naaman formerly had. He is unclean spiritually and physically. Like the rest of Israel, Gehazi did not value his incredible privileges! He was a servant to perhaps the most holy man alive. He regularly heard about the wisdom of God. He saw God work amazing miracles through Elisha. Gehazi knew God's power could multiply a widow's oil to pay her debts. He saw how a barren Shunammite woman gave birth to a little boy. And when the young child died, Gehazi saw the power of God raise the child to life. Gehazi's problem was, he was not satisfied with God, nor did he trust God for his future! His greedy heart thought God owed him more than he was getting and he was not willing to wait for it in faith.

God had already determined that Elisha (a picture of Jesus) would not and could not accept any money or gift for the healing of Naaman! God's grace in salvation is a free gift, which Naaman's healing is a picture of. But another reason is: God wants us to see, if we, like the greedy Gehazi, serve Him just for the money. If we do, then we are also unclean lepers! God wants us to be convicted about His sure judgment against greed! We read in 1 Corinthians 6, that the greedy will not inherit the kingdom of Heaven. God is making that point in giving us the example of Gehazi!

Prayer: Lord, we see how Gehazi has a common problem. He was so close to Your knowledge, but none of it was in his heart! The miracles Gehazi witnessed did not change him! May this be a warning for us today, who want to see miracles! How much better it is to hear and read Your Word and seek to be obedient! How foolish for Gehazi to covet the world's goods for a day, only to lose his soul for eternity! Lord, may we not be like him! In Jesus' name we pray. Amen.

JUNE

Josiah is crowned king

"The king stood by the pillar and renewed the covenant in the presence of the LORD - to follow the LORD, and keep His commands, regulations and decrees with all his heart and all his soul."
2 Kings 23:3a

June 1

"'Don't be afraid' the prophet answered. 'Those who are with us are more than those who are with them.'" 2 Kings 6:16

Elisha's elegant ears and eyes

"Don't be afraid." We so often need these three words! Elisha knew something we dearly need to know! He knew God protects us in big ways as well as in small ones! God in all of His Almighty power, is *"with us"*! His angels outnumber Satan's helpers and are more powerful! Hear and see: what is true for Elisha is true for us!

Now *"the king of Aram was at war with Israel,"* 2 Kings 6:8a. While this king discusses battle tactics with his officers, Elisha by the power of God hears them speak their plans and sends a word of warning to the king of Israel. So the king of Aram learns Elisha is listening in! He found out that Elijah is in the town of Dothan, so he sends horses, chariots, and a strong force of soldiers to capture him. In the morning Elisha's servant goes outside the city gates and sees that the city is surrounded by the enemy! In great fear, the servant asks Elisha, *"Oh, my Lord, what shall we do?"* 2 Kings 6:15b.

Elisha saw the battle clearly; his servant didn't! His servant thought the town was already defeated because the enemy was at the gate! He did not see God's protecting angels! By faith and experience, Elisha really did not even need to look! He knew as we must know, *"Those who are with us are more than those who are with them.' And Elisha prayed, 'Lord, open his eyes that he may see.' Then the Lord opened the servant's eyes, and he looked and saw the hills full of horses and chariots of fire all around Elisha,"* 2 Kings 6:16b-17.

Can we "hear" and "see" like Elisha? We can! James wrote about Elijah, Elisha's father in the faith, *"Elijah was a man just like us,"* James 5:17a. These prophets were common men! They were redeemed sinners just like us! They prayed in faith and God was <u>pleased</u> to answer them and protect them. Let us also pray!

Prayer: Lord, what a beautiful truth and reality! In Romans 15:4, You say, *"For whatever things were written before were written for our learning, that we through the patience and comfort of the Scriptures might have hope."* Lord, You give us hope! In Jesus' name we pray. Amen.

June 2

"Jehoram son of Jehoshaphat began his reign as king of Judah. He was thirty-two years old when he became king, and he reigned in Jerusalem eight years. He walked in the ways of the kings of Israel, as the house of Ahab had done, for he married a daughter of Ahab. He did evil in the eyes of the Lord." 2 Kings 8:16b-18

Jehoram, married evil and did evil

This particular Jehoram is the son of Jehoshaphat. His life shouts to us, "Don't do what I did." "If we do, our end will be horrible!" See what we must learn from the evil King Jehoram.

Jehoram's father was one of the best kings of Judah! Daddy Jehoshaphat had the grace of God in great measure, but he could not give that grace to his son! No parent can! If a child of good parents goes the evil way, the Bible shows they are normally worse than other unbelievers! Good parents need to understand also that King David and King Jehoshaphat had wayward children.

If you are that wayward child, beg God for His grace and mercy! God put you here on this earth to seek Him and find Him. We are all personally responsible, as Acts 17 teaches, to find and know God.

This Jehoram of Judah married Athaliah, a daughter of wicked Ahab and Jezebel of Israel. She was as wicked as her parents! As a result, Jehoram *"walked in the ways of the kings of Israel, as the house of Ahab had done."* Jehoram's poor choice for a spouse greatly added to his ruin! Surely he thought that marrying royalty and money would bless him. Instead it killed him! *"When Jehoram established himself firmly over his father's kingdom, he put all his brothers to the sword,"* 2 Chronicles 21:4a. He hated his brothers because he hated God!

Father Jehoshaphat made a mistake in promoting his son to succeed him. Privileges before responsibility is the ruin of many children! In the end, God's prophet Elijah sent a letter to Jehoram in 2 Chronicles 21:12-15. It said that God was going to strike Jehoram and his family with a *"heavy blow."* God also gave Jehoram a painful disease and took his life.

Prayer: Lord, how true it is that You will not be mocked! Jehoram not only failed in this life, he failed eternally! May we learn from him. In Jesus' name we pray. Amen.

June 3

"The driving is like that of Jehu son of Nimshi – he drives like a madman." 2 Kings 9:20b

Jehu, a hard charging man

Does this description of Jehu somehow fit our life-style? Are we a hard-charging and demanding person with little regard for others? Should our nickname be Mr. or Mrs. "Get it done." Today Jehu would be called an extreme "Type A" personality. Much of our population is like this! A Jehu "Type A," is always in a hurry. Delays of any kind frustrate him or her. A "Type A," is very competitive. They are quick to use others to achieve their own selfish and personal goals. Deep down, a "Type A" person has an inner hostility, a rotten attitude. Anyone or anything that hinders them in their current flurry of activity becomes an object of their wrath! Type A people often have quick tempers. Even this, they think helps them. Then, people are not as likely to get in their way. For if they do, they know what the consequences are! A Type A's mad pursuit of unreachable goals will never allow godly contentment!

Relaxation was not an option for Jehu! To relax and just sit would be stressful! He had to be moving! If Mrs. Jehu wanted to sit and talk he had a giant urge to get out and do some more work! Any task that needed to be done was far more important than any relationship! His plans were always more important than people.

Just because God used Jehu to be His missionary to implement His justice on wicked Ahab and Jezebel, does not mean that God approved of Jehu's spiritual life! It is not recorded that Jehu was a spiritually-minded man. In fact, *"Jehu was not careful to keep the law of the Lord, the God of Israel, with all his heart. He did not turn away from the sins of Jeroboam, which he had caused Israel to commit,"* 2 Kings 10:31. Jehu was big on speed and small on love! May we not copy him!

Prayer: Lord, You show us personality traits in the Bible that are in us. You tell us, "Type A" personalities, something we need to learn: *"Be still before the Lord and wait patiently for Him."* Lord change us for Your glory. Change us for the good of others, and for our good! Make us more heavenly-minded so that we do more earthly good. In Jesus' name we pray. Amen.

June 4

"Jehoiada brought out the king's son and put the crown on him; he presented him with a copy of the covenant and proclaimed him king. They anointed him, and the people clapped their hands and shouted, 'Long live the king!'" 2 Kings 11:12

Jehoiada the priest promotes King Joash

It is necessary to sort out the players in this drama to see who fits in where. Let us start with Jehoram, King of Judah. He married Athaliah, daughter of Israel's King Ahab and Jezebel. Jehoram's son Ahaziah became Judah's king. Jehu kills him. And the wicked Athaliah seizes the throne, killing her grandchildren. But her grandson Joash, is safely hidden from her! Joash's Aunt Jehosheba, his dad's sister, raises him. Jehosheba just happens to be married to Jehoiada the main priest. God provided a good priest in a time of great wickedness!

Jehoiada has a plan. He talks to 300 guards that are coming off duty and going on duty. They protect the young king with King David's swords that are in the temple. The wicked grandmother, Athaliah, is killed. Justice is served at last. Little Joash becomes king at age seven! What a beautiful sight this had to be. He is standing in the temple, holding "*a copy of the covenant.*" He has God's Holy Law in his hands and in his heart! After years of no law or justice, the law of love and justice for all is back, and they "*clapped their hands and shouted, 'Long live the king!'*"

"*Jehoiada then made a covenant between the Lord and the king and people that they would be the Lord's people. He also made a covenant between the king and the people,*" 2 Kings 11:17. The former leadership was unfaithful. So new vows were given by the boy king to pledge his allegiance to God and his faithfulness to the people.

Jehoiada is teaching us something important about seven year old Joash! Children are the current church as much as they are the future church. Secondly, spiritual maturity has more to do with love and obedience than age. Joash was spiritually mature at seven!

Prayer: Lord, surely the angels rejoiced in Heaven with You at this historical event! Lord, grant us faithful pastors like Jehoiada. Grant us repentance in our leaders! After all, we were created to worship You alone. In Jesus' name we pray. Amen.

June 5

"Jotham son of Uzziah king of Judah began to reign. He was twenty-five years old when he became king, and he reigned in Jerusalem sixteen years. His mother's name was Jerusha daughter of Zadok. <u>He did what was right in the eyes of the Lord,</u> just as his father Uzziah had done." 2 Kings 15:32b-34

Jotham, he made wise choices!

History is important! Jotham was a good man who lived and ruled well! *"<u>The people,</u> however, continued their corrupt practices,"* 2 Chronicles 27:2b. Jotham did not do what the young men of his age were doing! Jotham did what was right in the eyes of the Lord. He cared about what God cared about, which is mercy and justice for all! *"<u>Jotham grew powerful because he walked steadfastly before the Lord his God,</u>"* 2 Chronicles 27:6. Did you notice, Jotham promoted and honored the name of God in the midst of a wicked generation. The historian Josephus said Jotham was "pious towards God, just towards men and laid himself out for the public good." Jotham was serious about life. He knew well that God put him where he was so he could do good!

Jotham lived for the approval of God. Think about that! "Whose approval do we seek?" If we live to impress our friends, we are in for big trouble. Live for God is the message of the Bible. If we humble ourselves, God will lift us up. We must quit trying to lift up ourselves. We must not be so serious about what we look like to others! No one else really cares anyway, except God! Instead, we must care about the honor of God and the welfare of others. Jotham did this and notice, *"Jotham grew powerful because he walked steadfastly before the Lord his God."*

There is a warning here for children and grandchildren! Grandpa Uzziah was a godly man. His son Jotham, *"walked steadfastly before the Lord his God."* But, Jotham's son Ahaz went the other way. He lived a corrupt life. Don't waste your precious years! You only have one life! Live it wisely like Jotham did!

Prayer: Lord, how lovingly You warn us again and again! It matters how we live. It matters that we honor You! Strengthen us to live like Jotham who loved God first, others second and himself humbly last. Make us a servant like Jesus. In His name we pray. Amen.

"*Ahaz sent messengers to say to Tiglath-Pileser king of Assyria, 'I am your servant and vassal. Come up and save me out of the hand of the king of Aram and the king of Israel, who are attacking me.'*"
2 Kings 16:7

Ahaz bows to a foreign, pagan king

Through the wicked rule of King Ahaz, God shows us how quickly a country can go from strong to weak. Ahaz became king at age 20, nine generations after forefather David. "*He did not do what was right in the eyes of the Lord his God,*" 2 Kings 16:2b. Ahaz did not love God, His laws, or His people. His list of sins were long. His reign was short! He died hating God at age 36. A full chapter testifies to his horrible life!

In our text, Ahaz basically bows down to the king of Assyria which is present day Iraq. If only he had bowed down to God as his faithful forefathers had! If only he had asked God to save him, instead of asking a wicked king, then the glory of his country would not have departed.

Secondly, "*And Ahaz took the silver and gold found in the temple of the Lord and in the treasuries of the royal palace and sent it as a gift to the king of Assyria,*" 2 Kings 16:8. Ahaz gave away the wealth of his nation, for the supposed protection of a man who was only using him! What an offence to God who would have protected Judah!

Third, "*Then King Ahaz went to Damascus to meet Tiglath-Pileser king of Assyria. He saw an altar in Damascus and sent to Uriah the priest a sketch of the altar, with detailed plans for its construction,*" 2 Kings 16:10. Ahaz visits a foreign king and falls in love with his pagan worship practices. He has the same kind of altar built and put in God's holy temple. More on this tomorrow.

Fourth, "*When the king came back from Damascus and saw the altar, he approached it and presented offerings on it,*" 2 Kings 16:12. Ahaz now worships on this new altar, moving God's altar out of the way! Ahaz stops the worship of God in the temple and replaced it with the very practices that God hated! He led the people in a downward spiral!

Prayer: Dear Lord, we love You. We want to worship You alone. Please stop those who are trying to replace You with false gods of all kinds. May Your name be lifted up. In Jesus' name we pray. Amen.

June 7

"So Uriah the priest built an altar in accordance with all the plans that King Ahaz had sent from Damascus and finished it before King Ahaz returned." 2 Kings 16:11

Uriah the priest, builds the devil an altar

Ahaz was not the only one who had contempt for God, so did Uriah the priest. He who was in charge of the priests and all their functions, was tired of the old way of doing things. They were stale in their worship of God and wanted change. If only they knew their hearts were the problem! But they thought something more "exciting" would keep the people coming to church. This is so like today!

We have seen that Ahaz, *"saw an altar in Damascus and sent to Uriah the priest a sketch of the altar; with detailed plans for its construction,"* 2 Kings 16:10b. This was a pagan altar, built for pagan sacrifices, in the Lord's Holy temple. Uriah willingly built it, even before the wicked King Ahaz returned from his trip.

Think of what Uriah consented to. He now willingly offers sacrifices on a pagan altar. That's like taking Satan's dining room table with all of its demon carvings, and using it for the Lord's Supper! Uriah even took down the basins that the priest used for washing after doing a sacrifice for their own sin. The priests had to be clean before they sacrificed for the sins of the people. Uriah was not concerned about personal holiness! Can such a blind priest lead blind people to the Gospel light?

What King Ahaz commanded, Uriah did! *"He offered sacrifices to the gods of Damascus, who had defeated him; for he thought, 'Since the gods of the kings of Aram have helped them, I will sacrifice to them so they will help me.'"* But they were his downfall and the downfall of all Israel," 2 Chronicles 28:23. The altar of God was moved to the back corner of the temple.

Prayer: Lord, we see cold hearts in a king, in a priest, and in the people. Lord, we can see that wayward Judah is a warning to us in how they moved Your altar to the back of the temple. We too, move You to the back of our hearts and then wonder why You are not blessing us! O Lord, when You are not our all, You become our nothing! Be our everything Lord! In Jesus' name we pray. Amen.

June 8

"Hezekiah trusted in the Lord, the God of Israel. There was no one like him among all the kings of Judah, either before him or after him. He held fast to the Lord and did not cease to follow Him; he kept the commands the Lord had given Moses. And the Lord was with him; he was successful in whatever he undertook." 2 Kings 18:5-7a

Hezekiah, a man God gave more time to

Hezekiah was the son of wicked king Ahaz. He was everything his father wasn't! He *"trusted in the Lord"*! It is that simple. Trust, like faith, believes and hopes in God even when, or especially when we cannot see the way clearly. But our trust in God is not a blind trust! Just the opposite, we know that God's omniscience, power, wisdom and providence can do the impossible. It is instructive that Hezekiah *"rebelled against the king of Assyria and did not serve him,"* 2 Kings 18:7b. His wicked father Ahaz, bowed to this same king and was totally unsuccessful. Our text is a testimony to the faithfulness of God. Hezekiah *"was successful in whatever he undertook"*! The reason is, *"the Lord was with him."*

Hezekiah, unlike his father, did not find God's loving laws boring. He loved them, and God loved him in return. God teaches us by contrasting a wicked father and a good son. God wants us to see that worshiping Him and honoring His commandments makes a difference now and for all eternity.

Now the good king Hezekiah falls sick. The prophet Isaiah tells him he will die. This too is for the glory of God! But Hezekiah prays, *"'Remember, O Lord, how I have walked before you faithfully and with wholehearted devotion and have done what is good in Your eyes.' And Hezekiah wept bitterly,"* 2 Kings 20:3. God responds: *"I have heard your prayer and seen your tears, I will heal you,"* 2 Kings 20:5b. God gave Hezekiah 15 more years, and victory over his enemies.

Prayer: Lord, we can only say, wow! We have seen Hezekiah's faithfulness to You. Lord, how true it is, *"Blessed are the merciful, for they shall be shown mercy."* Lord, You are so faithful. We see that You healed Hezekiah for the sake of Your own name You show us Your mercy and faithfulness. May we be found faithful, for we too need Your mercy! In Jesus' name we pray. Amen.

June 9

"Manasseh was twelve years old when he became king, and he reigned in Jerusalem fifty-five years. His mother's name was Hephzibah. He did evil in the eyes of the Lord, following the detestable practices of the nations the Lord had driven out before the Israelites." 2 Kings 21:1-2

Manasseh, so evil, repented, was saved!

Manasseh had great parents! His father King Hezekiah and his mother Hephzibah were outstanding! Yet he was worse than any king in the history of Judah. Manasseh rebuilt the high places. He made altars to Baal, and erected an Asherah pole. He did and encouraged anything concerning sex. He built pagan altars in the temple and worshiped astrology. He sacrificed his own son on an altar to the god Molech in the valley of hell. He went to witches and worshiped demonic powers. *"The Lord said... 'Manasseh king of Judah has committed these detestable sins. He has done more evil than the Amorites who preceded him and has led Judah into sin with his idols," 2 Kings 21:10-11.* Manasseh filled Jerusalem with innocent blood!

God cannot be mocked! He brought in the Assyrians. They, *"took Manasseh prisoner, put a hook in his nose, bound him with bronze shackles and took him to Babylon," 2 Chronicles 33:11b.* Ouch, ouch, the way of a transgressor is hard! Can you imagine being led with hook in your nose? Manasseh went wherever he was led! God knows how to teach!

God moved Manasseh into full repentance! *"In his distress he sought the favor of the Lord his God and humbled himself greatly before the God of his fathers. And when he prayed to Him, the Lord was moved by his entreaty and listened to his plea; so He brought him back to Jerusalem and to his kingdom. Then Manasseh knew that the Lord is God," 2 Chronicles 33:12-13.* God can save the greatest sinner! Manasseh tried with all his heart to right his wrongs. How he regretted not serving the Lord from his youth!

Prayer: Lord, how amazing You are to wicked sinners like us! You tell us in Jeremiah that we are *"desperately wicked and beyond cure."* What cleansing power there is in Jesus' blood! Even now, Manasseh is probably leading the choir, singing "Amazing Grace." We praise You for our complete salvation! In Jesus' name we pray. Amen.

"Josiah was eight years old when he became king, and he reigned in Jerusalem thirty-one years... He did what was right in the eyes of the Lord and walked in all the ways of his father David, not turning aside to the right or to the left." 2 Kings 22:1-2

Josiah, a child king who loved God

Are we waiting to be older to start serving God? If we are, then take a lesson from the life of Josiah. He *"was eight years old when he became king."* What is even more important is: *"He did what was right in the eyes of the Lord."* He was an obedient boy. He did not do what he wanted, but what God wanted! He lived to please God, and he lived to follow grandpa David. Young Josiah's life must shout to us that we do not have to be old to be a mature Christian! Josiah was mature spiritually at age eight! This means that by habit, by his daily practice, Josiah put away living like the wicked kings before him! After Josiah put away the old habits, <u>he replaced them</u>! That is big boy living! He *"walked in all the ways of his father David."*

If a boy has the habit of doing wrong and keeps doing it, it quickly becomes a bad habit. Boys who start smoking before age 15 have the hardest time quitting! Boys who speak bad words at an early age have a hard time stopping their swearing! That is because these are the things practiced! This means we need to do the right practice, like studying, and then do it until it becomes a habit! It is true, those who do right and practice it, learn just like a good football player learns good skills by practicing. This is what Josiah did! He learned God's ways and followed them! The Bible holds him up as an example to us.

However, Josiah is not just an example to kids! There are lots of "old people" who keep doing the old habits instead of "repenting" and focusing on new godly ones! Make no mistake, Josiah was a solid confessing Church member at age eight. The love of God was in his heart and it showed by his doing *"what was right in the eyes of the Lord"*!

Prayer: Lord, You made the author of Hebrews write; *"Solid food is for the mature, who by constant use have trained themselves to distinguish good from evil."* Lord, make us obedient so we are mature like Josiah. In Jesus' name we pray. Amen.

June 11

"Saul died because he was unfaithful to the Lord; he did not keep the word of the Lord and even consulted a medium for guidance, and did not inquire of the Lord. So the Lord put him to death and turned the kingdom over to David son of Jesse." 1 Chronicles 10:13-14

Saul, the people's choice, removed by God

It was the people who wanted Saul as their king. God allowed it, but Saul was never God's choice. From the life of Saul, we learn that God can remove any leader, any time He pleases! However, to instruct us further, God does give us specific reasons in our text as to why He removed the unfaithful Saul. He *"did not keep the word of the Lord."* Through Samuel, God commanded Saul, *"Go and completely destroy those wicked people, the Amalekites,"* 1 Samuel 15:18b. King Saul did not listen. He kept what he wanted for himself and the people. But Saul was disobedient or rebellious in more than just this.

Saul, *"consulted a medium for guidance."* If we think this is not a big problem, we do not understand the Spirit/spirit world! There are two powerful forces in a war for our soul! God's Holy Spirit and Satan's devilish spirit, who is called a *"familiar spirit"* for a good reason. God warns us, *"And the person who turns after mediums and <u>familiar spirits</u>, to prostitute himself with them, <u>I will set My face against that person and cut him off from his people</u>. Sanctify yourselves therefore, and be holy, for I am the Lord your God,"* Leviticus 20:6-7 NKJV. God warns us because the *"familiar spirit"* pretends to be God's Holy Spirit. The evil *"familiar spirit"* world includes any who practice, *"divination or sorcery, interprets omens, engages in witchcraft, or casts spells, or who is a medium or spiritist or who consults the dead. Anyone who does these things is detestable to the Lord,"* Deuteronomy 18:10b-12a. King Saul knew the power behind these things was not holy, and he rebelliously chose to use them anyway. Today, many people think stories of demons and evil spirits are innocent! They are not. We must never think we are wiser than God concerning the spirit/Spirit world!

Prayer: Lord, we thank You for Your mercy in teaching us through the life of King Saul. We also thank You that You are the only One who makes us holy! In Jesus' name we pray. Amen.

June 12

"The Lord was with Jehoshaphat because in his early years he walked in the ways his father David had followed. He did not consult the Baals but sought the God of his father and followed his commands rather than the practices of Israel." 2 Chronicles 17:3-4

Jehoshaphat *"sought the God of his father"*

Did your grandparents love God and His ways, going back many generations? It is only by the covenant mercies of God if they did, and that is precious. In the second verse of the song, "Faith of Our Fathers," it says; "Our fathers, chained in prisons dark, were still in heart and conscience free; <u>How sure will be their children's peace if they, like them, contend for Thee.</u>" Jehoshaphat followed the good life habits or *"practices"* of his fathers. Jehoshaphat's good practices in Judah, are compared to Ahab and Jezebel's bad *"practices"* in Israel. So what did King Jehoshaphat do that God saw as righteous?

Jehoshaphat did not *"consult the Baals."* Ahab sought out these wicked priest and embraced evil rather than good. They encouraged the people into pleasing the flesh in ways that were the direct opposite of God's holy ways. In contrast to this evil, Jehoshaphat *"removed the high places and the Asherah poles from Judah."* The perverts and their ways were not welcome or permitted, and then the land flourished! It was God who made it flourish that is the loud message!

Jehoshaphat took to heart the verse, *"Remember your Creator in the days of your youth, before the days of trouble come and the years approach when you will say, 'I find no pleasure in them,'"* Ecclesiastes 12:1. Jehoshaphat *"<u>sought</u> the God of his father,"* meaning he <u>contended</u> for the faith in visible ways. He sent leaders to teach the *"Book of the Law."* How this stands in contrast to those today, who try to remove God's holy laws. Then we wonder why God allows adultery, stealing, lying and violence to increase. God will bless us personally, and our land, if we seek God like Jehoshaphat did!

Prayer: Lord, we need this constant reminder of how Your blessings are conditional to our faithfulness in loving You and Your holy ways. Grant us repentance for the glory of Your most holy name. In Jesus' name we pray. Amen.

June 13

"Amaziah asked the man of God, 'But what about the hundred talents I paid for these Israelite troops?' The man of God replied. 'The Lord can give you much more than that.'" 2 Chronicles 25:9

Amaziah learns a big money principle!

Amaziah was a king in Judah for 29 years. We read, *"He did what was right in the eyes of the Lord, but not wholeheartedly,"* 2 Chronicles 25:2. One of the things that Amaziah did do right was listen to an unnamed *"man of God."* This man came to him to teach us all a very important principle concerning money or wealth.

The situation is this: Amaziah was building an army. *"He also hired a hundred thousand fighting men from Israel for a hundred talents of silver,"* 2 Chronicles 25:6. The *"man of God,"* reminded Amaziah that God was presently frowning on unfaithful Israel and that he should dismiss the 100,000 Israelite men he had hired to fight for him. Then in the words of our text, Amaziah argues that he had already paid, a "hundred talents," for their services. If he dismisses them now, he will completely lose that money! Now we get to the point that God is trying to teach Amaziah and us.

"The Lord can give you much more than that." The man of God told Amaziah that if he was faithful that money he gave to those soldiers was nothing compared to what God can and will do for him! Amaziah sent them out and God gave him a great victory over his enemies. But now, we have a test! Will we bend the rules to try get ahead? Or, will we make a sacrifice for the sake of God's kingdom? If we are faithful, know this for sure! We can never out give God, for He is not a debtor to anyone; He fully repays! Beyond that, a good, clean conscience is worth more than a boat load of gold.

Prayer: Lord, You have told us that it is the meek that will inherit the earth. Your beloved King David said in Psalm 37:25, *"I was young and now I am old, yet I have never seen the righteous forsaken or their children begging bread."* Lord, may we never forget that You are the one who holds the purse strings! In Jesus' name we pray. Amen.

June 14

"Uzziah was sixteen years old when he became king, and he reigned in Jerusalem fifty-two years... He did what was right in the eyes of the Lord, just as his father Amaziah had done. He sought God during the days of Zechariah, who instructed him in the fear of God. <u>As long as he sought the Lord, God gave him success</u>." 2 Chronicles 26:3-5

Uzziah's life shows success is conditional

Early on in Uzziah's lengthy kingship, He walked closely with God. He *"did what was right."* He did not do what was right in his own eyes, but what was right *"in the eyes of the Lord."* At first, he kept the commandments of God, and God blessed him in return. Initially, Uzziah was faithful in keeping covenant with God. Remember how Deuteronomy 28 lists the blessings for obedience and the curses for disobedience. Uzziah's life pounds this point home to us!

"As long as he sought the Lord, God gave him success." What a statement this is! He tore down the enemies' walls and built up God's. God was for him both offensively and defensively! *"God helped him against the Philistines and against the Arabs,"* 2 Chronicles 26:7a. God blessed his livestock and fields. It also says that Uzziah *"loved the soil."* I like that! He also had a huge army. He made many weapons of war and became very powerful. In all of this, God blessed him.

"But after Uzziah became powerful, his pride led to his downfall. He was unfaithful to the Lord his God," 2 Chronicles 26:16a. Notice how Uzziah became proud, and what God did about it! *"Uzziah, who had a censer in his hand ready to burn incense, became angry. While he was raging at the priests in their presence before the incense altar in the Lord's temple, <u>leprosy broke out on his forehead</u>,"* 2 Chronicles 26:19.

Filled with pride, King Uzziah tried to take on the office of priest also! And do not miss the fact that he was angry! *"Man's anger does not bring about the righteous life that God desires,"* James 1:20! Like Uzziah, the hardest test we may ever face is when God blesses us! Will we then remain humble and committed to God?

Prayer: Lord, we see Your immediate and righteous displeasure with King Uzziah. You do judge pride! Make us humble and keep us there so we remain servants for Your Kingdom! In Jesus' name we pray. Amen.

June 15

"Now in the first year of Cyrus king of Persia, that the word of the Lord spoken by the mouth of Jeremiah might be fulfilled, the Lord stirred up the spirit of Cyrus king of Persia, so that he made a proclamation throughout all his kingdom, and also put it in writing."
Ezra 1:1 NKJV

Cyrus, a pagan king commissioned by God

Cyrus is a good example of how God places in power whomever He wants, on His time schedule! God said the Israelites would be in captivity for 70 years. Right at this point, *"The Lord stirred up the spirit of Cyrus."* God made Cyrus willing to do what he did. Isaiah said, *"Thus says the Lord to His anointed, to Cyrus, whose right hand I have held,"* Isaiah 45:1a NKJV. God appointed and anointed a pagan king to set His people free! Just think, if God can use a pagan king to liberate His people, how much more can He use His own Son, King Jesus to set us free?

Perhaps after reading our text, you came to the conclusion that Cyrus was a godly king! Not so! Cyrus was a blood thirsty, cruel, unbelieving king! Isaiah says about God's relationship to Cyrus, *"I have even called you by your name; I have named you, though you have not known Me,"* Isaiah 45:4b NKJV. Cyrus was moved by God to be a liberator so that: 1. *"Israel shall be saved by the Lord with an everlasting salvation; You shall not be ashamed or disgraced forever and ever,"* Isaiah 45:17 NKJV; 2. *"Look to Me, and be saved, all you ends of the earth! For I am God, and there is no other,"* Isaiah 45:22 NKJV.

In the end, who were the ones that went to rebuild Jerusalem and why did they choose to go? The answer is the same as with Cyrus! *"All those whose spirits God had moved, arose to go up and build the house of the Lord which is in Jerusalem,"* Ezra 1:5b NKJV. Christians are God's present day Israel by His will and grace alone! The only reason we choose God is because God moves our spirit to love Him!

Prayer: Dear Lord, how good it is for us to see how You moved Cyrus to act out Your will! For in the same way, You make our wicked hearts willing to love You. It is You who gathers us together in Your Heavenly Jerusalem. We worship You for Your grace to us sinners. In Jesus' name we pray. Amen.

June 16

"Ezra arrived in Jerusalem in the fifth month of the seventh year of the king. He had begun his journey from Babylon on the first day of the first month..., for the gracious hand of his God was upon him. For Ezra had devoted himself to the study and observance of the Law of the Lord, and to teaching its decrees and laws in Israel." Ezra 7:8-10

Ezra, faithful priest and teacher

Jewish tradition says that Ezra wrote both the book of Ezra and Nehemiah. Ezra's family line is traced back to Aaron, the family of priests. Over the years there were many priests, yet Ezra is singled out and honored here. The reason is: *"for Ezra had devoted himself to the <u>study</u> and <u>observance</u> of the Law of the Lord, and to <u>teaching</u> its decrees and laws in Israel.* Note the word, *"for."* God blessed Ezra *"for"* it because he loved God's holy rules for living, His Law. Ezra did not just study the Law. He <u>observed</u> it, meaning he <u>obeyed</u> it! Then he <u>taught</u> it.

See the sovereignty of God in moving powerful King Xerxes to send Ezra to rebuild Jerusalem. This is the same Xerxes who made Esther his queen, just five months after Ezra arrived in Jerusalem! Now we know more of the reason Satan entered the wicked official Haman! It was to try stop God's people from rebuilding Jerusalem!

God even moved King Xerxes to provide gold and silver in abundance for the rebuilding efforts and for purchasing animals to sacrifice. Furthermore, Xerxes even commanded Ezra to *"appoint magistrates and judges to administer justice to all the people,"* Ezra 7:25b. Ezra so loved the law of God that he set up a whole judicial system so all the people were treated justly! Wow! We supposedly live in a Christian land today with a democracy based on God's Law, yet our land is trying to remove the Ten Commandments! We are doing the exact opposite that Ezra did and then we wonder why there is an increase of corruption and violence. When we repent and once again love the Law of God, keeping it and teaching it will God's blessings return.

Prayer: Lord, we praise You for putting the love of Your holy laws in Ezra's heart and even in an unbelieving king's heart. Lord, we stand accused of not loving Your Law more. Forgive us and turn us back to You, we plead! In Jesus' name we pray. Amen.

June 17

"I confess the sins we Israelites, including myself and my father's house, have committed against You. We have acted very wickedly toward You. We have not obeyed the commands, decrees and laws You gave Your servant Moses. Remember the instruction You gave Your servant Moses, saying, 'If you are unfaithful, I will scatter you among the nations, but if you return to Me and obey My commands, then even if your exiled people are at the farthest horizon, I will gather them from there and bring them to the place I have chosen as a dwelling for My Name.'"
Nehemiah 1:6b-9

Nehemiah, chosen to rebuild Jerusalem

Nehemiah is in Susa, the winter capital of the Persian empire. It is just 446 years before the coming of Christ. Nehemiah and Ezra are the last books written before Jesus' birth. Nehemiah's name means, "consolation of Yahweh." God placed Nehemiah in a most important position as cupbearer to the king. He recommended and tasted what wine the king could safely enjoy. He discussed national concerns with the king. At this time, Nehemiah received news that the remnant in Jerusalem, 700 miles away, was not doing well. They were unable to rebuild Jerusalem! Notice what Nehemiah does about it!

In our text, he personally identifies himself with the national sins of Israel and confesses them clearly to God! Now, after confessing and humbling himself before God, the way is finally opened to rebuild Jerusalem. Nehemiah petitions Artaxerxes, the king of Persia, concerning the desolation of his native place in Judah. And the king, with the blessing of the queen, sends Nehemiah to rebuild Jerusalem. How true it is, he who kneels before God can stand before anyone!

Nehemiah is given provision and protection to build Jerusalem, the city Jesus walked in. Whenever God's people were repentant, whenever they confessed their sins and returned to Him, He restored them. God's protection was in the midst of great obstacles as we will see tomorrow.

Prayer: Lord, how quick You are to forgive us personally and nationally when we repent and turn back to You. We see that You always restored repentant Israel. Lord, may we learn from this today and humbly repent! In Jesus' name we pray. Amen.

June 18

"When Sanballat the Horonite and Tobiah the Ammonite official heard about this, (the rebuilding of Jerusalem) they were very much disturbed that someone had come to promote the welfare of the Israelites."
Nehemiah 2:10

Sanballat, Satan's agent to stop missions

Sanballat was a Samaritan government official who, like his fellow countrymen, hated the Jews. The name "Sanballat," means sin, for that is what he lived for. He did everything he could to stop Nehemiah from rebuilding Jerusalem. Do not think that the way the Arabs and other nations of the Middle East hate Israel is something new!

Sanballat first, *"ridiculed the Jews"* for their efforts to rebuild. He did this in front of the army and many people, to stir them up against God's people. After this, *"They all plotted together to come and fight against Jerusalem and stir up trouble against it,"* Nehemiah 4:8. Nehemiah's response to all of this was: *"But we prayed to our God and posted a guard day and night to meet this threat,"* Nehemiah 4:9. What a godly response! But still, the people, and we too, are afraid! To our fears, Nehemiah speaks, *"Don't be afraid of them. Remember the Lord, who is great and awesome, and fight for your brothers, your sons and your daughters, your wives and your homes,"* Nehemiah 4:14b.

Now the wall is built. So Sanballat has a new plan to kill Nehemiah. He invites Nehemiah to meet him with the purpose of ambushing him and taking his life. Wisely, Nehemiah refuses to meet. Again Sanballat tries a new scheme. He threatens to tell the king that Nehemiah is planning a revolt. The reason for all of this is that Satan is trying to discourage God's people so they would give up! At the same time God is testing His people to trust in His providence! Nehemiah passes the test by praying to God in Nehemiah 6:9b, *"Now strengthen my hands."* This will also happen to us! In the end God will build our weak faith as we witness His faithfulness firsthand! Our God is so good!

Prayer: Lord, William Carey was so right! "We are a thousand times safer in the most dangerous place on earth, in the center of God's will, than we are in the safest place on earth outside of His will." Lord, we worship You. In Jesus' name we pray. Amen.

June 19

"When the turn came for Esther (the girl Mordecai had adopted, the daughter of his uncle Abihail) to go to the king, she asked for nothing other than what Hegai, the king's eunuch who was in charge of the harem suggested. And Esther won the favor of everyone who saw her."
Esther 2:15

Esther, the girl who won a beauty contest

Esther was a young, orphan girl who became queen of the most powerful nation on earth. God raised up Esther to help deliver His people from His enemies. Uncle Mordecai adopted Esther. She grew up as a devout Jewish girl. When the former Queen Vashti lost her position, the king looked for a replacement among the most beautiful young girls of the land. Esther's outward beauty caught the eye of the king's officials, but her inner beauty won the king's heart!

The girls who wanted to be the Queen could select any of the jewels they wanted from the king's treasury, and they could keep them! Esther *"asked for nothing."* She went to the king with empty hands and was given a privileged position! Is this not true for all who go to King Jesus?

"Now the king was attracted to Esther more than to any of the other women, and she won his favor and approval more than any of the other virgins. So he set a royal crown on her head and made her queen instead of Vashti," Esther 2:17. What a verse to meditate on! Is this not true for every single Christian? In Christ, *"You are a chosen people, a royal priesthood, a holy nation, a people belonging to God,"* 1 Peter 2:9a. Esther is a beautiful picture of our *"chosen"* spiritual condition! As we shall see, Esther's deliverance from the wicked Haman is like our deliverance from the wicked Satan!

Esther's life teaches us to see the sovereign hand of God in the affairs of people. God has His hand on every life! How does our life fit into God eternal plan to redeem lost sinners? Like Esther, do we go to the King with empty hands, looking for His favor? Or, are we too busy looking for jewels and riches that we can keep only for this life?

Prayer: Lord, we thank You for showing us such a clear picture of how You are in total control of this world and how we must humbly approach You. Lord, be merciful to us. In Jesus' name we pray. Amen.

June 20

"All the king's officials and the people of the royal provinces know that for any man or woman who approaches the king in the inner court without being summoned the king has but one law: that he be put to death. The only exception to this is for the king to extend the gold scepter to him and spare his life." Esther 4:11a

King Ahasuerus, approach with caution!

Esther became the queen, the wife of the most famous and rich Persian King Ahasuerus, which is his Hebrew name. His Persian name was Xerxes. He lived 475 years before Christ and ruled the country from Ethiopia to India. His winter palace was in Susa, 200 miles from Babylon, in present day Iraq. His new Queen Esther, was chosen before hundreds of others. However, she keeps her Jewish identity a secret.

Fast forward five years. All the Jews are scheduled to be killed on a certain day. Uncle Mordecai convinces Esther that she must act and appeal to the king on behalf of her people. The wise words of Mordecai are insightful for us yet today! *"For if you remain silent at this time, relief and deliverance for the Jews will arise from another place, but you and your father's family will perish. And who knows but that you have come to royal position for such a time as this?" Esther 4:14.*

The rules for approaching the powerful Ahasuerus in the court, are in our text. It was almost certain death to approach the king and this applied to Esther too. In the same way, we too must go to King Jesus! If we don't, we will surely perish. It is 100% against the law for us to go to God, for we all deserve death, not mercy! Like Esther, we too are placed in this world to go to the King and ask for mercy! And even though it is against the law, it is not against the Gospel! Unlike Ahasuerus, God will surely reach out with His scepter and pardon us!

Prayer: Lord, what contrast there is between King Ahasuerus and King Jesus who said: *"Come to Me, all you who are weary and burdened, and I will give you rest,"* Matthew 11:28. Lord, You also command us, *"Approach the throne of grace with confidence, so that we may receive mercy and find grace to help us in our time of need."* We thank You for Your mercy. In Jesus' name we pray. Amen.

June 21

"Then Queen Esther answered, 'If I have found favor with you, O king, and if it pleases your majesty, grant me my life — this is my petition. And spare my people — this is my request.'" Esther 7:3

Esther's protection is Haman's judgment

From the beginning of history God has clearly shown His loving covenantal concern for those He is calling to Himself. He also shows that He judges evil even in this life! We do not normally see the spiritual and physical struggle going on in Heaven or on Earth for the souls of men. For this reason God gives us special events, like the protection of Esther and the destruction of Haman. This amazing event is a clear picture of the truth: *"For evil men will be cut off, but those who hope in the Lord will inherit the land,"* Psalm 37:9. Therefore may we keep our eyes on Him in true faith and in serious prayer.

In the book of Esther, the enemies of God <u>seem</u> to be in control. Esther, Mordecai and ultimately all Israel, <u>seem</u> to be doomed! But then, God removes the former queen, replacing her with the humble, prayerful and beautiful Esther. All this is happening in a pagan land! Then the wicked Haman, the most powerful prince, pounces on prayerful and honorable Mordecai, the uncle of Esther. We see humble Mordecai living to honor the Lord and the king. We see arrogant Haman living to honor himself! Mordecai refuses to bow to evil Haman and his wicked agenda, so Haman tries to eliminate him along with God chosen people!

God, who is always in total control of world events, parades the request of Esther in our text before the king. Suddenly, Haman's plans to eliminate Esther, Mordecai and all the Jews are exposed! Quickly, at the blink of an eye, Haman and his family are eliminated instead of God's people! How true it is, *"If God is for us, who can be against us?"* May we then, just like Esther and Mordecai, *"Come boldly to the throne of grace, that we may obtain mercy and find grace to help in time of need,"* Hebrews 4:16b NKJV.

Prayer: Lord, we see that, *"the power of the wicked will be broken, but the Lord upholds the righteous,"* Psalm 37:17. Lord, we are so grateful for Your protection and provision! In Jesus' name we pray. Amen.

"That same day King Xerxes gave Queen Esther the estate of Haman, the enemy of the Jews. And Mordecai came into the presence of the king, for Esther had told how he was related to her. The king took off his signet ring, which he had reclaimed from Haman, and presented it to Mordecai." Esther 8:1-2a

Mordecai, doorkeeper then Prime Minister

Mordecai sat at his post by the palace door. He fasted and prayed. He begged God to deliver His own people. He knew he was sentenced to death. God truly designed and allowed this great trial in the life of Mordecai, just to make his need of mercy clearer! God wanted to show Mordecai and us, His great power over the forces of evil.

What a picture of the sure mercy of God on display here! God promises His mercy and grace to every true believer. But still, God wants us to ask for it! "*Let us approach the throne of grace with confidence, so that we may receive mercy and find grace to help us <u>in our time of need</u>,*" Hebrews 4:16. Make note of the fact that Mordecai <u>wanted</u> "*mercy*" weeks before he received it. But when he really <u>needed</u> "*mercy,*" it was there just in time. God's mercy is never too early for then we would not learn to trust Him! Nor is God's "*mercy*" ever too late that we should despair! God's "*mercy*" is always just on time as He has the whole world and everyone in it, under His absolute sovereign control!

Mordecai received mercy because he was a humble, dependent believer! In fact, the humble Mordecai is contrasted with Haman the arrogant. Haman thought he was winning, but Mordecai was the one who prevailed. It is still true that, "*God opposes the proud but gives grace to the humble,*" 1 Peter 5:5b.

Mordecai is also a good example of how God turns our rather lukewarm prayers into fervent petitions for His specific mercy. And in turn, how specific God is in answering our cries for help. God does not, "*ignore the cry of the afflicted,*" Psalm 9:12b.

Prayer: Lord, sad to say we are often more like the proud Haman than the humble Mordecai. We have way too much pride! Lord, we humble ourselves before You! Lift us up Lord. Forgive us and grant us Your mercy. In Jesus' name we pray. Amen.

June 23

"'Does Job fear God for nothing?' Satan replied. 'Have You not put a hedge around him and his household and everything he has? You have blessed the work of his hands, so that his flocks and herds are spread throughout the land.'" Job 1:9-10

Satan, he knows what you are doing!

Here we see Satan having a meeting with God. The spiritual battle going on for the souls of men is an intense one! God shares Job's life with us in part, just to teach us something about Satan and the spiritual battle in the heavenly places! Twice, in Job 1 & 2, Satan addresses God and taunts Him. Twice, God said to Satan, *"Have you considered My servant Job?"* Twice, Satan was well aware of what the righteous Job was doing! He knows what we are doing too! How else can Satan tailor temptations specifically to target our spiritual weaknesses? <u>When we are in the will of God, we are out of Satan's will, and Satan hates that!</u>

We must learn from the origin of Satan when God said this about him: *"You were the model of perfection, full of wisdom and perfect in beauty. You were in Eden, the garden of God,"* Ezekiel 28:12b-13a. But then this most perfect and beautiful angel sinned as God tells it: *"Your heart became proud on account of your beauty, and you corrupted your wisdom because of your splendor. So I threw you to the earth,"* Ezekiel 28:17a. There it is! The one who guarded the most holy place in Heaven now wants to corrupt us here on earth. And Satan knows the temptation that best fits us personally.

Paul wrote about spiritual warfare; *"For our struggle is not against flesh and blood, but against the rulers, against the authorities, against the powers of this dark world and against the spiritual forces of evil in the heavenly realms,"* Ephesians 6:12. Jesus taught us to pray to God, *"'Deliver us from the evil one,"* Matthew 6:13b. The best way to be protected from Satan is to follow Job's example. Be righteous and true to God, pray to Him, and the victory will be ours.

Prayer: Lord, You know what Satan is up to. You control him. He still reports to You as we can see from Your discussion with him about Job. Satan knows when we are living for You and he is eager to stop us. Protect us Lord! Deliver us from this evil one. In Jesus' name we pray. Amen.

"Then Job arose and tore his robe and shaved his head, and he fell to the ground and worshiped. And he said: 'Naked I came from my mother's womb, and naked shall I return there. The Lord gave, and the Lord has taken away; blessed be the name of the Lord.' In all this Job did not sin nor charge God with wrong." Job 1:20-22

Job, tested by God, tempted by Satan

Nothing will test our faith more than a big trial! Well, Job had three great trials, in succession. Job lost all his possessions, all his servants, all his children, plus his health, all in just one day. Job knew that as a Christian, all things work together for good! But in the heat of the battle, a serious trial is not so easy! Our sinful human nature wants to question God and we want to demand an answer from God. The truth is, God allowed Job's difficult trial as He allows ours! More than that, God even designed Job's trial to test Job! <u>God will test all faith</u>, because all faith must be tested to see if it is real! With Job, as with us, God wanted to show Satan and us how a believer responds in a righteous way!

In Job's serious trial, we must also realize that <u>Satan is tempting Job</u> to curse God. Satan wanted Job to carry on like a wild man in response to his great affliction! Satan knew well that it was common for people to shake their fist at God, to get drunk and to demand why. Yet Job never asked why of God, for he knew something about the providence of God that we must understand. It was God who gave him so many blessings! Now God decided for some good reason to take them away. Job trusted the wisdom of God! Do we trust God when supposed "bad things" happen to us? My selfish experience says no, not at first. But then God makes us willing to accept what He gives us. Praise be to His holy name!

James tells us to "*consider it pure joy, my brothers, whenever you face trials of many kinds,*" James 1:2. <u>Have the right attitude</u>. God is testing our faith to build us up, to sanctifying us! He knows best how to bring us safely to Heaven as 2 Timothy 4:18 teaches!

Prayer: Lord, help us to see that we are just like Job. We too have difficult trials. In them, we need Your wisdom, which You give generously to those who ask. We are so thankful that You are with us in our trials, to help us pass them! In Jesus' name we pray. Amen.

Job had, "*painful sores from the soles of his feet to the top of his head. Then Job took a piece of broken pottery and scraped himself with it as he sat among the ashes. His wife said to him, 'Are you still holding on to your integrity? Curse God and die!'*" Job 2:7b-9

Job's wife doesn't stand by her man!

Job's wife had a life of privileges. She was the richest woman alive. She had servants for anything she wanted. She had a house that was the envy of the neighborhood. She had seven sons and three daughters. But even more than that she had the most righteous man on earth as a devoted husband to her and their children. How kindly Job treated her and prayed for the family! What a great example Job set for everyone to follow. Job's wife was blessed!

Job's wife surely made a marriage vow in the presence of the people and God. She said something like this: "I, Mrs. Job, take you Mr. Job to be my wedded husband. And I promise today, in the presence of God and those gathered here, that from this day forward, in sickness or in health, in poverty or in riches, with the gracious help of God, I will love, honor, and obey you in all things according to God's ordinance, and will never forsake Him or you as long as we both shall live."

After years of a good marriage, God takes her children and wealth away. Job is really sick! Job's wife has no hope and gives up! She placed too much of her hope in the "good life" continuing! Her trust in God is weak and she curses God and her husband. She wants to commit suicide and wants her husband to curse God and die with her. She has given in to the very temptation that Satan hoped to lure Job into. However, Job stays true to God and acts righteously. Job <u>kindly</u> rebukes his wife. "*You are talking like a foolish woman. Shall we accept good from God, and not trouble?*" Job 2:10a. What happened to Job's wife in life will happen to us in death! Our wealth will be gone! In the end, we will be separated from our children. What is our hope in?

Prayer: Lord, may we learn from Job's wife to stand by our spouse, and by You, our God. Lord, we also remember how Jesus' disciples left Him in His difficult trial. May we be as gracious as Job and Jesus when others fail to stand by us. In Jesus' name we pray. Amen.

June 26

"I know that my Redeemer lives, and that in the end He will stand upon the earth." Job 19:25

Job's faith grows, Satan's hope dims

There is so much we must learn from the faith of Job. We have seen that God loved Job and blessed him. We have seen how God allowed Satan to oppress Job and even take his wealth and children from him. We have seen Job, so sick and hurting that he was almost dead. And every one of these events only drove Job closer to God! The theme of Job is not only that Job's faith grows, but that Satan's hope dims!

Satan's best attempts to separate Job from God not only didn't work, but it served to drive Job closer to God! In the end Job could only say, *"My ears had heard of You but now my eyes have seen You,"* Job 42:5. A cancer patient said about her experience: "I never knew God like this before!" Oh, to be brought to the place where we have no one else to turn to, but God. It is an experience we really need, and in the end we are so grateful for this time!

God's persevering love to Job is the same for all believers! Someone asked the aging Billy Graham to give a good word about God. He simply said, "Jesus loves me this in know." That's really good! Job said, *"I know that my Redeemer lives, and that in the end He will stand upon the earth."* Job 19:25. I used to think this said, I would stand upon this earth. No, Jesus will *"stand upon the earth."* In Judgment, He will stand as our deliverer/redeemer and as Satan's executioner! Satan is already finished! He can't stop Jesus' appointment to *"stand upon the earth"*!

With Paul we must say: *"We believe that Jesus died and rose again and so we believe that God will bring with Jesus those who have fallen asleep in Him. According to the Lord's own word, we tell you that we who are still alive, who are left till the coming of the Lord, will certainly not precede those who have fallen asleep. For the Lord Himself will come down from Heaven,"* 1 Thessalonians 4:14-16a.

Prayer: Lord, how great is Your salvation. When You save us, You save us so completely that no one can snatch us out of Your hand, not even Satan. We praise You now and for all eternity! In Jesus' name we pray. Amen.

June 27

"For the sake of Your name, O Lord, forgive my iniquity, though it is great." Psalm 25:11

David's prayer of a sincere believer

This Psalm is so impressive! Every verse is the heartbeat of a believer who is dependent on God. The whole Psalm is actually a beautiful prayer of a humble and broken sinner reaching out to God for His mercy and grace! It goes on to say that those who put their hope in God will never be put to shame! That is a huge concern for each of us. We do not want to be personally put to shame. Verse seven asks God not to remember the sins of our youth or any of the ways we have rebelled. We are asking God to not give us what we deserve but instead, what we desperately need: His forgiveness! We are asking God to remember how He forgave us, how He took our sin and gave us the righteousness of Christ. So the prayer is asking God to see Christ perfect life, not our sinful one, which He does.

Our text now appeals to God to be merciful to us and forgive us for the sake of His Name! We pray for His Name to be more honored and more fully known. May the Lord give us the burden to pray this verse, not only for our forgiveness, but also that He is glorified through us!

In verse 15, David realizes that only God can release his feet from all the snares in his life! A rabbit or bird cannot free itself, and neither can we. God must do it! David is also *"lonely and afflicted."* He is in the throes of *"anguish"* and *"distress,"* and he calls out to God for mercy! *"Guard my life and rescue me; let me not be put to shame, for I take refuge in You."* How silly of us, not to pray this prayer!

What about us? Are we searching for a solution to our problem? Our anxiety must go down; our trust must go up! Amazingly, it is God who builds our faith and trust in Him as we experience His deliverance! It is His divine attributes that are for us now and forever!

Prayer: Lord, David expresses the deepest needs of our own hearts. His concerns are our concerns. We need You in every way to complete us and protect us. We cast all our cares on You, knowing that You really do care for us. You even promised to never leave or forsake us. You are a beautiful God! In Jesus' name we pray. Amen.

June 28

"O Lord, do not rebuke me in Your wrath, nor chasten me in Your hot displeasure! For Your arrows pierce me deeply, and Your hand presses me down." Psalm 38:1-2 NKJV

David's painful depression

Too often today people want to hide their depression from others. Praise God, He made David write about it for our benefit and for God's glory. Clearly David sinned when he committed adultery and murder and then did not confess it. He tried to ignore his wrong pattern of living at this point of his life, but God got his attention. God wanted David depressed! David says, *"Your hand presses me down."* David took the two pills of confession and repentance to come out of his depression!

See what David says in verse three about what he painfully knew! *"There is no soundness in my flesh because of Your anger, nor is there any health in my bones because of my sin."* Man's pride wants to overlook these two facts! Make no mistake, David's schedule stunk! God corrected it, as only the pain of discipline can. If we do not honor Him with our time, God has His own way changing us. David was playing playboy instead of being warboy! God raised up David to shine for Him, not to bring shame to His name. It is plain and simple, God put David back on course!

Understand this: David's <u>feelings</u> of depression were not sinful in any way, but his <u>actions</u> that led to depression were. Too often we only want to focus on fixing the feelings of depression. We make all kinds of excuses to ourselves and to others about why we are so down, thus delaying our healing! God wants us to get serious with the sin connected to our depression. Then He will quit pressing us down. Guilt hurts for a good reason: it is supposed to! Why do we try to numb it with drugs, alcohol, food, buying something, etc..

Read Psalm 38. Read about love in 1 Corinthians 13:4-8. See what needs to change in our relationships and responsibilities. Be specific in prayer about what needs to change. As we confess it and turn from it, God's Spirit will change our feelings to joy, instead of sadness!

Prayer: Lord, You are loving yet bluntly clear when our devotion to You needs to change. Thank You for making David write to us on this important subject. In Jesus' name we pray. Amen.

June 29

*"Have mercy on me, O God, according to Your unfailing love;
according to Your great compassion blot out my transgressions. Wash
away all my iniquity and cleanse me from my sin. For I know my
transgressions, and my sin is always before me."* Psalm 51:1-3

David's healing confession

Satan will try to convince us not to confess our sin! We must be fully
aware that he wants us to hide them. David listened to the devil for
some time. As a result, David was suffering physically as well as spiritually.
He was even greatly depressed from his failure to confess his sin as we
saw in Psalm 38 yesterday. David's healing started like this: God sends
the prophet Nathan to convict him and help him to see the importance
of confessing his sin. This confession of David here in Psalm 51, is one of
the spiritual highlights of his life and ministry!

David's adultery with Bathsheba and the murder of her husband is
now out in the open. Instead of being proud and ignoring his sin, he
humbly acknowledges it. After confessing it, he quickly experiences the
amazing forgiveness of God. O, that we might confess our sin more
often, more openly and more specifically!

David pleads with God, *"Restore to me the joy of Your salvation and
grant me a willing spirit, to sustain me,"* Psalm 51:12. He did not say, "my
salvation" but *"Your salvation."* Have we lost the joy of His salvation? A
failure to confess sin may be one reason! Granted, we are still saved!
But is our joy gone? If so, tell God about our sin in as much detail as we
can. Confess it specifically, for that is how we change! Often we are
way too vague in how we confess our sin. David said to God, "a *broken
spirit; a broken and contrite heart, O God, You will not despise,"* Psalm
51:17b. A big part of being broken is to finally be fed up with our sin
and cry to God about it clearly. That is what David did!

Prayer: Lord, like David, we have such a great stubbornness when it
comes to confession! How much we need Your Spirit to convict us and
for You to forgive us! How gracious Your forgiveness of sin really is! We
praise You for restoring us! In Jesus' name we pray. Amen.

June 30

"But as for me, my feet had almost slipped; I had nearly lost my foothold. For I envied the arrogant when I saw the prosperity of the wicked. They have no struggles; their bodies are healthy and strong. They are free from the burdens common to man; they are not plagued by human ills." Psalm 73:2-5

Asaph, from sinful envy to godly praise

Asaph the psalmist, is much like David the psalmist. He is transparent about what he has learned in the Christian life. If we have the courage to be so open, we too can be a teacher to many. We just need to be honest about what God is teaching us!

When Asaph wrote Psalm 73, he was close to being depressed and he admits it. He recalls his thoughts and actions at this time in his life. See how the first verses reveal a self-pity or a self-focus. He was fully loving himself the most, rather than God and then others as the Bible teaches. Count the personal pronouns in the first half of the psalm. Then count them in the second half. It is very revealing how self-centered he and we are in our journey through life.

Asaph admits his envy! He is thinking God is not fair! If that is true, then God is not perfect. If we think God is not fair, then we are saying that we know more than what God knows about our needs! We are the ones being arrogant, when we envy the arrogant! Asaph felt sorry for himself, *"till I entered the sanctuary of God; then I understood their final destiny,"* Psalm 73:17. Now Asaph has pity on the lost instead of self-pity! Now he starts to regain his spiritual senses. His confession is in verse 22. In the last six verses his mind is on God. Read the Psalm. Asaph changed and had a time of worship instead of a pity party!

Compare Asaph's Psalm 73 to David's Psalm 37. They are almost identical. David explains how to change from envy and from all sin! We must put off the sin of envy in verse one. Then we can replace it and start to *"trust in the Lord,"* in verse 3. We are now able to *"delight"* in the Lord in verse 4. We now can *"commit"* our way to the Lord in verse 5. Finally, we start to rest in the Lord or *"be still before the Lord"* in verse 7.

Prayer: Lord, the world's wisdom is foolishness. Your wisdom is incredible! We worship You. In Jesus' name we pray. Amen.

JULY

Shadrach, Meshach and Abednego in the fiery furnace

"If we are thrown into the blazing furnace, the
God we serve is able to save us from it, and He
will rescue us from your hand, O king."
Daniel 3:17

July 1

"I have hidden Your Word in my heart that I might not sin against You."
Psalm 119:11

David's delightful devotion

I recently met an older teenager who claimed to be Christian. She could proudly tell me the characters and details of countless, worthless movies! Yet she asked, "Who was Thomas in the Bible?" and she thought "Ecclesiastes" was a Tamil word. Her problem is our problem. We have the written Word of the living and eternal God, infallible, forever true, forever relevant, yet we read it so little!

What if a loved one overseas wrote us a personal letter? Would we open it? Would we not read every word carefully? Yet God our Creator, our King, Redeemer and best friend wrote us a letter. The dust on the cover of our Bibles shouts at us, "You hypocrite!"

If we have any hope to know the true God, any hope to know of His power and purposes, then we must know His Holy Word! David was said to be a man after God's own heart. Why? David really was devoted to God! Consider the many Psalms that David wrote. These were meditations of David's devotion as he recounted his experiences and how God's holy attributes gave him strength!

What can we say about David's devotion? Where did it come from? There is only one answer: God! *"The Lord said to Samuel... 'Fill your horn with oil, and go; I am sending you to Jesse the Bethlehemite. For I have provided Myself a king,'"* 1 Samuel 16:1 NKJV. See the big difference here between David and Saul! When God chose Saul, He said, *"Make them a king,"* 1 Samuel 8:22b. Why? The people did not want God. They rejected Him! If we want to be devoted to God we have to want God! We have to get serious, kneel down and pray and pour out our heart to God. Has He ever refused a beggar? No, He says, *"Come to Me, all you who are weary and burdened, and I will give you rest,"* Matthew 11:28.

Prayer: Lord, we desire a deeper relationship with You! We want to be devoted to You, yet we know that You must also draw us to Yourself! Lord, we can only humble ourselves in prayer and beg for more of Your mercy and grace! In Jesus' name we pray. Amen.

July 2

"A wife of noble character who can find? She is worth far more than rubies." Proverbs 31:10

The Proverbs 31 woman

The woman described here in Proverbs 31 does not have a name, but the description of her character describes a noble woman in the image of God! She lives an unselfish life-style. Character matters! Because she has this good character, she acts in a certain moral and upright way. She cares about relationships. She loves and respects her husband. She disciples her children and is a blessing to all those who are in her life. True love for God and for His kingdom shows in our relationships.

The Proverbs 31 woman is one great worker! God commanded the man and the woman to have dominion over the world. She does that. Verses 13-24 describe all the things she does. She is not a couch potato! *"She gets up while it is still dark."* Many men and woman need to take this verse to heart. She does not just pray, *"give us this day our daily bread,"* she does many things to earn it, which is consistent with her godly character. She understands that in doing her responsibilities and in managing her relationships, God guides and directs her.

She speaks with grace, meaning she speaks without anger and bitterness, which are the opposite of grace! *"She speaks with wisdom, and faithful instruction is on her tongue,"* Proverbs 31:26. Note how this verse fits with the next one. Her wise and faithful instruction in verse 26, is followed up with, *"She watches over the affairs of her household."* If she lived today she would not waste her time watching T. V. She disciples others in a gracious manner, teaching what is right, then follows it up to see that the wise instruction is followed!

Notice also, *"charm is deceptive, and beauty is fleeting"*! How many women of the world manipulate others with deceptive talk, trying to impress them with their outward beauty. Character and proper relationships are her talk and walk. She is one fulfilled woman; praised by God and by her loving family!

Prayer: Lord, we have much to learn about what it means to be a godly woman and a godly man. Thank You for showing us what kind of life-style is pleasing to You! In Jesus' name we pray. Amen.

July 3

"Remember your Creator in the days of your youth, before the days of trouble come and the years approach when you say, 'I find no pleasure in them.'" Ecclesiastes 12:1

Solomon, youth remember your Creator

Solomon had wisdom, a gift from God, but this does not mean that he had wisdom all at once. He had to learn wisdom, just as you do. If you asked those who are "older" if they would like to be young again, most will say, "Yes." They would then add, "But only if I can know what I know now." Well, Young Man and Woman, Solomon is teaching you those things that you need to know now. He understands that youth have passions! Use that passion. Treasure that passion! But keep in mind that God is your Creator. A fear of God is health food for you!

Solomon had the resources and power to try anything and everything, and he did. He admits looking for satisfaction and contentment in education, but it did not satisfy. He collected wives, horses, animals, birds and gardens, just to name a few. When reflecting on all this, Solomon said, *"banish anxiety from your heart and cast off the troubles of your body, for youth and vigor are meaningless,"* Ecclesiastes 11:10.

You see the same madness for "things." "If I can only have a good vehicle, I will be satisfied. If I only had this boy or girl for a spouse, I would be happy. If I only had a house of my own, better clothes, more money, I would be content." No way! Contentment is not what is in your hand; it's what's in your heart! That is what Solomon is teaching. Keep a fear of God as you move through life! Remember your Creator!

"Know that the Lord is God. It is He who made us, and we are His; we are His people, the sheep of His pasture," Psalm 100:3. Live in the light of eternity is another way to say this! You are not your own! You belong to God! His eye is always upon you. What a blessing that is yours, if you "Remember your Creator." What a curse if you try to be your own boss. God does not want to be your co-pilot, He demands to be your Pilot!

Prayer: Lord, our prayer is, "Jesus Savior pilot me over life's tempestuous seas! Unknown waves before me roll, hiding rocks and treacherous shoal. Chart and compass come from Thee, Jesus Savior pilot me!" In His name we pray. Amen.

July 4

"Now all has been heard; here is the conclusion of the matter: fear God and keep His commandments, for this is the whole duty of man. For God will bring every deed into judgment, including every hidden thing, whether it is good or evil." Ecclesiastes 12:13-14

Solomon's conclusions on life

In the end, life comes down to a few basic principles! We are the ones who make life a complicated mess; God keeps it simple. We have already seen the *"fear God"* part, in yesterday's message. Now it is time to *"Keep His commandments."* Another way to say this is: "trust and obey." That in a nutshell, is the purpose of every life. We were created by God to enjoy God forever! If we are going to enjoy Him forever, we need to obey Him today. God will test us every day, whether or not we love Him. The reason is in our text! As created beings, we have a sacred *"duty"* to our Creator God. There is only one God who is in this category!

When we die, *"God will bring every deed into judgment."* God reminds us of this because He loves us. *"Every deed"* will be judged, even every *"hidden thing, whether it is good or evil."* God does not forget our sin, as many think! When we die, it will not matter whether we were rich or poor! It will not matter what level of education we were able to complete. What will matter is, did we put to death the selfishness we were born with, and love God and others. That is exactly what the commandments direct us to do! God help us to curb our selfish desires!

Paul said, *"I eagerly expect and hope that I will in no way be ashamed, but will have sufficient courage so that now as always Christ will be exalted in my body, whether by life or by death. For to me, to live is Christ and to die is gain,"* Philippians 1:20-21.

Prayer: Lord, You are the holy One, the only One without sin. Only through You can we experience holiness. You became our substitute and saved us from our sins. Your grace is on us and we experience it. The way You loved Your disciples, You also love us. The way they learned to love You, we want to learn to love You too! Lord what power is in Your hands! What love is in Your heart! What peace there is with You! Make us like You. In Jesus' name we pray. Amen.

July 5

"Like a lily among thorns is my darling among the maidens."
Song of Songs 2:2

Solomon's wisdom to lovers

King Solomon wrote the Song of Songs with words that have a double meaning. He taught the right relationship of Christ to His church and the right relationship of a husband and wife. With this in mind, consider how as a Christian, you are *"a lily among thorns"* in Christ's eyes. Truly God loves all people, but you Christian, are here called by Christ, *"My darling."* You are nearest to the heart of God! Others are but "thorns" compared to how much more Christ loves you! When Jesus prayed to the Father, He said, *"I am not praying for the world, but for those You have given Me, for they are Yours,"* John 17:9b. You are precious to Jesus because you are precious to God! In fact, Jesus loves you with an everlasting love!

You are *"like a lily"* because of Jesus! And He said, *"I am a rose of Sharon, a lily of the valleys,"* Song of Songs 2:1. Because of Christ in you, your relationship to Christ makes you bloom more beautifully every day. Meditate on that and thank God! It is only because of His Spirit in you, that you are growing more gracious each day!

Secondly, a husband who sees his wife as a *"lily among thorns,"* is truly in love and can call his wife, *"my darling."* A wife who sees her husband *"like an apple tree among trees of the forest,"* in Song of Songs 2:3, can lovingly call her husband, *"my darling."* But if a man has a lust problem, his wife is no lily among thorns! She is a thorn among lilies! A woman with eyes of lust also sees her husband as just a plain tree, and other men are *"apple trees."* Just as Jesus loves us with an everlasting love, we too must have that same commitment to our spouse! Our God is jealous for a good reason, and our spouses are jealous for us also!

Prayer: Dear Father in Heaven, we thank You for changing us from thorns to lilies by Your grace. We deserve to be thorns, but we need to be lilies. The husband in Proverbs 31, looked at his darling wife and said, *"You excel them all."* So do You Lord. There is no god like You! We worship and adore You! In Jesus' name we pray. Amen.

"Wash and make yourselves clean. Take your evil deeds out of My sight! Stop doing wrong, learn to do right! Seek justice, encourage the oppressed. Defend the cause of the fatherless, plead the case of the widow." Isaiah 1:16-17

Isaiah's message is God's concern

Isaiah was a very special prophet of God. That is why he is listed first in a line of prophets, which are not listed in order, time wise. Isaiah was married and had two children. He ministered faithfully to the people of Israel from 740 to 701 B.C. It is believed that Isaiah was the martyr who was sawn in half in Hebrews 11:37. God gave Isaiah a vision as part of recorded Scripture. What God taught Isaiah, we need to learn! God is teaching Israel and us that we must change and what must change! This same godly process is laid out by Paul in Ephesians 4:22-24, in his famous, "change chapter."

God begins the book of Isaiah by showing Isaiah in a vision about the ways His people have greatly offended Him! For fourteen verses, God lays out their ugly sins! Then, God speaks just two clear verses to show us and Israel what our repentance must look like!

"Wash and make yourselves clean. Take your evil deeds out of My sight! Stop doing wrong," Isaiah 1:16. This is the first half of true Biblical repentance! God is saying, <u>confess</u> the sin, <u>stop</u> the old sinful behavior and <u>put it off</u>! Again that is the first half. When we do not do this part, we do not change! And we must do this half first.

Secondly, we must replace the sin! We must have a godly replacement for our sin, not a different sin! We must put on the new godly behavior. More than that we must focus intently on the new way of living! See the "focus" words God is careful to say here! *"<u>Learn</u> to do right! <u>Seek</u> justice, <u>encourage</u> the oppressed. <u>Defend</u> the cause of the fatherless, <u>plead</u> the case of the widow,"* Isaiah 1:17. These are actions we still need to be involved in, 2700 years after God gave these words to Isaiah!

Prayer: Lord, we can see that Your repentance process is not complicated. Help us to be specific in prayer, specific in our obedience and ever so active for You! In Jesus' name we pray. Amen.

"Do not let Hezekiah mislead you when he says, 'The Lord will deliver us.' Has the god of any nation ever delivered his land from the hand of the king of Assyria?" "How then can the Lord deliver Jerusalem from my hand." Isaiah 36:18 & 20b

Sennacherib, mocks God and loses

Our text are the words of Sennacherib to Judah, through his field commander. We also read about Sennacherib in 2 Kings and 2 Chronicles. We see how God can work through leaders and nations to carry out His divine will. God sometimes used a wicked leader like Sennacherib, to defeat apostate and unrepentant Israel. God did this, *"because they had not obeyed the Lord their God, but had violated His covenant – all that Moses the servant of the Lord commanded. They neither listened to the commands nor carried them out,"* 2 Kings 18:12.

However, King Sennacherib is still personally accountable to God for his own actions. Sennacherib had already defeated Israel before his boasting words in our text. Sennacherib is now turning his sights on Judah. His problem is, he now blasphemes God! He has no respect for the Lord and His Almighty power. In fact, Sennacherib says that he is more powerful than God is!

It is interesting to see Hezekiah's response to Sennacherib and his ambassadors. He did not go out to see them to reason with them! He did not allow his people to reason with this wicked king who was threatening Jerusalem. *"When Hezekiah heard this, he tore his clothes and put on sackcloth and went into the temple of the Lord,"* Isaiah 37:1. Hezekiah knew God could completely stop this wicked king who blasphemed God! Hezekiah puts his hope in God, not in the size of his army! Is this our response to such wickedness? These are important questions that we need to deal with. Like Hezekiah, we need to humble ourselves and go to God in serious prayer.

Prayer: Lord, You told us, *"If My people, who are called by My name, will humble themselves and pray and seek My face and turn from their wicked ways, then will I hear from Heaven and will forgive their sin and will heal their land,"* (2 Chronicles 7:14). Lord, please move us to seek Your face if we are unwilling. In Jesus' name we pray. Amen.

July 8

"'If you keep your feet from breaking the Sabbath and <u>from doing as you please</u> on My holy day, if you <u>call the Sabbath a delight</u> and the Lord's holy day honorable, and if you honor it by <u>not going your own way</u> and not doing as you please or speaking idle words, <u>then you will find your joy in the Lord</u>, and I will cause you to ride on the heights of the land and to feast on the inheritance of your father Jacob.' The mouth of the Lord has spoken." Isaiah 58:13-14

Corporate worshipers, the blessed ones

Corporate Sabbath worship has never been optional. The seven day week was established by God for the good of man and for the honor of Himself. God made us for Himself! Even though the honor of God is the main issue when we fail to worship, so is His desire to bless us! See how "*If*," is used three times in our text! Our blessings from God are conditional! If we honor God and keep <u>His day</u> holy then He honors us!

"Observe the Sabbath day by keeping it holy, as the Lord your God has commanded you. Six days you shall labor and do all your work, but the seventh day is a Sabbath to the Lord your God," Deut. 5:12-14a. The fourth commandment is the longest of the ten. In it we see God's will for us on the Sabbath day. It is God's day to do as He commands us, meaning, the day is not ours to do as we please!

On the Sabbath, we need to hear the Word of God. We need to participate in the sacraments, per 1 Corinthians 11:23-26. We need to sing songs, and pray publicly according to Colossians 3:16 and 1 Timothy 2:1. *"Six days you shall labor and do all your work."* God rested on the seventh day, just to show us that we need to also!

The Sabbath is a taste of Heaven. An important question is: "Does it taste good to us?" If not, pray that God will quicken our taste buds. *"Let us not give up meeting together, as some are in the habit of doing, but let us encourage one another-and all the more as you see the Day approaching,"* Hebrews 10:25.

Prayer: Lord, how our observance of Sunday worship reveals the condition of our hearts! You show us that when our worship fails, we will soon fail. Lord, move us to worship You! For we need to seek after more of Your Kingdom and less of ours. In Jesus' name we pray. Amen.

July 9

"The Word of the Lord came to me, saying. 'Before I formed you in the womb I knew you, before you were born I set you apart; I appointed you as a prophet to the nations.' 'Ah, Sovereign Lord,' I said, 'I do not know how to speak; I am only a child.' But the Lord said to me, 'Do not say, "I am only a child," you must go to everyone I send you to and say whatever I command you. Do not be afraid of them, for I am with you and will rescue you,' declares the Lord." Jeremiah 1:4-8

Jeremiah's call from God

Jeremiah is informed (and so are we) that God had His eye on him while he was still in the womb. The great Creator knows why He put Jeremiah and us here in this world! How encouraging! Jeremiah now has a purpose! Youth want and need a purpose. They see the broken and careless way people live. We must study the Word of God to see His response to a broken world. God says of all Christians, young or old, *"We are God's workmanship, created in Christ Jesus to do good works, which God prepared in advance for us to do,"* Ephesians 2:10. We must talk to God about what He wants us to do!

God not only sends young Jeremiah, He gives him His message. *"Say whatever I command you"*! Do we not also have God's message and a command to teach others *"everything I have commanded you"* in Matthew 28:19-20? We have not only a full Old Testament but also a complete New one. We can see more clearly the empty tomb. We more completely have His Spirit in us!.

"Go," don't say, "No." Jeremiah was reluctant at first. He said *"I do not know how to speak; I am only a child."* Yes, but God uses children. It was little Samuel who spoke God's message to Eli. No one else had the conviction or the guts to speak. It was a little girl who pointed Naaman to the God of Israel! It was a little boy who gave his fish to Jesus. The question is not, "Can God use us?" but "Are we willing to be used by God!" *"Do not be afraid of them, for I am with you and will rescue you."* How encouraging and comforting God's protection is!

Prayer: Lord, we thank You for sharing Jeremiah's call with us. We see almost this same message to us in the Great Commission. Impress it on our hearts Lord. In Jesus' name we pray. Amen.

July 10

"The Word of the Lord has brought me insult and reproach all day long. But if I say, 'I will not mention Him or speak any more in His name,' His Word is in my heart like a fire, a fire shut up in my bones. I am weary of holding it in; indeed, I cannot.*"* Jeremiah 20:8b-9

Jeremiah's burning desire for evangelism

Jeremiah teaches the people about the holiness of God whom they have offended. Jeremiah knows for certain that they are doomed if they continue the way they are going and do not repent. He cares about the glory of God! He cares about their lost souls!

By Chapter 17, we see Jeremiah preaching by every city gate in Jerusalem. His message is: *"This is what the Lord says: Be careful not to carry a load on the Sabbath day or bring it through the gates of Jerusalem. Do not bring a load out of your houses or do any work on the Sabbath, but keep the Sabbath day holy, as I commanded your forefathers,"* Jeremiah 17:21-22. Jeremiah warns, but he also offers hope. He says in Jeremiah 17:24a, *"But if you are careful to obey Me, declares the Lord, and bring no load through the gates of this city on the Sabbath, but keep the Sabbath day holy,"* then God will bless!

The "official" religious leaders have had enough! They think they alone are God's mouthpiece! *"When the priest Pashhur son of Immer, the chief officer in the temple of the Lord, heard Jeremiah prophesying these things, he had Jeremiah the prophet beaten and put into stocks,"* Jeremiah 20:1-2a. In this context, Jeremiah says he must speak the Word of God!

What about us? If we are not willing to speak the Word of God in "good times," what will we do when we are forbidden to speak it? Can we go from Sunday to Sunday without opening the Word of God? If we can, then it's no wonder we have no fire in our heart! Do not say, "I am just a common man!" Jeremiah was that! Do not say, "I am not ordained!" The ordained priests were not teaching God's message! As a result, there was no conviction, no repentance and no change! That is why God still uses common people like Jeremiah!

Prayer: Lord, we see the same evil conditions, and the same attitude to hearing and speaking God's message that Jeremiah did. Lord convict us and use us. In Jesus' name we pray. Amen.

July 11

"The Word came to Jeremiah from the Lord when King Zedekiah sent to him Pashhur son of Malkijah and the priest Zephaniah son of Masseiah. They said: 'Inquire now of the Lord for us because Nebuchadnezzar king of Babylon is attacking us. Perhaps the Lord will perform wonders for us as in times past so that he will withdraw from us.'" Jeremiah 21:1-2

King Zedekiah & Priest Pashhur panic

What a turn of events here, which could also happen to us at any time. Jeremiah has been teaching the people to repent and turn to God. Pashhur, the leader of the priest, was wrongly teaching that God wanted to give the people peace and prosperity. Opposite messages were being taught! Look around! How many people are still teaching peace and prosperity like it is God's message? Who is really concerned about repentance and the honor of God's name?

A few years back, I was teaching in Chennai, India, and a man told me this was the first time in 10 years he ever heard that God wanted him to repent of anything! All he had heard was, "give money and God will bless you!" It is interesting that Pashhur's name means the same as what he taught, "prosperity everywhere." Jeremiah knew something we need to know! Past spiritual blessings are not a guarantee of future blessings when people reject God!

Suddenly, as our text shows, *"Nebuchadnezzar king of Babylon is attacking."* King Zedekiah and Pashhur are finally forced to admit what they tried to deny: Jeremiah was God's servant. He was speaking God's truth! They panic and ask Jeremiah to intercede for them! They hope God will do a miracle like He did in the past and deliver them. But God does not deliver unrepentant people. He humbles them with oppression, until they see the error of their ways, repent, and then call upon Him. God never restored Israel when they were unrepentant!

Prayer: Lord, forgive us for the error of our ways. May we turn to You in true repentance and faith. For You our God are holy, concerned that we live holy lives. Raise up more Jeremiahs in our day who are willing to speak Your truth, regardless of the cost. In Jesus' name we pray. Amen.

July 12

"The Lord has done what He purposed; He has fulfilled His Word which He commanded in days of old. He has thrown down and has not pitied, and He has caused your enemy to rejoice over you; He has exalted the horn of your adversaries." Lamentations 2:17 NKJV

Judah, devastated, cried and wept!

Lamentations is a funeral poem in five chapters. The book is meant to shock us into repentance and renew our faith in God. Lamentations shows us that when God's patience runs out with a country and its people, it will be a Hell on earth! Starvation, continual grief, crying and lamenting describes the current pain and brokenness of the people of Judah! Children slowly dying, starving in their mothers' arms! Jerusalem is empty. The temple is defiled. The holy place where the people would not go is a urinal for the pagans! The proud priest who prophesied prosperity and peace, have ashes on their heads or are dead. A lovely princess has *"become a slave!"* The blood runs in the streets. Both young men and women are bleeding and dying. Some are taken captive! And guess what, *"The Lord has afflicted her,"* Lamentations 1:5b NKJV. God said it would happen, and now it has! The first half of the book describes the pain, the hopelessness and the horribleness of it all! Suddenly, some of the people remember the character of their God! Hope is dawning! They start crying out to God. Humility is finally replacing their anger!

"This I recall to mind, <u>therefore I have hope</u>. Through the Lord's mercies we are not consumed, because His compassions fail not. They are new every morning; great is Your faithfulness," Lamentations 3:21-23 NKJV.

Hope, is that part of our faith that gives us a purpose for living. Like Israel, we may have little or nothing in our hand! But, if we have God in our heart, we have everything. Hope sustains us!

Prayer: Lord, we see Judah had no hope because they were angry at You! Their memory served them poorly when they experienced difficult times! But then, You jogged their memory to see that You are a God of mercy and grace, just what they needed! They looked to You for what they needed, not what they deserved! May we do the same, for Lord we need You! In Jesus' name we pray. Amen.

July 13

"He asked me, 'Son of man, can these bones live?'" Ezekiel 37:3a

Ezekiel, and the million dollar question

What a great question God asks Ezekiel and us! There is a valley full of dry bones before Ezekiel! There are acres of sleeping bones. Can God make these bones live? Ezekiel is not quite sure. So God tells him and us what will happen. *"These bones are the whole house of Israel. They say, 'Our bones are dried up and our hope is gone; we are cut off.' Therefore prophesy and say to them: '<u>This is what the Sovereign Lord says: O My people, I am going to open your graves and bring you up from them,</u>'"* Ezekiel 37:11b-12a.

We have more information than Ezekiel did. We have seen in the Bible that the grave could not hold Jesus. Our Lord and Savior is called the first fruits of those who are made alive. Since all believers are "God's Israel," this resurrection promise is for us! We shall be like Him! We can count on it. It is going to happen. God will open up every grave and all living people will come out!

Jesus Himself taught on the subject of the coming resurrection. He said, *"Do not be amazed at this, for a time is coming when all who are in their graves will hear His voice and come out - those who have done good will rise to live, and those who have done evil will rise to be condemned,"* John 5:28-29. Not just believers, but all people will come out of the grave. It does not matter if we believe it or not! The resurrection is going to happen! God will make it happen!

Some of the people in Ezekiel's time were having a lot of problems. They were in captivity again. They were slaves. They had cruel masters and they suffered much. They wondered, if it would always be like this? The answer is "No." There is a day coming when every person will be given a glorified body that will never die. Jesus proved that by rising from the dead Himself and also by raising Lazarus from the dead.

Prayer: Dear Lord, we are convinced that You can and will raise up everyone who ever died! The question for us is: Where will our body, and soul be going after our resurrection? Lord, we thank You that You cover our sins and bring us to Heaven forever. In Jesus' name we pray. Amen.

July 14

"Daniel purposed in his heart that he would not defile himself."
Daniel 1:8a NKJV

Daniel, student with a purpose!

When Daniel was about 14 years of age he was taken captive to Babylon. The authorities recognized Daniel as a young man with a quick mind. So they trained him. Soon Daniel did better than the other students; his competition was fierce! His classmates were *"some of the king's descendents and some of the nobles, young men in whom there was no blemish, but good-looking, gifted in all wisdom, possessing knowledge and quick to understand,"* Daniel 1:3b-4a NKJV. But Daniel was the best student for a good reason! God makes a difference! Daniel was committed to God, thus God was for Daniel. The life of Daniel is a good example for us! *"Whatever things were written before were written for our learning, that we through the patience and comfort of the Scriptures might have hope,"* Romans 15:4 NKJV. What did Daniel do?

Daniel did not compete against the other students, he lived for God. When we compete with others, our minds are more on what they are doing, than what we are doing! Competing with others creates turmoil and wastes much time and energy. Daniel's mind was on what God wanted him to do. As Daniel continued in school, the other students conspired to take Daniel down. But Daniel still did not give in to the temptation to fight them! Daniel knew that it was God's problem, not his. Other students tried to get him expelled from school because he refused to do the evil things the other students did. Can you say the same thing?

Are you willing to try drugs, alcohol, sex and other distractions just to fit in with the popular kids? Did you know that bad habits which start in your youth, usually continue into adulthood? Daniel didn't do the evil stuff. He knew that God would not protect him if he did! A song says, "Give of your best to the Master, give of the strength of your youth." Daniel lived that song, and God blessed him! God was Daniel's strength and shield! God is your strength and shield, if you put your trust in Him!

Prayer: Lord, we thank You for the life of Daniel. You gave us such a good example to follow. May we see that giving in to sin is never a good idea. In Jesus' name we pray. Amen.

July 15

"Is it true, Shadrach, Meshach and Abednego, that you do not serve my gods or worship the image of gold I have set up." Daniel 3:14b

Shadrach, Meshach and Abednego's furnace

What was true of Daniel is also true of his three friends. They were all outstanding, promising young men who loved God no matter what anyone else thought. They daily experienced a close communion with God. They were fully satisfied with God, and God was fully satisfied with them! Contrast this fullness with God, to the emptiness the pagans had with their gods. They now add a new god, a ninety-foot tall idol, all because they were not yet satisfied! But then, they will never be satisfied. These gods did not make them, know them, nor were they capable of loving them in return!

The command comes, *"Whoever does not fall down and worship will immediately be thrown into a blazing furnace,'"* Daniel 3:6. Shadrach, Meshach, and Abednego refuse. They are arrested and brought to this powerful pagan king. He heats up the furnace seven times more than normal. He orders the three to be bound, with their clothes on, and thrown into the furnace! The strong men who throw them in, die from the intense heat. Shadrach, Meshach, and Abednego are not hurt. The ropes are burned off as they walk in the fire, yet they do not try to get out. The fires has no effect on them. A fourth Person is in the fire with them. It is an angel, God himself, Jesus, we believe. When the king calls the three out of the furnace they do not have one hair burned. They do not even smell like smoke!

God will do for us what He did for Shadrach, Meshach and Abednego. Jesus will come to our rescue. In fact, He already has. He spent three hours experiencing the pain of Hell on that Cross. This was our furnace of pain! Remember this, the very strongest without Jesus, died at the door of that furnace! But we will not be harmed if Jesus is with us, for He has taken the wrath of the King (His Father) upon Himself!

Prayer: Lord, what a beautiful picture of how much You are with us in the furnace of affliction. Truly, nothing can separate us from the love of God in Christ Jesus! We praise You for Your amazing love. In Jesus' name we pray. Amen.

July 16

"Therefore, O king, be pleased to accept my advice: Renounce your sins by doing what is right, and your wickedness by being kind to the oppressed. It may be that then your prosperity will continue."
Daniel 4:27

Daniel's alarming advice!

Daniel was a mild mannered man and well respected. He had a great concern for the welfare of the king, which was why he was a faithful and trusted adviser to four kings. <u>Daniel was bold, always straight forward with the truth, always tactful</u>. He speaks the words of our text to the most powerful king in the world. He is not afraid!

Daniel's message is straight from God! Daniel is willing to tell the king that he is sinning! Too often we don't even want to tell a child that much! Daniel is speaking the truth with love, and that makes all the difference! We can say hard things to people, if we love them, and say it kindly! We can say hard things if we clearly show that we have their best interest in mind. I doubt if any other advisers of the king could be so open and honest. Because of a fear of man, they were quicker to tell the king what he wanted to hear. But that is not what he needed! It is a sign of spiritual maturity when we give people what they need, and not what they want, and do it in a respectful way!

Daniel's alarming advice is a big personal lesson for us. If God tells a prideful king to, *"renounce your sins by doing what is right,"* then it is also good advice for us who can also be very proud in how we live! Are we trying to use people or somehow hurt them to advance our reputation, or even our prosperity? We may seem to succeed like the king did, for a little while! BUT, God is watching! God is testing us! God will hold us accountable for how we treat others. May we listen to God who boldly tells us the truth about what is important in life!

Prayer: Lord, we too need a rebuke for being too proud, for not reaching out to the *"oppressed"* in Your name and for Your glory. In Isaiah it says that Jesus *"was oppressed and afflicted."* He knows the pain. He sees and hears the pain of those who are physically and spiritually *"afflicted."* Lord humble us and equip us to see and hear what You see and hear! In Jesus' name we pray. Amen.

July 17

"Twelve months later, as the king was walking on the roof of the royal palace of Babylon, he said, 'Is not this the great Babylon I have built as the royal residence, by my mighty power and <u>for the glory of my majesty</u>?' The words were still on his lips when a voice came from Heaven, 'This is what is decreed for you, King Nebuchadnezzar: Your royal authority has been taken from you.'" Daniel 4:29-31

Nebuchadnezzar, one proud builder

God warned Nebuchadnezzar, but he did not change! *"Twelve months later."* God did what He said He would do. God brought down a proud man who was also a tyrant! Nebuchadnezzar could, with one word or gesture, put a person to death or bless them! And this is exactly what he did to try maintain absolute control. It is what dictators still do! It's true that God put King Nebuchadnezzar in power to discipline His wayward children of Israel. Every leader is responsible to God to rule with justice. Nebuchadnezzar didn't do that. God saw how this man literally *"oppressed"* the people so that he could have every luxury he wanted. In time, the king became so proud that he even bragged about how he built up Babylon.

You may remember that Babylon had its beginning at the Tower of Babel. Do you know what they said before God busted up that building program? *"Come, let us build ourselves a city, with a tower that reaches to the heavens."* Why were they doing this? *"So that we may make a name for ourselves,"* Genesis 11:4a. Nebuchadnezzar built up Babylon to make a name for himself! God immediately suspends Nebuchadnezzar's building program!

Today many will labor to build their own "Babylon!" Few will labor to build Jerusalem, that is, build up the body of Christ! Both will be costly to build. When we turn to the book of Revelation we can see which one will last for all eternity! *"The great city of Babylon will be thrown down, never to be found again,"* Revelation 18:21b. Are we laboring to build that which will last?

Prayer: Lord, may we not possess the spirit of Babylon! Forgive us where we have lived to exalt ourselves instead of You! Move us to the safest place on earth, at the foot of the cross. In Jesus' name we pray. Amen.

July 18

"Daniel distinguished himself above the governors and satraps, because an excellent spirit was in him; and the king gave thought to setting him over the whole realm." Daniel 6:3 NKJV

Daniel, a spirit with a purpose!

Why was Daniel so "distinguished"? Our text gives us an immediate answer. There was, *"an excellent spirit in him."* Yes, it was this *"spirit"* that set Daniel so noticeably apart from the rest! So what is it that Daniel had that the others didn't? First of all, Daniel knew full well, what was completed in the Bible up to his day. It says in Daniel 9:2, 11 and 13 that Daniel was familiar with Moses' books and also the prophets. It was his reading of Jeremiah that led him to pray in such a powerful manner. For us also, how much easier it is to pray after reading the Bible. The Spirit of God wrote the Bible! Through reading and applying the Word, God's Spirit dwells in us and makes our spirit after His Spirit. Daniel was not only right in what he said, but in how he said it graciously. *"An excellent spirit was in him,"* Daniel 6:3a NKJV. Many preachers and teachers may teach truth today, but ungraciously scream their message.

Because of Daniel's *"excellent spirit,"* his personality was almost flawless! The reason is: God's personality is flawless! <u>Daniel was a great example of what it really means to be a "spirit-filled" Christian.</u> *"The fruit of the Spirit is love, joy, peace, longsuffering, kindness, goodness, faithfulness, gentleness, self-control,"* Galatians 5:22-23a NKJV. These words clearly describe Daniel's personality or character. Daniel's three friends were likewise devoted to God and were also blessed by God. The difference is: God. *"For these four young men, God gave them knowledge and skill in all literature and wisdom,"* Daniel 1:17a NKJV. If we think that God cannot do this yet today, then we really do have a faith problem! God gives wisdom to His children. That is why the fear of the Lord is just the beginning of true wisdom!

Prayer: Lord, You are the God who does not change, from everlasting to everlasting You are God. You still bless our life if we will but put our faith in You and honor You! For that purpose You created us! Forgive us when we want to learn from the world and from Satan. Lord, put Your spirit in us. In Jesus' name we pray. Amen.

July 19

"They could find no corruption in him, because he was trustworthy and neither corrupt nor negligent," Daniel 6:4b.

Daniel, dare to be one!

Our text is quite a testimony to the life of Daniel. Here he was a pilgrim in a foreign land! (Are not we all?) By the time of our text in Daniel 6, four successive foreign kings or rulers have been in power over Israel. The people are still in exile. Through it all, Daniel remains faithful to God and each king. What a lesson for us! Surely Daniel is a type of Jesus. Since we are called Christians, should we not be the same? Daniel did three things in our text that set him apart!

First, there was *"no corruption in him."* No one could bribe Daniel or get him to do anything that would hurt his God or his king. In Daniel's day, people used their positions to get favors of all kinds. Daniel did not do that, not even once! Daniel did what was right all the time. Daniel was right not only in what he said but he was right in how he said it! His words were seasoned with grace, just like Jesus!

Second, *"he was trustworthy."* You could tell Daniel anything and he would only use that information to be a blessing to his God and to his country. He never had a selfish agenda. *"Not my will but Thine be done,"* was true of Daniel as well as it was with Jesus. Are we trustworthy? Are we completely trustworthy?

Daniel was never "negligent" in his duty. This means that Daniel was absolutely dedicated in his service to the king, and in his worship to his God. For a very good reason the words "worship" and "service" are almost identical in the Greek. There are many brilliant and gifted people in this world. But if they are negligent in their duties then they are basically a waste. Jesus was also faithful in all that He did. We are also called to a life of faithfulness. The reason is: faithfulness is driven by the grace of God. Faithfulness is a fruit of God's grace. Whether we are faithful or sinfully negligent is a big issue. Dare to be a Daniel!

Prayer: Dear Lord, how often we do what we feel like doing instead of what we should do! Forgive us for our selfish habits! Give us a heart like Daniel and Jesus! May we do what is right all the time, and then, leave the results to You. In Jesus' name we pray. Amen.

"In his upper room, with his windows open towards Jerusalem, he knelt down on his knees three times that day, and prayed and gave thanks before his God, as was his custom since early days." Daniel 6:10b NKJV

Daniel, praying with a purpose!

When Daniel's fellow workers tried to frame him and set him up for failure, Daniel went home and *"knelt down."* Daniel knew for certain that God was his protector. Hours later, in answer to Daniel's prayer, God closed the mouths of the lions and *"no injury whatever was found on him, because he believed in his God,"* Daniel 6:23b NKJV. Yet, his prayerless accusers, when they were put in that same lions' den, *"the lions overpowered them, and broke all of their bones in pieces before they ever came to the bottom of the den,"* Daniel 6:24 NKJV.

How did Daniel pray so powerfully? Daniel confessed sin! We included part of his prayer here because it is so instructive! Daniel included himself in the corporate sins of Israel! *"I prayed to the Lord my God, and made confession, and said, 'O Lord, great and awesome God, who keeps His covenant and mercy with those who love Him, and with those who keep His commandments, we have sinned and committed iniquity, we have done wickedly and rebelled, even by departing from Your precepts and Your judgments. Neither have we heeded Your servants the prophets, who spoke in Your name to our kings and our princes, to our fathers and to all the people of the land. O Lord, righteousness belongs to You, but to us shame of face, as it is this day - to the men of Judah..."* *"Yes, all Israel has transgressed Your law, and has departed so as not to obey Your voice; therefore the curse and the oath written in the Law of Moses the servant of God have been poured out on us, because we have sinned against Him."* *"We do not present our supplications before You because of our righteous deeds, but because of Your great mercies. O Lord, hear! O Lord, forgive! O Lord, listen and act! Do not delay for Your Own sake, my God, for Your city and Your people are called by Your name,"* Daniel 9:4-7a, 11, 18b-19.

Prayer: Lord, we see that confession of sin humbles us and elevates You! You show us that prayer is a great strength, not a weakness. Give us prayerful hearts like Daniel! In Jesus' name we pray. Amen.

July 21

"My God sent His angel, and He shut the mouths of the lions. They have not hurt me." Daniel 6:22a

Daniel's dazzling deliverance!

Daniel's life of faith comes to us from a time in the history of the church when it was difficult to be a Christian. We have seen how Daniel was a great student, chose good friends and spoke the truth. He warned kings and had an excellent spirit. Daniel was not corrupt or negligent in his duties. He was faithful. Daniel was one of the best ever in ministry! We need to see what Daniel was not, as well as what he was!

Paul David Tripp wrote an excellent book called "Dangerous Calling." He challenges pastors and all of us about the most dangerous pitfalls in ministry. These are the very things Daniel was wise to avoid. Mr. Tripp, a pastor, writes: "I wish I could say that my story is unique, that most pastors don't struggle the way I did. I wish I could say that in the lives of the vast majority of pastors there is no disconnect between their public ministry personas and the details of their private lives. I wish I could say that most pastors are as skilled at preaching the Gospel to themselves as they are to others. I wish I could say that relationships between pastors and their staff are seldom tense and seldom break down. I wish I could report that a few pastors are angry and bitter. I wish I could tell you that my experience is that most churches' pastor their pastor well. I wish I could encourage you with the fact that most pastors are known for their humility and approachability. I wish I could say that most pastors minister out of a deep sense of their own need. Yes, I wish I could say all these things, but I can't."

Contrast this honest statement to Daniel who was faithful in all things! After Daniel came out of the lions' den, the king wrote: *"I issue a decree that in every part of my kingdom people must fear and reverence the God of Daniel,"* Daniel 6:26a. God the real King delivered Daniel completely. Our God is still the great deliverer!

Prayer: Lord, we stand amazed as we meditate on our responsibility to be faithful like Daniel. May You give us strength and boldness. Savior like a Shepherd lead us! In Jesus' name we pray. Amen.

July 22

"*When the Lord began to speak through Hosea, the Lord said to him, 'Go, take to yourself an adulterous wife and children of unfaithfulness, because the land is guilty of the vilest adultery in departing from the Lord.' So he married Gomer.*" Hosea 1:2-3a

Prostitute Gomer, points us to God's love

The book of Hosea begins with God telling Prophet Hosea to marry a prostitute named Gomer. How shocking we may think! Yet God with compassion and holiness wants Israel and us to see what we are doing to Him. God cares that His people have spiritually and physically forsaken Him for other gods. Israel was "*guilty of the vilest adultery in departing from the Lord.*" Hosea is the first prophet of seven, (God's perfect number) who all lived at the same time. All warned the people to turn back to God. Isaiah, Joel, Amos, Obadiah, Jonah and Micah give the same warnings. How many more wake-up calls will God give us?

Hosea and Gomer's first son, Jezreel, was named by God. "Jezreel," was also a place located in the middle of the country! Israel was rotten to the core and God cuts on the core. Their first daughter God calls, "Lo-Ruhamah" meaning to have pity. God pitied Israel because they would be invaded by the Assyrians. What they did to the people of Israel is too graphic to explain here. But God took pity on Judah and saved them for many years yet.

Their third child was a son and God named him, Lo-Ammi. It means you are not my people and I am not your God. Neither was Lo-Ammi Hosea's child. He was fathered by another man. Gomer, like Israel, committed adultery and gave birth to a child born in sin, content to sin, died sinful, and was cut off from God. Romans 1:18-23 also teaches how wicked man willfully left God!

The people of Israel saw clearly how God spoke directly to them through the lives of Hosea and his prostitute wife and children! This scandal was more talked about than a serial on T.V. But still, the people refused to repent!

Prayer: Lord, what great lengths You go through to warn us. We know You are a jealous God. You made us and care for us. Forgive us for not loving You more. In Jesus' name we pray. Amen.

July 23

"The Lord said to me, 'Go show your love to your wife again, though she is loved by another and is an adulteress. Love her as the Lord loves the Israelites, though they turn to other gods and love the sacred raisin cakes.' So I bought her for fifteen shekels of silver and about a homer and a lethek of barley." Hosea 3:1-2

Hosea, buys Gomer from slavery

Gomer left her husband thinking, *"I will go after my lovers,"* Hosea 2:5b. She was not content with her marriage. She thought her problem was her husband, not her own heart, so she leaves! But Gomer forgot something! Almighty God is sovereign! God says, *"she will chase after her lovers but not catch them; she will look for them but not find them. Then she will say, 'I will go back to my husband as at first, for then I was better off than now,'"* Hosea 2:7. Like many women before her and after her, she found out that the way of the transgressor is hard when God has His eye on you!

It is believed that when Gomer left Hosea, she most likely sold herself to one of the pagan temples. They in turn, rented her out each day to various men. It is in this kind of situation in our text, that God instructs Hosea to buy her back! We may think, "How disgusting." But before we shake our finger at Gomer, see how this is a picture of exactly what God did for us when He gave us salvation. We too were bought by Satan. We were born in sin. We were then redeemed, not by a mere *"fifteen shekels"* and a little *"barley."* We were redeemed by the costly blood of Christ, God's own Son.

Gomer left Hosea for what she wanted, that is to sin. God intervened and gave her what she needed, a restored marriage. Better yet she was restored to God Himself! How great is the grace of God to us who are such great sinners!

Prayer: Lord, we are so amazed how much You loved us dirty sinners! We too were literally in bondage, unable to come to You. Lord, You took pity on our hopeless situation and came to us. You bought our souls, and bodies too, for all eternity. We give You our thanks. And if we are not yet Your child, we plead with You to redeem us too! In Jesus' name we pray. Amen.

July 24

"For strong is the One who executes His Word. For the day of the Lord is great and very terrible; who can endure it? 'Now, therefore,' says the Lord, 'Turn to Me with all your heart, with fasting, with weeping, and with mourning.' So rend your heart, and not your garments; return to the Lord your God, for He is gracious and merciful, slow to anger, and of great kindness; and He relents from doing harm.'" Joel 2:11b-13 NKJV

Joel, the day of the Lord is coming!

The book of Joel starts with a word of warning and moves on to a source of hope. A main concern is the coming *"day of the Lord,"* or Judgment Day! We don't know when this book was written. It was either after Judah had two wicked kings and then Athaliah, or it was after the exile and captivity. Either way, Joel saw the locust come and devour everything! The locust was one of the plagues God put on Egypt. The locust were a promised judgment if God's people were unfaithful. He said, *"Swarms of locust will take over all your trees and the crops of your land,"* Deuteronomy 28:42. God's punishment happened!

Learn from the locust in Joel 2:4-11. God leads them and they follow! *"Like swift steeds, so they run."* Relentless, they march in perfect formation! *"They run like mighty men."* No one can steer them off course. *"They do not push one another."* The locust never tries to stop others from God's marching orders! They march miles deep, united and focused, with purpose! The locust teach us history is marching on. God is in total control! The church must follow God like locust! There is a judgment coming! *"The day of the Lord is great and very terrible; who can endure it?*

We must repent today so we can face the Judgment. That is Joel's message of hope! God gives an invitation in verse 12, *"'Turn to Me with all your heart, with fasting, with weeping, and with mourning.' So rend your heart, and not your garments; return to the Lord your God, for He is gracious and merciful."* What a relevant message for us today. We can flee from the wrath that is to come.

Prayer: Lord, we hear Your message! Time is marching on like an army of locust. Minute after minute the clock ticks closer to Your coming Judgment Day. No one can stop it. May we be ready! In Jesus' name we pray. Amen.

July 25

"Amos answered Amaziah, 'I was neither a prophet nor a prophet's son, but I was a shepherd, and I also took care of sycamore-fig trees. But the Lord took me from tending the flock and said to me, 'Go prophesy to My people Israel.'" Amos 7:14-15

Amos, a common man, called by God

God's people of Israel became increasingly unrepentant and uncaring about living for God. They ignored the loving laws of God. Instead they did what was right in their own eyes. They decided to write their own version of right and wrong. The priests taught what the people wanted to hear! Does this sound familiar? Well, God finally had His fill of the people's wickedness and He sent a common man, Amos, to give them His message! God's message through Amos is still relevant!

Amos was a shepherd and he took care of some trees. Instead of tending these, God told him to tend to the needs of His covenant breaking Israel. It is the wisdom and power of God that called Amos, equipped him, and used him. It is the wisdom of God that calls and equips us to be used by Him! It is important to know that it is God who is calling, because tough times will come. People will trouble us, like they did to Amos. Then Amos reminded them, he was called by God to do what he is doing! God calls. God equips. And God goes with us!

Amos clearly told the people of God's coming judgment. But he also gave a promise of God's grace, if the people would repent. In the midst of God's promised destruction in chapter nine, we finally come to Amos 9:11, where God talks about restoration. We need to see this! For we need not fear God's judgment now or at the end of time if we repent and live for Him today!

God's message through Amos is clear, righteousness and justice are important to Him. God holds us personally accountable to keep His righteous laws. But He also holds nations accountable to obey His laws, as evidenced in Chapter 1 and 2. God will not be mocked! He made us and has a right to rule us.

Prayer: Lord, Your timeless Word is so relevant! May we be convicted of our national sins and personal sins too. May we heed the call to repentance. In Jesus' holy and righteous name we pray. Amen.

July 26

"See I will make you small among the nations; you will be utterly despised. The pride of your heart has deceived you." Obadiah 2-3a

Obadiah, says our persecutions will end!

Every book of the Bible has a specific purpose in redemptive history. The short book of Obadiah shows God's coming judgment on Edom, the descendants of Esau. But this is also a snapshot of how God will deal with all of His enemies and ours. So if we are persecuted today, read Obadiah! It was written to encourage us!

Esau brought his condemnation on himself. Remember how he despised his covenant upbringing, his birthright and even his parents. He despised God's rules for marriage by taking two pagan wives. But most of all Esau despised God! His big problem was that he had a mountain of pride. Esau wanted to set his own rules for life. He thought neither God or man could stop him from doing what he wanted to do! It may sound good that a person should be able to do what he or she wants in life. But what if that "something" is harmful to others or to God. For this very reason God gave His people the Ten Commandments. However, these commandments were far from Esau's way of living! All through the Bible this is called rebellion and unbelief.

Esau's descendants presently live in the area of Jordan, and they still hate God and Israel. It is recorded that in pride Edom thought, *"Who can bring me down to the ground?"* Obadiah 3b. He thought he would get away with his violence and persecution of others, but God tells him, *"You will be utterly despised."* God also says, *"I will bring you down,"* Obadiah 4b.

We must learn from the book of Obadiah that it is the righteous purposes of God, not the evil will of men like Esau, Hitler etc, that will determine the course of history! Now that is comforting! God cares about His persecuted people. Behind their present difficult circumstances He is always at work for them! So let us trust in God!

Prayer: Lord, You tell us that, *"a man's pride will bring him low, but the humble in spirit will retain honor,"* (Proverbs 29:23 NKJV). What an eternal truth this is! We praise You for Your persevering promises! Please give us humble spirits. In Jesus' name we pray. Amen.

July 27

"The Word of the Lord came to Jonah son of Amittai: 'Go to the great city of Nineveh and preach against it, because its wickedness has come up before Me.' But Jonah ran from the Lord." Jonah 1:1-3a

Jonah, made willing to serve God

Jonah was a marked man when God had His eye on him to go and be His missionary to a pagan nation! Jonah was not willing to serve God, at first! Initially, neither are we! But then, God made Jonah willing to serve Him. Here we see the sovereign hand of God at work in Jonah's life. We say sovereign because of this truth! *"For it is God who works in you to will and to act according to His good purpose,"* Philippians 2:13.

"The Word of the Lord came to Jonah." He did not come to God and say, "I am willing to serve You!" Jonah only came after God made him willing to do so! And so it is with us! God made Jonah minister in Nineveh from 785 B.C. to 775 B.C. In the book of Jonah, we learn two important things about the sovereignty of God.

1. God is the Creator of everything. In today's day and age this needs to be said. Belief in evolution is poor science and a terrible religion. Imagine that you made the world in six days and admired the work of your hands, calling it good. Then the devil's assistant comes along and says the world "evolved" into what it is today. Don't believe it. It is God who made us and everything else.

2. The creation responds to the Creator. All creation responds to God! All creation serves God! The book of Jonah shouts this fact! The sailors, the waves, the great fish, the vine, the scorching heat, all respond to God! *"The heavens declare the glory of God; the skies proclaim the work of His hands,"* Psalm 19:1. A great number of people repented because God made them respond to Him! It is not any different for all who turn to God! *"But because of His great love for us, God, who is rich in mercy, made us alive with Christ even when we were dead in transgressions - it is by grace you have been saved,"* Ephesians 2:4-5.

Prayer: Lord, how true it is that You make us willing to love and serve You, when we were not yet willing to do so. Even the leaves on the trees wave praises to You, the One who made them! What a great God and Savior You are. In Jesus' name we pray. Amen.

July 28

"In my distress I called to the Lord, and He answered me. From the depths of the grave I called for help, and You listened to my cry."
Jonah 2:2b

Jonah's fishy prayer

In Jonah 2:1-10, we have a great lesson on serious prayer! There are some very important prayer points that we must learn from the life of Jonah.

Jonah was honest in prayer. There is no ritual here! There are no weather reports or history lessons given to God. Jonah didn't have time for empty formalities and neither do we! Jonah's heart simply cried out to God's heart! Like Jonah, let us not give God instructions, but just report for duty! "Lord, I am all Yours! Speak to me and use me for Your name's sake!"

Jonah prayer was dependent on God's mercy. Jonah's self-righteousness is 100% gone! Jonah needed mercy now, immediately! When we urgently cry, "God be merciful to me now! God save me now! God help me now!" He will hear us. Spiritual urgency is most pleasing to God, because He is a merciful and compassionate God, timely with His mercy! God specifically told us, *"Call upon Me in the day of trouble; I will deliver you, and you will honor me,"* Psalm 50:15. We can depend on the mercy of God!

Jonah was repentant in prayer. Jonah with a sudden change of heart said: *"I remembered You, Lord,"* Jonah 2:7b. Confession is good for the soul! Before this Jonah went his selfish way. Now he goes God's way! Jonah knew by sudden experience what Jesus later said, *"'The time has come,' He said. 'The kingdom of God is near. Repent and believe the good news!'"* Mark 1:15. Jesus did not separate repenting and believing, neither must we. Salvation includes both!

Prayer: Dear Lord, like Jonah we must learn that the task ahead of us is never as great as the Power behind us. Lord, things are never out of control, but under Your control. Help us Lord! When we cannot clearly trace the workings of Your Almighty hand, help us to trust Your loving heart. In Christ's most holy name we pray. Amen.

July 29

"He has showed you, O man, what is good. And what does the Lord require of you? To act justly and to love mercy and to walk humbly with your God." Micah 6:8

Micah, who is like our God?

A young man drank too much. He talked bad language and was intimately involved with two girls. He was angry and held a grudge against many, including so many of his relatives. But he went to church regularly. He took communion and taught a Sunday School class. He expected to go to Heaven! Now we know what Israel's problem was! And then they had the nerve to ask these questions: *"With what shall I come before the Lord and bow down before the exalted God? Shall I come before Him with burnt offerings, with calves a year old? Will the Lord be pleased with thousands of rams, with ten thousand rivers of oil?"* Micah 6:6-7a. God, what is it going to take for You to bless us?

God's answer through the prophet is: *"He has showed you, O man, what is good. And what does the Lord require of you? To act justly and to love mercy and to walk humbly with your God,"* Micah 6:8. "Walk" with your God, because worship without obedience, is worthless! More than that, worship without obedience is offensive to God! God desires godly children! Who is willing to be like our God? That is the issue. And guess what? Micah's name means, "Who is like our God."

God acts justly; God loves mercy; Jesus walked humbly. These are not three separate issues. If we act justly, or care about justice, then we will love mercy. When we love mercy, we will walk humbly! We will make sure everyone in treated fairly. It's all about compassion! Visit the widow; feed the poor; help the needy and the oppressed. Seek out ways to be a blessing to them! When we are blessed by God, we have a responsibility to be a blessing to others. We are called to be a missionary for God. Our God is just and holy and want us to be the same. That is the best worship! "Who is like our God?" is a good question!

Prayer: Lord, we cannot pretend to love You for Your eyes see through everything. We cannot buy You, for You already own everything. We cannot work for our salvation; Jesus did the work. Lord forgive our pride and make us *"act justly"*! In Jesus' name we pray. Amen.

July 30

*"The Lord is a jealous and avenging God; the Lord takes vengeance
and is filled with wrath. The Lord takes vengeance on His foes and
maintains His wrath against His enemies." "The Lord is good, a refuge in
times of trouble. He cares for those who trust in Him."* Nahum 1:2 & 7

Nahum, God's judgment on evil nations

The prophet Nahum enters the world scene 100 to 150 years after
Jonah preached to Nineveh. Today, Nineveh is the city of Mosul, in Iraq.
God allowed them prosperity and power, but then, they forgot God
again! Nahum's message is to Nineveh, but it's also to Israel and to us
who are flirting with evil. Nahum's name means comfort. His message
was mostly judgment, but mercy too. Nahum was in ministry for 50 years,
from 663 to 612 B.C.

Even though Nahum emphasizes God's wrath over His love, the Bible
is balanced! We must see and understand the perfect balance between
God's wrath and His love! Nahum tells us how God exercises His jealous
wrath. The reason is: God created us and everything! He has the holy
right to be angry when we worship other gods! The subject of God's
wrath is not just Old Testament, it's in every New Testament book! We
must understand God's wrath before we can understand how Jesus'
love saves us from God's wrath. His wrath on sinners is not just future, it
is present day also, as John 3:18b & 3:36b so clearly teach!

*"The Lord is good, a refuge in times of trouble. He cares for those
who trust in Him."* God Himself supplies the refuge from His wrath. God
poured out His wrath fully on sinless Jesus, saving us from His own wrath!
But Nineveh no longer wanted to serve God! They wanted to do
wickedness and serve their gods. So God destroyed them even though
the walls of the city were 100 feet thick! The palace covered 100 acres
and could take a 20 year siege, but that was no problem for God! He
predicts a flood in 1:8 and 2:6, and it happened! It was not until 1842
A.D., 165 years ago that Nineveh was finally rebuilt. No one can stand
before the wrath of God apart from the covering of love of Jesus'
atoning blood!

Prayer: Lord, how horrible is Your wrath, but how great is Your grace to
those who believe in Jesus! Make us believe Lord. In Jesus' name we
plead and pray! Amen.

July 31

"How long, O Lord, must I cry for help, but You do not listen? Or cry out to You, 'Violence!' but You do not save? Why do You make me look at injustice? Why do You tolerate wrong? Destruction and violence are before me; there is strife, and conflict abounds. Therefore the law is paralyzed, and justice never prevails. The wicked hem in the righteous so that justice is perverted." Habakkuk 1:2-4

Habakkuk, pleading with God in prayer!

Habakkuk was God's prophet from 612-588 B.C. He wrote his book around 600 B.C. Jeremiah was also a prophet then, but he was older and had already been serving God for about 30 years. In 597 B.C. Assyrian rule gave way to Babylonian rule under Nebuchadnezzar 2. King Jehoiachin of Judah, was taken captive to Babylon.

Habakkuk brought the people's needs to God. He also brought the needs of God to the people. Basically, this is what a prophet is, a mediator. Habakkuk's passion was thus two-fold, the honor of God and the sin of the people in breaking covenant with Him.

Habakkuk cries to God for mercy! He now knows that God has said to him: "*I am raising up the Babylonians,* (which is Nebuchadnezzar 2) *that ruthless and impetuous people, who sweep across the whole earth to seize dwelling places not their own,*" Habakkuk 1:6. He pleads with God to shorten the years that God planned to afflict His people! His prayer is: "*O Lord, are You not from everlasting? My God, my Holy One, we will not die. O Lord, You have appointed them to execute judgment; O Rock, You have ordained them to punish,*" Habakkuk 1:12

Habakkuk knew repentance was the critical need for the nation! He knew they did not primarily need a better leader or a better economy! When they had those things, they left God, and grew in their wickedness! God is going to punish them and it has already started! Habakkuk knows God will never restore Israel until she repents, so this is his prayer and it must also be ours today!

Prayer: Lord, hear our prayer from Your prophet, (Habakkuk 3:2). "*Lord, I have heard of Your fame; I stand in awe of your deeds. O Lord. Renew them in our day, in our time make them known; in wrath remember mercy.*" In Jesus' name we pray. Amen.

AUGUST

Wise men worshiping Baby Jesus in the manger

"Today in the town of David a Savior has
been born to you; He is Christ the Lord."
Luke 2:11

August 1

"The whole world will be consumed by the fire of My jealous anger."
"But I will leave within you the meek and the humble, who trust in the name of the Lord." Zephaniah 3:8b &12

Zephaniah, from judgment to joy

From 640 to 615 B.C., Zephaniah and Jeremiah were prophets, servants of God. Zephaniah was a relative of the good kings, Hezekiah and Josiah. Yet, Judah still has a problem! Even though Judah just had two good kings, their daily lives never turned from their wickedness! They never stopped serving other gods. They enjoyed sinning and kept on doing it! What about us? Do we blame our government for the moral lapse in the land? It is we who need to change our ugly living habits!

Note especially, God had Zephaniah preach His judgment on the unrepentant people for their ongoing wickedness. But then, at the end of 3:8, suddenly God's instruction to Zephaniah changes. He now gives great hope to those who were faithfully serving the Lord. God says, *"But I will leave within you the meek and the humble, who trust in the name of the Lord."* The grace of God never stops within a country. God always has His remnant! What hope and joy we have in our God! Even though His wrath is poured out; even though the unrepentant will be judged severely, He will never forsake His own. Zephaniah teaches us to trust in God when the going gets tough and to stay faithful! Zephaniah knows that God has everything under His total sovereign control. So, as believers, we must rejoice in the Lord!

For nine verses Zephaniah tells us why we, as believers, should rejoice when God's judgment is all around us! *"The Lord has taken away your punishment,"* Zephaniah 3:15a. *"The Lord your God is with you, He is mighty to save. He will take great delight in you, He will quiet you with His love, He will rejoice over you with singing,"* Zephaniah 3:17. It is what God continues to do that will cause us to rejoice!

Prayer: Lord, how You love us in Christ! You save us, delight in us, quiet us, and rejoice over us with singing! How blessed we are, all because of Your abundant and never ending grace! We worship You, our tender Shepherd! In Jesus' name we pray. Amen.

August 2

"So the Lord (through Haggai) stirred up the spirit of Zerubbabel son of Shealtiel, governor of Judah, and the spirit of Joshua son of Jehozadak, the high priest, and the spirit of the whole remnant of the people. They came and began to work on the house of the Lord Almighty, their God." Haggai 1:14

Haggai, concerned about God's honor!

In 586 B.C., Jerusalem fell to Persia. Forty-eight years later, in 538, the first Jews returned to Jerusalem. Starting in 520 B.C. until 480, the Prophet Haggai worked alongside Zechariah to encourage the rebuilding of the temple. Haggai's book that bears his name, was written about 520. As the temple was finally rebuilt four years later, in 516 B.C., Haggai concern was the building of the temple.

God moves to convict the Jewish settlers to rebuild the temple. For 20 years they plowed their fields, planted and rebuilt their own houses, but the temple "remains a ruin." God tells them they were "spinning their wheels" because they were not serious about a relationship with God!

"This is what the Almighty says: 'Give careful thought to your ways. You have planted much, but harvested little. You eat, but never have enough. You drink, but never have your fill. You put on clothes, but are not warm. You earn wages, only to put them in a purse with holes in it,'" Haggai 1:5-6.

God tells the people: *"'Go up into the mountains and bring down timber and build the house, so that I may take pleasure in it and be honored,' says the Lord,"* Haggai 1:8. God, "blew away" what they tried to gain, all because they did not honor Him!

God's principles of His honor and His blessing us, is a covenantal issue for all times! We never read something like this in a newspaper! Instead we hear some "scientific explanation" of why conditions are not more favorable. Why do people hate the obvious truth? When we honor God little, He blesses us little!

Prayer: Lord, it is good that You speak clearly to us! We are too much like Israel! Convict us to care more about Your house being built! Lord, may Your name be praised! In Jesus' name we pray. Amen.

August 3

"He showed me Joshua the high priest standing before the angel of the Lord, and Satan standing at his right side to accuse him. The Lord said to Satan, 'The Lord rebuke you, Satan! The Lord, who has chosen Jerusalem, rebuke you! Is not this man a burning stick snatched from the fire?' Now Joshua was dressed in filthy clothes as he stood before the angel. The angel said to those who were standing before him, 'Take off his filthy clothes.' Then he said to Joshua, 'See, I have taken away your sin, and I will put rich garments on you.'" Zechariah 3:1-4

Zechariah, trading old garments for new ones

The Prophet Zechariah lived around 520 B.C. The seventy years of exile are now over. Zechariah has eight visions concerning the present and future restoration of Israel. We have an awesome scene of a court room in Heaven. Priest Joshua in the text, is a picture of God's chosen remnant coming to Himself. It is an incredible real picture of our amazing salvation by grace alone.

In Zechariah's fourth vision, Satan is standing in God's court as the accuser. In Israel, the accuser stands to the right of the accused. Satan is accusing those God wants to forgive and send to Jerusalem. But, this is also all Christians! The thing is: Satan is right! We are all guilty and do not deserve to be forgiven! We have all broken the law of God. Like Israel, we too have seventy years or a lifetime of captive sinning! Joshua was "dressed in filthy clothes as he stood before the angel." "Filthy clothes" means covered with people dung, excrement. This is our "dirty" condition before God who is our holy Judge! People go to court in good clothes, to look good. We go to God a stinking mess, and God forgives us! What grace!

Zechariah's prophetic truth looks at the remnant already saved in the course of history. Zechariah also looks ahead to those God will save! Zechariah sees Jesus rescue the burning sticks from the fire. That's us, saved from Hell, along with the redeemed from every century. We are on our way to Heaven and Satan can't do one thing about it! Satan is standing. Our God is sitting, totally victorious!

Prayer: Lord, what a pathetic mess we are! You literally rescued us from the fire, from Satan and from Your wrath! How can we not live for You? We worship You. In Jesus' name we pray. Amen.

August 4

"'Bring the whole tithe into the storehouse, that there may be food in My house. Test Me in this,' says the Lord Almighty, 'and see if I will not throw open the floodgates of Heaven and pour out so much blessing that you will not have room enough for it.'" Malachi 3:10

Malachi, teaches us to tithe

In the book of Malachi, God points out that Israel, from the beginning, was loved and favored by Him. But now, their sacrifices were *"blemished."* Their priest did not *"honor"* God. The people were not *"thankful."* And the whole nation was *"robbing"* Him! So God issues a most solemn warning. *"'Return to Me and I will return to you,' says the Lord Almighty,"* Malachi 3:7b. We are at the same critical crossroad and this warning is now ours!

God gives Israel and us a command! Start tithing! Give back to God the 10% tithe! Give 10% of what you make or earn, for the building of God's kingdom. Give to the church, the orphan and widow. The poor and needy are the Church's responsibility, not the government's. We, the Church, are not doing our job!

"Bring the <u>whole tithe</u> into the storehouse." Give the full 10%, don't cheat God! And as we shall see, don't cheat ourselves either! For if we faithfully give, God here promises us, *"so much blessing that you will not have room enough for it."* God challenges us directly in this by saying, *"Test Me in this."* This is the only place in the Bible we are told to test God and it is commanded here!

Four promises are given if we are obedient in giving the tithe. 1. God promises <u>abundance</u> in verse 10; *"I will pour out so much blessing."* 2. God promises <u>protection</u> in verse 11; *"I will prevent pests from devouring your crops."* 3. God promises <u>reputation</u> in verse 12; *"Then all the nations will call you blessed."* 4. God also guarantees, the <u>certainty</u> that the blessings will come with these words; *"Test Me in this."* Four promises from God, based on the faithfulness of God, are a guarantee!

Prayer: Lord, we know that You do not need our money but want to test our hearts to see if we love You and trust in Your faithfulness. Lord, give us good hearts, good jobs and good strength so we can give more! Thank You for blessing us! In Jesus' name we pray. Amen.

August 5

"In those days John the Baptist came, preaching in the Desert of Judea and saying, 'Repent for the kingdom of Heaven is near." "And with many other words John exhorted the people and preached the good news to them." Matthew 3:1-2, Luke 3:18

John the Baptist's message: Repent!

John knew many in Israel had a false confidence that they were children of God! John was bold to speak a loving warning concerning their lost condition. He did not want them to perish! His strong message was not condemnation, but to wake them up to their need of a Savior. The people thought that because Abraham was their father, they were automatically Heaven bound. They thought their ethnic heritage guaranteed their salvation! This is still a problem with the Jews to this day!

Do we as Gentiles make this same kind of covenant presumption? Yes, we may think that because we are born in Christian homes, because we go to church and are baptized, we are automatically God's children. When it says in Romans 3:10, *"there is no one righteous, not even one,"* we think this warning is for others!

John's preaching of a baptism for repentance was not new! Formerly it was reserved for non-Israelite people like Tamar, Ruth or Rahab. But now John is preaching this message to covenant Israel, and they are greatly offended! Today, there are many who go regularly to church, yet the deeds of the flesh in Galatians 5:19-21 describe how they live. If we warn them to repent, they too are greatly offended. They will even call us judgmental, arrogant and self-righteous.

Real repentance is not just a sorrow for sin like the world's kind of repentance. Biblical repentance leads to salvation, forgiveness and a turning from sin. Worldly repentance is being sorry for the consequences of a particular sin, for what it does to us. Whereas, Biblical repentance is being sorry for what our sin cost God and what it continues to do to His holy name!

Prayer: Lord, John said *"the time has come"* concerning repentance. You tell us that there are many in Hell today who missed their time to repent. May we listen to Your servant John and repent of our sinful ways. In Jesus' name we pray. Amen.

August 6

"After Jesus was born in Bethlehem in Judea, during the time of King Herod, Magi from the east came to Jerusalem and asked, 'Where is the one who has been born king of the Jews? We saw His star in the east and have come to worship Him.'" Matthew 2:1-2

Magi worship; covenant leaders don't!

Lowly shepherds were the first to receive Jesus and bring honor to Him. After leaving Mary and Joseph, *"they spread the word concerning what had been told them about this child,"* Luke 2:17b. Old Simeon and Anna also received Him and glorified God. So the word was out about the Messiah being born, but only a few cared! The comment in our text, *"after Jesus was born,"* is about two years later! The Magi are Gentiles! They are the scientific wise men of the day. Observing Jesus' star, they go to Herod! They knew, a *"king of the Jews"* was born. In saying, *"Where is the one,"* they were affirming their belief of Jesus' coming!

Herod is *"disturbed."* After all, he is Herod the Great, king of the Jews! Alarmed and afraid, he calls the Jewish church leaders. He *"asks them where the Christ was to be born, 'in Bethlehem of Judea,' they replied,"* Matthew 2:4b-5a. So Herod asks the Magi to tell him where the child is, so he too can worship Him! What a lie! God warns the Magi and they do not tell Herod anything. *"When Herod realized that he had been outwitted by the Magi, he was furious, and he gave orders to kill all the boys in Bethlehem and its vicinity who were <u>two years old</u> and under,"* Matthew 2:16a. *"Two years,"* because the baby Jesus was almost that age by now.

Imagine this, the Magi are magicians and astrologers, completely pagan! They came a huge distance to worship Jesus! The Jewish leaders had event after event pointing to Christ, and did not care about Him from day one! This is exactly why John wrote, *"the world did not recognize Him,"* or *"receive Him,"* John 1:10-11!

Prayer: Lord, You brought the Magi from great distance to worship You! Today, many in the church are a great distance from You! Call sinners Lord, far and near! Give us all the same strong assurance of who Jesus is. And Lord, may many sinners see that You are just a humble prayer away from salvation! In Jesus' name we pray. Amen.

August 7

"When they had gone (the Magi), an angel of the Lord appeared to Joseph in a dream. 'Get up,' he said, 'take the child and his mother and escape to Egypt. Stay there until I tell you, for Herod is going to search for the child to kill Him.'" Matthew 2:13

Herod the Great vs. God the Greatest

At this time there was a Jewish religions system of government and also a Roman civil one. God in His wisdom put the family of Herod in office as the successive heads of the religious Jewish government. There are eight Herods listed in the Bible. In the next four devotions, we will focus on the four main ones: Herod the Great, Herod Antipas, Herod Agrippa 1 and Herod Agrippa 2. We will study them in order.

Herod the Great was actually an Edomite, a descendent of Esau. It was the Roman leaders, Augustus and Antonius Caesar that gave Herod his position. This is all the more reason that the "Herod family," tried to stop the spread of the Gospel! Yet, God in His amazing sovereign control of everything, uses this family of rulers to actually spread the Gospel far and wide. Herod the Great, the first Herod, was the king when Jesus was born. He ruled from 37 B.C. to 4 B.C.

We already know from yesterday's devotion and our text how the Magi came a great distance to worship Jesus. We saw how King Herod the Great did everything he could to kill Jesus in His infancy. But praise be to God, He sent an angel to warn Jesus' father and mother. Herod could not touch Him! God is the Great Protector!

We too live in perilous times! There are still so many enemies of the Cross! In Christ, we are 100% spiritually protected. We are physically protected also, far more than we will ever know. After all, Jesus is our Good Shepherd. There is none better. God still has His protecting angels who save us from disasters of many kinds. Satan still needs permission to afflict us, just like he did with Job and Jesus. The glaring truth is: If God the Greatest is for us, who can be against us?

Prayer: Lord, how You protected Your Son in His hostile environment. How You protect us! *"Surely goodness and mercy shall follow me all the days of my life, and I will dwell in the house of the Lord forever."* We worship You, our Great God. In Jesus' name we pray. Amen.

August 8

"Some Pharisees came to Jesus and said to Him, 'Leave this place and go somewhere else. Herod wants to kill you.' He replied 'Go tell that fox, I will drive out demons today and tomorrow, and on the third day I will reach My goal.'" Luke 13:31-32

Herod Antipas, "that fox"

When Herod the Great died, his will gave the kingdom to his three sons. They were Antipas, Archelaus and Philip. Antipas got Galilee and Perea, which is in the north. Philip received the area east of Galilee. Young Archelaus, got Samaria and Judea and also Idumea. He was so evil that the people pleaded with the Roman government to remove him, and they did. Herod Antipas, also called the tetrarch, was the Jewish ruler from 4 B. C. to 39 A. D.

Herod Antipas put John the Baptist in prison. John rebuked Herod for marring Herodias, for she was his brother's wife. We will discuss Herod's marriage and his killing of John the Baptist, in our study of Herodias in Mark 6:17.

Herod Antipas was ruler over the Jewish religious system. The Pharisees threatened Jesus that He should leave town or their Herod boss would kill Him. Jesus' responds, *"'Go tell that fox..."* Jesus is aware that Herod acts like a fox guarding the hen house! <u>Herod, does not love Jesus' church</u>. <u>He loves his own "ministry!</u>" He loves his own power, his position, his privileges. How may leaders today, are just like Herod? Jesus said, *"I will drive out demons today and tomorrow, and on the third day I will reach My goal."* Herod cannot stop the church of the Lord Jesus Christ! No one can! The gates of Hell cannot prevail against it!

Jesus later stood trial before this same Herod Antipas. *"When Herod saw Jesus, he was greatly pleased, because for a long time he had been wanting to see Him. From what he had heard about Him, he hoped to see Him perform some miracle,"* Luke 23:8. Herod was <u>curious </u>about Jesus, not <u>serious</u>! *"He hoped to see Him perform some miracle."* How many millions today, are like Herod, *"curious,"* not *"serious"* in having a relationship with Jesus!

Prayer: Lord, You know, there is still so much corruption. Lord, purify Your church! You deserve the glory! In Jesus' name we pray. Amen.

August 9

"On the appointed day Herod, wearing his royal robes, sat on his throne and delivered a public address to the people. They shouted, 'This is the voice of a god, not of a man.' Immediately, because Herod did not give praise to God, an angel of the Lord struck him down, and he was eaten by worms and died.'" Acts 12:21-23

Herod Agrippa 1, in power, temporarily

Herod Agrippa was one proud and arrogant man. If he were a bird he would be a peacock. He ruled from 37 A.D. to 44 A.D., just seven years. We first read about him in Acts 12 where, *"King Herod arrested some who belonged to the church, intending to persecute them. He had James, the brother of John, put to death with the sword,"* Acts 12:1b-2. Then when he saw that this persecution and the subsequent killing of James pleased the unbelieving Jews, he seized Peter. He intended to put Peter on trial and kill him, to make a big show, for his own popularity. But then, God miraculously makes a bigger show of delivering Peter from prison. God snatches him from between powerful guards, locked cells and gates. Now, the wicked Herod searches for Peter. Since God hid Peter, there is no way he will be found! So now Herod Agrippa 1, kills the ones who were guarding Peter. Herod was such a ruthless man!

We then learn much from our text about how God in trinity, is the One who is in control! It is true what was said about Jesus, *"the government will be on His shoulders,"* Isaiah 9:6. Wicked rulers like Herod, even to this day, do not have the last word about who is king, president or ruler of any country! Their position in government is given to them by God and He can take it back at any time. All rulers are accountable to God to rule according to His standard of justice!

Prayer: Lord, we read how Herod does everything in his power to bring down Your church and Your believers. Yet he cannot do it. How suddenly Mr. Herod is dead, eaten by worms, on his way to a place where worms will chew on him forever! And then, we read the amazing words, *"But the Word of God continued to increase and spread,"* (Acts 12:24). Isaiah was right! *"The grass withers and the flowers fall, but the word of our God stands forever."* Lord, how eternal is Your power and glory! In Jesus' name we pray. Amen.

August 10

"Then Agrippa said to Paul, 'You almost persuade me to become a Christian.'" Acts 26:28 NKJV

Herod Agrippa 2, *"almost persuaded"*

I recently read, "The Robe." It showed how the crooked, Jewish leaders under "the Herods," helped the Roman government stay in power. These Jewish leaders lived very well, while their own Jewish brothers suffered. It was these powerful high priest and chief men who wanted Paul out of the way. Paul was a threat to their wicked comforts!

In Acts 24:27, Porcius Festus has just come to power, succeeding Felix as the Roman governor. Festus wants to do the powerful, but crooked, Jewish leaders a favor, just so they would submit to his rule. Knowing this, the *"high priest and chief men of the Jews,"* Acts 25:2 NKJV, sent Paul to Festus, charged with disturbing the peace. Festus knew Paul was innocent when he sent Paul to Herod Agrippa 2, the head of the whole Jewish political system. Argippa 2, ruled from 53 to 70 A.D.

Paul spends most of Acts 26, telling Agrippa and Festus how the whole Old Testament pointed to Jesus Christ. King Agrippa clearly heard the Gospel message from the lips of Paul. He knew it was the truth. But because he was the head of the Jewish system, he could not openly accept that Jesus had replaced the Jewish traditions. He would be out of a job if he accepted Paul's Savior. It is in this context that Herod King Agrippa the second said to Paul, *"You almost persuade me to be a Christian."*

Well, what about us? How persuaded are we that Jesus Christ is who Paul said He was? Do we almost believe? Or do we truly believe? King Agrippa would give anything to go back and change his bad decision that cast him into Hell. He refused the One that all the Old Testament law and sacrifices pointed to. Now, we have the New Testament as well as the Old! Agrippa's *"almost persuaded"* decision screams to us that the offer of salvation is for today.

Prayer: Lord, what a sad story. So close, yet so eternally dead. May this be a warning for all those who delay to embrace Christ. May we also see the seriousness of faithfully presenting Christ as Paul did. In Jesus' name we pray. Amen.

August 11

"This is how the birth of Jesus Christ came about: His mother Mary was pledged to be married to Joseph, but before they came together, she was found to be with child through the Holy Spirit. Because Joseph her husband was a righteous man and did not want to expose her to public disgrace, he had in mind to divorce her quietly." Matthew 1:18-19

Joseph, God's chosen father for Jesus

God chose Joseph to be Jesus' earthly father for a very good reason. He was a great father! It is good for us to look at his character and some of the things he did to raise up a Son of God. The fact that Joseph was righteous and merciful is already seen in our text. Joseph's character stands out!

"Joseph her husband was a righteous man." Since God is righteous, He wanted an earthly father who was also righteous! Joseph did the right things. He taught his boy to be a man. He taught him how to pray and how to work. He taught his son the trade of carpentry. He taught his son to be honest and true to his word. He taught him how to love and forgive. Most of this Joseph taught by example! Jesus did not hear mommy and daddy arguing. In fact, <u>where in the Bible did Joseph even speak one word</u>? <u>He led by righteous example</u>!

Joseph, *"did not want to expose her to public disgrace."* He was merciful and gracious! What would we say if we were presented with a pregnant bride who said she was a virgin? Joseph's first thoughts were he did not want to disgrace her. Here is a good example of how God's law must guide a home, but His grace must govern it also! Law without grace creates rebellion. Grace without law is chaos. Joseph was upright, gentle and hard working too. We need fathers like this!

Joseph *"did what the angel of the Lord had commanded him,"* Matthew 1:24b. Joseph had a faithful character. When God or an angel spoke, Joseph listened and obeyed immediately, first time fast! He moved when God told him to. He endured hardship and disappointment without complaining, without a bitter attitude! That's character!

Prayer: Lord, what a great benefit to see who You chose to be Your Son's earthly father. Move us to follow his righteous, merciful and faithful leadership example. In Jesus' name we pray. Amen.

August 12

"As soon as Jesus was baptized, He went up out of the water. At that moment Heaven was opened, and He saw the Spirit of God descending like a dove and lighting on Him. And a voice from Heaven said, 'This is My Son, whom I love; with Him I am well pleased.'" Matthew 3:16-17

Jesus' baptism and ours

We know baptism is important because it is one of just two sacraments that God in His wisdom gave to us. But why was Jesus Himself baptized? What is the real value of our baptism?

Jesus gave the reason He was baptized. *"It is proper to do this to fulfill all righteousness,"* Matthew 3:15b. It was the will of God for Jesus to be baptized. Jesus had to be like us in every way, except sin. He who is fully righteous, humbled Himself to be baptized. Interestingly, when John baptized someone, that person would confess his sins. But *"as soon as Jesus was baptized,"* He immediately came out of the water. He had nothing to confess! Jesus completely kept the old covenant of works for us to be perfect before God.

Baptism is not a religious ritual. Like circumcision before it, it is a sign of the covenant. The real question is: What is the value of having the sign of the covenant? We are marked by God! We have His Spirit. We have His seal of approval and ownership. We have His promises.

Think about the questions Paul asked the Romans! *"What advantage, then, is there in being a Jew, or what value is there in circumcision? Much in every way! First of all, they have been entrusted with the very words of God,"* Romans 3:1-2. Just think, we have a far more complete Bible, a loving letter from God Himself. We no longer see Christ as a shadow like the Jews did. We can see Him clearly and all He has done and recorded. We have the truth to guide us to Christ for forgiveness and for direction for all of life. The washing with water is a visible sign to always remind us that Christ alone washes us completely from our sin.

Prayer: Lord, we thank You for baptism and for the covenant privileges we have. Thank You for Jesus, for Your Word and Spirit! You not only dwell with us, but in us. Lord, help us to remember baptism, Your sign that points to Your complete ownership! May we live like we are Your child! In Jesus' name we pray. Amen.

August 13

"Therefore, if you are offering your gift at the altar and there remember that your brother has something against you, leave your gift there in front of the altar. First go and be reconciled to your brother; then come and offer your gift." Matthew 5:23-24

A brother, *"has something against you"*

We are talking to our friends when another person walks by and she gives us "the look" that says, "I don't like you!" We say in a disgusted voice, "I don't know what I ever did to her, but she sure has some issue with me!" If the offended is one of us, then Jesus is talking to us to do what we can to mend our relationships!

The first word of the text *"therefore,"* connects two thoughts. First, Jesus tells us, *"I tell you that anyone who is angry with his brother will be subject to judgment,"* Matthew 5:22a. This is a major point of our growing up as Christians! We are talking about our sanctification process. We are talking about a change Jesus demands that we make in our spiritual journey. We must put off the old habits, especially our anger and bitterness. This begins the process of repairing relationships.

Secondly, forgiveness must <u>replace</u> our anger that is not *"righteous,"* in James 1:20 Forgiveness must also replace our bitterness that is *"of the devil,"* in James 3:15b. Both need to be confessed to God and replaced! In our text, Jesus demands we model forgiveness! The number one lasting beauty treatment ever, for our spiritual and physical life is forgiveness! This means we give someone what they need, not what they deserve. No one ever deserves forgiveness. The forgiveness we must give others must exactly model the forgiveness that Jesus gives to us. He forgives all our sins! Jesus even forgave us when we were giving Him that hateful "look." Now we must forgive, in the same way!

Jesus here connects forgiving a "brother" to offering our tithe gift. Like the tithe, forgiveness is a test of our faith. Our heart has passed the tithe test when we are on our way to the altar with the gift! Now, we must make sure there is nothing in our heart against another brother!

Prayer: Lord, You here teach us one of life's greatest lessons. May we hear it and do it, knowing You are commanding us to forgive others. In Jesus' name we pray. Amen.

August 14

"O you of little faith." Matthew 6:30b

The disciples' *"little faith"*

Four times in Matthew, Jesus said the words, *"O you of little faith."* Why? What exactly is this *"little faith"* Jesus is referring to? The first time Jesus said it, the disciples were worried about having enough money for food and clothing. Their problem and ours is that we quickly rely on our money rather than God. We cannot serve two masters. So Jesus gives us an illustration to convince us that we need to trust in God. *"Now if God so clothes the grass of the field, which today is, and tomorrow is thrown into the oven, will He not much more clothe you, O you of little faith?"* Matthew 6:30 NKJV. Jesus has complete control over the needs of His children!

The second time Jesus said *"O you of little faith,"* the disciples were fearful of a storm while on the sea. *"But He said to them, 'Why are you fearful, O you of little faith?' Then He arose and rebuked the winds and the sea. And there was a great calm,"* Matthew 8:26 NKJV. Jesus has absolute authority over the weather!

The third time Jesus said *"O you of little faith,"* the disciples were at sea and they were afraid thinking they saw a ghost or spirit walking on the water. But it was Jesus. *"When he (Peter) saw that the wind was boisterous, he was afraid; and beginning to sink he cried out, saying, 'Lord save me!' And immediately Jesus stretched out His hand and caught him and said to him, 'O you of little faith, why did you doubt?"* Matthew 14:31. Here Jesus calls Peter's fear of the spirits, *"little faith."* Jesus' Spirit is far stronger than the evil spirit world!

The fourth time Jesus said, *"O you of little faith,"* was because the disciples acted like the self-righteous and wicked Pharisees. *"O you of little faith, why do you reason among yourselves because you have brought no bread?"* Matthew 16:8b NKJV. Jesus wanted His disciples to trust Him and rely on Him for everything! Jesus owns the world's largest storehouse!

Prayer: Dear Father, we can see that fear of all kinds is "little faith." Even Adam did not fear until he sinned against You. Lord help us to trust in You more and more! For You have forgiven our past. You provide for us in the present. Our future is fully secured for us by Your power and provision. Thank You Lord! In Jesus' name we pray. Amen.

August 15

"The centurion replied, 'Lord, I do not deserve to have you come under my roof. But just say the word, and my servant will be healed. For I myself am a man under authority, with soldiers under me. I tell this one, "Go," and he goes; and that one, "Come," and he comes. I say to my servant, "Do this," and he does it.'" Matthew 8:8-9

The Centurion has a great faith

A centurion was a Roman officer who had 100 soldiers under him. A Roman soldier is a Gentile, normally an enemy of the church. You may remember that when Jesus was presented in the temple by His parents, the devout Simeon prophesied that Jesus would be, *"a light for revelation to the Gentiles,"* Luke 2:32a. The centurion here is one of the first Gentile believers. This centurion is perhaps the only example of a master who is concerned about his worker, pointing to the Greater Jesus who as Master is very concerned about those who serve Him!

Notice how and why Jesus comments on the extraordinary faith of the centurion! *"When Jesus heard this* (the way the request came for the healing of the centurion's servant), *He was astonished and said to those following Him, 'I tell you the truth, I have not found anyone in Israel with such great faith,"* Matthew 8:10. The Jews thought the size of their faith was superior to anyone else's! A Gentile was considered a dog, not able to have or even understand what faith was about! Do we sometimes look at others that way? I know that I have!

Jesus' pattern of teaching led up to this healing of the centurion's servant! In Matthew 7, Jesus said not to judge others but consider our own spiritual walk. Then He told us to ask, seek and knock for a relationship with Him! He told us the road was wide that led to destruction. He said we could tell a tree by its fruit and that some people were wise builders and others were foolish! These statements all fit the unbelieving Jews and showed the great faith of the centurion.

Prayer: Lord, we are so guilty. Our judgmental attitude only underlines our lack of faith! We have not been all that fruitful for You, and our pride has led to much foolishness! Lord, increase our faith personally and may we have a burden for the physical and spiritual needs of others! In Jesus' name we pray. Amen.

August 16

"As Jesus went on from there, He saw a man named Matthew sitting at the tax collector's booth. 'Follow Me,' He told him, and Matthew got up and followed Him." Matthew 9:9

Matthew, a cheater Jesus chose!

Matthew was a Jew who collected taxes for the Roman government. Such a person is called a publican. His Jewish countrymen hated him and considered him an apostate Jew! Normally the ruling Sanhedrin would excommunicate a publican for his role in collecting extra money from the people. Keep in mind, the ruling Jewish Sanhedrin wanted the people's money and goods for themselves.

Jesus chose Matthew to be one of His twelve disciples to show the depths of His grace. Jesus likely gave Matthew his name which means, "the gift of God." Matthew was called by the name of Levi in Mark and Luke. Matthew was a pastor type who reached out to other sinners with the Gospel message that Jesus saves sinners. Matthew knew what it meant for a stealing and cheating man to be forgiven!

Matthew was not praying when Jesus found him. Matthew was busy sinning in his *"tax collector's booth."* He was cheating people. Jesus comes and says, *"Follow Me."* But then, Jesus does the same for us! He convicts us by His Spirit to stop sinning and start following His way of living. It is not we who initiate the desire to follow Him, but He who makes us willing to follow! We now see the response of Matthew's new life.

Immediately, in this next verse, Matthew reaches out to others! "*While Jesus was having dinner at Matthew's house, many tax collectors and 'sinners' came and ate with Him and His disciples.*" Matthew also wrote a book to convince the Jews that Jesus was the Christ, the promised Messiah. What is our response to Jesus? Do we invite others into our homes. Do we make an honest effort to tell others about the Christ who forgives great sinners like us? See more on Matthew the pastor tomorrow.

Prayer: Lord, You begin Matthew 9 healing a paralytic. You move to calling Matthew, another kind of paralytic to be Your disciple. Then You use Matthew to call out to paralytics like us! Lord, we thank You for making us willing and able to follow You when we can't move a muscle towards You! In Jesus' name we pray. Amen.

August 17

*"'Why does your Teacher eat with tax collectors and 'sinners'?' On
hearing this, Jesus said, 'It is not the healthy who need a doctor, but the
sick. But go and learn what this means: "I desire mercy, not sacrifice."
For I have not come to call the righteous, but sinners.'"*
Matthew 9:11b-13

Sinners, Jesus ate with them!

Your pastor was involved in the conversion of the biggest cheat in the
city! Now this man who cheated many, throws a big dinner party. He
invites other cheaters that he knows. Many male and female prostitutes,
pedophiles, thieves, and blackmailers also come. Your pastor goes too,
and enjoys their company! The big dinner is next to city hall, where truth
be known, most got their positions by bribery and fraud. These "city
fathers" confront your pastor and want to arrest him. However, the same
people your pastor is eating with helped get these "city fathers" into
office. This is basically what is happening in our text!

Contrast how the tax collectors and sinners were conscious of their
spiritual poverty. The Pharisees were proud of their religious upbringing.
The sinners humbly asked Jesus for mercy. The leaders proudly thought
they had no sin problem. The sinners loved Jesus' company, thankful to
learn from Him. The church leaders hated Jesus, jealous of how the
people loved Him. The sinners praised and worshiped Jesus; the
Pharisees wanted to kill Him.

Matthew knew what the grace of the Lord Jesus Christ could do to
a person. He wanted others to experience that freedom! Matthew had
the means and the desire to present Christ to sick people, and he does
it with compassion, not with a self-righteous attitude. Matthew knew by
experience what we sinners must experience from Jesus healing us.

Man's religion says, "I obey, therefore I am accepted." God's Gospel
says, "I'm accepted, therefore I obey." Jesus said, *"I desire mercy, not
sacrifice"*! We can't work for our salvation, but once saved, like Matthew
and a good pastor, we must work for the salvation of others!

Prayer: Lord, help us to extend Your mercy to many who are in dire
need of Your healing touch for their souls! It is the least we can do for
You, our Savior who mercifully healed us! In Jesus' name we pray. Amen.

August 18

"Jesus went through all the towns and villages, teaching in their synagogues, preaching the Good News of the kingdom and healing every disease and sickness. When He saw the crowds, He had compassion on them, because they were harassed and helpless, like sheep without a shepherd. Then He said to His disciples, 'The harvest is plentiful but the workers are few.'" Matthew 9:35-37

Jesus' teaching example

"Jesus went." The first two words already convict us. A farmer knows the harvest in the field does not just show up in the grain bin. We have to labor and go out into the fields! In evangelism, we are guilty of waiting for the harvest to come to us. We hang a sign on the church and then think we've done our evangelism duty! It will not happen that way!

A big problem is: We are too comfortable to "do evangelism." Jesus became uncomfortable just coming to this world. He was born in a dirty stable. He went into the dirty streets. He touched dirty people with filthy diseases. He cleansed them from their dirty sins. The spotless Lamb of God got dirty doing the work of evangelism! We often say we don't know how to do evangelism. It seems to be more, we want to stay "clean" and we don't want to "work."

"He had compassion on them." What is our compassion spent on? Let's be honest! Do we really want lost souls to be reconciled to God? What is our passion in life? If we are honest, it is our idols that keep us from doing the work of evangelism and discipleship! Most people sitting in good churches have the knowledge, but they lack the desire.

"They were harassed and helpless." People are still being bombarded by that which is not true. The world will not teach truth! They do not know truth! God's Son, Spirit and Word is what is true and they do not have it. Who will go and teach the *"harassed and helpless"* the truth? The harvest is out there! May we not wait until we are qualified to go. Go and God will qualify us! *"The harvest is plentiful but the workers are few"*! God loves good workers!

Prayer: Dear Heavenly Father, Jesus said, *"Ask the Lord of the harvest, therefore, to send out workers into His harvest field."* Lord, send us! We don't want the harvest to spoil. In Jesus' name we pray. Amen.

August 19

"Come to Me all you who are weary and burdened and I will give you rest. Take my yoke upon you and learn from Me."
Matthew 11:28-29a

Jesus' "yoke," His Lordship of us

Jesus here directs His hearers how He is Lord of all of life. Christ was aware that the Jews considered the Torah or the Law of God, a "yoke" that God put on them. Jesus knew His followers still needed to keep the law as a guide for living. He also knew the people needed to have a new heart or mind. No one, not one single person, can possibly serve Christ until they are intellectually changed. And who of us can claim to have a new mind, the mind of Christ, if we are unwilling to summit to the authority of Jesus as Lord?

The Christian looks to Jesus as His Lord, to instruct him and to command him. Jesus is our teacher about God the Father, man, duty, life, death, truth, righteousness, the Word of God, even tradition or cultural practices. Any part of the Christian faith or life that Jesus Christ has taught on is part of the "yoke" to which we must submit to. No Christian is at liberty to disagree with Jesus!

Jesus as Lord means that God and the Bible are not interested in doctrine without practice! Truth in the Bible is always something to be known, something to be done! With that in mind, the doctrine that Jesus Christ is Lord has practical implications for how we live today! Notice here just four implications of the Lordship of Jesus.

First, knowing that Jesus is Lord has implications for our minds. Our minds control our actions! As we think, so we are! Second, Jesus is the Lord of our moral life. How we behave matters! Third, Jesus is Lord of our daily work. We must follow His example of working! Work is both service and ministry. We give ourselves in the service of God and man, under the Lordship of Christ! Fourth, Jesus is Lord of the church! We don't do "church" our way. We do it His way. It is His church.

Prayer: Lord, You are both our Savior and Lord. We belong to You. We were purchased by You, for You. We don't make You Lord. You are Lord! Direct us for Your glory. In Jesus, our Lord and Savior's name we pray. Amen.

August 20

"A bruised reed He will not break, and a smoldering wick He will not snuff out." Matthew 12:20a

Christ shows us complete perseverance

A *"reed"* in the swamp sways in just a little wind. *"Bruised,"* it very quickly breaks. *"A smoldering wick,"* is barely burning. It is just a tiny spark! Both of these examples are a symbol of extreme weakness, *"a bruised reed,"* and *"a smoldering wick,"* are pictures of us as fragile and weak believers. It fits us! We have a wandering and weak faith. If it were not for the love, the gentleness, the protection, and the perseverance of the Father, Son and Spirit, our spiritual life would be snuffed out in a moment! We could not possibly make it to Heaven.

In our text, Jesus gives us a most beautiful promise, true for every single believer! And this promise that He will not break a *"bruised reed"* is reliable because it is carried out by the powerful attributes of God. Yes, by the grace of God we will arrive at that distant shore!

There is a doctrine called, "The perseverance of the saints." It is a true doctrine, but it seems to be misnamed. It would be more accurately called, "The perseverance of Christ in a believer's life." Christ causes our perseverance to happen! *"He is able to save completely those who come to God through Him, because He <u>always lives</u> to intercede for them,"* Hebrews 7:25. Isn't that verse beautiful? We see why our weak faith doesn't break or die! Christ keeps it alive, and He promises always to keep it alive! We have the world's best Mediator!

Think too of when Jesus prayed for Peter in Luke 22:32a, that his *"faith would not fail."* Jesus told Peter there was a reason that his faith did not completely fail. *"Simon, Simon* (put your name here), *Satan has asked to sift you as wheat. But <u>I have prayed for you</u>, Simon, <u>that your faith may not fail</u>,"* Luke 22:31-32a. That prayer is exactly why our faith like a bruised reed does not fail! How can we ever fall short of Heaven if Jesus is praying for us? There is a house in Heaven reserved for us!

Prayer: Lord, Your loving eye watches out for us weak lambs! May the tender and persevering love that You have for us, move us to love You more and more! In Christ's name we pray. Amen.

August 21

"Then Peter came to Jesus and asked, 'Lord, how many times shall I forgive my brother when he sins against me? Up to seven times?' Jesus answered, 'I tell you, not seven times but seventy-seven times.'"
Matthew 18:21-22

Peter asks a big question on forgiveness

Peter, the Type A, the hard-charging man, asks Jesus one of the most important questions in the Bible! Peter had just heard Jesus discuss the six verses in Matthew 18:15-20. He had serious personal problems in his relationships. Jesus knew that the great amounts of anger and bitterness in Peter's relationships had to be put-off. He knew that forgiveness was the only replacement that had to be put-on to complete the process in overcoming these great sins.

Peter was trying to figure this all out, as we must also! Peter remembered that Jesus had already taught them on forgiveness in the Lord's prayer. There, we believers petition God to forgive us because we have already forgiven others who sinned against us! Then after the Lord's prayer, Jesus lovingly warned His disciples, *"For if you forgive men when they sin against you, your Heavenly Father will also forgive you. But if you do not forgive men their sins, your Father will not forgive your sins,"* Matthew 6:14-15.

Peter thought he was being generous when he asked Jesus if seven times was sufficient to forgive another person who has hurt us. And Peter was thinking of seven times in a lifetime! Jesus totally shocks Peter by telling him we must forgive 77 times, or in the KJV, 70 times 7, which is 490 times a day. Jesus did not teach the reason for this here but in Ephesians 4:32 the Bible is clear. *"Be kind and compassionate to one another, forgiving each other, just as in Christ God forgave you."*

Jesus knew Peter did not yet completely understand the importance of forgiveness so He told Peter a story. This will be tomorrow's lesson as we learn that our forgiveness must be an act of grace.

Prayer: Lord, how completely and beautifully You teach us about the importance of forgiveness in all of our relationships. Help us to understand this important act of sacrificial love and forgive others. In His name we pray. Amen.

"'You wicked servant,' he said, 'I canceled all that debt of yours because you begged me to. Shouldn't you have had mercy on your fellow servant just as I had on you?' In anger his master turned him over to the jailers to be tortured, until he should pay back all that he owed. This is how My Heavenly Father will treat each of you unless you forgive your brother from your heart." Matthew 18:32b-35

The unmerciful servant won't forgive

What if Jesus told us we were wicked for not forgiving someone? Well, the *"king"* in the parable represents Jesus. The *"servant,"* who was forgiven a debt so big that he could never pay it, is like us Christians. The *"fellow servant"* who owed the unmerciful servant some money is our Christian brother or sister. *"The jailers"* are Satan and his demon helpers.

The unmerciful servant then is us, who have been forgiven much, even all our sins. Now we refuse to show mercy in various ways in our everyday living. Our anger and bitter thoughts, words and actions are unmerciful to others. We unmercifully hang on to grudges. We are "choking" others as the unmerciful servant does in the parable. We say we can't (won't is the truth) forgive this or that person for what they have done to us! We argue that they do not deserve our forgiveness. Correct, they don't! But mercy is the giving of our forgiveness to those who don't deserve it! Jesus knows, no one ever deserves mercy, nor did we when He forgave us our big debt of sin!

What did the master (Jesus) do to the unmerciful servant? *"His master turned him over to the jailers to be tortured, until he should pay back all that he owed."* Jesus gives the stingy and unmerciful Christian to Satan for some pain and difficult times. Yes, Jesus will allow the physical body of any hard-hearted believer feel pain to turn them back to Himself. The moral of the story is: <u>No</u> mercy, <u>know</u> pain. It is the wisdom of God to use pain to train our brain, to love again!

Prayer: Lord, in love You tell us some hard things. You demand that our hearts are clean, which You inspect carefully! You don't want to see hardness in our hearts, but instead see mercy for others who need it. Lord, help us to be constantly forgiving just as You are constantly forgiving us. In Jesus' name we pray. Amen.

August 23

"Now a man came to Jesus and asked, 'Teacher, what good thing must I do to get eternal life?'" Matthew 19:16

The young ruler and his deceptive riches

This man had it all according the world's way of thinking. He had youth, vitality, wealth, power, and position! He had all the latest gadgets! He even had knowledge about Jesus in his head. He addresses Jesus as *"Teacher"* here in the NIV; *"Good Teacher"* in the NKJV; and *"Good Master"* in the KJV. He goes to the right person, to the only One who can give eternal life! So, he asks the right questions, to the right person, for the right reasons, *"to get eternal life"*! Intellectually, he was right where he needed to be! But Jesus is going to show him and us that knowing about God is not enough!

Jesus exposes the young man's religion as being of the head but not of the heart! Jesus lays bare the self-righteous heart of this young man when he asks Jesus about doing some *"good thing,"* to enter Heaven. Jesus points out *"there is only One who is good,"* Matthew 19:17b, pointing to His own perfect life as the only life that God accepts as *"good."* By doing so, <u>Jesus was telling the young man that he had to be perfect, not just good, to enter Heaven</u>. And that perfection was the life of Christ Himself. So, even though the man knew Jesus was good, he still thought his own goodness might get him to Heaven!

To test the man's *idea of "good,"* Jesus asks a simple question that shows the mans lack of love for God in commandments 1-4, and his lack of love for others in commands 5-10. So Jesus asks him, *"If you want to be perfect, go, sell your possessions and give to the poor, and you will have treasure in Heaven. Then come, follow Me,"* Matthew 19:21. The young man was not willing! It turns out that this young man loved his possessions the most, not God, not others, but self! We do not need to have many possessions to have this idol problem! Poor people also lie, cheat, and steal to get more!

Prayer: Lord, You expose our hearts. We claim to love You with our mouths, but our life proves that we have idols that we love more. Lord, make us willing to love You and others for Your glory and for our eternal good! In Christ's name we pray. Amen.

August 24

"Peter answered Him, 'We have left everything to follow You! What then will there be for us?' Jesus said to them, 'I tell you the truth, at the renewal of all things, when the Son of Man sits on His glorious throne, you who have followed Me will also sit on twelve thrones, judging the twelve tribes of Israel. And everyone who has left houses or brothers or sisters or father or mother or children or fields for My sake will receive a hundred times as much and will inherit eternal life.'" Matthew 19:27-29

Twelve disciples, and you, are rewarded

Jesus knew serving God the Father was a sacrificial task! To encourage His disciples, He tells them that they will be rewarded for their difficult service. This is for us too! Many do not believe in rewards in the hereafter. They say, "I would be happy to be a doorkeeper in Heaven." True, but what about Jesus' words in our text? He promised rewards and eternal life, to give us hope and to spur us on to greater devotion to Him.

As Christian parents we will be greatly rewarded for our sacrifice, now and in eternity! God notices as we work and give of ourselves, our time and our precious resources! The Living Bible says it so well, *"For God is not unfair. How can He forget your hard work for Him, or forget the way you used to show your love for Him – and still do – by helping His children,"* Hebrews 6:10. God is by far, the most just employer we will ever work for!

"Everyone who has left houses or brothers or sisters or father or mother or children or fields for My sake will receive a hundred times as much and will inherit eternal life." The Bible ends with the following promise. The Lord Jesus said, *"Behold, I am coming soon! My reward is with Me, and I will give to everyone according to what he has done,"* Revelation 22:12.

"Rejoice and be glad, because great is your reward in Heaven," Matthew 5:12a. The older I get, the more I see, we cannot out give God in this life! He knows our heart, our sacrifice, our pain, and the ridicule we put up with in serving Him. He will never forget any of His precious children!

Prayer: Lord, You tell us, *"If anyone gives even a cup of cold water... he will certainly not lose his reward,"* (Matthew 10:4). Lord, help us to be sacrificial in our life. You are awesome! In Jesus' name we pray. Amen.

August 25

"You know that the rulers of the Gentiles lord it over them, and their high officials exercise authority over them. Not so with you. Instead, whoever wants to become great among you must be your servant."
Matthew 20:25b-26

"Servants must lead My church," says Jesus!

Servants are the most important character in the Bible. Jesus even washed His disciples feet to make the point even clearer. So often we have a problem in leadership. How wrong it is when a church leader thinks that he is the boss, the head of his church! That is trying to steal the headship of the Church from our Lord Jesus Christ! That, dear friends, is clericalism, the domination of the clergy to keep the laity in submission. Jesus never squashed His disciples like a bug. He allowed and encouraged His disciples to take responsibility in the work of the church!

Clericalism in the protestant church is as bad as it is with the pope! Jesus pointed out that the secular community lords it over one another also. They manipulate people. They push people around. They boss one another. Don't do that! Jesus emphasized, *"Not so with you."* This is My Church and I want servant leaders. Our text is a Biblical mandate for all of us in the church to be like Jesus, serve others. That can never happen until we first accept that Jesus is the Lord of the Church! Only then will the Church be delivered from the powerful, clerical union that is doing so much to destroy the Church!

In Matthew 23, Jesus said the Pharisees loved it when the people gave them big titles and bowed down to them. But <u>not you</u> Jesus said! You are all brothers and sisters. His Church must look to Him and depend on Him. Clericalism does far more to stop the work of evangelism, than advance it! Jesus never required an extensive education for His uneducated disciples? Why do we think that the more education a person has the better he or she is at soul winning. Was that ever true in the Bible? Servant leaders by their example, must train others to be servants.

Prayer: Lord, You said, *"The harvest is plentiful but <u>the workers</u> are few. Ask the Lord of the harvest, therefore to send out <u>workers</u> into His harvest field."* Lord forgive us for thinking we need more supervisors instead of more workers. May we serve You. In Jesus' name we pray. Amen.

August 26

"Jesus entered the temple area and drove out all who were buying and selling there. He overturned the tables of the money changers and the benches of those selling doves. 'It is written,' He said to them. 'My house will be called a house of prayer, but you are making it a "den of robbers."'" Matthew 21:12-13

Money changers, meet the Reformer

Jesus the Judge comes into town on a white donkey. In that day judges rode white donkeys. The people are shouting, *"Hosanna in the highest!"* His Highness fittingly goes straight to the temple, for He presides over His Church! He is not impressed! He should have seen worshipers, souls that love Him, but instead He saw at a lot of busy activities!

By this time, Jesus was recognized as a great Prophet. The people now need to realize that Jesus is also their Priest. And what are priests supposed to do? They are to pray and provide for the people to have their sins forgiven. Then they can stand before God clean! But this was not happening in the temple area. Where are the "spiritual activities"? Where are the people confessing their sins? Where are the priest praying and praising God? The primary purpose of the temple was gone and Jesus came to reform it!

"The blind and the lame came to Him at the temple," Matthew 21:14. Just one verse! How it accuses us! Which one are we in the temple? Are we the *"money changers"* or the *"blind and the lame?"* Take a test.

Do we take our work or play into church with us? Little boy or girl, are you thinking of who you are going to play with tomorrow? Student, are you thinking of tomorrow's test or what you are going to wear to school? Mom, are you making preparations for dinner? Dad, are you thinking of tomorrow's work? All are good things, but not in church! The people were selling doves in the temple; we are trying to get our "ducks" in a row during church! Jesus turns over our "duck" table also. Jesus says, "Not here, this is a place for prayer and worship of Me!"

Prayer: Lord, we are so in love with the world that we take it into church with us. Lord, reform our worship of You. Drive out our personal ambitions. Make us say, *"Hosanna in the Highest"* along with the other blind and lame who came to worship! In Jesus' name we pray. Amen.

August 27

"Then one of them, a lawyer, asked Him a question, testing Him, and saying, 'Teacher, which is the great commandment in the law?'"
Matthew 22:35-36 NKJV

Mr. Lawyer questions Jesus, and us

God shows us many pictures in the Bible, to help us remember what is being taught. In the verses before us, a hotshot lawyer tried to trick Jesus with a loaded question! This lawyer tried to get Jesus to say that one commandment was more important than the other. Then they could say that Jesus had no respect for the law of God. No doubt, all of the Ten Commandments are to love God. But Jesus broke down the Ten Commandments to two. It is to love God in commands 1 to 4 and to love others in commands 5 to 10. There is no command to love self! We are to love others as ourselves! We already know how to love self!

The lawyer had a problem. Jesus knew man's basic problem, since the fall in the Garden of Eden, was to love self more than God or others. Jesus knows how selfish this lawyer and we are. When I teach Jesus' point here, I put a "J" on the board for loving Jesus, commands 1 to 4. Then I put an "O "on the board for loving others in commands 5 to 10. Last, I put a "Y" on the board for you. J.O.Y. spells joy. When we put the "Y" first, (selfishness), we lose our JOY. It really is this simple!

I read a story about a minister of the Gospel who became a doctor. He said he did so because people will pay more to care for their body than they will pay to care for their souls. Then this same man became a lawyer. He did so because he learned that people will pay more money to get their own selfish way than they will pay to take care of their body.

Jesus' point is: We are born selfish, totally depraved! We do not need to love self more! That's what our problem is! And this is the test of every life! Will we, who are born a child of Adam, seek a relationship with God through Jesus, and love God and others more than our selfish self? We will have joy in eternity if we have passed that one test!

Prayer: Lord, we can see that tricky Mr. Lawyer asks a very good question. We must admit that our natural desire as sinners is to do the opposite of what is holy and pleasing to You. Lord, move us away from self to You and into the lives of others. In Jesus' name we pray. Amen.

August 28

"The Kingdom of Heaven will be like ten virgins who took their lamps and went out to meet the bridegroom." Matthew 25:1b

The ten virgins, "Which one am I?"

Ten virgins teach us urgency concerning the kingdom of God in Matthew 25:1-13. Jesus is speaking a solemn warning, two days before His death. He tells a parable, a story the people could understand. Weddings were in the evening. The bride and her female friends would be assembled in the wedding house. The groom and his friends went to the "bride house" when they were ready. The bride and her friends waited to see the lights of the groom's party approaching. Then they lit their lamps and went out to meet them. Together they would enter the marriage hall and then the doors were locked.

Five of the ten virgins had a lamp (or soul), but did not have the oil (the spirit or presence of God). So they blindly went out into the night to try to find the necessary oil to light their lamps. But the marriage feast already started and the house was locked when they finally tried to get in. No one would open the door. They missed the celebration!

The wedding feast is a picture of Jesus' Second Coming. The five wise virgins are true believers. The five foolish ones are those who know about Jesus, but have no true relationship with Him. The question is: How is it that someone knows about Jesus, but is not ready for Heaven? After all, the five foolish ones expected to go to Heaven! But they were so busy about the cares and snares of this world that they took no time to develop a relationship with the Lord Jesus Christ. They knew about their sins, but did not ask for forgiveness or turn from them.

The visible church today still has the foolish and the wise sitting side by side. Which camp are we in? Are we serious, or are we cold to the Lord and His eternal kingdom? <u>We may think we know Jesus, but does Jesus know us</u>? The parable ends with Jesus words to the foolish five: "*I tell you the truth, I don't know you,*" Matthew 25:12b.

Prayer: Lord, David wisely prayed, *"search me and know me"*! Lord move us to the Cross. If we are unwilling to kneel there, make us willing! Give us Your grace and mercy that we need, and not Your wrath that we deserve. Make us fit for Heaven! In Jesus' name we pray. Amen.

August 29

"I was afraid and went out and hid Your talent in the ground..." "His Master replied, 'You wicked and lazy servant!...'" 'Throw that worthless servant outside, into the darkness, where there will be weeping and gnashing of teeth." Matthew 25:25-26a & 30

Three servants, Heaven and Hell

We have great joy and great sadness before us in the Parable of the Talents. Jesus adds to what He taught in the Parable of the Ten Virgins, from our lesson yesterday. Jesus now shows us what kind of person goes to Heaven and what kind of person enters hell.

There are three servants. The servants are us! Their master gives talents to the three, because he is going on a *"journey."* The Master is Jesus who left for Heaven. The first servant is given 5 talents and gains 5 more by the time the Master returns. The second servant is given 2 and gains 2 more. Jesus said to them on His return, *"Well done, good and faithful servant! You have been faithful with a few things; I will put you in charge of many things. Come and share your Master's happiness!"* Matthew 25:23b. We want to hear these words when our Savior meets us!

"Faithful," is the issue! Their faithfulness did not save them, but it was proof that they were saved! Their hearts were filled with love for the Master and for His kingdom! Jesus said, *"I will put you in charge of many things."* There are rewards in Heaven. *"Share your Master's happiness!"* There is great joy in Heaven!

The third servant was given one talent. He, *"dug a hole in the ground and hid his Master's money,"* Matthew 25:18b. When the Master returned, the servant told Him, *"I was afraid and went out and hid your talent in the ground."* Jesus' responds, "You wicked, lazy *servant!"* Why? *"Afraid"* is the opposite of trust and obey! *"Afraid"* is so paranoid about what happened in the past, so worried about what could happen in the future, that <u>nothing is happening in the present!</u> Jesus sent this person *"outside, into the darkness,"* to hell itself.

Prayer: Lord, what a horrible test The Judgment is if we do not serve You in this life. What a blessed thing it is when we do love and serve You. Lord, fill us with Your Spirit more and more. Use us for Your glory! In Jesus' name we pray. Amen.

August 30

"Now when evening had come, He sat down with the twelve. Now as they were eating, He said, 'Assuredly, I say to you, one of you will betray Me.' And they were exceedingly sorrowful, and each of them began to say to Him, 'Lord, is it I?'" Matthew 26:20-22 NKJV

Judas, the betrayer

We are either going through a hard trial or we will be. We have been betrayed, deceived and cheated. We cry out to God, "Why Lord? Why am I going through so much suffering? Life was going so well until this 'someone' (like Judas) came into my life! I have been betrayed by the very one who was supposed to love me! Worse yet, I was made to look like I am the one who was guilty! Why did You, my omnipotent God, allow these things to happen?"

Look to our text, see how our perfect Savior was treated! Jesus announced that one of the twelve would betray Him. He expected to be betrayed! Think of how different our attitude would be if we expected it, rather than thinking no one will ever betray us! Also, the other disciples did not know who His betrayer was! They all said, "*Is it I?*" Expect that others will be unaware that we are being betrayed! But Jesus knows! Just as Jesus knew from the beginning He was going to be betrayed by Judas. He knows our betrayers!

We will be charged with being negligent when someone betrays us! Some will say we should have done more to protect ourselves. Would our accusers dare charge Jesus for being negligent in choosing Judas, and for not removing him from his "treasurer office"? Why did Jesus allow Judas to betray Him? Yes, it was so the Scriptures could be fulfilled! But Jesus was also betrayed because He had to be afflicted in all the ways we are! If we are followers of Jesus, what happened to Him, will likely happen to us! So let us keep our eyes on Him who is the Author and Perfecter of our faith. He knows best how to perfect our faith and it just may include betrayal!

Prayer: Lord, how it hurts to be betrayed! It is so embarrassing. Our reputations are threatened. We can't see the way out. But praise be to You our God! You promise to bring us through every trial! In Jesus' name we pray. Amen.

August 31

"So Judas threw the money into the temple and left. Then he went away and hanged himself." Matthew 27:5

Judas' suicide - Part 1

Judas was wrong when he decided to end his life. He knew the sixth commandment, *"You shall not murder,"* Deuteronomy 5:17. Judas knew the first commandment that said, *"You shall have no other gods before Me,"* Deuteronomy 5:7. Judas acted as a god, in the place of God, when he took his own life. Judas had a lot of guilt and remorse from his sin. The result was, he was down and depressed. What was he supposed to do with his guilt? He needed to go to Christ and confess it. Instead, Judas confessed his sins to the corrupt church leaders, to others, but not to Jesus. This added to his load of guilt. How often do we go to others with our guilt instead of to God? How many lonely people are there in bars that tell their problems to those who cannot help them?

Like Judas, those who commit suicide lack hope. Self-pity is their attitude of choice. They are self-focused and selfish in how they are living! It is all a very wrong response to what has happened to them! A selfish fear of what is happening to "me" is pulling them lower and lower. "No man hates himself" is the truth. Too much self-esteem, not too little, is behind all suicidal thinking. *"After all, no one ever hated his own body, but he feeds and cares for it, just as Christ does the church,"* Ephesians 5:29.

God teaches us to put our hope in Him! Suicide does not trust in the providence of God. *"No temptation has seized you except what is common to man,"* 1 Corinthians 10:13a. God fully understands our trial and He promises to help us! *"God is faithful; He will not let you be tempted beyond what you can bear,"* 1 Corinthians 10:13b. If we will go to Him and handle our problem His way, with His wisdom and with His resources, He will provide a way out of the problem that we are facing!

Prayer: Lord, how often You allow Your children to face difficult situations, to test them to see if they will rely on You and Your love for them. Lord, strengthen us to trust You more! Deliver us from the evil one. In Jesus' name we pray. Amen.

SEPTEMBER

The disciples catching many fish

"He called out to them, 'Friends, haven't you any fish?' 'No,' they answered. He said, 'Throw your net on the right side of the boat and you will find some.' When they did, they were unable to haul the net in because of the large number of fish."
John 21:5-6

September 1

"Judas threw the money into the temple and left. Then he went away and hanged himself." Matthew 27:5

Judas' suicide - Part 2

The subject of suicide needs more discussion. For even the great prophet Elijah selfishly *"prayed that he might die"* in 1 Kings 19:4. So, what if a suicide does happen in our Christian circles? How will we react? It is too common for us to stand in judgment, wanting to fix the blame for what happened! Could the family have done more? Could the church have done more? Could the spouse, parent or child have done more? Of course, we all could have done more! Perhaps we expected too much from the one who committed suicide! In a suicide situation, it is more important to be driven to the Cross than to explanations! We cannot fix the suicide situation, but Jesus can comfort us all!

Concerning Judas, should we dwell on his performance? No, it would be more profitable to think about our own performance! Does not our own performance fall short every day, and some days more than others? Are we accepted by God and on our way to Heaven, based on our performance? No! Then why are we tempted to condemn any suicidal person because their performance failed? If any of us believe that we will get to Heaven based on our performance, then it is we who have a performance problem and are lost! What we do will not get us into Heaven, or out of Heaven! God the Father accepts the perfect work of Christ on the Cross for our sin! *"It is finished"*! The *"good work"* has been done by Christ! Salvation is by grace alone, never by works! So if we still think a suicide person cannot go to Heaven based on some "bad work," we have a big Gospel problem!

But what about Judas? We know from Jesus own words that Judas was not a Christian, even though he was called a disciple. Judas was lost because his sins were not covered by Jesus. This does not mean that all who commit suicide are lost just because Judas was.

Prayer: Lord, we all have a small amount of faith! It is a good thing that it's not the size of our faith that saves us! Lord, comfort the families with the many difficult issues concerning suicide. And we thank You for the comfort You give. In Jesus' name we pray. Amen.

September 2

"The angel said to the women, 'Do not be afraid, for I know that you are looking for Jesus, who was crucified. He is not here; He is risen, just as He said. Come and see the place where He lay.'" Matthew 28:5-6

Jesus' resurrection and ours

"Do not be afraid." The angel of God speaks to these believing women about the fears they had of death, of dying and of the tomb. If Jesus is our Lord, we have nothing to fear! Just before this, unbelieving soldiers were shaking with fear when they saw the same angel of God. The angel did not tell them, *"Do not fear,"* for they had great reason to fear! They did not follow this Jesus.

"He is not here." Jesus could not stay in the grave because the wages of sin is death and He had no sin of His own. His death was for us who believe! After paying for our sin, He left the tomb to go where He can be of most benefit to us and to His Father's kingdom! So when we gaze at His empty tomb, think of how Jesus left it to go to that great throne room in Heaven. There He is our Advocate in the court of Heaven. There, He mediates for us. He has a great interest in us! For us He suffered so much. *"He is not here."* He is in Heaven, for us!

Believers, *"Come and see the place where He lay."* The innocent Son of God died and was in the tomb! See how He had to die and lie there for our sins to unite us to His Father! See how He took our sins to the grave. See His resurrection. It is proof for us that our sins are fully forgiven! The immortal Jesus still lives! He will never be in a tomb again, and neither will we! <u>Because of Jesus' resurrection, all believers will merely sleep in the grave, totally sinless, waiting for Jesus to bring their souls from Heaven to be reunited with their bodies.</u>

Unbelievers, *"Come and see the place where He lay."* You too will come out of your grave. Your body will not sleep forever either! *"<u>A time is coming when all who are in their graves will hear His voice and come out</u> — those who have done good will rise to live, and those who have done evil will rise to be condemned,"* John 5:28b-29. See the empty tomb and repent while there is still time!

Prayer: Lord, may Your resurrection change us, even as it changed Your disciples. Move us to fully believe. In Jesus' name we pray. Amen.

September 3

"Jesus came to them and said, 'All authority in Heaven and on earth has been given to Me. Therefore go and make disciples of all nations, baptizing them in the name of the Father and of the Son and of the Holy Spirit, and teaching them to obey everything I have commanded you. And surely I am with you always, to the very end of the age.'"
Matthew 28:18-20

Jesus' command, our commission or omission?

Only a commander can give a commission! After Jesus rose from the dead, all authority was given to Him. As Commander in Chief, He passes it on. But is this command just to the disciples? Is it just to pastors and ministers? Or, is the Great Commission to all believers?

First of all, Jesus said "Go." He did not say, "Send." "Go" to all nations, to all the ethnic groups. Israel was located at the crossroads of the world, but they were not an effective witness to the world. Do the work of discipleship and baptize. Jesus says, *"Surely I am with you,"* even, *"to the very end of the age."* That also includes you and I. Thinking the commission is only for the "ordained" has been our "Great Omission"!

Our commission is in Mark 16:15b-16. *"Go into all the world and preach the good news to all creation. Whoever believes and is baptized will be saved, but whoever does not believe will be condemned."* The word *"go"* is again used. We are also to teach about Heaven and warn unbelievers about Hell. Jesus last words on earth were, *"But you will receive power when the Holy Spirit comes on you; and you will be My witnesses in Jerusalem, and in all Judea and Samaria, and to the ends of the earth,"* Acts 1:8. What are the reasons we do not *"go"*?

1. We care so little about our own sin, why should we care about the sins of others? 2. We have idols. Other things are more important to us! 3. We are lazy. 4. We don't understand the reward. 5. We are too busy preaching our own kingdom to talk about His kingdom. 6. The devil tells us we are not "qualified" and many churches buy into his line of thinking. May we listen to Jesus who said, "go."

Prayer: Lord, we have one life to live. May we live it for You. May we love Your kingdom! May we come rejoicing, bringing in the sheaves! In Jesus' name we pray. Amen.

September 4

"As soon as they left the synagogue, they went with James and John to the house of Simon and Andrew. Simon's mother-in-law was in bed with a fever, and they told Jesus about her. So He went to her, took her hand and helped her up. The fever left her and she began to wait on them." Mark 1:29-31

Simon Peter's mother-in-law

Jesus went to Simon Peter's house on a mission to bring His healing grace. There Peter's mother-in-law was very sick with a fever. She was burning up physically, unable to get up, unable to do anything about her sickness. Even though she had a physical ailment, her life points to a person burning up spiritually. She needed Jesus in a big way, and Jesus brought her His grace and forgiveness that healed her inside out!

Do not miss the point that Jesus works in families. Brother Andrew had just brought Simon to meet Jesus. After Jesus accepted Simon as His disciple, He changed his name to Peter. God uses family members to introduce Jesus. Mary and Martha brought brother Lazarus to Jesus. Family influence is a responsibility and privilege no one can ignore! Our influence on others will speak either bad or good for all eternity. God will use us to be an instrument to conversion, or Satan will use us to be an instrument to destruction. Which will it be?

So grace not only went to Simon's house, it did something when it arrived. And not only did it do something inside the house, but the news quickly travelled outside the house also! *"That evening after sunset the people brought to Jesus all the sick and demon-possessed. The whole town gathered at the door, and Jesus healed many who had various diseases,"* Mark 1:32-34a.

God transformed a simple fisherman's home to be one of the most important places in the city! May God use our houses to share the healing power of the Lord Jesus Christ.

Prayer: Lord, we are so thankful that You still heal the sick physically and spiritually. We need Your divine healing. How wonderful is the truth that after You healed this dear lady, she immediately served You and others. What a testimony to what You want us to do. Strengthen us to serve! In Jesus' name we pray. Amen.

September 5

"A man with leprosy came to Him and begged Him on his knees, 'If You are willing, You can make me clean.' Filled with compassion, Jesus reached out His hand and touched the man. 'I am willing,' He said. 'Be clean!' Immediately the leprosy left him and he was cured."
Mark 1:40-42

A leper is made clean

Leprosy was just horrible. Leprosy started with spots on the skin. In time open sores came with pus draining out and they smelled bad. Eventually, their fingers and toes rotted off. A leper lived for up to ten years and literally rotted away. When diagnosed, they had to leave their family and live in a leper colony, totally isolated. A leper had to cry "Unclean," and had to stay at least 50 feet from another person. Doctor Luke said, this man was "*covered in leprosy*," in the last stages of the disease.

A leper was seen as cursed by God! And this leper is a picture of us and how filthy our sin is to God! Like leprosy, our sin starts small, spreads, and is far greater than skin deep. When a leper died, everything was burned up! And so do we if we die in our sins!

This leper came to Jesus! He "*begged Him on his knees, 'If You are willing, You can make me clean.'*" Jesus touched this untouchable leper and no one else ever did that! "*Immediately the leprosy left him and he was cured.*" Note that this man's disease did not corrupt Jesus! Instead, Jesus' cleansing power went into the leper! Cured, Jesus said to him, "*show yourself to the priest and offer the sacrifices that Moses commanded for your cleansing, as a testimony to them,*" Mark 1:44b.

In Leviticus 14, a priest had to examine the leper to pronounce him clean. Then the priest would take two birds, kill one, sprinkle its blood, and release the other bird. It was a sign that atonement was made and the leper was free. What a beautiful picture of how Jesus cleanses us dirty sinners! Redeemed by the blood of the lamb, this leper is like all of us who are bound for Heaven!

Prayer: Lord, our sin rots us away! Just as You caused this leper to approach You, move us to You also! For it was not the leper's faith that healed him, but it was Your willingness that did! Heal us Lord! In Jesus' name we pray. Amen.

September 6

"'But that you may know that the Son of Man has authority on earth to forgive sins...' He said to the paralytic, 'I tell you, get up, take your mat and go home.' He got up, took his mat and walked out in full view of them all. This amazed everyone and they praised God, saying, 'We have never seen anything like this.'" Mark 2:10-12

The paralytic, forgiven and healed

Jesus is home in Capernaum. The house is overflowing. No more can get in. Jesus *"preached the Word to them,"* Mark 2:2b. That in itself is so instructive. The Word must be preached! Four men bring their friend who is paralyzed. They are expecting a healing, for Jesus has been doing that in meetings. But they can't get in! Luke tells us why! *"One day as He was teaching, Pharisees and teachers of the law, who had come from every village in Galilee and from Judea and Jerusalem, were sitting there,"* Luke 5:17a. How many people can fit in a house if they sit? Is this a sit down strike? Why didn't they move? Because sitting showed authority, so their pompus butts sat. But can they stop the Gospel from going out? No! Four men take the roof apart and drop the paralytic in. It sounds like it was four ropes on the corners of the bed.

The paralytic said nothing! Jesus said, *"Friend, your sins are forgiven,"* Luke 5:20b. What a shock! His friends were looking for healing! After all, this man is paralyzed! Yes, but even for him, Jesus' forgiveness was more important than the health of his body! Do we know this? Another reason Jesus said that the paralytic was forgiven was so, *"that you may know that the Son of Man has authority on earth to forgive sins."* When we observe the Lord's Supper, we celebrate our complete forgiveness, not our physical health! In salvation, we are forgiven our past, present and future sins! We dying people need God's forgiveness!

The Pharisees knew that Jesus just claimed to be God. For only God can forgive sins! Now Jesus *"said to the Paralytic, 'I tell you, get up, take your mat and go home.'"* His healing was immediate. His healing was complete. His healing was eternal! This paralytic is us!

Prayer: Lord, what beautiful words, *"your sins are forgiven."* No one can forgive sins but You, O God! We worship You for Your grace and mercy. In Jesus' name we pray. Amen.

September 7

"Then He looked at those seated in a circle around Him and said, 'Here are My mother and My brothers!'" Mark 3:34

Mary, a mother who learns to let go

Jesus teaches His family and us here, what we don't see so clearly in other Bible characters. At eight days old, baby Jesus was brought to the temple for the sign of circumcision, (Luke 2:21.) God's covenant mark is on this child as belonging to Him for life! Forty days after birth, the mother and father again returned to the temple for a purification rite for their own sins, and to present baby Jesus to the Lord. The parents are starting to let go of the child who is on loan to them from God.

"Every year His parents went to Jerusalem for the Feast of the Passover," Luke 2:41. On this yearly pilgrimage, Jesus, at the age of 12, stayed back in Jerusalem. His parents were unaware of it as they traveled home. *"After three days they found Him in the temple courts, sitting among the teachers, listening to them and asking them questions,"* Luke 2:46. One of the main points of this event was that Jesus is now teaching His parents, and us too, something important! That is, *"Didn't you know I had to be in My Father's house?"* Jesus is saying that He had God-ordained work to do that must take Him out of His family home! Part of the implication is: "Mom and Dad, you need to begin to let go."

In Mark 3:31-35, Jesus teaches more on His family letting go. Jesus had already appointed His 12 disciples. He was teaching them and a crowd of others. *"Then Jesus' mother and brothers arrived. Standing outside, they sent someone in to call Him."* The crowd told Him, *"Your mother and brothers are outside looking for You."* *"Then He looked at those seated in a circle and said, 'Here are My mother and brothers!'"* And the exclamation point is in the text. Jesus was teaching His family, and us, the importance of evangelism and that these believers were His mother and brothers! Are we willing to love others like that?

Prayer: Lord, we must admit, we are selfish. Like Mary, we may know that a family member is called to leave home and do Your work; may we not try to call them back, but bless their work. Lord, may Your kingdom come! In Jesus' name we pray. Amen.

September 8

"Listen! A farmer went out to sow his seed." Mark 4:3

A farmer *"went out"*!

Jesus left the streets of gold for the dusty fields of Nazareth! This Farmer is Jesus. But, the farmer must also be us! This farmer has no name, for he must have many faces in many countries. He is a picture of God's child, serious about getting the Gospel out.

To sow, a farmer has to get up and go out! He can't just stay in the house! He must make an effort to go out! He can't say "It's too hot or too cold." He should not think that any field is too small to plant. After all, good produce grows in small gardens! Why is it, we never *"went out"* to do the important work of evangelism? Jesus showed us by example not to be a couch potato but to go out and be a soul-winner!

We must prepare to be used by God. A farmer must make an effort to get his seed ready! The seed is the Word of God. We must study and pray about the Word. Too often we are a picture of a lazy farmer. When it is time to plant, our planter is still broken from last year! The chains are off and it is not greased! The mice ate our seed and the fertilizer is hard from leaving it in the planter a year ago. Suddenly, it's time to plant, and we are not prepared! Today, most seed has a coating on it to protect it and give it a boost when it goes in the ground! We need to coat our planting of God's Word with prayer and ask for the Spirit's blessing! The Spirit who wrote that Word, certainly will bless it. If we coat it with prayer and meditate on it, He will give the seed of His Word a boost! We should know that bad seed does not germinate!

A good farmer sowed the seed and went out in the field, like a fisherman must go out on the sea. We can't sow the seed or cast our net in the house. A sign board on our church or house is not evangelism either! A farmer must get in the field and sow the seed where it has a chance to grow! Leave home. Launch the boat. Start the motor. Bait the hook. Cast the line. Fish with prayer. Catch fish!

Prayer: Lord, how we need to *"listen"* to these first few words of Yours! Prepare our hearts to go out; and push us if we don't! Bless our going and bring in Your precious harvest of souls. In Jesus' name we pray. Amen.

September 9

"Listen! A farmer went out to sow his seed. As he was scattering his seed, some fell along the path... Some fell in rocky places... Other seed fell among thorns... Still other seed fell on good soil." Mark 4:3-8a

A farmer's four types of soil

When Jesus told "The Parable of the Soils," He was comparing the people's response to hearing the Gospel, to the different soil conditions that farmers have. We will use four D's to described the spiritual condition of those who hear the Word of God. They are: Deceived, Demonstrative, Distracted, Discerning.

"Some fell along the path." <u>Deceived,</u> they saw no need for God. There was no coverage or amount of soil over the seed, so, the birds ate the seed. Satan took away any desire for God. They simply did not care about spiritual things. They were deceived about the importance of a real relationship with God.

"Some fell in rocky places." <u>Demonstrative,</u> would describe their worship pattern. They have an emotional response to the Gospel, but there was no change in how they live. Their hearts were not changed. They liked Christ and even thought He was a good man. But their problem was: They demonstrated lip service to God but not heart service!

"Other seed fell among thorns." <u>Distracted,</u> wealth, jobs, worries of many kinds were described by Jesus as, *"thorns which grew up and choked the plants."* Such people go to church, but other things, even good things, distract them from the sincere worship of God.

"Still other seed fell on good soil." <u>Discerning,</u> they heard the Word, accepted it, and responded to it. Their life was changed. They knew right from wrong and pursued right living. Trust and obey was their motto and great desire. Their faith believed and trusted in God even when it could not see! Discerning, they made wise decisions based on God's Word and will.

Prayer: Lord, we can see from Your teaching that there is nothing wrong with You or Your Seed, the Word. Help us to receive You, believe in You, then live for You. Fill us with Your presence Lord. In Jesus' name we pray. Amen.

September 10

"A furious squall came up, and the waves broke over the boat, so that it was nearly swamped. Jesus was in the stern, sleeping on a cushion. The disciples woke Him and said to Him, 'Teacher, don't you care if we drown?'" Mark 4:37-38

The Teacher tames the tempest

The chapter begins with Jesus preaching from His ship pulpit. The congregation has gone home. The disciples alone are left. They have so much to learn yet, and such a short time to learn it! (True for us also, isn't it?) Jesus has another important message to teach them, but He will use no words this time! He has a quicker plan in mind.

Jesus asks the disciples to go to the other side of the lake, where He has work to do. We will see that sometimes it's not what we do at our destination that's so important, but what we learn along the way! A really strong storm comes up, as we can see in our text. The ship "seems" to be on its way to the bottom of the sea! The disciples are in a panic. Jesus, in total control, is comfortably sleeping!

The ship is a good picture of the church which includes us. The storm is a symbol of the serious problems that it endures on its journey. Trials come, testing our faith. Our patience and our perseverance is built up. Like with the disciples, Jesus allows our trials, tailoring them to fit what we still need to learn. James said in 1:2; "*Consider it pure joy, my brothers, whenever you face trials of many kinds.*" Why, because God is about to teach us something important! Part of that lesson will be to trust Him more as He miraculously stills the storm in our breast.

Know this for sure! God is faithful, He will not allow His child to be tested or tempted beyond what we can endure. He has a way out for us! Don't panic, He isn't. Look to Him and ask for His wisdom! Don't be bitter or angry! Trust that He knows what's best! Don't give up! The boat may rock, but we won't drown! Christ owns us! No one can pluck us out of His hand. We need to learn that lesson well as the disciples did!

Prayer: Lord, we must admit Your hardest lessons are the very ones we learn the most from. We never forget them, just as You intended. We thank You for building us up in the faith and preserving us for eternity. In Jesus' name we pray. Amen.

September 11

"Then one of the synagogue rulers, named Jairus, came there. Seeing Jesus, he fell at His feet and pleaded earnestly with Him, 'My little daughter is dying. Please come and put Your hands on her so that she will be healed and live.' So Jesus went with him." Mark 5:22-24a

Jairus, "Don't be afraid, just believe"

Jairus, like other "synagogue rulers," probably had much unbelief and criticism concerning who Jesus was. But now his little daughter is sick and dying. So he pleads with Jesus "Come and heal my daughter!" Jesus goes, but on the way, messengers tell Jairus, *"Your daughter is dead."* Jesus says to Jairus and to us, five beautiful words; *"Don't be afraid, just believe,"* Mark 5:36b. May these five words sink to the bottom of our souls! *"Believe,"* Jesus can still do something! *"Believe,"* your daughter's death is just a short nap! Is it not the same for us? When compared to eternity, our physical bodies will also sleep in the grave for a little time!

Jesus arrives and says to the people, *"Why all this commotion and wailing?"* Jesus then speaks to the little girl who has died. *"Little girl, I say to you, get up!"* *"Immediately the girl stood up and walked around... At this they were completely astonished,"* Mark 5:42. Jesus' words to us are basically the same! *"Do not be amazed at this, for a time is coming when all who are in their graves will hear His voice and come out — those who have done good will rise to live, and those who have done evil will rise to be condemned,"* John 5:28-29. Jesus has resurrection power!

Jesus will do far more for us than He did for this little girl! His resurrection power will raise and transform us into a new glorified body, just like His own! *"We shall be like Him, for we shall see Him as He is."* We will never sin again, never get sick or ever be in pain again! We will never need to sleep again! There will be day and night fellowship with God and others. More than that, if Jesus can wake up dead bodies and transform them into a glorified body, how much more can He wake up dead sinners and change our rebellious proud hearts! Our God is an awesome God!

Prayer: Lord, how wonderfully You teach us about Your resurrection power through events like the daughter of Jarius. What a privilege it is to be Your child. In Jesus' name we pray. Amen.

September 12

"For Herod himself had given orders to have John arrested, and he had him bound and put in prison. He did this because of Herodias, his brother Philip's wife, whom he had married. For John had been saying to Herod; 'It is not lawful for you to have your brother's wife.'"
Mark 6:17

Herodias, she *"nursed a grudge"*

Herod the Great had three sons, Antipas, Archelaus and Philip. Herodias was married to Philip. Then brother Antipas married her. Philip was not dead, so Herodias was not a widow! Mark calls her *"brother Philip's wife."* Historian Josephus said that Herod Antipas was also still married to his first wife. Jewish law stoned adulterers. But when the leader of the church is guilty, who needs to obey? John the Baptist was right in telling Herod he was wrong.

Herodias absolutely hated John the Baptist. It says, *"Herodias nursed a grudge against John and wanted to kill him. But she was not able to,"* Mark 6:19. Her "husband" Herod, *"feared John and protected him."* Herod liked to listen to John, but was *"puzzled"* about repentance! Imagine that, the head religious leader of Israel is puzzled about repentance! So Herodias resorts to trickery to get at John.

Herod gives a banquet and the daughter of Herodias danced. Pleased, Herod said he would give her any gift she wanted. She asked for John's head. This grieved Herod, but because of peer pressure and pride he did it. Herodias and her daughter are also guilty! Herodias nursed a "grudge," and it led to murder! Do we have a grudge against anyone? If so, we must listen to John's words to Herod: Repent! We must live by grace!

Herodias is never heard from again. She pretended to be somebody but ends up a nobody. Herodias' dancing daughter was Salome. Josephus says she later died when the ice broke on a frozen river. She was on "thin ice" when she asked for John's head. God, who is jealous for His name and for His servants, paid her back!

Prayer: Lord, You clearly teach us not to *"nurse a grudge"* like the wicked Herodias did. Lord, forgive us when we have! Strengthen us to be forgiving, thus gracious! In Jesus' name we pray. Amen.

September 13

"'First let the children eat all they want,' He told her, 'for it is not right to take the children's bread and toss it to their dogs.' 'Yes Lord,' she replied, 'but even the dogs under the table eat the children's crumbs.' Then He told her, 'For such a reply, you may go; the demon has left your daughter.'" Mark 7:27-29

The begging woman of Canaan

The Pharisees are angry at Jesus and His disciples. They say the disciples are spiritually unclean for not washing their hands before eating. Jesus tells them, that a man is not unclean from what goes into his mouth, but by what comes out of it! Jesus then list many evil sins. Now in our text, we have a Greek Syrian woman coming to Jesus She is begging for her unclean daughter to be healed of serious demon-possession!

Jesus found very little faith in Israel! Yet just across the border is a woman who only heard about Jesus' healing power! To prove a big faith point, Jesus at first pushes her away, saying He has to minister to the Jews and doesn't have time to teach the neighbors of Israel. Jesus even calls her the common slang for a non-Jew, a dog.

Now we see the deep faith of this woman. She says even a dog is allowed to eat the crumbs that fall under the table when the children eat. She is begging for just a crumb of mercy from Jesus! <u>By faith, she knows just a crumb of blessing from Jesus is enough to heal her daughter from the demons that have been troubling her</u>!

Contrast is what we see here! And this contrast is still in our world today! The Jewish leaders who Jesus called *"hypocrites,"* in Mark 7:6, thought they were clean, but they were unclean. This woman knew she and her daughter were unclean and they wanted to be clean, free from the power of Satan! And Jesus heals them!

The big question in front of us is, which of these two groups describes us. Do we think we have arrived spiritually, because we were born in the covenant to Christian parents? Or do we see that we are sinners in need of the healing touch of Jesus Christ?

Prayer: Lord, we come before you humbly, like this woman from Canaan. Lord be merciful to us! We need mercy from Your Almighty hand. Deliver us from the power of Satan. In Jesus' name we pray. Amen.

September 14

"For even the Son of Man did not come to be served, but to serve, and to give His life as a ransom for many." Mark 10:45

Mark, the one who learned to serve

The theme of John Mark's life and book was one of service. Mark was a lot like us in his Christian struggles! He knew that Jesus Christ suffered for him personally. At an early age Mark thought, "What can I do to pattern my life after the life of my Master, Jesus Christ." What a beautiful response! But then Mark failed in his service to God, only to learn from that failure. So his Gospel is of much practical use to us!

Mark had a promising beginning as a servant. Mark was the cousin of Barnabas. His mother must have been a solid Christian because in Acts 12:12 it says, *"many people had gathered and were praying"* in her house when Peter was in prison. Also, Barnabas and Saul took young John Mark along on a missionary journey in Acts 13.

Mark then failed as a servant. For some reason, Mark abandoned Barnabas and Saul. It appears he didn't even consult them but left them and went home. Later, in Acts 15, *"Barnabas wanted to take John, also called Mark, with them, but Paul did not think it wise to take him, because he had deserted them in Pamphylia and had not continued with them in the work,"* Acts 15:37-38. Do we walk away from the Lord's work for the comfort of our homes?

Mark learned to serve faithfully! Again Mark went with Barnabas on a mission journey. The book of 1 Peter ends with Peter saying that Mark was with him. And at the end of Paul's life he writes to Timothy, *"Get Mark and bring him with you, because he is helpful to me in my ministry,"* 2 Timothy 4:11b. Truly Mark learned to follow Jesus' example of being a servant! Are we learning?

Prayer: Dear Lord, You told Your disciples and us (Mark 9:35) that, *"If anyone wants to be first, he must be the very last, and the servant of all."* We see that Your dear disciple Mark learned to serve others for the sake of the Gospel. Lord help us to do that also. Give us that willingness and protection to do those good things that build Your kingdom. In Jesus' name we pray. Amen.

September 15

"Jesus, Son of David, have mercy on me!" Mark 10:47b

Blind Bartimaeus, he cried for mercy

It is mentioned in Mark 10:46b that, *"a blind man, Bartimaeus (that is, the Son of Timaeus), was sitting by the roadside begging."* Did you see how the son's name is like the father's? Many think the meaning is that the father was also born blind. I don't know if that is true but it sure fits with what Jesus is teaching in the story.

Jesus had just taught in verse 45 that He came *"to give His life as a ransom for many."* Then immediately we read of this blind man. Perhaps the biggest shock of all is that this blind man is really you and I. Spiritually, we are blind to our spiritual condition! We cannot open our eyes any more than that blind man could. In fact his father was blind before him just as our fathers were spiritually blind all the way to Adam. This blind man actually had an advantage over us! He knew he was blind. He cries out because he is blind. He is desperate to see! Are we?

Think of the other people in the Bible who cried for mercy and received it! David cried *"Have mercy on me, O God,"* in Psalm 51. The Canaanite woman said, *"Have mercy on me, O Lord."* The Bible is showing us, if we cry out to God like that, we will also receive mercy! Grace and mercy is our biggest need, because we too are guilty. We too need a pardon from God to turn away His just wrath!

God's grace is even in our crying out, *"Have mercy on me, a sinner."* We cry out only because before the world was created, before we were even born, the Triune God had already put that desire for Him in our heart! That happened when the Father gave His sheep to His Son! Christ knew us and loved us already then. In fact, that is exactly why Christ came to world. He came to rescue His elect sheep who were lost! This is also why Paul, along with us, still teach the Gospel message. Paul begins his letter to Titus, *"Paul, a servant of God and an apostle of Jesus Christ for the faith of God's elect."* If you are reading this, God is calling out to you!

Prayer: Lord, you know all those who You marked as Your own. Work in them to cry out to You. Save them for Your own name's sake. Use them for Your name's sake also. In Jesus' name we pray. Amen.

September 16

"Jesus sat down opposite the place where the offerings were put and watched the crowd putting their money into the temple treasury. Many rich people threw in large amounts. But a poor widow came and put in two very small copper coins, worth only a fraction of a penny."
Mark 12:41-42

The widow's mite shows her mighty heart

We don't normally sit and watch what people give for their offering. The giving of tithes and offerings is a private matter that is given to God, for His kingdom work. So the real picture of this poor widow is quite simple: Jesus sees every single penny we give and He sees our reason for giving it. *"Jesus said, 'I tell you the truth, this poor widow has put more into the treasury than all the others. They all gave out of their wealth, but she, out of her poverty, put in everything – all she had to live on,'"* Mark 12:43b-44. It is not what we give that matters to Jesus! It is what we have left after we give.

The love of God and His kingdom was in the heart of this widow. It is our hearts that Jesus wants also, not our money! He owns the cattle on a thousand hills, the wealth in every mine. The giving of gifts and tithes is an act of worship, and it is a big test of our hearts. The widow passed that test! *"Each man should give what he has decided in his heart to give, not reluctantly or under compulsion; for God loves a cheerful giver,"* 2 Corinthians 9:7. It's not even the size of our purse that determines our giving; it's the size of our hearts!

"Remember this: Whoever sows sparingly will also reap sparingly, and whoever sows generously will also reap generously," 2 Corinthians 9:6. We give to God; He blesses us in return. However, this "giving to get," is of secondary importance. But we are reminded of our blessing, because we have many important needs and God has unlimited blessings. *"God is able to make all grace abound to you, so that in all things at all times, having all that you need, you will abound in every good work,"* 2 Corinthians 9:8. Four "alls" from our Al-mighty God, when we give heart worship to God through our giving!

Prayer: Lord, forgive us for being selfish with what we have. May we honor You like this dear widow lady! In Jesus' name we pray. Amen.

September 17

"A certain man from Cyrene, Simon, the father of Alexander and Rufus, was passing by on his way in from the country, and they forced him to carry the cross." Mark 15:21

Simon of Cyrene has a divine detour

Simon had one thing in mind! He was going to Jerusalem to celebrate the Passover. He wanted to experience that once a year event that pointed to the blood of the lamb on the doorpost and their deliverance from Egypt. Simon's journey was about 1000 miles. It was a long distance from his hometown of Cyrene which is currently called Libya, in Africa. Simon was a devout Jew, a proselyte, that is a pagan who was converted to Judaism. Surely he had already been in Jerusalem for a few days. Now he gets up early to go into the city when suddenly, out of the city comes a noisy procession. Some poor, beaten up man is struggling with a cross and He falls down, totally exhausted.

We read that the Romans *"forced"* Simon or *"compelled"* him, as the NKJV reads, to carry the cross. We do not know why the Romans picked Simon, maybe because he looked with pity on Jesus. Or maybe it was because he was a foreigner from Africa. Surely Simon was *"compelled,"* for he would not willingly defile himself and not be able partake of the Passover meal. Simon the Cyrene had no choice but to carry that cross. He had a divine appointment, one of those "divine detours," that changes one's life forever. His service to Christ was planned before the foundation of the world, (Ephesians 2:10), just like every true Christian! Little did Simon know that his unplanned meeting would not only change his life, but privilege him to carry the cross of our Lord Jesus Christ!

Years later Paul writes about what Mark hints at in our text. *"Greet Rufus, chosen in the Lord, and his mother, who has been a mother to me, too,"* Romans 16:13. Simon's wife and his son Rufus, were like family to Paul. Simon's family was used mightily to carry the Gospel of Jesus to many places. May we do the same, without being forced!

Prayer: Lord, Your sovereignty is amazing! You time events perfectly to advance Your kingdom. Make us willing to lift up Your Cross, teaching Christ crucified. Make us willing to serve You for Your glory and for our good. In Jesus' name we pray. Amen.

September 18

"At the sixth hour darkness came over the whole land until the ninth hour. And at the ninth hour Jesus cried out in a loud voice; 'Eloi, Eloi, lama sabachthani?' which means, 'My God, My God, why have You forsaken Me?' And when the centurion, who stood there in front of Jesus, heard His cry and saw how He died, he said, 'Surely this Man was the Son of God!'" Mark 15:33-34 & 39

The Centurion sees Jesus die and believes

The darkness spoken of here is not an eclipse as some would have us believe. The yearly Passover was always celebrated at full moon. Nor could this have been a dust storm, as it was the rainy season! This is what the prophet Amos spoke of! *"'In that day,' declares the Sovereign Lord, 'I will make the sun go down at noon and darken the earth in broad daylight,'"* Amos 8:9. Darkness indicates judgment! The last of the ten plagues was also total darkness. God is judging Jesus for our sin, that is, if we are a Christian! If we are not a Christian yet, we are still guilty, and we must face eternally what Jesus is facing on the Cross, which is the wrath and judgment of God.

Jesus' cry on the Cross was the wild kind of cry we would make if someone held us over a fire! In fact, Jesus' bloodcurdling scream is that cry of a person who is experiencing the pain of Hell! When He cried, "My God, My God, why have You forsaken Me," Jesus had been in incredible anguish for three hours. Literal Hell is a separation from God's love where His wrath is present against sinners. All of God's wrath is on Jesus, who is screaming the cry of the damned, so we don't have to!

The centurion had seen may people die. They usually hang on to life for two days or so. Jesus' death was quick, just six hours. Nothing about Jesus' death was normal! But then, Jesus had to die at the exact time the priest entered the Holy of Holies to make atonement for the sins of the people. Can you imagine how shocked the priest was when the 60 foot tall curtain *"was torn in two from top to bottom"* in verse 38? No longer needed, that bloodstained curtain, was destroyed by God!

Prayer: Lord, by grace we can with the centurion say, *"Surely this Man was the Son of God!"* What a great price You paid to save us! We will praise You forever! In Jesus' name we pray. Amen.

September 19

"Some women were watching from a distance. Among them were Mary Magdaline, Mary the mother of James the younger and of Joses, and Salome. In Galilee these women had followed Him and cared for His needs. Many other women who had come up with Him to Jerusalem were also there." Mark 15:40-41

Many women care about Jesus

Luke and Mark record some important matters concerning four main women who were at Jesus' crucifixion. Plus there were *"many other women"* following Jesus. What made these women follow Jesus? *"In Galilee these women had followed Him and cared for His needs."* The men got more of the ink, the ladies got more of the work. The men sat and ate with the Master, while the ladies were busy in the market, in the kitchen, in the washroom, raising the children and nursing any who needed attention. The men disciples are not mentioned here, because all but John, left Jesus! Even though every disciple except Judas was from Nazareth in Galilee, they were not at the Cross!

"Many other women who had come up with Him to Jerusalem were also there," Mark 15:41. In His ministry Jesus noticed women and even talked to them. He didn't treat them like they were second class citizens. He understood their difficult lot in life. He watched many sons "get spoiled," while the girls were made to serve the entire household. Jesus, and Christianity after Him, did much to elevate the status of women. The women in turn, responded to Jesus!

Jesus Himself created the first woman, Eve, to be a helper to the task and to be a source of affection in the home. For this reason, women are better at "relationships," better in keeping the peace and love in the home, and in the church too! These women were like family to Jesus. And did you notice, Jesus spent more time with those whom He knew would cry at His funeral!

Prayer: Lord, the way these women cared for Jesus and for His kingdom accuses us! Forgive us for how little we care about You and Your kingdom. Like Jesus, may we also encourage women to use their gifts to build the Church of our Lord Jesus Christ. In Jesus' name we pray. Amen.

"Then an angel of the Lord appeared to him, standing at the right side of the altar of incense. When Zechariah saw him, he was startled and was gripped with fear. But the angel said to him: 'Do not be afraid, Zechariah; your prayer has been heard. Your wife Elizabeth will bear you a son, and you are to give him the name John.'" Luke 1:11-13

Zechariah, God remembers His covenant

Zechariah was a Levite priest. He lived in a small town outside Jerusalem. His wife was Elizabeth, (tomorrow's topic). *"But they had no children, because Elizabeth was barren; and they were both well on in years,"* Luke 1:7. Zechariah's name means, God remembers His covenant. This elderly couple was righteous, when unrighteousness was the norm.

Priests served on a team. On one of these teams, Zechariah *"was chosen by lot, according to the custom of the priesthood, to go into the temple of the Lord and burn incense,"* Luke 1:9. He was alone, when burning incense, and an angel appeared to him! *"Your prayer has been heard. Your wife Elizabeth will have a son."* Like Abraham and Sarah, Zechariah and Elizabeth had a miracle child in their old age. *"What is impossible with men is possible with God,"* Luke 18:27b. We must remember this when we pray!

"You are to give him the name John." The angel maked a point of this! God, with complete authority, named the child, John. Everyone assumed his name would be Zechariah, like his father. After all, sons carried on the family name. Back then, people had one name! God went against tradition to show the special relationship He would have with John. God showed that John would be different than his priest father. John was to be God's prophet, the only one who bridged two testaments. John will usher in the new Covenant. God did not forget His promises, nor will He ever! What a good picture of a believer Zechariah was. He followed God's plan for his life, not his own. Zechariah was a man who prayed and depended on God. Faith must still do that!

Prayer: Lord, by covenant You also name us. You call us Christian, in honor of Your only Son. You constantly remember that we are related to You. May we remember that You are our loving Father. In Jesus' name we pray. Amen.

September 21

"When his time of service was completed, he returned home. After this his wife Elizabeth became pregnant and for five months remained in seclusion. 'The Lord has done this for me,' she said. 'In these days He has shown His favor and taken away my disgrace among the people.'"
Luke 1:23-25

Elizabeth, a good wife and mother!

Elizabeth is the wife of Zechariah and the mother of John the Baptist. Like her husband, she is a Levite, tracing her descendants way back to Aaron. Elizabeth is a relative of Mary, Jesus' mother. Elizabeth's name means "God is my oath." God is keeping His covenant promises! He is about to send the long awaited Savior. Elizabeth's disgrace is removed! To not have a child was thought to be cursed by God. Now God is giving her a miracle child, a special child. As parents they were told, *"He will be a joy and a delight to you, and many will rejoice because of his birth,"* Luke 1:14. Godly parents and godly children make for a very happy family! They are satisfied with God and with each other!

Once I was at a business meeting, the participants were taking turns telling about themselves. A common confession was, "in five years my kids will be out of the house and then my life will begin." I did not share their sentiments! Like Zechariah and Elizabeth, we must be happy to have our child or children in our home!

John, *"will be great in the sight of the Lord. He is never to take wine or other fermented drink, and he will be filled with the Holy Spirit even from birth,"* Luke 1:15. The child was to be a Nazirite. John was given by God, set apart for God, to live for God! And godly parents were needed to prepare him. Our children are in the same situation!

"You are to give him the name John." His name means, "the Lord is merciful." Think of how many times old Zechariah and Elizabeth were reminded of God's mercy! We too need a reminder to stay humble and thankful! Let us pray about that.

Prayer: Lord, how You were faithful in keeping Your covenant promises to Abraham, Isaac, Jacob and now to us also! We praise You for Your mercy, that is greater than all our sin. Along with Zechariah and Elizabeth, we worship You. In Jesus' name we pray. Amen.

"'I am the Lord's servant,' Mary answered. 'May it be to me as You have said.' Then the angel left her." Luke 1:38

Mary, the mother of my Lord

Our introduction of the mother of Jesus is in the following verses: *"God sent the angel Gabriel to Nazareth, a town in Galilee, to a virgin pledged to be married to a man named Joseph, a descendant of David. The virgin's name was Mary. The angel went to her and said, 'Greetings, you who are highly favored! The Lord is with you,'"* Luke 1:26b-28. These words took Mary completely by surprise! She was, *"greatly troubled."* But the angel calmed her and told her how she would have a baby, literally the Son of God, the Messiah in the flesh, baby Jesus.

See God's words of grace to Mary, *"you are highly favored."* Mary was righteous, but there were other righteous women. Also think of the angel's words, *"The Lord is with you."* Are these words not true for every believer? Properly understood, the grace of God to each believer makes us all *"highly favored,"* and *"the Lord is with you"*!

Mary's response are the words in our text. Even though she was *"highly favored,"* she remained a humble servant of God! One of the first things Mary did was share the Good News in a visit with her cousin Elizabeth, who was also pregnant with little John the Baptist. What a meeting this must have been! They shared their secrets and had such happy fellowship together.

Elizabeth understood that Mary was giving birth to the long-awaited Messiah. In Luke 1:42, *"In a loud voice she exclaimed: 'Blessed are you among women, and blessed is the child you will bear!'"* Also note the words in the next verse that show the deep faith of Elizabeth! *"But why am I so favored, that the mother of my Lord should come to me?"* She recognizes Jesus as Lord before He is even born. Her faith accuses us if we, who have far more knowledge, do not see Jesus as Lord!

Prayer: Lord, we read that Jesus' mother broke out in a song of worship to You! She realized that *"from now on all generations will call me blessed,"* (Luke 1:48b). Lord, You have a blessed, believing mother. How blessed are we also to have believing mothers. We thank You for this grace also. In Jesus' name we pray. Amen.

September 23

"And it came to pass in those days that a decree went out from Caesar Augustus that all the world should be registered. So all went to be registered, everyone to his own city." Luke 2:1 & 3 NKJV

Caesar Augustus, moves on God's schedule

The <u>Roman government</u> is at the very peak of its power. The family of the Caesars has another son on the throne. Caesar Augustus was adopted by his great uncle, the famous Julius Caesar. Uncle Julius was murdered and now Caesar Augustus is made the ruler. He was the ruling Caesar from 44 B.C. to 14 A.D. In this time he became so powerful that the former ruling senate became almost powerless. There is a lot written about Caesar Augustus in his reign of 58 years. But he gets just one verse in the Bible. Only Luke mentions his name. He records in our text that Caesar made a decree to register everyone in his then, worldwide kingdom!

Augustus called for the most famous census ever. He wanted a registration of all people, so he could tax them. It is likely Caesar Augustus also wanted to know how many people were subject to his rule. But there was something Caesar did not understand. *"The king's heart is in the hand of the Lord, like the rivers of water; He turns it wherever He wishes,"* Proverbs 21:1 NKJV. It is on God's schedule for Jesus to be born. But, Jesus' mother Mary and father Joseph are in Nazareth. In Micah 5:2 it says that the Messiah would be born in Bethlehem! No problem! God moves the father, mother and Child at exactly the right time, to exactly the right place, by the decree of Caesar Augustus!

God is totally in control of this world! A mouse doesn't move without His knowledge. Every event in every life is according to the sovereignty of God. According to Acts 17:26, we too are born in exactly the place and time God wanted us to arrive, even to the parents of God's choosing. May we see more clearly how great and awesome our God is, and worship Him more!

Prayer: Lord, we are in awe of Your majesty. How completely You move world events according to Your divine schedule, to accomplish Your divine purposes. May we learn to trust and worship You more. In Jesus' name we pray. Amen.

September 24

"Do not be afraid. I bring <u>you</u> Good News of great joy that will be for all the people. Today in the town of David a Savior has been born to you; He is Christ the Lord." Luke 2:10b-11

Baby Jesus, born "Lord," for you!

The best birth announcement ever, was announced by God's holy angels! They spoke so clearly to the shepherd but also to "*you*" who are alive today. Baby Jesus is now born. And He was born "Lord," the one and only Lord Jesus Christ. Lord, because He never ceased to be God! Jesus, because He is the one and only Savior. Christ, because He is the Lord's anointed to hold the offices of prophet, priest and king. The whole Old Testament pointed to Him. He is now here! Come and worship Him! Don't be afraid. He will receive "*you*"!

Of what benefit is it that Jesus is Lord? By being related to Him, "*you*" are brought into the kingdom of God! Yes, He is the King of His kingdom. It's that simple. His birth day long ago in the Bethlehem manger was His incarnation, meaning, God came into the world in the flesh, as a human being. Jesus is now fully human as well as fully God. And the day Jesus entered the world, He also became your servant. That's what He told His disciples when He washed their feet. What an amazing reality that Jesus is your Lord and your servant. What greater evidence is there that He is fully God as well as fully man?

Saying the words, *"Jesus is Lord"* was the earliest Christian creed. Any unbeliever confessing that Jesus Christ is Lord could be baptized. The reason is, nobody can say, *"Jesus is Lord,"* except by the Holy Spirit, 1 Corinthians 12:3. Still today, *"If you confess with your mouth, 'Jesus is Lord,' and believe in your heart that God raised Him from the dead, you will be saved,"* Romans 10:9. Do you know why? By saying *"Jesus is Lord,"* you have a Biblical conviction about Christ and a personal commitment to Him as your Lord! See Acts 2:36-37 to learn more on the importance of Christ's Lordship.

Prayer: Lord, what love You showered on us in giving us Jesus! You sent Him to this sinful earth to pay a debt He didn't owe, because we owed a debt we couldn't pay! How we love and worship You for it! May we live for You. In the Lord Jesus' name we pray. Amen.

September 25

"Now there was a man in Jerusalem called Simeon, who was righteous and devout. He was waiting for the consolation of Israel, and the Holy Spirit was upon him." Luke 2:25

Grandpa Simeon blesses Jesus' family

Simeon is introduced to us as *"righteous and devout."* He spent much time in prayer and in communion with the Lord. It is specifically recorded that Simeon was *"waiting for the consolation of Israel,"* for the coming of the Messiah. God had revealed to him that the Christ, the long-awaited one in the Old Testament, would be seen with Simeon's own eyes before he died. So Simeon is waiting in the temple courtyard, knowing that someday Jesus would show up. Finally the big day came. And the result was Simeon praised God even more. He said, *"My eyes have seen Your salvation,"* Luke 2:30. That brings up a good question. What do we see by faith? If we search the Scriptures, if we are righteous and devout before God, we too will be able to say with Simeon, *"My eyes have seen Your salvation"*! And Simeon was filled with peace as he left the temple. We have peace when we hold Jesus close in our heart.

In Jesus day, it was customary for Jewish parents to take their firstborn boy to the temple to give a sacrifice and then to receive a blessing. It appears that Simeon is the priest. Jesus totally fulfilled the Old Testament in going to the temple. When giving the blessing to the Child, Simeon knew who he was holding! With great foresight the first part of his blessing was, *"This child is destined to cause the falling and rising of many in Israel,"* Luke 2:34b.

How are we doing spiritually speaking? Are we *"rising"* or *"falling"* in our faith? What is our response to this Jesus who is the Lord? If an Old Testament person like Simeon could see the divine Child so clearly, how much more should we who have a crucified and ascended Jesus!

Prayer: Lord, little is said about the childhood of Jesus. Yet here we see that He humbly went to the temple as a baby. Lord, You saw fit to glorify Your Son through the actions of this devout Simeon whom You raised up! Lord, raise us up to be a blessing to Your kingdom also. In Jesus' name we pray. Amen.

September 26

"There was also a prophetess, Anna, the daughter of Phanuel, of the tribe of Asher. She was very old; she had lived with her husband seven years after her marriage, and then she was a widow until she was eighty-four. She never left the temple but worshiped night and day, fasting and praying." Luke 2:36-37

Grandma Anna, thankful, not bitter!

What a woman Anna was! She had just seven years of marriage and was a widow for probably sixty years! A widow in any culture is most difficult, but a widow in Israel was doubly hard. What a response of grace to the hardships she faced in life! What hope she had! How did she do it?

Anna obviously got rid of all bitterness. Many people in her situation don't do that! Anna could have been filled with self-pity, for that was the temptation she faced! Anna could have been paralyzed by fear, but she was too close to God to go down that rough road. Anna had a response of grace because the grace of God was deep in her! Gracious responses come from the grace of God in us all.

Anna had hope! Her hope was in God and in His promises to her! Anna knew much of the Old Testament, as she was in the temple *"night and day."* She was close to God, real close. Hope from God is not dependent on our health, on other people, or in circumstances being just right! Biblical hope does not depend on what we have in our hand but what we hold in our heart!

There is another part to Anna's hope! She hoped and prayed for the coming Messiah that God promised! The verse after our text says; *"Coming up to them* (that is Joseph, Mary, Baby Jesus and old Simeon) *at that very moment, she gave thanks to God and spoke about the Child to all who were looking forward to the redemption of Jerusalem,"* Luke 2:38. Anna saw Jesus, her hoped for Messiah. Now she lives on to tell others about Him! Do we hope for the Messiah's return? Do we tell others about Him as Anna did? If we do, that is thankful living!

Prayer: Lord, Your grace in Anna made all the difference! Instead of wasting her life on self-pity and bitterness, she lived her life in thanksgiving. Fill us with Your grace so we too live graciously! In Jesus' name we pray. Amen.

September 27

"And the child grew and became strong; he was filled with wisdom, and the grace of God was upon Him." Luke 2:40

Jesus' leadership training started young

We need solid leaders in our churches! How should they be trained? Jesus' training as a leader started young! Too often this time of His life is overlooked! Two year old Hebrew children learned and recited daily the following Shema. *"Hear, O Israel: The Lord our God, the Lord is one. Love the Lord your God with all your heart and with all your soul and with all your strength. These commandments that I give you today are to be upon your hearts. Impress them on your children. Talk about them when you sit at home and when you walk along the road, when you lie down and when you get up. Tie them as symbols on your hands and bind them on your foreheads. Write them on the doorframes of your houses and on your gates,"* Deuteronomy 6:4-9. All children needed to learn these truths early. Wise leader training starts in infancy! Three points we must learn from Jesus' training.

1. <u>Leadership is about relationships</u>. Jesus loved God. As a human being Jesus loved God. Children must learn to love God. The next point tomorrow is on obedience. Not one of us is interested in obedience, if we do not first love God. Besides loving God, we must love the ones we lead. *"If someone says, 'I love God,' and hates his brother, he is a liar; for he who does not love his brother whom he has seen, how can he love God whom he has not seen?"* 1 John 4:20 NKJV. We hate others and God, because our love for self is so far out front.

A selfish leader is into "privileges" not "servant-hood." How do leaders get so selfish? They are born selfish, and many parents make their child more selfish from infancy! They get what they want, when they want it, as often as they want it! The parents jump when the child moans. They laugh at their child's prideful acts as they grow! Then, suddenly, the parent is crying, wondering what went wrong! And we in turn wonder, why real leaders are so few?

Prayer: Lord, forgive us for learning leadership from the world instead of from Him who is the Way, the Truth and the Life. How timeless and priceless are His ways. In His name we pray. Amen.

September 28

"And Jesus grew in wisdom and stature, and in favor with God and men." Luke 2:52

Jesus' leadership training "*grew*"

We continue to look at the training that Jesus received.

2. <u>Jesus learned obedience as He "grew</u>." A child must learn about obedience before age one! An undisciplined child is the opposite of the way Jesus learned to "do right." Leadership that tells others to "do right," is not enough. Leaders themselves, must "do right." Leaders must reverence God's commandments. This means they must also respect authority, not lie, not cheat, not steal, not commit adultery, and not covet. Jesus learned godly obedience very young.

3. <u>Jesus learned valuable skills as He "grew</u>." He learned discipleship skills before He taught others! As a young carpenter, Jesus learned <u>how to work</u>. He knew the importance and satisfaction of hard, sacrificial, physical work for the benefit of others. Today, too many leaders don't know how to work! Jesus learned about <u>work process</u>. He learned to take wood, steel and stone from a rough shape, and mold it into a finished product. Using the very same process, Jesus took "rough fishermen," that He shaped into vessels for The King.

Jesus learned <u>character</u> as He grew. Today, many leaders know much about books, little about character. When knowledge trumps character we have a king, not a servant-leader like Jesus!

Jesus learned to <u>manage</u> as He "*grew*." With limited time and resources, He learned to schedule, budget, prioritize and constantly evaluate. Later Jesus had three years, a stone for a pillow and little food to feed many. He prioritized events to teach the right things in the right order. He evaluated His disciples with gentle rebukes and encouragement.

Jesus had the <u>opportunity</u> to display His skills and delegate responsibilities. Today many leaders hang on to absolute control, without practicing discipleship. Jesus knew how the multiplication of discipleship worked. Too many leaders pretend about disciples "developing their gifts," but do little in allowing or encouraging them to use them.

Prayer: Lord, impress on our hearts what You taught Jesus about leadership. Help us to follow Your example. In His name we pray. Amen.

September 29

"The Word of the God came to John son of Zechariah in the desert. He went into all the country around the Jordan, preaching a baptism of repentance for the forgiveness of sins." Luke 3:2b-3

John's mission, prepare for the Messiah

John the Baptist was a unique character in the Bible with a specific mission. He is the last Old Testament prophet, almost 400 years after Malachi. We see in our text that the word of the Lord came to him in the desert. This is a common way prophets were called. John was a Levite, a descendant of Aaron who's office was in the wilderness, not in any temple. His mission was to prepare people spiritually and morally for Jesus arrival. That is exactly why John preaches about repentance, forgiveness and the need of a Savior. John was telling the people to turn to Christ? When Jesus' comes, according to Matthew 21:43, He was going to remove the kingdom from unbelieving and unrepentant Israel and give it to the other nations, to the Gentiles! This is why John is so serious! This is why he is crying out!

What is true for the Israelites in John's day, is true for us today. John did not beat around the bush when he said about Jesus, *"His winnowing fork is in His hand to clear His threshing floor and to gather the wheat into the barn, but He will burn the chaff with unquenchable fire,"* Luke 3:17. The Israelites who repented and turned to Jesus Christ would be saved, the others, burned up. Jesus came with a ministry of salvation for all nations, but He is also coming in judgment for those who don't believe.

Do not be mistaken. Repentance does not save us any more than our faith saves us! Jesus alone saves! John's message was repent and have your sins forgiven by Jesus Christ! John's approach in calling for repentance and pointing to Jesus is what we still need! God help us to believe in Jesus!

Prayer: Dear Lord, we can see how You used John the Baptist, a man who dressed funny, used hard language and told people what they did not want to hear! Yet You wanted to get the attention of sinners. You knew we needed Jesus. O Lord, how we need all of His holiness and none of our sinfulness! Fill us with Him. In Jesus' name we pray. Amen.

September 30

"When a woman who had lived a sinful life in that town learned that Jesus was eating at the Pharisee's house, she brought an alabaster jar of perfume, and as she stood behind Him at His feet weeping, she began to wet His feet with her tears. Then she wiped them with her hair, kissed them and poured perfume on them." Luke 7:37-38

A woman who anointed the feet of Jesus

The Bible shows us how a common woman was sincere in how she loved Jesus. She went against cultural practice to show her love. The setting is this: A Pharisee invited Jesus to dinner. Perhaps they thought they were showing their love to Jesus by doing this. But Jesus in typical form used this common woman who was a sinner, to teach them what real love looked like. So this woman with a "shady past," shows up with an expensive jar of perfume. She is in tears. She cries so much that she washes Jesus feet with her tears and dries them with her hair. And then, she kisses His feet and applies the perfume! The host Pharisee observes this. He thinks that a true prophet would not come near this woman, for a prophet would know the kind of sinner she was!

Jesus knew the thoughts of His Pharisee host. So He tells him about two men. One owed a moneylender 500 days' wages, another owed 50 days' wages. Neither could pay. Then both were forgiven their huge debt. Jesus asked, "Who would be the most grateful?" The Pharisee said, "The one who owed the most!" Yes, and this woman with the greater sin debt owed the most! *"Then Jesus said to her, your sins are forgiven,"* Luke 7:48. Did one of these cruel moneylenders ever forgive a debt? No, they had someone beaten if they didn't pay! But Jesus forgives!

No one has sins so great that Jesus cannot completely forgive them! His grace is greater than all our sin. If this woman who was known in the community as a great sinner could be forgiven, then so can we be forgiven. And then secondly, how much do we love Jesus for His forgiveness? Do we openly display our love to Him? *"He who has been forgiven little loves little,"* Luke 7:47b.

Prayer: Lord, this woman who sinned much puts us to shame! We too are great sinners who cannot pay our huge sin debt! May we love as this woman did, unashamedly! In Jesus' name we pray. Amen.

OCTOBER

Women looking for Jesus at the tomb

"When the Sabbath was over, Mary Magdalene, Mary the mother of James, and Salome bought spices so that they might go to anoint Jesus' body." Mark 16:1

October 1

"A man was going down from Jerusalem to Jericho, when he fell into the hands of robbers. They stripped him of his clothes, beat him, and went away leaving him half-dead... A priest... and... a Levite... passed by on the other side. But a Samaritan, as he traveled, came where the man was; and when he saw him, he took pity on him." Luke 10:30b-33

The Good Samaritan, who is He?

A proud lawyer asked Jesus, "Who is this neighbor that I must love to inherit eternal life?" The better lawyer, Jesus, asks him a question in return. (We must learn from Jesus; don't argue, ask questions.) Jesus' parable on the "Good Samaritan," is His response to the "expert."

A man is beaten up, robbed, half-dead, laying on the road. The priest and Levite passed by, (these were the wicked teachers of the law, the Pharisees). They daily traveled the Jericho to Jerusalem road.

The wounded, half-dead man is you and I, dying sinners! It is a picture of our spiritual condition! Only we were not *"half-dead."* We "were dead in our trespasses and sins," Ephesians 2:1b. Satan was the robber who beat us and tore our robes of righteousness! Satan stole our identity with God in the Garden of Eden!

Who was this mixed breed Samaritan who came and rescued us? It was Jesus! We can know this from history. *"The king of Assyria brought people from Babylon, (and other towns) and settled them in the towns of Samaria to replace the Israelites. They took over Samaria and lived in its towns,"* 2 Kings 17:24. The Jews were racist. They hated the Gentile Samaritans who were a mixture of people from all races! Gentiles, Tamar, Ruth and Rahab were Jesus' grandmothers! He is the Good Samaritan in more ways than one!

Jesus *"was a neighbor to the man who fell into the hands of the robbers"*! So Jesus' question is an evangelism question! Do we go to the other side of the road to avoid half-dead sinners? The religious leaders of Jesus' day did that every day! "Church" to them, was a selfish, comfortable business! What is it to us?

Prayer: Lord, we thank You for caring about our lost condition! You bound our wounds and paid the price to restore us! You bring us to that Great Inn, Heaven. We worship You. In Jesus' name we pray. Amen.

October 2

"She (Martha) had a sister called Mary, who sat at the Lord's feet listening to what He said." Luke 10:39

Mary, the one who sat at Jesus' feet

Jesus and His disciples were invited into the home of Martha. Her sister, Mary, also lived with her, along with a brother Lazarus, of whom we will learn about later. Jesus enters the home of these believers because He needs food and a place to stay. But there is another important reason. Our God wants to show us how two sisters handle life differently. They share the same home. They face the same issues. But they handle their day to day problems differently. Their different response to Jesus, is significant! Jesus points out this difference to help us learn an important lesson in life.

Mary, *"sat at the Lord's feet listening to what He said."* Martha on the other hand, was busy in the kitchen, anxious about the food she would serve and getting everything "just right." Serving others is good! But Jesus is far more concerned about what we are <u>becoming</u>, than what we are <u>doing</u>! That is the reason Jesus said to Martha, *"Mary has chosen what is better, and it will not be taken away from her,"* Luke 10:42b. Working on a relationship with Jesus has eternal benefits. Mary was <u>acting</u> on getting to know Jesus better!

This story really challenges our daily habits. Could it be that we have been so busy serving the Lord, like Martha, that we do not have a very close relationship with Him? But do not take this the wrong way. To separate ourself from all duties and society to "get holy," is not the point here either. Duties do matter. But our time at Jesus' feet prepares us to do our work to the honor and glory of God! It is also a point here that Jesus is teaching women! In some cultures, it was commonly thought that women did not need to learn, but that they only needed to serve.

Mary *"sat at the Lord's feet,"* a sign of her humility and her spiritual hunger. Mary was quiet before the Lord. In summary, we can see that Martha fed Jesus, but more importantly Jesus fed Mary!

Prayer: Lord, we see the heart of Mary here who wanted to learn about You and Your kingdom. O Lord, put that desire in us we pray. In Jesus' name we pray. Amen.

October 3

"But Martha was distracted by all the preparations that had to be made. She came to Him and asked, 'Lord, don't you care that my sister has left me to do the work myself? Tell her to help me!'" Luke 10:40

Martha, the *"distracted"* one

Today and again tomorrow, we want to study more on the Mary and Martha contrast. *"But Martha was distracted."* The question for each of us is: "What is it, that distracts me from sitting at Jesus feet?" Whatever that "distraction" is, it really is an idol. Even ministry work can be our idol! Was Martha guilty of serving the Lord Jesus Christ but not really listening to Him? Is it possible that Martha was quite proud of her ministry to Jesus and wanted others to notice her great job? Was Martha more concerned about her reputation than knowing Jesus?

What about Martha's statement? *"Lord, don't You care that my sister has left me to do the work myself? Tell her to help me!"* Martha is quite filled with self-pity! I call it the "martyr syndrome." That is a "look at me" mentality. That kind of love turns the message of the Bible upside down! God first, others second, self last, is what the commandments and the Bible teach. Martha did not have the order of her love right! Jesus tells her and us: *"'Love the Lord your God with all your heart and with all your soul and with all your mind.' This is the first and greatest commandment. And the second is like it: 'Love your neighbor as yourself.' All the Law and the Prophets hang on these two commandments."* Matthew 22:37-40. Martha was not living like this!

Jesus was kind in His gentle rebuke to Martha. He did not tell her that serving Him was not needed. He simply said, *"'Martha, Martha,' the Lord answered, 'You are worried and upset about many things, but only one thing is needed,'"* Luke 10:41-42a. Jesus is basically saying, "Good job Martha, but *'one thing,'* <u>sit</u> at My feet." Once again we must come back to the question. What is it that is distracting us from that *"one thing,"* from knowing Jesus better? What is it that keeps us from having a vibrant prayer life and from studying His Word more?

Prayer: Lord, we need Your gentle corrections! You never crushed people's spirit, but lovingly corrected them for a closer relationship with You. May we do the same. In Jesus' name we pray. Amen.

October 4

"And Jesus answered and said to her, 'Martha, Martha, <u>you are worried</u> and troubled about many things. But one thing is needed, and Mary has chosen that good part, which will not be taken away from her.'" Luke 10:41-42 NKJV

Martha, "worried and troubled"

Jesus here draws attention to Martha's worry to show us a real personality problem. In Matthew 6:30b, "worry" is called by Jesus, "little faith." That truth must get our attention! "Worry" is not a Christian virtue! Worry may be the most socially acceptable sin in the Christian camp, but Jesus is not impressed with it! When teaching on the subject elsewhere, He said, "Do not worry, saying, 'What shall we eat?' or, 'What shall we drink?' or 'What shall we wear?' For the pagans run after all these things," Matthew 6:31-32a. Ouch! Like Martha, we sometimes act like unbelieving pagans! Do you know why? "Worry," is the complete opposite of trusting in God to supply our needs!

We have a Heavenly Father in Heaven! He controls the whole world. He controls us too. Our loving Father feeds the birds of the air and dresses up the lily in the field. He will care even more than that for us who are His prized possession in Christ! We are His adopted sons and daughters! He is "able to do exceedingly abundantly above all that we ask or think," Ephesians 3:20b NKJV.

Being "worried and troubled about many things," is anxiety! "Anxiety in the heart of man causes depression, but a good word makes it glad," Proverbs 12:25 NKJV. So being worried, troubled, anxious and fearful, can very easily lead to depression. <u>As busy as we are, our schedule is lacking if we do not go to the feet of Jesus</u>. A "good word" from Him is what we need! "Mary has chosen the good part." We too must work on our relationship with Him. "He who pursues righteousness and love finds life, prosperity and honor," Proverbs 21:21. Twenty-one is sometimes called the "adult age." Proverbs 21:21, is spiritual maturity!

Prayer: Lord, we don't want to act like pagans! We don't want to have little faith! We want to trust You more! Lord fill us with Your Spirit so that we trust and obey, for there is no other way to be happy in Jesus! In Jesus' name we pray. Amen.

October 5

"On a Sabbath Jesus was teaching in one of the synagogues, and a woman was there who had been crippled by a spirit for eighteen years. She was bent over and could not straighten up at all. When Jesus saw her, He called her forward and said to her, 'Woman, you are set free from your infirmity.' Then He put His hands on her, and immediately she straightened up and praised God." Luke 13:10-13

A crippled woman who was "set free"

Luke 13 begins with Jesus discussing how some Galileans had shed their own blood as part of a "religious ceremony." Then, 18 people died when a wall fell on them. Jesus asked, do you think these people were "*worse sinners*" because they suffered like this? "*I tell you, no! But unless you repent, you too will all perish,*" Luke 13:3. All of us are guilty and must repent or die. All of us are <u>totally depraved</u>!

The opening details of the chapter apply to this crippled woman! Note that this woman had 18 years of enslavement to a spirit, not God's Spirit! The picture is, "*she was bent over and could not straighten up at all,*" Luke 13:11b. She could not remove her sin burden on her own!

This spiritually and physically crippled woman now goes to Jesus. His <u>irresistible grace</u> pulls her! "*When Jesus saw her, <u>He called her forward</u> and said to her, 'Woman, you are set free.'*" Now the religious leaders are "*indignant*" at Jesus because He "*worked*" on the Sabbath. So Jesus asks them if they gave their animals water on the Sabbath? They did, and before them was a woman who needed "living water."

Jesus healed this unnamed woman, pointing us to the truth of <u>election</u>! "*Should not this woman, <u>a daughter of Abraham</u>, whom Satan has kept bound for eighteen long years, be set free on the Sabbath day from what bound her?*" Luke 13:16. She should. She must. She will. Her name was written on Jesus' hands before time began! She was healed, in God's perfect timing.

Prayer: Lord, what a complete picture of the Gospel this crippled woman is. We see her original sin. We see You pulling her to Yourself! We see her being selected by You. We see Your removal of her sin burden. Lord how true this is for all who believe! "*And she immediately straightened up and praised God,*" and so do we! In Jesus' name we pray. Amen.

October 6

"The younger son got together all he had, set off for a distant country and there squandered his wealth in wild living." Luke 15:13b

Prodigal son, forever changed!

I believe that the people and events surrounding this prodigal son teach us more about the amazing grace of God, than in any other place in the Bible. I will number the important grace points, to highlight the grace of God to us who are sinners.

First, this spoiled youngest prodigal is a picture of: (1) our <u>totally depraved nature</u>! He has a totally different idea about how he wants to live as compared to the father, a picture of our God and Father in Heaven. So he leaves the father to get in his opinion a "real life"! And suddenly, he becomes a slave to his passions, eating with pigs. This is quite the picture of our sinful, depraved spiritual condition.

Second, since no slave can set himself free, God alone, by His Spirit, convicts this wayward son of his sinful living pattern! (2) <u>God had to completely select/elect this sinner,</u> just as God elects all sinners! The prodigal learned the hard way that his life was very quickly going from bad to worse. But God's Spirit made him come to his senses!

Third, the father draws the prodigal to himself, and the son (3) <u>cannot resist</u> the pull of the father. In fact, the father is looking down the road for the son to appear knowing the exact time the son is coming! Then, to highlight the grace of God, the father embraces the son <u>before</u> the son even opens his mouth to confess his sin!

Fourth, the father puts new clothes on the son, new sandals on his feet and (4) a ring on his finer to symbolize the fact that he is now a son <u>forever</u>! The son will now <u>persevere</u> in his new relationship because of what the father did in making him a royal heir! Still, another point of grace we will see tomorrow.

Prayer: Dear Lord, Your grace is so amazing in showing us how great a sinner we are! And then, You free us from our sin by the blood of Your perfect Son, making us perfectly righteous! How You pull us to Yourself when we are bent on living wickedly. And You so completely save us that we will never for one moment be lost again! Lord, we worship and praise You for Your grace! In Jesus' name we pray. Amen.

October 7

"The older brother became angry and refused to go in. So his father went out and pleaded with him. But he answered his father, 'Look! All these years I've been slaving for you and never disobeyed your orders; Yet you never gave me even a young goat so I could celebrate with my friends.'" Luke 15:28-29

Older brother, refuses to celebrate

To understand who the Older Son is, we need to know that the parable of the lost sheep, the lost coin and the prodigal son are just one parable, told three ways. Secondly, we must know who Jesus' audience is. We know that from how the parable begins. *"Now the tax collectors and 'sinners' were all gathering around to hear Him. But the Pharisees and the teachers of the law muttered, 'This man welcomes sinners and eats with them,'"* Luke 15:1-2.

"The older brother became angry." This is exactly the attitude of the self-righteous Pharisees and teachers of the law towards Jesus and His disciples. They are the ones who, *"refused to go in."* They would not welcome a sinner who was saved by Christ! In fact, the Pharisees looked at a sinner with contempt! *"His father went out and pleaded with him."* God sent priests, judges, prophets and kings to direct them to Himself. Jesus filled all of these offices and they rejected Jesus also!

The older brother said, *"I've been slaving for you."* He thought he had earned his righteousness! He even claimed perfect obedience saying, I *"never disobeyed your orders."* He didn't know a relationship with Jesus! He had no reason to celebrate. This sour attitude defined the Pharisees!

The disciples once asked Jesus, *"'Why do You speak to them in parables?' He answered and said to them, 'Because it has been given to you to know the mysteries of the kingdom of Heaven, but to them it has not been given,'"* Matthew 13:10b-11 NKJV. And there is the fifth (5) and last point of grace, *"limited atonement."* Grace is limited to those Christ gives it to. If a prisoner's sentence is commuted by the judge, he is a free man. But not all prisoners are set free!

Prayer: Lord, Your grace to us gets more amazing every day! We are so undeserving and You are so gracious. We worship You for forgiving us and saving us! In Jesus' name we pray. Amen.

October 8

"There was a rich man who was dressed in purple and fine linen and lived in luxury every day. At his gate was laid a beggar named Lazarus, covered with sores and longing to eat what fell from the rich man's table. Even the dogs came and licked his sores." Luke 16:19-21

The rich man, Lazarus and us - Part 1

We have before us a *"rich man"* and a poor man to get our attention on the value of eternal things, as compared to money and the comforts it can buy! The problem with this *"rich man"* was not so much his riches, but that he was uncaring! His arrogant attitude on earth, placed him in Hell for eternity. When the reality of his eternal torment was suddenly experienced, the *"rich man"* wanted to warn his *"brothers"* not to live like he did! Dear friend, these *"brothers"* he wanted to warn are us!

Jesus would not allow the *"rich man"* to warn anyone! The reason is, we already have "*Moses and the Prophets*," to warn us! We have the Old Testament, and a complete New Testament telling us to care about the poor and to seek a relationship with God and man.

Moses said to the rich man, "*When you have finished setting aside a tenth of all your produce in the third year, the year of the tithe, you shall give it to the Levite, the alien, the fatherless and the widow*," Deuteronomy 26:12a. The rich man failed this 10% tithe test! He did not give to the "Levite," the organized church, nor did he, as part of his tithe, help those in need! God gives us all the responsibility to help care for those who cannot care for themselves!

Ezekiel said to the rich man, "*Now this was the sin of your sister: She and her daughters were arrogant, overfed and unconcerned; they did not help the poor and needy. They were haughty and did detestable things before Me. Therefore I did away with them as you have seen*," Ezekiel 16:49-50. The wicked in Israel were "*detestable*" unconcerned about the "*poor and needy*." If they had known Jesus personally, they would have cared about the things that Jesus cared about!

Prayer: Lord, what sobering words, You destroyed this *"rich man"* because he was selfish, unconcerned about God and man! Change our hearts Lord! Forgive us and use us to be a blessing to many! In Jesus' name we pray. Amen.

October 9

"There was a rich man who was dressed in purple and fine linen and lived in luxury every day. At his gate was laid a beggar named Lazarus, covered with sores and longing to eat what fell from the rich man's table. Even the dogs came and licked his sores." Luke 16:19-21

The rich man, Lazarus and us - Part 2

The parable is not teaching that giving to the poor saves us. Jesus alone saves. But after one is saved, he or she will care about what moves the heart of God! Particularly notice the order of things here in Luke's Gospel. First, the parable of the Prodigal Son in Luke 15 shows us the real grace of God in saving a repentant sinner. Now we have the parable of the "Rich Man," to contrast for us the very real wrath of God, in condemning an unrepentant sinner!

Like the Pharisees in Jesus' day, many people still mock the doctrine of Hell. The Sadducees denied the possibility of a coming resurrection. These people did not want to believe that anyone deserves eternal punishment, for then they too would also be deserving of it personally! Jesus tells us this story of the rich man and Lazarus to get us more serious about the reality and the difference between Heaven and Hell in the soon to come afterlife!

We have before us the godly Lazarus who was so horribly treated in this world. But he was never forgotten by God. Lazarus's name itself means "God has helped." There are many "Lazarus" in this world who need to be reminded that God sees and cares about them! Do we?

This parable presents some good questions! Will we from Heaven see loved ones in Hell? No! Will we miss those we once loved on earth? The answer has to be "No" once more! The only possibility I can think of is that there will be no loved ones in Hell, but only those we once loved! In Heaven, we will be completely in love with those we are with, and with God. Even more than that, we will truly see Jesus, "*as He is*"! Formerly, we loved the image of God in many different people. But if anyone dies without Christ, there remains none of God's beauty in them!

Prayer: Lord, too often we are this unbelieving rich man. We are unwilling to help those You lay on our doorstep. Lord, help us to see that we too are beggars for Your grace and love! In Jesus' name we pray! Amen.

October 10

"Then Jesus told His disciples a parable to show them that they should always pray and not give up. He said: 'In a certain town there was a judge who neither feared God nor cared about men. And there was a widow in that town who kept coming to him with the plea, "Grant me justice against my adversary."'" Luke 18:1-3

Persistent widow, she prevails

In our text, Jesus desires that all of His dear children, *"should always pray and not give up."* For this reason, Jesus tells His disciples and us about a widow woman who was being mistreated badly. He does not say exactly what the gross injustice was to this woman. Perhaps Jesus wanted us to know that He, as a just and holy God, cares much about every injustice we will ever face. So make no mistake dear believer, this widow who is suffering at the hands of others, is us! She has no one to help her out. Her only possibility for relief is to go to the local judge who is totally unjust in how he operates. This wicked judge's common practice is to make a decision based on how much it would benefit him personally.

This persistent widow has nothing. She has no money. She has no "rights." She has so little of this world's goods that she can't even give a small bribe to move this judge to act on her behalf. All this widow can do is bombard Mr. Unjust Judge day and night with her cries for mercy! This is exactly our position as poor sinners.

Do we recognize that we stand before the just judge Jesus Christ, just like this widow lady? We must be persistent and earnest! Jesus is encouraging us to do just that. His point is: If an unjust judge is willing to give mercy to an undeserving sinner, how much more will Jesus our Just Judge, give mercy to His own children!

Prayer: Lord, we thank You for showing us the truth about persistently coming to You, pleading for Your mercy. Not just Your saving mercy do we seek, but Your protecting and providing mercy. Lord, how we need You to move mountains for us. Do that so we can see even more clearly Your abundant grace. Awe us with Your presence so that we testify of Your goodness! In Jesus' name we pray. Amen.

October 11

"To some who were confident of their own righteousness and looked down on everybody else, Jesus told this parable: 'Two men went up to the temple to pray, one a Pharisee and the other a tax collector. The Pharisee stood up and prayed about himself: "God, I thank you that I am not like other men — robbers, evildoers, adulterers or even like this tax collector. I fast twice a week and give a tenth of all I get.""
Luke 18:9-12

Proud Pharisee, he fails

We have just seen Mrs. Persistent Widow who humbly cried for mercy. Now Jesus shows us the worthless prayer of a "Proud Pharisee." Yes, he did pray, but the content of his prayer was telling God how good he was! This Pharisee represents proud people everywhere and Jesus points out two problems. First, they "<u>were confident of their own righteousness</u>," and second, they "<u>looked down on everybody else</u>," Luke 18:9. The big question is, "Am I like that?" What does a self-righteous person do that is so "*confident of their own righteousness*"?

A Pharisee never mentions his own sin. Not once is it ever recorded that a Pharisee confessed any sin of his own. In fact, when he prays, he does the opposite. He pats himself on the back for how good he is! His mountain of pride thinks that he is a gift to God's kingdom! He therefore sees no need for the Gift of God, which is Jesus Himself. Never, not even once, did a Pharisee ask God for his daily bread either! A Pharisee prays, "*about himself*" and lifts up his own name. He really wants people to bow to him, not to God!

The Pharisee was so self-centered that he "*looked down on everybody else.*" This means that he saw others as "despicable," as his and God's enemies! This is what a proud self-righteous person does yet today! Other religious leanings are offensive to him. Plus, "*robbers, evildoers and adulterers*" were dirty people to him. The Pharisee did not see that he was the most offensive and dirtiest one of all!

Prayer: Lord, open our eyes to the ways we are proud and self-righteous. Lord, help us to see our own faults, our own blemishes. May we turn from them. Convict us of all the ways we sin against You. Forgive our sins. In Jesus' name we pray. Amen.

October 12

"When Jesus reached the spot, He looked up and said to him, 'Zacchaeus, come down immediately. I must stay at your house today.' So he came down at once and welcomed Him gladly." Luke 19:5-6

Zacchaeus, a weird, despicable man

There is a lot to learn in the life of Zacchaeus that is important! This is one of the few places in Scripture where Jesus calls out to a man. Normally, we see the people calling out to Jesus for mercy! Yet the amazing truth of grace is: God always starts the new, spiritual birth process in all people! Jesus said in John 15:16a, *"You did not choose Me, but I choose you and appointed you to go and bear fruit – fruit that will last."* We see not only ourselves but others crying out to God. We can't see the Holy Spirit convicting us of our sin, drawing us to God.

Why *"must"* Jesus go to this man's house? One reason is because Zacchaeus' name was written on Jesus' hands as one of His own! Now Jesus is claiming him! In Jesus' own prayer He said, *"Father, I want those You have given Me to be with Me where I am, and to see My glory, the glory You have given Me because You loved Me before the creation of the world,"* John 17:24.

What better way could Jesus show the power of His sovereign, transforming grace, than in Zacchaeus, a really nasty person. <u>Zacchaeus was a Jew who worked for foreigners to collect unreasonable taxes on fellow Jews!</u> He was an obnoxious, little man who was very rich with money taken from his own people. He was a traitor. He was weird. He ran fast through a crowd and climbed a tree. His social skills were a complete failure. He was a publican, which means he was most likely excommunicated by the ruling Sanhedrin.

Jesus' grace to Zacchaeus was immediate! He said, *"Here and now I give half of my possessions to the poor, and if I have cheated anybody out of anything, I will pay back four times the amount,"* Luke 19:8b.

Prayer: Lord, we are as nasty and naughty as this little man! And then You came to our house, just as You did to the house of Zacchaeus! You came into our hearts and put Your grace into us! We pray that Your grace would be as evident in our lives as it was in the life of Zacchaeus! In Jesus' name we pray. Amen.

October 13

Jesus said, *"But the hand of him who is going to betray Me is with Mine on the table." "They began to question among themselves which of them it might be who would do this."* Luke 22:21 & 23

Judas and persecution

The ultimate persecution ever, was the betrayal and subsequent death of the holy, God-man Jesus. Now we would think that this attempt to stop Jesus' ministry and life would come from the age old enemies of God, the heathen of the surrounding lands. But no, it came from among His twelve disciples. It came from those who knew Him. In the book, "Back to Jerusalem," the author tells about the persecution in China from unbelievers. The author compared that to the West where persecution is mainly from within the church, as we see here with Jesus. How do we respond to those who persecute us?

First, we must expect to be persecuted! Jesus said, *"If they persecuted Me, they will persecute you also,"* John 15:20b. If we do not expect persecution, we will have a very bitter attitude when it does come! I have done that! And my bitterness towards those who tried to stop me from doing the Lord's work was wrong. Your attitude will not be very positive either if you do not expect persecution!

Second, in the midst of persecution, stay faithful to what God has called us to! Jesus' response to persecution was that He lived for the will of the Father and still faithfully carried out the work that God had called Him to do! We must do the same. We must stay focused on God's work and a deeper relationship to Him, even as people try to stop us!

Third, at first others will be blind to the church members who are trying to stop the Gospel. When Jesus said to the disciples in Matthew 26:21, *"one of you will betray Me,"* they had no clue which disciple would do this! The person persecuting us will have some self-righteous reason for trying to put the brakes on us for teaching others to follow Christ. Again, stay faithful! Don't get sidetracked!

Prayer: Dear Lord, we have so much to learn about persecution. Continue to teach us. Forgive us for taking our eyes off from You as events develop to stop the Gospel. May we be faithful stewards of the truths of the Gospel. In Christ's name we pray. Amen.

October 14

"Simon, Simon, Satan has asked to sift you as wheat. But I have prayed for you, Simon, that your faith may not fail. And when you have turned back, strengthen your brothers." Luke 22:31-32

Simon Peter, Satan desires you!

Precious to God, all disciples of Jesus are important to Satan! Jesus tells Simon this by saying his name three times. Jesus said "Simon" as a kind rebuke to remind him of his old habits of being proud and loud! Jesus used the name "Peter" when he acted spiritually mature.

"Satan has asked to sift you." This first *"you"* is plural in the Greek meaning all the disciples. The following *"you"* and *"yours"* are for Peter personally. Satan knows Peter and the other ten disciples were chosen to carry on Jesus' work on earth. Satan hears his damnation clock ticking! He wants all leaders to fail. He wants national leaders, church leaders, and leaders of all kinds to fail, including those in the home! If the shepherd fails, Satan knows, the sheep will scatter.

"But I have prayed for you, Simon." Jesus will never let Satan have more of any believer, than what will benefit him in the end! *"He will not let you be tempted beyond what you can bear,"* 1 Corinthians 10:13b. Satan is allowed to afflict Simon thus he denies Jesus three times, the same amount of times he was called *"Simon."* Now, Peter feels the pain of guilt and weeps over his sin. Now, he is serious about changing. We don't change either until we weep over our sin. Jesus gave Satan just enough room, to force the pain of guilt on Peter, pushing him to repent! C. S. Lewis said, "Pain insists upon being attended to, God whispers to us in our pleasures, speaks in our conscience, but shouts in our pains; it is His megaphone to rouse a deaf world."

Jesus used Satan to wake Peter up! Jesus did not protect the other disciples like He protected Peter! And here's why! *"When you have turned back, strengthen your brothers."* Now it's Peter's mission to strengthen the others. Jesus provided for the ten, by providing for Peter.

Prayer: Lord, what a huge responsibility we now have as teachers and parents. How we too must overcome our personal sin, so that like Peter, we can teach others. Lord, we thank You for Your Spirit that gives us guilt, forcing us to change! In Jesus' name we pray. Amen.

October 15

"With one voice they cried out, 'Away with this man! Release Barabbas to us!' (Barabbas had been thrown into prison for an insurrection in the city, and for murder.)" Luke 23:18-19

Barabbas set free, like us!

The Roman government had a custom. Once a year at Passover time, a guilty man was released from prison and allowed to freely live again in society. It was intended to show that the government was gracious. The Roman governor of Judea and Samaria was Pilate. His job as governor, was to control the people and collect taxes for Rome. Pilate was the one who set a guilty person free. Pilate knew that Jesus was innocent. Herod Antipas, the Jewish leader knew it too. Justice would have been served if they had released the innocent Jesus. But Pilate had a problem. The chief priest and the people wanted Jesus killed. Pilate and Herod Antipas, both had their own dirty secrets. They could not afford a confrontation with the people.

Barabbas was a criminal. He was in prison *"for an insurrection in the city, and for murder."* He was a real enemy of both the Jews and the Roman government. Barabbas was a dangerous man! Politician Pilate offered the people a choice. You can have the innocent Jesus or the guilty Barabbas. Yet the people wanted Jesus dead. Perfect Jesus was killed on the Cross. Guilty Barabbas was set free. But then, is not this *"Barabbas"* really you and me?

It was ultimately God who put Jesus on that Cross. Jesus is the first and only one to perfectly keep the Old Testament "covenant of works"! Now, the New Testament "covenant of grace" can be implemented. God provided the Passover Lamb once, for all. The Jewish system is over! The final sacrifice has been made. We too are set free. Jesus took our place. In our place condemned He stood! In Christ, we are now just like Adam was before he sinned. *"God made Him who had no sin to be sin for us, so that in Him we might become the righteousness of God,"* 2 Corinthians 5:21. The Judge's hammer comes down; we are set free!

Prayer: Lord, how amazing that this Barabbas is like us! We are set free with the perfect obedience of Christ; He takes our sin. Lord, Your grace is beyond amazing! In Christ's name we pray. Amen.

October 16

"'We are punished justly, for we are getting what our deeds deserve. But this Man has done nothing wrong.' Then he said, 'Jesus, remember me when You come into Your kingdom.'" Luke 23:41-42

The dying thief, he saw and believed

The believing of the dying thief is quite something to meditate on! We usually just observe the last minute nature of his salvation experience. How important to see this, as it gives us hope for those who are not yet serious with God! There is hope for salvation while there is still breath! But there is so much more that God wants to teach us about what changed the mind of this Jewish bandit.

Think about what this dying thief saw. He saw Jesus beaten, scourged, and mocked. He saw some women who *"mourned and wailed for"* Jesus. He saw Jesus, on the way to be executed, tell these women, *"Daughters of Jerusalem, do not weep for Me; weep for yourselves and your children,"* Luke 23:28. The thief was moved by what Jesus said, and how He tenderly looked at the people with such concern and love!

The dying thief felt the nails go into his own hands and feet while he loudly cursed those who were doing it! Then he saw the soldiers lay Jesus on that Cross and drive those nails right through His hands and feet! But Jesus did not curse His executioners! Instead, He prayed, *"Father, forgive them, for they know not what they do."* He saw Jesus pray for His enemies when He was being put to death!

The thief saw the sign that said, *"This is the King of the Jews."* This Jewish thief was familiar with the Scriptures. His first thoughts of repentance had to be, "This may be the promised Messiah." And then he realized, "This is the promised Messiah!" Then in Luke 23:42, he said, *"Jesus, remember me when You come into Your kingdom,"* Luke 23:42. His faith was confirmed immediately. *"Jesus answered him, 'I tell you the truth, today you will be with Me in Paradise,"* Luke 23:43.

Prayer: Lord, what a beautiful picture of the Gospel of grace we see here. The thief's feet and hands were nailed down. He could do no work to "get saved." Your grace that saved him, also saves us sinners! We praise You for it! In Jesus' name we pray. Amen.

October 17

"Now there was a man named Joseph, a member of the Council, a good and upright man, who had not consented to their decision and action. He came from the Judean town of Arimathea and he was waiting for the kingdom of God." Luke 23:50-51

Joseph of Arimathea, a rich, godly man

Joseph was a man of means. He had money. He had reputation. He was honest. He had the respect of others. He was a counselor or senator. Joseph had spiritual wisdom. He did not consent to what the other wicked leaders were doing! He was a compassionate and godly man! Joseph had courage or boldness that he used to do good. He was one of the most qualified to be in a position of "spiritual leadership." He had a servant's heart. It was safe for God to bless this man because he stayed humble! It was this man, Joseph of Arimathea, that God raised up to give our Lord and Savior His earthly tomb.

What about us who by the grace of God are Christians? *"We are God's workmanship, created in Christ Jesus to do good works, which God prepared in advance for us to do,"* Ephesians 2:10. Do we, like this Joseph, look for opportunities to do good to others? Paul wrote; *"Let us not become weary in doing good, for at the proper time we will reap a harvest if we do not give up. Therefore, as we have opportunity, let us do good to all people, especially to those who belong to the family of believers,"* Galatians 6:9-10.

I know some "Josephs of Arimathea." They are a breath of fresh air. They are encouraging in the midst of so many discouragers! God has raised them up to be a blessing to others, all for the advancement of His kingdom! We praise God for these godly people. They are so needed. Like the original Joseph of Arimathea, they are humble servants of God, seeking to do good. May we all look for opportunities to do the same!

Prayer: Lord, bless our world with more who are like "Joseph of Arimathea." May we all step forward to be a blessing to You and to Your kingdom! Your kingdom endures forever! In Jesus' name we pray. Amen.

October 18

"The Word became flesh and made His dwelling among us. We have seen His glory, the glory of the One and Only, who came from the Father, full of grace and truth." John 1:14

Jesus the Man, full of grace and truth

John presents to us here the humble character of the Man Jesus. Yes, Jesus was fully God and He never ceased to be that. But here we are observing in just five words what the character of Jesus the Man was like. He was *"full of grace and truth."* As Christ's followers, both *"grace and truth"* must fill us! The problem we commonly have is: we are "full of truth," yet weak on grace; or, we are "full of grace" yet weak on truth doctrines. We need to be like Jesus, full of both.

How important it is to have a balance of grace and truth for parenting and evangelism! *"Truth,"* without grace is legalistic, which is what the Pharisees were. They thought they were fulfilling the law. So too, graceless people hate others who are not "doctrinally" just like them. And then they wonder why their parenting and evangelism efforts are not working! One man forced his children to repeat Sunday sermons after returning home. Yet he was the coldest fish I ever saw. He knew nothing about being kind and loving to his wife or children. She was a battered wife who lived a horrible life! His children couldn't wait to leave home and they do not go to church today! Truth without grace is harsh and promotes rebellion in others.

"Grace," without truth is pointless as far as the Gospel is concerned. Without the truth there is no conviction of sin. There is no confession. There is no repentance! There is no need for a Savior. When grace is big and truth is small, people are seen as big and God is seen as small. Grace without truth is spiritual ignorance!

We need to be like Jesus. He was, *"full of grace and truth."* We need to boldly speak the truth about people's spiritual condition, in a loving way. We need to know the grace of God and then live it out as worship to God and as a blessing to others!

Prayer: Lord, make us more like You, doctrinally pure and so very gracious in dealing with others. May we hate the sin and love the sinner, just like You did. In Jesus' name we pray. Amen.

October 19

"Andrew, Simon Peter's brother, was one of the two who heard what John had said and who had followed Jesus. The first thing Andrew did was to find his brother Simon and tell him, 'We have found the Messiah' (that is, the Christ). And he brought him to Jesus."
John 1:40-42a

Andrew, he brought people to Jesus!

Andrew was the younger brother of Peter. In fact, it was Andrew who brought Peter to Jesus. As we shall see, this was a pattern of how Andrew operated. He introduced people to Jesus. Andrew was a fisherman from Bethsaida. He surely was friends with the two fishermen brothers, James and John, from Bethsaida. These two sets of brothers, James and John; Peter and Andrew, made up the inner circle of Jesus' disciples. They were by God's design, common men and not the religious elite.

Andrew, of all the disciples, was the most thoughtful of others and the most easy to get along with. This fact made him approachable by members of the community. Andrew did not seek the spotlight or attention. He was especially willing to serve in the background. He humbly did the little things that kept Jesus' agenda running smooth. In the feeding of the 5,000 in John 6:8-9, Andrew took the initiative to find food for the huge crowd. He brought the boy with those five loaves and two fish to Jesus, trusting Jesus could do much with little!

Andrew was the first home missionary of the church when he brought Peter to Christ. He was also the first foreign missionary when he brought some Greek speaking people to Jesus. Andrew shows us that he believed in personal evangelism, which is still the most effective way to practically help people. Jesus Christ was precious to Andrew! The question is, how precious is Christ to us? Do we work to introduce others to Christ like Andrew did? Andrew's brother Peter wrote, *"Therefore, to you who believe, He is precious,"* 1 Peter 2:7a NKJV.

Prayer: Lord, You chose hard working men to teach us about the importance of obediently serving You and others. May we follow the example of Andrew who didn't care who got the glory, just so the job got done. Forgive us for our proud and selfish ways. In Jesus' name we pray. Amen.

October 20

"The next day, Jesus decided to leave for Galilee. Finding Philip, He said to him, "Follow Me.' Philip, like Andrew and Peter, was from the town of Bethsaida. Philip found Nathanael and told him, 'We have found the One Moses wrote about in the Law, and about whom the prophets also wrote-Jesus of Nazareth, the son of Joseph.'"
John 1:43-45

Philip, the one who willing followed

Jesus said but two words to Philip! *"Follow Me."* Those two words are sufficient for Jesus to make a sinner come to Him. It is good for our understanding of the grace of God, for the worship of God, that Jesus is the one who calls out to Philip. It was not the other way around. Philip did not ask Jesus if he could follow Him. There is much grace here in these two words, *"Follow Me."* They are a command that is obeyed every time, by every believer! Philip had to follow Jesus. Paul wrote, *"Those He called, He also justified,"* Romans 8:30b. Jesus' grace is irresistible! His calling is irrevocable.

Philip was also a fisherman just like Andrew and Peter. What stands out with Philip is he simply got the job done! Our Lord could have called more educated and refined men! After all, Nicodemus and Joseph of Arimathea were also available! But Jesus preferred simple, rough fishermen who could relate to the common man. Jesus loved His simple but willing and devoted disciples as we can see in Jesus' prayer in John 17. The disciples, with the exception of Judas, modeled the beatitudes. They were the poor in spirit. They were hungry and the mournful. The disciples were meek, merciful and pure in heart. They suffered much for righteousness sake! Are we willing to suffer for Him who suffered for us? The answer to that question is important now and it will echo throughout all eternity!

Prayer: Lord, we are humbled that You call simple people like Your disciples to take Your Word to the ends of the earth. May we be like Your precious disciples who were obedient to Your call to evangelize. For Lord, You are worthy of our worship and service! Fill us with your Spirit! In Jesus' name we pray. Amen.

October 21

"Jesus saw Nathanael coming to Him, and saith of him, Behold an Israelite indeed, in whom is no guile." John 1:47 KJV

Nathanael, a man without guile

What a great compliment Jesus gives to Nathanael. *"Guile"* is an older word, but we should know its meaning. The NKJV translates guile as *"no deceit."* The NIV says, *"nothing false."* In other words, Nathanael had integrity, he cheated no one,. He was completely honest, he openly spoke the truth boldly, yet lovingly. You knew what he was thinking, if he had a doubt he shared it. You could say, he wore his heart on his sleeve. If something had to be done he did it quickly and right. He was not selfish, but was a great friend to many.

When Jesus called Philip to be His disciple, Philip immediately went to his friend Nathanael telling him, *"We have found the One Moses wrote about in the Law, and about whom the prophets also wrote-Jesus of Nazareth, the son of Joseph,"* John 1:45b. Nathanael was shocked! *"'Nazareth! Can anything good come from there?' Nathanael asked."* John 1:46a. These words show an immediate response to a piece of news, as well as moving forward at the request of a friend. When Philip said, *"Come and see,"* Nathanael willingly went with him. He did not have some other selfish thing to do instead!

Our text in the NIV says, *"When Jesus saw Nathanael approaching, He said of him, 'Here is a true Israelite, in whom there is nothing false.'"* Jesus points out to us the noble character of Nathanael to teach us something important! That is, Jesus knows exactly how truthful we are in all of our dealings with both God and man! Jesus, the Judge of Heaven and earth, knows our character! If this fact does not create in us a fear of God, then we are spiritually, quite dead!

Would we cheat if we knew we would not be caught by man? Would we tell a "little lie" or "stretch the truth a little," to make us look better. Nathanael wouldn't, and Jesus recognized this!

Prayer: Lord, we so often hear it said, "Be true to yourself." Lord, may we be true to You because self is a mess. Like Nathanael, we want to be Your disciple. Put Your truth in us and use us for Your glory just like You did with Nathanael. In Jesus' name we pray. Amen.

October 22

"Now there was a man of the Pharisees named Nicodemus, a member of the Jewish ruling council. He came to Jesus at night and said, 'Rabbi, we know that you are a teacher who has come from God. For no one could perform the miraculous signs You are doing if God were not with him.'" John 3:1-2

Nicodemus learns from Jesus about salvation

Nicodemus heard of Jesus' miracles and had surely seen them. He comes to Jesus at night, secretly. He really wants to know who Jesus is and Jesus immediately tells Nicodemus about the need to be born again. Jesus gives us some points on salvation.

"Flesh gives birth to flesh," John 3:6a. We inherit Adam's sin and are born sinners. *"Spirit gives birth to spirit,"* John 3:6b. God's Spirit is an irresistible gift to our spirit or soul. He wakes us up. He convicts us of our sin. *"The wind blows wherever it pleases,"* John 3:8a. God calls some people to Himself, limited to who He pleases. *"But whoever lives by the truth comes into the light, so that it may be seen plainly that what he has done has been done through God,"* John 3:21. God's Spirit makes us walk with Him. He gives us guilt when we sin. He gives us peace and joy when we are faithful. He grows us up. It is His process of sanctification.

Nicodemus learned that <u>God's sovereignty saves</u>. He also learned <u>it's man's responsibility to be saved</u>! Both are true. If we lean too much either way, we have a problem! If a person goes to Hell, it's their own fault. *"Just as Moses lifted up the snake in the desert, so the Son of Man must be lifted up, that <u>everyone who believes in Him</u> may have eternal life,"* John 3:14-15. The chart below explains man's spiritual condition.

Pre-fall — able to not sin — able to sin — has free will
Post-fall — able to sin — not able to not sin — has only will to sin
Regenerate — able to sin — able to not sin — free will regained
Glorified— not able to sin — able to not sin — impossible to sin

Prayer: Lord, we see that Nicodemus believed. He even helped Joseph of Arimathea with Your burial. We praise You for teaching us through him. In Jesus' name we pray. Amen.

October 23

"He must increase, but I must decrease." John 3:30 NKJV

John the Baptist, increasingly decreasing

John the Baptist was the last of the Old Testament prophets and the first voice here in the New Testament. John the Baptist and the whole Old Testament pointed to Christ. John was a rabbi himself. Yet he said of Jesus, *"This was He of whom I said, 'He who comes after me has surpassed because He was before me,'"* John 1:15b. This is not some riddle. Jesus did come both before and after John. Jesus, as God, always existed before John did! As man, Jesus also came after John.

John the Baptist spoke the words of our text in response to his own disciples. They were telling him about how another Rabbi, Jesus, was baptizing many people. John had been busy teaching the Gospel of repentance and then baptizing people, and so did Jesus. John's important ministry of pointing to Jesus was predicted by Isaiah fully 700 years before this. As important as John's ministry was, it lasted just 18 months. God also puts us in a time slot for His purposes.

<u>John knew he was in the world to point to Christ</u>. John said from his heart, *"He must increase, but I must decrease."* But then, are we not all in the world for the same reason as John? Do we have the same attitude as John? Are our lives pointing to the greatness of Jesus, or do we point to who we are and what we do? What do we want more of? Do we want people to accept us? Or, do we want people to accept Jesus? Our answer to this question is our true motive for living and for ministry!

May God forgive us for pointing to ourselves so much! May He forgive us for spending so much time in wanting people to somehow love us more. We have it so backwards. It is Christ they must love more! Lord, it is You who must *"increase"* in our lives! But, that is not very possible until we first *"decrease."* Biblical change, as taught in Ephesians 4:22-24, says the put-off must happen before the put-on can! May God work this change in us!

Prayer: Lord, we admit that we have given You more lip service than real heart service. We say we want people to love You more, but that is not how we live! Lord, take our pride and bury it in the deepest sea! May You be the apple of our eye! In Christ's name we pray! Amen.

October 24

"Jesus, tired as He was from the journey, sat down by the well... When a Samaritan woman came to draw water, Jesus said to her, 'Will you give Me a drink?'... The Samaritan woman said to Him, 'You are a Jew and I am a Samaritan woman. How can You ask me for a drink?' (For Jews do not associate with Samaritans.)" John 4:6b-9

The Samaritan woman, Jesus talked to her

Jesus teaches us about evangelism and mission work in His meeting with the Samaritan woman. The Jews could not do mission work with the Samaritans because they would not talk to them! Plus a man would not talk to a woman. But more than that, the Jews looked down on the Samaritans. Six hundred years earlier, in an act of ethnic cleansing, the Jews' Assyrian enemies settled "foreigners" in Jewish towns. Now 600 years later Samaria is made up of mixed races. The Jews were racist! They refused to deal with these people! But Jesus loves every race of people and tribe. Therefore He ministered to them and many were saved. This Samaritan woman is one example!

By talking to this woman, Jesus shows us something about evangelism. He started by simply asking for a drink? Then He used her response to dig deeper into her life in a friendly way. Jesus cared for the condition of her lost soul. She was religious, but wrong in what she believed. She thought she "got holy" by going to a particular mountain where she worshiped God and idols. Jesus lovingly shows her, it's not the place, of worship that is important, but the Person! Jesus gently shows her who He is! We too must show others who Jesus is! But we cannot do that if we don't care about their lost condition or we won't talk to them!

Many don't do evangelism because they are afraid! Evangelism is outside their comfort zone. *"Jesus, tired as He was,"* did evangelism outside His comfort zone. It is the devil that convinces us that evangelism is off limits! It is people like this Samaritan woman who are spiritually hungry! Will we give them, *"living water,"* Jesus Himself, or will we keep silent?

Prayer: Lord Jesus, You not only instruct us here, You rebuke us for not opening our mouths! Lord, fill us with boldness to be gentle and caring like You, then we can minister to many, just as You direct us to do. In Jesus' name we pray. Amen.

October 25

"True worshipers will worship the Father in spirit and truth, for they are the kind of worshipers the Father seeks." John 4:23b

Jesus teaches about true worshipers

How do we fail to worship *"in spirit and truth"*? One glaring example is our love affair with cell phones! The poorest of the poor may have nothing in the cupboard, but they have a cell phone in their hand that means everything to them! The youth today hold their "cell" so tight. They resemble a baby sucking its thumb while holding a security blanket. During the week it is bad enough, but why do so many hold their phones in church? Recently, one man got up three times to answer his cell during one sermon, and he was sitting in the front row!

If we went to a job interview, would we switch off our cell? If we answered it, any employer would see that our phone is more important than a customer! A phone as our slave is one thing, but it has become the master for so many! People worship their cell phones in church, because they worship it all week long! *"No man can serve two masters."*

Recently a number of pastors were annoyingly walking out of class to answer their phones. It was clear, they did not see a problem! I asked these men, "Do you switch off your cell phone when you want intimacy with your wife at night?" They openly said, "Yes." WHY then, are phones not turned off when the people come to church to be intimate with God? They were shocked by the connection!

Has the cell phone replaced the Bible in our homes and has the virus also moved into the church? Is not that cell phone an Idol? Can we really worship God, *"in spirit and truth"* if primary importance is given to phone calls or text messages? Satan is so happy with this. And then there are kindles, i-pads and electronic toys also in church! Who in the spirit world that does not want us to worship God? It is Satan himself!

Prayer: Lord, You said of the Pharisees, *"These people honor Me with their lips but their hearts are far from Me."* Lord, we have a heart problem; forgive us! Convict us to respect You and Your Holy Bible. May we never forget it, but carry it in our pockets and flip through it constantly! Lord teach us to say with David, *"I delight in Your decrees, I will not neglect Your Word."* In Jesus' name we pray. Amen.

October 26

"Here is a boy with five small barley loaves and two small fish, but how far will they go among so many?" John 6:9

A boy is used by Jesus to feed thousands

Jesus knew His disciples! They were ordinary people, who didn't have much faith. They did not see how it was possible to feed 5000 people with so little! The situation was a crisis for them, but not for Jesus! He knew that He could move mountains if it was necessary! So once again, Jesus arranges a specific opportunity just so He can teach His disciples and us an important life lesson about faith and works!

The boy who has the bread and fish is not even named! Jesus gave his bread and fish to His disciples. They in turn gave and there was even more to give, so they kept giving. The disciples saw God's resources in abundance to supply the need. Hmm! How the providence and goodness of God is at work, just in time, to those in need.

Often our resources seem so small. Our abilities seem so limited. Our needs seem so overwhelming! And this is so often right where Jesus wants us to be, dependent on Him! If God is for us, who can be against us? But, there is much more we need to learn from this miracle!

Jesus *"gave thanks,"* then He went and gave to His disciples! What would have happened if the disciples just gave thanks again and again for the food and blessings, but did not distribute it? Surely, Jesus would have rebuked them most strongly! Are we guilty of having much food and many blessings, and even though we are thanking God for them, we are not sharing? This miracle is more about how Jesus gives us an overabundance of spiritual blessings, to share! Jesus is the true Bread of Life! If Jesus can use an unnamed boy to feed His people, what is our excuse for not being willing to be availiable to Jesus?

Prayer: Lord, how completely You care for us! You give us physical and spiritual food! You build our weak faith and then use us even as You used this little boy. Use us more to give out Your name for You are the Bread of Life! Just as You used Your disciples, use us! Multiply our efforts. May a real spiritual life be completed in us and in others! In Jesus' name we pray. Amen.

October 27

"'You do not want to leave too, do you?' Jesus asked the Twelve. Simon Peter answered Him, 'Lord, to whom shall we go? You have the words of eternal life. We believe and know that You are the Holy One of God.'" John 6:67-69

Jesus, our Prophet, Priest and King

Jesus was specifically anointed by God to be our Prophet, Priest and King, fulfilling all of these Old Testament offices. But now, as believers, Jesus anoints us to be His prophets, priests and kings!

1. Jesus is our Prophet. A prophet reveals the will of God. In John 17:8 Jesus said, *"I gave them the words You gave Me and they accepted them. They knew with certainty that I came from You, and they believed that You sent Me."* Do you know what this means for us as Christians? We are anointed to be prophets also! We are to receive Christ and share Christ to a dying world!

2. Jesus is our Priest. A priest works for reconciliation. And yes, we too are to be priest unto God, working for the reconciliation of others to God! We must be in intercession for others as a good priest does. We are told to *"pray continually,"* in 1 Thessalonians 5:17. Jesus set the example when He said, *"I pray also for those who will believe in Me through their (the disciples') message,"* John 17:20b.

3. Jesus is our King. A king rules and defends his people. Jesus rules and defends His Church. He is the King of kings, and the Lord of lords. As Lord of His Church, He sends us to go, to be on the offensive for Him. He wants us to be courageous in His service, for He promised to be with us! To not go because of fear, is to have a weak faith that doubts God. We must be especially devoted to our Lord's kingdom because His kingdom will not fail!

Prayer: Lord, how amazing it is that You anoint us to be Your prophets, priests and kings. You fill us and make us bold for Your kingdom. You tell us, *"You are a chosen people, a royal priesthood, a holy nation, a people belonging to God, that you may declare the praises of Him who called you out of darkness into His wonderful light,"* (1 Peter 2:9) Strengthen us Lord to serve You faithfully! In Jesus' name we pray. Amen.

October 28

"He replied, 'The man they call Jesus made some mud and put it on my eyes. He told me to go to Siloam and wash. So I went and washed, and then I could see.'" John 9:11

The blind man's three point sermon

Jesus gave His second *"I Am"* statement about who He is, when He said, *"I Am the Light of the world,"* John 8:12b. Right after this, the miracle of giving sight to a blind man happens, proving that Jesus is God. This uneducated blind beggar man suddenly can see!

Jesus put mud on the blind man's eyes and told him to wash in that famous pool of Siloam, the one that gets its water from Mt. Zion. Did the blind man need the mud and the washing to be healed? No, but Jesus was testing his obedience as compared to the disobedience of the Pharisees. The man did as Jesus told him; he was immediately healed. And now hear the simple but brilliant testimony of this blind man.

In simple words, he gives a beautiful three point sermon. 1. *"So I went,"* 2. *"and washed"* 3. *"and then I could see."* His healing was primarily a spiritual healing. His experience is true for every Christian. God moves us to the Cross where we can also say, *"I went."* We too lay our sins at the Cross. We receive the righteousness of Christ and therefore can say, *"I washed."* Our dirty sins are fully washed away. We are so spiritually clean, it's as if we had never sinned. Our spiritual eyes are opened so that we can also say, *"then I could see."*

It was the hard-hearted Pharisees who were really blind to who Jesus was. They could not understand this eye opening experience of the blind man. It was not their experience! And Jesus did this on the Sabbath. Why? Jesus is showing us that it is on Sunday that we primarily get our eyes opened to the Light of the world.

Jesus later found this formerly blind man. He asked him, *"'Do you believe in the Son of Man?' 'Who is He, sir?' the man asked. 'Tell me so that I may believe in Him,'"* John 9:35b-36. And the man believed and worshiped Jesus. Do we believe in the Son of Man?

Prayer: Lord, what a privilege it is to be able to say with this formerly blind man, "I went, I washed, I see." Lord, we believe and worship You. In Jesus' name we pray. Amen.

October 29

"Jesus wept." John 11:35

Christ's crying concern!

The Bible teaches us to weep with those who weep. The Word of God emphasizes compassion. It is not a sign of weakness to cry! Tough guys can and should cry. Jesus did, and He is the Author and Perfector of our faith and life! If we were to take God's loving concern for us, and our responsibility to love Him and others out of the Bible, it would be a very small book. Jesus was a Man, a perfect Man, filled with compassion and willing to show it!

Jesus had close friends in Bethany. He was especially close to Mary, Martha and their brother Lazarus. The context of John 11 is the demonstrated care that Jesus had with this family in Bethany and their love for Him. One day, *"the sisters sent word to Jesus, 'Lord, the one You love is sick,'"* John 11:3, meaning Lazarus. Jesus was in a different town and purposely delayed His going to them so Lazarus would die!

Jesus now goes to Bethany to see this family that He loved. *"When Jesus saw her weeping* (Mary), *and the Jews who had come along with her also weeping, He was deeply moved in spirit and troubled,"* John 11:33. Jesus was moved to tears that good friends of His were hurting! But is there a deeper reason for Jesus' weeping? He was *"deeply troubled."* What does this mean?

Perhaps *"Jesus wept"* because not one of His disciples expressed the hope that Jesus could raise Lazarus from the dead. Jesus raises Lazarus to prove that He has complete control over both life and death, now and for all eternity. Or, perhaps *"Jesus wept"* because Lazarus would have to leave the glory of Heaven and come back to a sinful earth. Whatever all the reasons are for Jesus' weeping, He shows Himself to be a tender Shepherd who cares when His lambs are hurting. Do we care when others hurt?

Prayer: Lord, You sent Your Son to a cruel world to love the unlovable. Your tender compassion is so needed in all of us. Lord, be the master of our emotions! Make us love what You love. Have us weep over what You weep over! You are the Author and Perfector of our faith. We pray this in Jesus' name. Amen.

October 30

"Jesus called in a loud voice, 'Lazarus, come out!' The dead man came out, his hands and feet wrapped with strips of linen, and a cloth around his face." John 11:43b-44a

Lazarus' resurrection is ours in Christ

When Jesus arrived in Bethany, Lazarus had already been dead four days. His body was rotting in the grave, returning to dust. Then by the Word of God Jesus calls him out of the grave. Jesus' beloved Lazarus comes out of his tomb to live again. Amazing? No, not from God's standpoint! We should not be amazed either! Jesus said: *"Do not be amazed at this, for a time is coming when all who are in their graves will hear His voice and come out – those who have done good will rise to live, and those who have done evil will rise to be condemned,"* John 5:28-29. If we are a friend of Jesus, we too will come out of our grave to live forever with our beautiful Savior.

In fact, *"all who are in their graves will hear His voice and come out."* Unbelievers will *"come out"* of their graves also! Only they will see the face of their righteous Judge who will condemn them to an eternity of living in that place of suffering, called Hell!

<u>Every single person will come out of their graves the same way they went in</u>! Lazarus went into his grave a righteous man. He came out a righteous man. A wicked man goes into the grave wicked and comes out the same way. There is no possibility of repentance in the grave!

How much good must a person do to go into the grave righteous? Must our good simply be more than our bad? No, for the Bible says, *"There is no one who does good, not even one,"* Romans 3:12b. What then can we do to be righteous? Turn to Jesus. He alone is the Mediator to God to forgive our sin. He alone can give us His perfect righteousness! If we despise His grace before we go into the grave, we will see His wrath when we come out! Jesus made man from the dust once, He can and will do it again!

Prayer: Lord, we can plainly see that You gave us the life of Lazarus, as another example, to remind us that You have the power to make us come out of our tombs. May we not only turn to You today for Your righteousness, but live for You also. In Jesus' name we pray. Amen.

October 31

"Then one of them, named Caiaphas, who was high priest that year, spoke up, 'You know nothing at all! You do not realize that it is better for you that one man die for the people than that the whole nation perish.'" John 11:49-50

Caiaphas, more guilty than Pilate

Caiaphas is the new Jewish high priest. He is the arrogant son-in-law of Annas the high priest. He is young and bold and wants to make a name for himself! Just the kind of person not needed in leadership! See why and how he stirs up other leaders to kill Jesus.

Jesus had just raised Lazarus from the dead causing many to believe. *"Then, (at this point) the chief priests and the Pharisees called a meeting of the Sanhedrin,"* John 11:47a. See their wicked and selfish hearts! *"'What are we accomplishing?' they asked. 'Here is this Man performing many miraculous signs. If we let Him go on like this, everyone will believe in Him, and then the Romans will come and take away our place and our nation,'"* John 11:47b-48. They were not for God's kingdom! They were for their own! How evil! They were supposed to be in office to bring people into the Lord's presence, but they hated God and man.

Caiaphas is a ring leader of liberal theologians! See here one of the best descriptions of liberal theology ever: *"Then the Jews led Jesus from Caiaphas to the palace of the Roman governor. By now it was early morning, and to avoid ceremonial uncleanness, the Jews did not enter the palace; they wanted to be able to eat the Passover,"* John 18:28. What hypocrisy! To get away with trying Jesus, they had their own mock trial in the middle of the night! When the Roman court opened at 6 a.m., they were at Pilate's door! But, they would not go into Pilate's house thinking it would make them unclean for the Passover! This is their own ceremonial law, not God's! Liberals do that. They bind the real Passover Lamb and rush to kill Him. Then they go and worship the one they do not know. How is that possible?

Prayer: Lord, we see Caiaphas, a church leader who rejected Christ! Lord, forgive our blindness. May we examine our own hearts and worship You! Deepen our faith and loyalty to You! In Jesus' name we pray. Amen.

NOVEMBER

Paul and Silas with the Philippian jailor

"The jailer called for lights, rushed in and fell trembling before Paul and Silas. He then brought them out and asked, 'Sirs, what must I do to be saved?'"
Acts 16:29-30

November 1

"Pilate came out to them and asked, 'What charges are you bringing against this Man?' 'If He were not a criminal' they replied, 'we would not have handed Him over to you.' Pilate said, 'Take Him yourselves and judge Him by your own law.' 'But we have no right to execute anyone,' the Jews objected. This happened so that the words Jesus had spoken indicating the kind of death He was going to die would be fulfilled." John 18:29-32

Pilate, judged by the Perfect Judge

This is the biggest trial ever in the history of the world! In fact, the results of this trial have been reprinted in thousands of languages. We are privileged to study the transcripts and benefit from them.

Pilate is a Roman judge, in office from A.D. 26-36. Pilate is in charge of the praetorium, which means hall of judgment in Latin. We call this the courthouse. There, Pilate has many soldiers.

Pilate is not the main judge of this trial; Jesus is! That truth becomes so clear as we study the proceedings. Like a news reporter, I have made an acronym, PILATES, to show how Jesus is really judging Pilate as He teaches both Pilate and us, who He is!

Perfect Man	**T**ruth Teller
Immanuel predicted	**E**ternal Savior
Lord and King	**S**acramentally perfect
Almighty and Man	

Perfect Man – Pilate rightly asked the Jewish leaders a good question: *"What charges are you bringing against this Man?"* Pilate tells them to judge Him yourself. Pilate knew Jesus was perfectly innocent!

Immanuel predicted – Pilate was not answered when he asked the Jewish leaders to kill Jesus themselves. There is only one good reason for this! Our Immanuel predicted in John 12:32-33, how He would be killed! Our text points to His complete sovereign prediction!

Prayer: Lord, You arranged a mock trial so You could die as a sacrifice for our sin! We praise You for such a precious salvation. In Jesus' name we pray. Amen.

November 2

"*Pilate... summoned Jesus and asked Him, 'Are You the King of the Jews?' 'Is that your own idea,' Jesus asked, 'or did others talk to you about Me?' 'Am I a Jew?' Pilate replied. 'It was Your people and Your chief priests who handed You over to me. What is it You have done?' Jesus said, 'My kingdom is not of this world. If it were, My servants would fight to prevent My arrest by the Jews. But now My kingdom is from another place.' 'You are a king, then!' said Pilate. Jesus answered, 'You are right in saying I am a king. In fact, for this reason I was born, and for this I came into the world, to testify to the truth.'*" John 18:33-37a

Pilate said, "You are a king, then!"

History tells us that Pilate took Roman pictures and insignia with him when he set up office in Jerusalem. The Jewish rulers could not accept his idolatry! Pilate threatened to kill them. They said, "Go ahead!" Pilate backed down, but kept Caesar's picture up. The Jewish leaders appealed to Caesar, Pilate's boss. Caesar made Pilate take down the pictures. So Pilate knows the Jews will go to Caesar if he does not kill Jesus. This is Pilate's problem. But, back to Jesus' judgment of Pilate.

Lord and King – Jesus agreed with Pilate's statement, then used it against him. "*Jesus said, 'My kingdom is from another place.' 'You are a king, then!' said Pilate. Jesus answered, "You are right in saying I am king.*" Jesus tells Pilate that He eternally existed as Lord and King!

Almighty and Man - Jesus answered, "*You are right in saying I am king. In fact, for this reason I was born, and for this I came into the world.*" Jesus testifies that he was both God and incarnate Man.

Truth Teller - "*I came into the world, to testify to the truth.*" Pilate was not interested in truth. Pilate, who thought he was free, was the one who was really bound. Jesus with His truth could have set Pilate free. But Pilate wanted to decide for himself what was true!

Prayer: O Lord, help many to see that Pilate gave up Your truth for the lie of the world. He forsook Your love for God's eternal wrath. What a poor investment! Lord, how we need Your mercy and we plead for it. In Jesus' name we pray. Amen.

November 3

"'I came into the world, to testify to the truth. Everyone on the side of truth listens to Me.' 'What is truth?' Pilate asked. With this he went out again to the Jews and said, 'I find no basis for a charge against Him. But it is your custom for me to release to you one prisoner at the time of the Passover. Do you want me to release 'the King of the Jews?'"
John 18:37b-39

Pilate kills the Passover Lamb

Eternal Savior – *"Everyone on the side of truth listens to Me!"* There is an invitation of the Good News, the Gospel of salvation. Jesus offered it to Pilate, but Pilate was not interested in truth or in Jesus. If Pilate was to believe in Jesus, he would have to proclaim to the world that Jesus was innocent. Then the Jewish leaders would rebel and go to Caesar. Pilate would not keep his job if an insurrection broke out. It was his responsibility to keep the peace! Pilate's wife also told him the truth, warning him about Jesus! *"His wife sent him this message: 'Don't have anything to do with that innocent Man, for I have suffered a great deal today in a dream because of Him,'"* Matthew 27:19b. Pilate made a fatal choice! He chose living his life the way he wanted, over accepting Jesus as his "Eternal Savior." What will we do? *"Choose you this day whom you will serve."* What do we choose?

Sacra mentally perfect – Pilate, the one who hated the Jewish system, kills the Sacra mentally perfect Passover Lamb. Is this not the complete insanity of all wicked people? <u>Insane Pilate, judged mentally perfect Jesus, guilty</u>! Why? Just one reason for this! So that we, like Pilate, who are mentally and spiritually off, can stand before God sane and innocent! Thank you Pilate! You are the only judge in the history of the world to condemn a completely innocent man to death! But know this: Like you, each of us will also be judged by Jesus!

Prayer: Father, in our place condemned He stood! You did this Father, so we can stand innocent on the Judgment Day, in the presence of Judge Jesus! Glory to You God, for giving us Your only Son to be our personal Passover Lamb. In Jesus' name we pray. Amen.

November 4

"Mary stood outside the tomb crying. As she wept, she bent over to look into the tomb and saw two angels in white, seated where Jesus' body had been, one at the head and the other at the foot. They asked her, 'Woman, why are you crying?' 'They have taken my Lord away,' she said, 'and I don't know where they have put Him.'"
John 20:11-13

Mary Magdalene and our grieving

The angels teach us something about the difficult process of grieving. How practically they minister to a grieving Mary Magdalene. This was the Mary that Jesus had cast seven demons out of in Luke 8:2. She knew what Jesus did for her and she loved Him much! Now that Jesus' body is missing, she is crying! Notice the question the angels ask Mary! And when Mary turns around, Jesus asks her the same question, "Why are you crying?" Mary, Jesus is by you! He is alive! He is with you!

The angels and Jesus did not say, "Don't grieve." However, we should never grieve like an unbeliever does, who is without hope! Many Christian parents say they grieve long and hard because they lost such a dear child. But, a child of a believer is with the angels and is also with Christ. The child is not lost! You will see that child again! Even David quit grieving once his child died. Instead he cried out hard and long to God while the child yet lived.

These are difficult points to talk about. Death tests our trust in God. We know that our caring God will never send any difficult trial into our lives that is not somehow a blessing to us. But now we have to believe it in the midst of our pain. How we must have a good and trusting attitude towards God in our grieving process. May we always keep our eye on Him who always has His eye on us! And when it is our time, to go *"through the valley of the shadow of death,"* may we remember, a shadow cannot hurt us, and Jesus is with us!

Prayer: Lord, help us to grieve with the hope of the resurrection in mind. Even Mary Magdalene could instantly quit grieving because Jesus was alive. We praise You that Jesus is still alive and He still gently asks us, "Why are you grieving?" Lord, fill all our crying and grieving with hope. In Jesus' name we pray. Amen.

November 5

"Now Thomas (called Didymus), one of the Twelve, was not with the disciples when Jesus came. So the other disciples told him, 'We have seen the Lord!' But he said to them, 'Unless I see the nail marks in His hands and put my fingers where the nails were, and put my hand into His side, I will not believe it.'" John 20:24-25

Thomas, a doubter who learned to trust

On first day of the week, early in the morning, Jesus arose and appeared to Mary and she worshiped Him. Jesus then told Mary to let the disciples know that He would be returning to the Father. So Mary informs the disciples and they gather together. Jesus comes and meets with them!

What you have just seen is the first two Christian worship services on the new Sabbath (Sunday). There was one worship service in the morning. Now there is one in the evening! The reason for these meetings is to meet with Jesus and celebrate the fact that He is risen. All the disciples are present except for Judas who is dead, and Thomas, who likely is afraid of the Jews. But for our instruction, the *"first day of the week"* is pointed out clearly.

Later, Thomas is told, *"We have seen the Lord!"* Thomas responds, *"Unless I see the nail marks in His hands and put my fingers where the nails were, and put my hand into His side, I will not believe it."* *"A week later,"* we read (hint, hint) it's the Sabbath and time to meet with Jesus. And when we worship, Jesus is always there! Notice, it is Jesus who approaches Thomas to convict him of who He is! *"Then He said to Thomas, 'Put your finger here; see My hands. Reach out your hand and put it into My side. Stop doubting and believe,'"* John 20:27.

Is it not the purpose of every Sabbath worship service, to *"stop doubting and believe"*? Thomas now believes in his heart and confesses with his mouth that Jesus is Lord! Thomas simply says, *"My Lord and my God."* May we too stop doubting, believe, and start confessing with our mouth that Jesus is Lord! For thus it is for those who are saved!

Prayer: Lord, just as You showed Yourself to Thomas, show Yourself to us. We believe You died for our sins. The nail prints in Your hands were because of the sin on our hands! With Thomas we confess, *"My Lord and my God."* In Jesus' name we pray. Amen.

November 6

"'Therefore let all Israel be assured of this: God has made this Jesus, whom you crucified, both Lord and Christ.' When the people heard this, they were cut to the heart and said to Peter and the other apostles, 'Brothers, what shall we do?'" Acts 2:36-37

Peter's 1ˢᵗ sermon – "Jesus is Lord"

At Pentecost Peter gave the first Christian sermon. When they understood that Jesus was the Son of God, the Lord Jesus Christ in the flesh, they were shocked! Peter explained the Lordship of Christ to them this way: *"Men of Israel, listen to this: Jesus of Nazareth was a Man accredited by God to you by miracles, wonders and signs, which God did among you through Him, as you yourselves know. This Man was handed over to you by God's set purpose and foreknowledge; and you, with the help of wicked men, put Him to death by nailing Him to the cross. But God raised Him from the dead, freeing Him from the agony of death, because it was impossible for death to keep its hold on Him,"* Acts 2:22-24.

After this introduction, Peter uses the words of our text to convince them that *"Jesus is Lord."* Their eyes are opened. They had killed Jesus who is equal to God. And as God, Jesus deserved to be worshiped, not killed. But <u>Peter did not leave them long in their guilt! He showed Jesus' killers that Jesus is Savior, as well as Lord</u>. Quite an important fact! Peter told them, *"Repent and be baptized, every one of you, in the name of Jesus Christ for the forgiveness of your sins,"* Acts 2:38b.

Do you remember Jesus' prayer on the Cross for His killers? It was, *"Father, forgive them, for they know not what they are doing."* That prayer was just answered in Peter's first sermon! *"Those who accepted his message were baptized, and about three thousand were added to their number that day,"* Acts 2:41.

Prayer: Father in Heaven, You teach us so much about the Lordship of Jesus! You show us that He has power over Satan and all his demon helpers! We see that all principalities and powers are under His feet, fully defeated. And by doing so, our Lord Jesus rescued us from the grip of Satan. Our Lord Jesus destroyed death and him who had the power over death, that is the devil! We praise and worship You, our Lord. In Jesus' name we pray. Amen.

"Then Peter said, 'Silver or gold I do not have, but what I have I give you. In the name of Jesus Christ of Nazareth, walk.' Taking him by the right hand, he helped him up, and instantly the man's feet and ankles became strong. He jumped to his feet and began to walk. Then he went with them into the temple courts, walking and jumping, and praising God." Acts 3:6-8

The lame man, he leaped into church!

Devout Jews went to the temple at 9 in the morning, 3 in the afternoon, and at sunset. At these times, beggars and lepers sat at the entrance, hoping to get an offering. Still today, we see this in many places. This was the life of a beggar in Jesus' day. Peter and John came along and the man held up his can, waiting for the music of the money to drop!

Peter's beautiful words, *"What I have I give you,"* contain a miracle itself. It is Peter's confession of his personal faith. Before Jesus healed Peter, he was a different man. He could not walk spiritually speaking! So when Peter gave the right hand of fellowship, he invited the lame man into communion with God and those who were already redeemed by the blood of the Lamb.

The reaction is instant! The lame man, *"jumped to his feet and began to walk."* It was a complete physical and spiritual healing! Immediately, the healed man went *"into the temple courts, walking and jumping, and praising God."* What a celebration! He worshiped God with Peter and John on this earth! If we are healed spiritually, we too will praise God with Peter and John in Heaven some day.

A young calf jumping and dancing when released from its imprisoned stall brings a smile to our face, just to see its joy. This man had more joy than that! He was free, eternally free! Immediately, he praises God for His grace and mercy. What do we think of when we enter the sanctuary? David said, *"I rejoiced with those who said to me, 'Let us go to the house of the Lord,'"* Psalm 122:1. May we too, leap with rejoicing into church!

Prayer: Lord, we know that You rejoiced in Heaven with the salvation of this lame man. But Lord, we too have a big problem. Some of us "churchgoers" are frowning in church. O Lord, heal us too! In Jesus' name we pray. Amen.

November 8

"You have not lied to men but to God." Acts 5:4b

Ananias and Sapphira, dying for lying!

All was not well in this fast growing church! A blemish shows up like a poisonous weed in a garden. The Bible is so open and honest! It is for our good and for God's glory to expose evil. Lying breaks the ninth commandment. God hates every lie. Satan is the author of them all. That's why Peter said to Ananias and Sapphira, *"Satan has so filled your heart,"* and for that reason, they lied *"to the Holy Spirit."* God's Spirit searches the heart of everyone. No one can fool God with a lie! Instant death was their punishment. What a vivid reminder on how wrong a lie is!

Ananias and Sapphira *"sold a piece of property,"* and *"kept back part of the money,"* Acts 5:1-2. They could have kept it all! The problem was, they were saying, *"that is the price."* But why did God strike them dead? He wanted to warn the early Christians and us that lying is eternally serious! Plus, God's Spirit is not in all who claim to love Christ!

Today, lying is so widespread. People do it without even thinking about it. They want a day off for personal reasons, they say "I am sick." When we cheat on our test scores, we are lying. When we adjust the scales in our store, we are lying. When we promise to give quality in business, but cheat, we are lying! We even lie when someone asks us if we want more food. We say "No" when we mean "Yes," knowing the host will ask again!

We can lie so easily and so often that after a while we don't even think about it. God warns us all: *"The good man brings good things out of the good stored up in his heart, and the evil man brings evil things out of the evil stored up in his heart. For out of the overflow of his heart his mouth speaks,"* Luke 6:45.

Two things in the Bible are clear. 1. All liars are hypocrites who say one thing and do another. 2. *"And all liars-their place will be in the fiery lake of burning sulfur,"* Revelation 21:8b.

Prayer: Lord, You know us completely! You tell us that You search our hearts. You examine us. And You will reward each of us according to what our deeds deserve. Lord, clean our hearts so our lips honor You! In Jesus' name we pray. Amen.

November 9

"*Because the patriarchs were jealous of Joseph, they sold him as a slave into Egypt. But <u>God was with him</u> and rescued him from all his troubles. He gave Joseph wisdom and enabled him to gain the goodwill of Pharaoh king of Egypt; so he made him ruler over Egypt and all his palace.*" Acts 7:9-10

Joseph, "*God was with him*"

Joseph suffered! A main reason Joseph suffered was due to the jealousy of others. The same issue will be a big problem for us. Surely that's why the subject comes up again in the New Testament. The knowledge of how "*God was with him*" is important for our right response.

Just think, it was the new leaders of Israel, "*the patriarchs*," who were against Joseph. He was the favorite of the father! If we are a Christian, we are also a favorite of the Father! Joseph had a special coat of many colors. We have Jesus' robes of righteousness! By reminding us again about the life of Joseph, we are encouraged to not give up hope. God's Almighty hand is still there to stop or limit what others try to do to us! God's omniscient (all-seeing) eyes see all of our struggles! The knowledge of this must compel us to keep our eyes on Him!

In his sermon, Stephen brings up the life of Joseph because he personally learned something the others seemed to have missed! That is: Joseph had courage in his trials! This does not mean that Joseph did not have some fears! But he courageously went forward in the face of fear! God saw the courage of Joseph that was grounded in a trust in Him. God still rewards a working faith like that!

It "seemed like" Joseph was done for! His faith was being severely tested, as ours will be! It will "seem like" we are losing the battle also. What will we do when it happens? Our response will define who we are, for that is our true character! If we get in the habit of trusting in God like Joseph did, it will become a pattern of living for us! Then it will be said of us, "*God was with him,*" or her!

Prayer: Lord, if Your powerful attributes are for us, who can ever harm us? Somehow, You will turn their every attempt to hurt us, for our eventual good. You are so good to us. We praise You. In Jesus' name we pray. Amen.

"You stiff-necked people, with uncircumcised hearts and ears! You are just like your fathers: You always resist the Holy Spirit! Was there ever a prophet your fathers did not persecute? They even killed those who predicted the coming of the Righteous One. And now you have betrayed and murdered Him — you who have received the law that was put into effect through angels but have not obeyed it." Acts 7:51-53

Stephen, courage for the Gospel

We used a long text here because these are the very words Stephen boldly spoke to the unbelieving Jews in defense of the Gospel. Stephen was one of the first deacons. He helped care for the poor and distributed gifts to the people. But Deacon Stephen was also a great teacher/preacher. *"Now Stephen, a man full of God's grace and power, did great wonders and miraculous signs among the people,"* Acts 6:8. *"Opposition arose,"* are the next words! Why? Because Stephen was very effective in his teaching, the religious leaders persecuted him. It will happen to us also. We must learn from Stephen!

Those who tried to stop Stephen, believed in "religious ritual," not in the Lord Jesus Christ! For this reason, it is very necessary to know what we believe, and why we believe it! Beyond that, we need to learn to say clearly what we believe, as Stephen did. We must know that the cost of commitment to Christ is high! Stephen had fears! But we can take heart! Courage for the sake of the Gospel is not the absence of fear, it is moving forward in the very face of fear!

Stephen copied Jesus in so many ways! Both were judged wrongly, both were rejected! Both in the face of death, prayed for God not to hold this sin against their tormentors! If both could have courage in death, we must have courage as we live day to day! We need to have the same mind as Stephen and Jesus! Their lives are on the pages of Scripture for us to see and to copy! May God help us!

Prayer: Lord, give us the strength and courage of Stephen! Lord, we know You hate cowards who will not stand up for the truth of the Gospel. Plant Your truth in us more and more. May truth be on our lips as well is in our hearts! In Jesus' name we pray. Amen.

November 11

"But Stephen, full of the Holy Spirit, looked up to Heaven and saw the glory of God, and Jesus standing at the right hand of God." Acts 7:55

Stephen, his Savior stands!

The context of our text is that Stephen is suffering to the point of death. And Jesus notices! We know that God's omniscient eye is always upon us and nothing escapes His perfect vision. But it is also true, nothing ever escapes our God's tender heart towards His children. Our text is absolute proof of God's tender eye!

Jesus is normally sitting at the right hand of God, as a reigning King. Sitting shows how Jesus is in complete control of all things. Yet in our text, notice Jesus is "*standing at the right hand of God*." The King of Heaven rises as if it were out of respect to how much Stephen is suffering. Or, perhaps Jesus stands to be nearer to Stephen. Or even, Jesus may getting up to greet Stephen as he is about to enter Heaven's doors. Regardless of reasons for Jesus standing, the text indicates the tender compassion of Jesus. May this be a great comfort to us! Jesus cares about what happens to us. His eye of compassion is on us! He especially loves His chosen and adopted children!

A loving and patient father is grieved and greatly moved when anyone injures his children. He may normally be a calm and patient man, but that quickly changes when someone puts a hand on his children. He simply cannot stand to see his children abused in any way! We have a powerful Savior who is similarly moved with a perfect sense of justice! He knows when we suffer unjustly!

In Zechariah's book, a protecting angel speaks out to believers; "*Whoever touches you touches the apple of His eye-I will surely raise My hand against them so that their slaves will plunder them. Then you will know that the Lord Almighty has sent me,*" Zechariah 2:8b-9. We have God's angels here on earth! We have the Father. We have the Son. We have the Spirit. Do not fear! God loves us deeply!

Prayer: Dear Lord, we are comforted that You were so moved by the suffering and dying Stephen. Lord, we thank You for Your eye that is always upon us. Give us the faith of Stephen to stand firm to the end! May Your holy name be lifted up. In Jesus' name we pray. Amen.

November 12

"Now for some time a man named Simon had practiced sorcery in the city and amazed all the people of Samaria. He boasted that he was someone great, and all the people, both high and low, gave him their attention and exclaimed, 'This man is the divine power known as the Great Power.' They followed him because he had amazed them for a long time with his magic." Acts 8:9-11

Simon the sorcerer, he's multiplied!

He's back! He really is! I'm not talking about Elvis either, although there are some similarities. Simon the sorcerer is in some churches. He is on T.V. too. He has much charisma! There is no need to mention any names. The list is too big anyway. Let us look closer at Simon the sorcerer, for he is doing so much damage in the church.

"Simon practiced sorcery." He was into magic, demonic powers through trances and demonic incantations. He was mediator to Satan, to get people "connected." Satan is a spirit, not the Holy Spirit, not God, but the opposite of God. Satan is powerful. He is tricky! Satan works to give a "religious experience" that will intoxicate! Simon the sorcerer was filled with his power. There are many "Simons" today!

Listen to the Spirit of God who knows all about imposter spirits! *"You shall keep My Sabbaths and reverence My sanctuary: I am the Lord. Give no regard to mediums and <u>familiar spirits</u>; do not seek after them, to be defiled by them: I am the Lord your God,"* Leviticus 19:30-31 NKJV. God hates imposters like Simon the sorcerer who tap into Satan's power sources to try fool us into thinking it's God's Holy Spirit.

Let me tell you of one, "Simon the sorcerer." I met this pastor, in southern Tamil Nadu. Like in our text, *"He boasted that he was someone great."* He had returned from South Africa where he was recognized as a "Divine Power." There he slayed hundreds of pastors in the "spirit." They went down under his command. He said he could feel the power going through his hand. Scores of others came to get the "feeling." They finally had the "spirit." In their delusion, they thought they had God's Spirit but it was Satan. How Satan wants people to "feel" holy, not be holy!

Prayer: Lord, protect us by Your Holy Spirit, for You alone make us holy! We worship You! In Jesus' name we pray. Amen.

November 13

"Now the angel of the Lord said to Philip, 'Go south to the road – the desert road – that goes down from Jerusalem to Gaza.'" Acts 8:26

Philip, the running evangelist

Philip is first mentioned in Acts 6:5-6, as one of the seven deacons that were appointed and ordained. The church is growing quickly! Chapter 6 ends with another deacon named Stephen who was teaching. Then in Acts 7 Stephen defends the Gospel before the Sanhedrin, and is martyred for teaching the truth! In God's providence, the Christians are persecuted and scattered from Jerusalem, *"except the apostles,"* Acts 8:1b. The church grew rapidly outside Jerusalem, even though the apostles remained in Jerusalem! This fact is too often overlooked, diminishing the responsibility of every Christian! God through an angel sends Philip to teach the Ethiopian eunuch. Later in this chapter Philip is, *"preaching the Gospel in all the towns until he reached Caesarea,"* Acts 8:40b.

God <u>calls</u>. Philip <u>goes immediately</u>! *"So he started out,"* Acts 8:27a. This sounds like God's call and Abram's obedience. So Philip, *"arose and went. And behold,"* Acts 8:27a NKJV. This *"behold"* is no accident! *"A man of Ethiopia,"* the queen's treasurer, was *"in his chariot, he was reading Isaiah the prophet,"* from a moving chariot! *"Then the Spirit said to Philip: 'Go near and <u>overtake</u> this chariot,'"* Acts 8:29b NKJV. I just love this! Picture this running evangelist catching a chariot! Still running, he asks, *"Do you understand what you are reading!"* God told him to run, so he ran! Some of us don't even want to walk for God, let alone run!

The Ethiopian is confused. Philip has the answer! Philip was competent in the Scriptures, thoroughly equipped as 2 Timothy teaches! We too must be <u>equipped</u>, and <u>available</u>! Or, are we too busy doing our own thing? Will what we are so busy doing, burn in the Judgment? Or will it last? Only that which is done for Christ will last! Philip was a common man who was equipped and available! Are we?

Prayer: Lord, Your call to Philip and his quick obedience is good to see. Help us to see our call also. *"You will be My witnesses in Jerusalem, and in all Judea and Samaria, and to the ends of the earth,"* (Acts 1:8b). You send us to our cities, our states and to our world! May we be available! In Jesus' name we pray. Amen.

November 14

"As he neared Damascus on his journey, suddenly a light from Heaven flashed around him. He fell to the ground and heard a voice say to him, 'Saul, Saul, why do you persecute Me?' 'Who are You, Lord?' Saul asked. 'I am Jesus, whom you are persecuting,' He replied. 'Now get up and go into the city, and you will be told what you must do.'"
Acts 9:3-6

Saul or Paul, called while still a sinner!

In recent days I have found this fact about Paul's calling very encouraging. We read in Acts 8:3, *"Saul began to destroy the church. Going from house to house, he dragged off men and women and put them into prison."* Then we see, *"Saul was still breathing out murderous threats against the Lord's disciples,"* Acts 9:1b. Saul was on his way to a distant city to hurt the name of Jesus Christ and to stop God's church from being built! We do the same thing! Our multitude of sins are also against Christ and His church! Did we also not try to stop others from serving the Lord? Did not our actions try to imprison others into the hands of Satan? See how this can be encouraging to us!

God calls us to be His witnesses! There will be times when Satan will discourage us by telling us that we should not be doing the work of the Lord because we had evil sins in our past. May this then be encouraging: God called Paul, while he was still a sinner!

Paul never let his past sins disqualify him for his present service! He looked to Christ who qualified him! Paul knew he was forgiven of his past sins. Paul also knew that he still sinned! He said, *"the evil that I do not want to do – this I keep on doing,"* Romans 7:19b. He did not allow Satan to take weeks, days, hours or minutes off from his service to Jesus Christ, and neither must we! Thanks be to God, through Jesus Christ our Lord! For this same Jesus who came to Paul, comes to us while we are still sinners! Jesus still has a plan to use redeemed sinners like us, to witness to other sinners who are lost!

Prayer: Lord, we pray Paul's prayer for the Ephesians in 3:16-17b. *"I pray that out of His glorious riches He may strengthen you with power through His Spirit in your inner being, so that Christ may dwell in your hearts through faith."* In Jesus' name we pray. Amen.

November 15

"In Damascus there was a disciple named Ananias. The Lord called to him in a vision, 'Ananias!' 'Yes, Lord,' he answered. The Lord told him, 'Go to the house of Judas on Straight Street and ask for a man from Tarsus named Saul, for he is praying.'" Acts 9:10-11

Ananias, reluctant but obedient

Ananias is an example of a good believer, a disciple who was available to be used by God for His purposes. The term *"disciple"* means that he was learning and growing in faith and in obedience. God is able to use such a person! God called to Ananias by name in a vision. Ananias' response is simply, *"Yes, Lord."* Ananias was actively listening for the voice of God, not too busy doing something else! Ananias was ready to be used by God. His response, *"Yes, Lord"* shows his close communication with God. Do our prayers reflect a close relationship with God? He uses those of us who are one in heart with Him!

God has a mission for Ananias. *"Go to the house of Judas on Straight Street."* God wanted Ananias to meet with Saul the great persecutor. It was God's will for Ananias to pray and help Paul see. However, Ananias is afraid to go. His fear problem is like ours! How often we don't do evangelism because of fear! But God comes to Ananias and says, *"Go."* Has not God done the same for us in the Great Commission? God's missionaries are often fearful, I know I am. But we must go because God says, *"Go"*! Ananias is convinced he must *"go."* So he goes in spite of difficult circumstances. He is convinced this is God's will!

God had plans to use Saul to become a great missionary. Ananias was aware of this because God told him. We have examples like Ananias, so that we will obey, even if we do not know what God will do with our witness for Him. However, we always know this: His Word will not return void but will accomplish His purposes (as seen in Isaiah 55:11).

Prayer: Lord, we see that You did not send Ananias to convict or to change Paul! Nor do You send us to convict anyone either. You do the convicting and changing! Your Holy Spirit makes people holy! You tell us it is our job to go and to speak Your Words. May we obediently go to build Your kingdom! In Jesus' name we pray. Amen.

November 16

"This man is My chosen instrument to carry My name before the Gentiles and their kings and before the people of Israel." Acts 9:15b

Paul, an apostle to the Gentiles

Paul was from Tarsus, the city where he was brought up. He was exposed to many different ideas and people. He was a student of the famous rabbi Gamaliel. He was a Pharisee, through and through. We have seen how Paul was a chief persecutor of Christians, hauling believers off to prison. But one day on his way to Damascus, Jesus met him, and Paul's life was changed and totally redirected!

Now this same Paul, is going to introduce himself to us. What will he say about himself? Will he tell us he is from Tarsus? Will he talk about his family? Will he mention that he had Gamaliel as a teacher? Will he brag about his higher education? Will he tell us about all his degrees? Paul never once mentions one of these in any of his letters' opening introductions? Then why do we so proudly bring up our education or status in life?

Paul identifies himself completely with Jesus Christ and Him alone! Every letter he writes, begins something like this: *"Paul, a servant of Christ Jesus, called to be an apostle and set apart for the Gospel of God,"* Romans 1:1. Jesus was clearly the Lord of Paul's life. In fact, Paul counted his life apart from Christ to be cow dung, or manure.

This of course demands a very good question. Who do we say that we are? What do others say about us? How would they define us? Does our relationship with Christ stand out? If not, why not? God still intends for the Gospel to go out into all the world! We live on the same side of the cross that Paul did! We either witness for Christ, or we witness against Christ. There is no neutral ground! To say nothing about Christ is to be against Him. Paul is not the only one that had to let his light shine. We not only have the Great Commission, we have the power of God to identify with Christ. What will people say about us after we are gone? What does God really think of us and our witness for Him?

Prayer: Lord, You were an eye opener to Paul. Open our eyes to that same relationship with You. We want our relationship with You to completely define who we are. In Christ's name we pray. Amen.

November 17

"In Joppa, there was a disciple named Tabitha (which, when translated, is Dorcas), who was always doing good and helping the poor."
Acts 9:36

Dorcas, she sewed and sowed!

Dorcas had many friends because she was a friend to many! She showed her faith by her good works! What little we do read about Dorcas' life, is that she, *"was always doing good and helping the poor."* She lived to be a blessing to as many people as she could.

Dorcas was not commended here for being a good talker but a good worker! How many people would rather "talk religion" than to practically show it! Another mistake we make is that we would willingly give for the poor, but not mingle with them. Dorcas did both. She was comfortable in getting her hands dirty for the sake of God's kingdom. She was not ashamed to take the role of a servant.

Dorcas was comfortable in moving with poor sinners. To mingle with "high society" is not wrong, but to do so without considering the poor is not how Dorcas lived! Our problem is that we do not want to be uncomfortable, even if it does advance the kingdom of God! Dorcas was not the only one who left many comforts behind to help the poor, so did Jesus. He left the streets of gold in Heaven to wash the feet of dirty fishermen. What do you think they stepped in as they cleaned fish?

Dorcas spent much time planning how to do good and then carried it out! Here also is where we tend to fail. We may know we need to do good, but because we plan nothing, we do nothing! Dorcas thought much about the things she could do to help others. She sewed and she sowed. What do we think about? Dorcas wisely spent much time with those whom Jesus also loved! She knew what was honoring to God and what was a blessing to others. Dorcas was not selfish!

Prayer: Lord, You shout to us with the simple but productive life of Dorcas! We are reminded of what one wise missionary said, "He is no fool who gives what he cannot keep, to gain what he cannot lose!" Lord, give us this kind of wisdom in our hearts! In Jesus' name we pray. Amen.

November 18

"At Caesarea there was a man named Cornelius, a centurion... He and all his family were devout and God-fearing; he gave generously to those in need and prayed to God regularly. One day at about three in the afternoon he had a vision. He distinctly saw an angel of God, who came to him and said, 'Cornelius!'... 'What is it, Lord?' he asked. The angel answered, 'Your prayers and gifts to the poor have come up as a memorial offering before God.'" Acts 10:1-4

Cornelius, a Gentile believer who did good

God is working. Gentiles are believing. Why are they believing? Did Cornelius believe because Peter came to him, pressing him to make a decision for Christ? No, not at all! Peter comes to Caesarea in the middle of Acts 10. Cornelius was *"God-fearing,"* <u>before</u> Peter came. Cornelius, *"gave generously to those in need,"* <u>before</u> Peter preached to him. Cornelius *"prayed to God regularly,"* <u>before</u> Peter's visit! Did Cornelius believe because he accepted Christ when Peter came? No, Cornelius was accepted by God <u>before</u> Peter came.

We attach too much importance to people making decisions, and to preachers pressing for them. God is the author of salvation to all who believe! Then why did God send a vision to both Cornelius and Peter so that they would meet one another. Both Peter and the Jews needed to accept that God's salvation is for all people! Peter's first words were, *"<u>I now realize how true it is that God does not show favoritism but accepts men from every nation</u>,"* Acts 10:34b-35a. God's calling of *"every nation"* keeps the promise He made to Abraham.

Peter also came because Cornelius needed encouragement and assurance of salvation, and to courageously preach the Gospel. Peter said, *"He commanded us to preach to the people and to testify that He is the One whom God appointed as Judge of the living and the dead. All the prophets testify about Him that everyone who believes in Him receives forgiveness of sins through His name,"* Acts 10:42-43.

Prayer: Lord, we see that Cornelius is a trophy of Your grace and power. As a result of Your love in his heart, he went around doing much good. May Your love be a motivating lesson to us all. Thank You for sharing the life of Cornelius. In Jesus' name we pray. Amen.

November 19

"He saw Heaven opened and something like a large sheet being let down to earth by its four corners. It contained all kinds of four-footed animals, as well as reptiles of the earth and birds of the air. Then a voice told him, 'Get up, Peter. Kill and eat.' 'Surely not, Lord!' Peter replied. 'I have never eaten anything impure or unclean.'"
Acts 10:11-14

Peter's vision, a command to disciple all

Peter is convinced, by way of a vision, to start bringing the Gospel to all people, to the Gentiles also. This is a huge shift in how God is moving to bring His kingdom to fulfillment. First, we had our ancient forefathers from Adam to Abraham. Then we had the Jewish Age. Now the Gentile Age is beginning to replace it. The Gentile Age got a big jump start beginning with Pentecost and now we have Peter's vision here.

Christ is now giving salvation to multitudes. God is beginning the process of reversing the order of who the Gospel is going to! Before, there were just a few Gentiles, like Rahab and Ruth. Now it will be the Gentiles first with just a few Jews. Paul explains it like this. "*Israel has experienced a hardening in part, until the full number of the Gentiles has come in,*" Romans 11:25b. That "*full number*" is the Gentiles, the rest of those promised to Abraham are now coming to faith and obedience!

Other changes are taking place. Before what was unclean (the Gentiles) contaminated the Jews! Now, with Christ's atoning death, those who were unclean become clean through the sinless Jesus. That is why Peter is told, "*Do not call anything impure that God has made clean.*" This is a major change in who is to be evangelized, thus the vision!

A vision is different than a dream in that it happens when we are awake, usually during the daytime. Even as Peter is trying to understand his vision to take the Gospel to the Gentiles, Cornelius is knocking at his door. God is so in control of who comes into His kingdom. Are we available like Peter to tell the truth of the Gospel to all people?

Prayer: Lord, we see Your Gospel of grace expanding! You are incredible, unbelievable, unchangeable and unstoppable in the hearts of all those You call into Your kingdom! We thank You for including us Gentiles! In Jesus' name we pray. Amen.

November 20

"Men from Cyprus and Cyrene, went to Antioch and began to speak to Greeks also, telling them the Good News about the Lord Jesus. The Lord's hand was with them, and a great number of people believed and turned to the Lord." Acts 11:20b-21

Cyprus and Cyrene men tell *"the Good News"*

God is building His church! The pouring out of the Holy Spirit on believers of every tongue (language) happened in Acts 2. Stephen is stoned to death in Acts 7. Peter has a dream that the Gospel must go to all people. Paul is converted to be an apostle to the Gentiles. *"Now those who had been scattered by the persecution in connection with Stephen traveled as far as Phoenicia, Cyprus and Antioch, telling the message only to Jews,"* Acts 11:19. The persecuted church is suddenly a growing church! Evil people try to make the Gospel stop, but God causes it to pop elsewhere! The church is now growing outside of Canaan, where Luke, the author of Acts is from.

Who were these *"men from Cyprus and Cyrene"*? What were they preaching and teaching so that, *"a great number of people believed and turned to the Lord"*? The church leaders in Jerusalem didn't know. So they sent Barnabas to check it out! What a great lesson to be learned concerning missions here! *"When he (Barnabas) arrived and saw the evidence of the grace of God, he was glad and encouraged them all to remain true to the Lord with all their hearts,"* Acts 11:23. Barnabas did not go with a proud "Jerusalem" agenda to stop the work, but to examine the fruit of what was happening! And Barnabas did what he did best, he encouraged them!

Too often those in a position of leadership think they are the only ones who should be teaching. This kind of jealous attitude is not present in Acts. May we follow the example of the Cyprus and Cyrene men and tell *"the good news."* For *"the Lord's hand was with them"* and a *"great number"* turned to the Lord! And the Gospel grows!

Prayer: Lord, how good of You to show us clearly how Your Church grows! We pray that we might all have the attitude of Barnabas! May we come alongside and encourage Your work wherever it is, for in this You are glorified! In Jesus' name we pray. Amen.

November 21

"They traveled through the whole island until they came to Paphos. There they met a Jewish sorcerer and false prophet named Bar-Jesus, who was an attendant of the proconsul, Sergius Paulus. The proconsul, an intelligent man, sent for Barnabas and Saul because he wanted to hear the Word of God. But Elymas the sorcerer (for that is what his name means) opposed them and tried to turn the proconsul from the faith." Acts 13:6-8

Sergius Paulus, an intelligent, new believer

Barnabas, Saul and Mark are on Paul's first missionary journey. They are on the island of Cyprus, the home of Barnabas. The group now comes to Paphos, the capital of Cyprus. Note that Paul comes to Paphos with the name Saul (his Jewish name), but leaves with the name Paul, (his Roman name). From here on he is called Paul, a missionary to the Gentiles!

Sergius Paulus was the main government official in Cyprus. Historians have said Luke was wrong, there never was a Sergius Paulus. But recently coins were dug up with his name on them. When it comes to truth, the Bible always wins over history and science. Sergius Paulus was governor from 47 to 48 AD. He was formerly an engineer, in charge of the waterways, *"an intelligent man."* The Gospel is also for intelligent people.

Sergius Paulus calls for this missionary team. He has heard of their teaching success on the island. *"He wanted to hear the Word of God."* *"Intelligent"* leaders need truth to govern well! *"But,"* there is opposition to him about learning the truth. The age old Satan is ever against the truth. He has an agent in place to stop the truth!

"Elymas the sorcerer (for that is what his name means) opposed them and tried to turn the proconsul from the faith." This Elymas was an advisor to Sergius Paulus. He knew that Paul was teaching the truth and wanted to stop it. After all, he would not have a job if Sergius Paulus believed! Paul immediately recognized that and did something about it. Tomorrow we see what Paul did. May we recognize that same opposition today and react to it also!

Prayer: Lord, You are the Author of truth. The fear of You is a beginning of real wisdom. Fill us with Your Spirit to teach Your truth. For Your truth alone sets us free. In Jesus' name we pray. Amen.

November 22

"Then Saul, who was also called Paul, filled with the Holy Spirit, looked straight at Elymas and said, 'You are a child of the devil and an enemy of everything that is right! You are full of all kinds of deceit and trickery. Will you never stop perverting the right ways of the Lord?'"
Acts 13:9-10

Paul & Elymas, missionary vs. magician

In just about every book of the Bible we are warned about false teachers, that is, those who teach and live out false doctrine. Elymas was such a man. His Jewish name was Bar-Jesus, meaning "Son of salvation." Paul calls him Elymas, "Son of the devil," for that is what he was. Elymas was a sorcerer and magician with power, but it was demonic in nature.

We have seen in verse seven, how Sergius Paulus is embracing the truth of Jesus. Elymas moves in to stop the truth from being believed! Elymas did this because he is a real disciple of Venus, a sex god. Anthanasius called Venus the god of lust. Venus is still powerful yet today, not only in the world, but in the church. The motive of Venus worshipers, like Elymas, is still the same: rewrite what is true to stop believers from believing in Jesus. Elymas types are imposters! They teach weird and wild things. The devil is their real master.

Sergius Paulus believes, especially now! He witnesses what Paul says and does to Elymas! *"'Now the hand of the Lord is against you. You are going to be blind, and for a time you will be unable to see the light of the sun.' Immediately mist and darkness came over him, and he groped about, seeking someone to lead him by the hand,"* Acts 13:11. Elymas goes into darkness, to where all the unredeemed will go! Light triumphs over darkness. The missionary is more powerful than the magician and the Gospel advances! *"When the proconsul saw what had happened, he believed, for he was amazed at the teaching about the Lord,"* Acts 13:12. May this be a lesson to us today! God's Word is the truth about life!

Prayer: Lord, we rejoice in Your truth and power! How Your miracles in the Bible point to who You are. Lord, help us to see Your truth. We worship You. In Jesus' name we pray. Amen.

November 23

"Barnabas wanted to take John, also called Mark, with them, but Paul did not think it wise to take him, because he had deserted them in Pamphylia and had not continued with them in the work. They had such a sharp disagreement that they parted company. Barnabas took Mark and sailed for Cyprus." Acts 15:37-39

Barnabas and Paul, fighting in the church

We see a big argument! Barnabas and Paul are so disgusted with each other about taking Mark along on the next journey that they refused to travel together! Yes, ministers and missionaries fight. This is perhaps the primary reason people leave the mission field and churches!

Imagine that, co-workers, two members of one body, fighting! That is like your arm fighting your leg saying, "I don't want to share the body with you!" Surely both were at fault. Barnabas perhaps played the family favoritism game too much. Paul perhaps was not forgiving enough of the young man's earlier mistakes. These kinds of "church problems," are often used by us, to make excuses for our shortcomings! *"The anger of man does not bring about the righteous life that God desires,"* James 1:20 applies here! This was not some righteous thing when they *"had such a sharp disagreement"*!

Just think, the persecutions of the Jews did not separate Paul and Barnabas. Famine, beatings and shipwrecks did not separate them. Yet this matter of John Mark ruined their relationship! God calls His <u>co-workers</u> to lift His name up, not to be <u>competitors</u> to tear each other up!

Barnabas left for Cyprus, his native place, which we know from Acts 4:36. We trust that Barnabas was true to the meaning of his name, "Son of Encouragement." Surely that was his nature, because the disciples gave him this name when they changed it from Joses. We know that Barnabas did a good job in training Mark.

Paul went to his native place also. Both Barnabas and Paul were successful. Nothing can stop the Gospel, not even our fighting. But that does not mean that our competitive spirits are pleasing to God!

Prayer: Lord, You tell us, *"How good and pleasant it is when brothers live together in unity,"* (Psalm 133). Lord, change our hearts so that we will work together for Your glory. In Jesus' name we pray. Amen.

November 24

"On the Sabbath we went outside the city gate to the river, where we expected to find a place of prayer. We sat down and began to speak to the women who had gathered there. One of those listening was a woman named Lydia, a dealer in purple cloth from the city of Thyatira, who <u>was a worshiper of God</u>. <u>The Lord opened her heart</u> to respond to Paul's message." Acts 16:13-14

Lydia believed and was baptized

In a vision, God spoke to Paul to go to the area of Philippi, which was a big city. When God called, Paul obediently went. God has a divine appointment for Lydia which she is yet unaware of. With Paul were Dr. Luke the writer of Acts, Silas and Timothy.

Paul's group found Lydia and other women by the river worshiping because there was no synagogue in Philippi. There needed to be ten Jewish men to start one. So a few of the Jews were meeting by the river. Lydia is called here a *"worshiper of God,"* because she was now practicing the Jewish faith, a convert from paganism. Before this, Lydia was from the pagan city of Thyatira.

Like so many today, Lydia went to a church service and worshiped God, but she was not a Christian! She was an unbelieving Jew. She was still guilty before the Law of God, exactly like we are. Paul preached how Jesus kept the law perfectly for her salvation. He told her how Jesus died and shed His blood as the Lamb of God, rising to life again. Then, after His disciples and many others saw Him, He returned to Heaven to be with His Father. Paul also told Lydia that now she could confess her sins to Him. He hears our prayers and forgives us sinners!

"The Lord opened her heart"! Lydia believed. She is now a Christian! Then notice, *"She and the members of her household were baptized, she invited us to her home. 'If you consider me a believer in the Lord,' she said, 'come and stay at my house.' And she persuaded us,"* Acts 16:15.

Prayer: Lord, we need Jesus, just like Lydia did. How good of You to save her and then use her for Your glory! Open our hearts Lord and use us too. In Jesus' name we pray. Amen.

November 25

"Once when we were going to the place of prayer, we were met by a slave girl who had a spirit by which she predicted the future. She earned a great deal of money for her owners by fortune-telling. This girl followed Paul and the rest of us, shouting, 'These men are servants of the Most High God, who are telling you the way to be saved.'"
Acts 16:16-17

A slave girl who was a fortune-teller

First, let us look at this "slave girl" who is demon-possessed. God through Paul acted in love to rescue this girl. As a slave, she was being mistreated. Just as God cares for the orphan and widow, so He cares for this young girl who is unable to free herself! Before this in Acts 16, Lydia was set free. Now the slave girl is saved. After this, the love of God rescues Paul and Silas as their chains fall off. Then the jailer and his whole family are set free from their bondage to sin. The message of the 16th chapter is that freedom is available in Christ! Also God loves to use His children to set others free! God loves the evangelist!

Notice, this fortune-telling girl knew who the Most High God was, but that fact, in itself, did not save her. Christ through Paul delivered her <u>from</u> her bondage, <u>to</u> a real life in Christ. How different this is than some are doing! Paul commanded the evil spirit to come out of this girl, yes, but Christ coming in, after that, was her salvation.

Secondly, the girl's owners are the object of Paul's (and God's) wrath or judgment. Contrast that to Paul's owner, the living God! In a real life situation which one is stronger? God stops their wicked means of earning a living. The owners complain to the authorities about Paul's teaching. But the truth is, they are mad because their easy money was stopped! God hates dishonest gain and He hates spirits that try to imitate and replace His Holy Spirit. These evil spirits were telling the future, most often falsely. Our God alone knows the future. He wants us to look to Him and trust Him for it. He is still the Great Deliverer!

Prayer: Dear Lord, we praise and worship You for being the only Holy Spirit! And because You are holy, You can make us holy today and for all eternity. Protect us from the evil spirit Satan, who wants to steal our joy and fellowship with You. In Jesus' name we pray. Amen.

November 26

"About midnight Paul and Silas were praying and singing hymns to God, and the other prisoners were listening to them. Suddenly there was such a violent earthquake that the foundations of the prison were shaken. At once all the prison doors flew open, and everybody's chains came loose. The jailer woke up, and when he saw the prison doors open, he drew his sword and was about to kill himself because he thought the prisoners had escaped. But Paul shouted, 'Don't harm yourself! We are all here!'" Acts 16:25-28

Paul and Silas, music, ministry, miracles

The newspaper called the "Philippian Pulse" reads: "Mother nature opens the prison with an earthquake, but the police keep all from escaping!" But know the real story. God controls everything in His creation, and the creation must listen to Him, for He owns it!

Paul and Silas were put in prison for casting an evil spirit out of a slave girl. In prison, they are now having a beautiful worship service with a captive audience, when suddenly *"all"* the doors come open. *"All"* the chains come off, from *"everybody."* Now how many miracles is that already? But it gets even better!

The jailer wakes up "spiritually," not just physically! The main concern of the jailer is that the prisoners may have escaped. If they have, he would be killed! However, they are all there, held by God! But you know that is not the end of the story! Mr. Jailer asks Paul and Silas, *"Sirs, what must I do to be saved*?" The shaking man is given the shocking truth, not a lengthy sermon. *"They replied; 'Believe in the Lord Jesus, and you will be saved - you and your household,'"* Acts 16:31. The jailer and all his household believe and are baptized! It was a divine appointment!

This was one happy household! Sure, they saw the miracles, but the miracles led to what was even more important. *"He was filled with joy because he had come to believe in God — he and his whole family,"* Acts 16:34b. Transformed, the jailer washes Paul's wounds instead of putting chains on his hands and feet!

Prayer: Lord, how awesome! May we too pray and sing! For You open the prison doors of our hearts and save us! You remove our chains. You wash our wounds! Thank You! In Jesus' name we pray. Amen!

November 27

"A Jew named Apollos, a native of Alexandria, came to Ephesus. He was a learned man, with a thorough knowledge of the Scriptures... though he knew only the baptism of John. He began to speak boldly in the synagogue. When Priscilla and Aquila heard him, they invited him to their home and explained to him the way of God more adequately."
Acts 18:24-26

Priscilla and Aquila, a gifted, married couple

Priscilla and Aquila are mentioned six times as a God-gifted, married couple. They quietly did the Lord's work together. They are a great example of a husband and wife working together in the ministry. Paul said about the rights of an apostle, *"Don't we have the right to take a believing wife along with us, as do other apostles and the Lord's brothers and Cephas? Or is it only I and Barnabas who must work for a living?"* 1 Corinthians 9:5-6. The other apostles had wives, *"along"*!

Wives were and are an important part of ministry that too often gets over looked! As a missionary, I know how big a blessing my wife is! What does a wife do on the mission field. Everything a wife does at home, and much more! Is it easy? No! But it is eternally worth it! He who gave His all for us, demands we all make sacrifices also!

Paul commended this excellent couple to the Romans. *"Greet Priscilla and Aquila"* calling them *"my fellow workers in Christ Jesus."* Paul then adds, *"They risked their lives for me. Not only I but all the churches of the Gentiles are grateful to them,"* Romans 16:3-4. Priscilla and Aquila were leaders in *"the church that meets at their house,"* Romans 16:5a. And Priscilla is listed first! She is a faithful wife.

The great teacher Apollos made "doctrinal errors." When *"Priscilla and Aquila heard him, they invited him to their home and explained to him the way of God more adequately."* Priscilla and Aquila did not argue with Apollo when, or right after he spoke! They did not confront him in front of others! They invited him to their house and helped him know the truth. They humbly worked to advance the Lord's kingdom!

Prayer: Lord, how You instruct us with Bible characters so that we may know how to carry out Your Great Commission. Forgive us for our mistakes. Lead us by Your Spirit. In Jesus' name we pray Amen.

> *"When it was decided that we would sail for Italy, Paul and some other prisoners were handed over to a centurion named Julius... and Julius, in kindness to Paul, allowed him to go to his friends so they might provide for his needs."* Acts 27:1-3

Julius, a kind man supplied by God

God determined Paul would go to Rome. God's sovereign hand makes the Roman governor Festus send Paul there! Julius, a Roman centurion is God's chosen escort to bring Paul and the other prisoners. The *"we"* that sailed with Paul is Dr. Luke, the author of the book of Acts! They boarded the ship in Africa, destination Syria. The *"kind man,"* Julius, allowed Paul freedom on the ship. Kind Jesus gives us freedom also! Dr. Luke was one of the, *"his friends"* who gave Paul the needed attention. God graciously provides *"friends"* to uphold us in our weaknesses and trials!

The group now gets on a ship for Italy. Problems begin and the winds are against them! We can relate to that! They finally came to *"Fair Havens,"* a safe harbor! Paul advises Julius to stay at *"Fair Havens"* or the ship and cargo will be lost, but the captain and owner of the ship overrule. How often we think that we are the "captain" of our ship and take unnecessary risks, going our own way headlong into danger!

The storm comes with disastrous consequences! *"We finally gave up all hope of being saved,"* Acts 27:20b. Man's effort still can't save himself! Paul now counsels all 260 on board, *"not one of you will be lost; only the ship will be destroyed,"* Acts 27:22b. Paul who is their prisoner now becomes their counselor! Our ship is going down also someday. Our earthly goods will be lost. But if we are in the Christian camp, we will be saved! Like Paul, we must take others with us to that safe shore!

The ship is grounded, then smashed. The soldiers want to kill the prisoners but kind Julius prevents them. Paul later wrote in 2 Timothy 4:18, *"The Lord will rescue me from every evil attack and will bring me safely to His heavenly kingdom. To Him be glory forever and ever. Amen."*

Prayer: Lord, so many valuable lessons are here. May we take courage. The storms You allow only strengthen our faith by Your preserving grace! We too will arrive safely on the shore because of Your kindness. We worship You! In Jesus' name we pray. Amen.

November 29

"Paul gathered a pile of brushwood and, as he put it on the fire, a viper, driven out by the heat, fastened itself on his hand. When the islanders saw the snake hanging from his hand, they said to each other, 'This man must be a murderer; for though he escaped from the sea, justice has not allowed him to live.' But Paul shook the snake off into the fire and suffered no ill effects." Acts 28:3-5

Paul's shipwreck, a ministry opportunity!

By God's design, Paul and crew are all saved and live on Malta for three months. Luke points out, *"The islanders showed us unusual kindness. They built a fire and welcomed us all because it was raining and cold,"* Acts 28:2. Paul, the servant apostle, puts wood on the fire. A viper, a deadly snake, bites Paul. God allows Satan's poisonous cousin to bite Paul. Satan is fully aware of how God is using Paul to bring many to Christ. But as we learned with Job and others, Satan still reports to God. He still needs God's permission to afflict any believer, including us.

Picture the viper hanging from Paul's hand. He is not alarmed or in a hurry to get it off. There in itself is a sermon in progress without using words. As the snake hangs on, the island people discuss how he must be a guilty murderer, that God is killing him despite surviving the shipwreck! These people are uneducated, barbarians, yet they have a sense of God's justice! It only proves, *"Since the creation of the world God's invisible qualities-His eternal power and divine nature-have been clearly seen, being understood from what has been made, so that men are without excuse,"* Romans 1:20. Do we think about the justice of God?

The viper has no affect on Paul, and in the fire it goes, to the eternal home of Satan, his demons and all who do not believe. Now, the people consider Paul a god. He is taken to the house of Publius, the *"chief official"* of the island. There Paul heals Publius' very sick father. *"When this had happened, the rest of the sick on the island came and were cured,"* Acts 28:9. God's detours are ministry opportunities of the best kind. Like Paul, may we use them to further God's kingdom.

Prayer: Lord, Paul's amazing God, is our God! Your divine attributes still work together to praise You, to benefit others, and to bless us! Lord, we worship You. In Jesus' name we pray. Amen.

November 30

"Therefore, I urge you, brothers, (and sisters) in view of God's mercy, to offer your bodies as living sacrifices, holy and pleasing to God - this is your spiritual act of worship. Do not conform any longer to the pattern of this world, but be transformed by the renewing of your mind. Then you will be able to test and approve what God's will is - His good, pleasing and perfect will." Romans 12:1-2

Paul's purity principle

We go to church to worship God. But then, during the week we willingly engage in practices that worship our selfish desires. For this reason, Paul says, *"I urge you"* to present your body to God as worship, all week long. *"I urge you,"* is a plea to be surrendered to God. Once a little girl had no money to give as an offering to God. So she walked up in the front of church and stood in the offering plate. She wanted to give herself to God! That is the right idea.

"In view of God's mercy." God gives us mercy upon mercy. *"Praise the Lord, for His mercy endures forever,"* 2 Chronicles 20:21b NKJV. His mercy to us never ends and this is primarily the mercy of salvation. In view of His gift that keeps on giving, we must give ourself completely to Him! Just think. What if a son or daughter living in a slum, is given a new house they could never afford. Then they offer themselves in adoration to our worst enemy. Would we not feel betrayed and hurt? Well, God did more than that for us!

"This is your spiritual act of worship." In the Old Testament, the priest sacrificed the offering, but the individual offered it! As Christians, our bodies are the temples of God! He lives in us! Should not our bodies then be a holy place? If we try to give a blemished sacrifice to God, He is offended. We cannot possibly give our spirits to God in worship, if we are unwilling to give our bodies also! *"Do not conform any longer to the pattern of this world."* The world does not love God. In fact they hate God. *"The Lord detests the thoughts of the wicked, but those of the pure are pleasing to Him,"* Proverbs 15:26.

Prayer: Lord, make us living sacrifices, holy and pleasing to You. For Lord, it is only reasonable for us to dedicate our bodies, as well as our spirits, to You and to Your service. In Jesus' name we pray. Amen.

DECEMBER

Paul escapes Damascus in a basket

"In Damascus the governor under King Aretas had the city of the Damascenes guarded in order to arrest me. But I was lowered in a basket from a window in the wall and slipped through his hands."
2 Corinthians 11:32-33

December 1

"Now, however, I am on my way to Jerusalem in the service of the saints there. For Macedonia and Achaia were pleased to make a contribution for the poor among the saints in Jerusalem. They were pleased to do it, and indeed they owe it to them. For if the Gentiles have shared in the Jews' spiritual blessings, they owe it to the Jews to share with them their material blessings." Romans 15:25-27

Poor Jews, why Paul gave to them

Our text contains not only information on giving, but an important reason we should give to the poor in the Jewish community. Paul's inspired logic is, we *"Gentiles have shared in the Jews' spiritual blessings."* Think of how the ancient Jewish fathers and mothers were the seed of the church. Abraham, Isaac, Joseph, Moses, Joshua, Samuel, David, Esther and eventually Christ were all Jewish. They worked and gave their lives so that the Gospel could eventually go to us Gentiles also. There were Jewish Christians who gave even their homes and lands to help finance the early church! Now, in our text, these same Jewish Christians and descendants of them, are poor and needy. There is a horrible famine in the land. Paul and the new Gentile churches, *"owe it to the Jews to share with them their material blessings."*

When God shared the riches of Christ with the Gentiles, He took away some of the favored status of the Jews, including some of their material blessings! *"For you know the grace of our Lord Jesus Christ, that though He was rich, yet for your sakes He became poor, so that you through His poverty might become rich,"* 2 Corinthians 8:9.

Spiritual and material blessings come to us all with responsibilities! We too, *"owe it to the Jews to share with them"* our blessings! More than that, we must be *"pleased to do it,"* as our text shows. Material and spiritual blessings are a literal test from God! Will we in turn be a blessing to others in the same way we were blessed? God wants us to know, *"Blessed is he who is kind to the needy,"* Proverbs 14:21b.

Prayer: Lord, You remind us often in Your Word (including Isaiah 58) how we must notice the poor and reach out to them! Then in return You give us mercy when we need it. May we love what You love and help the poor. You are so good to all Your children. In Jesus' name we pray. Amen.

December 2

"For I do not want you to be ignorant of the fact, brothers, that our forefathers were all under the cloud and that they all passed through the sea. They were all baptized into Moses in the cloud and in the sea."
1 Corinthians 10:1-2

Moses' and our own Red Sea crossing

This Red Sea crossing and the events shortly after are still meaningful for us today! The spiritual picture is profound. God says, I do " *not want you to be ignorant of the fact*"! The cloud shone on the path the Israelites needed to follow. The same cloud was above them to protect them from the sun, behind them to protect them from the enemy! "*They all passed through the sea*" God saved them all. So completely He saved them that the ground was even dry! God then kills the enemy completely! Both God's mercy and judgment are clearly seen.

"*They all ate the same spiritual food and drank the same spiritual drink; for they drank from the spiritual rock that accompanied them, and that rock was Christ.*" 1 Corinthians 10:3-4. They had manna, which was Jesus. The rock they got water from was Jesus. Jesus was with them! See the sacrament of baptism as they cross the sea. See the sacrament of communion by how they were fed by Christ in the wilderness! Both sacraments were given, after their deliverance from Egypt!

Neglecting baptism and communion has consequences! To their shame, many of our "*forefathers*" went to their eternal destruction! Our warning is, they ate and drank and got up to play! They played seriously and worshiped reluctantly. They were interested in "*pagan revelry*"! Twice God says, "*These things happened to them as examples and were written down as warnings for us, on whom the fulfillment of the ages has come,*" 1 Corinthians 10:11. These Corinthians had a temple for Venus (goddess of lust) where 1000 priestesses lived! Paul says, "Don't go there!" Today we have T.V. and the Internet. Be careful! Remember the Red Sea crossing is our baptism. May we live as God's children.

Prayer: Lord, what privileges we have! You deliver us from sin. You wash us and then remind us about how we belong to You! Again You warn us to take our physical and spiritual life seriously. Help us weaklings to do that! In Jesus' name we pray! Amen.

December 3

"Whoever eats the bread or drinks the cup of the Lord in an unworthy manner will be guilty of sinning against the body and blood of the Lord. A man ought to examine himself before he eats of the bread and drinks of the cup. For anyone who eats or drinks without recognizing the body of the Lord eats and drinks judgment on himself."
1 Corinthians 11:27-29

Paul's communion warning!

The Lord's Supper is an act of worship, one of two sacraments that Jesus gave us. Paul now gives us a serious warning concerning communion, because there were, and still are, abuses of it. Paul is concerned about the glory of God and our spiritual and physical welfare.

Many were seriously sinning *"against the body and blood of the Lord,"* which communion is a symbol and a memorial of. As we see and eat the bread and wine, we celebrate that Jesus is living in us spiritually, and physically too. Is He? Some were literally living like a child of Hell, thinking they were going to Heaven, just because they took this communion meal! Such sacramentalism is nonsense!

To get our attention, Paul warns us that some are bringing God's judgment on themselves. We may think we are getting God's blessing in communion, but the unrepentant get God's judgment! In fact, *"Many among you are weak and sick, and a number of you have fallen asleep,"* 1 Corinthians 11:30b. Some among us are sick and dying physically because of our spiritual neglect! This is a serious issue.

Members were being selfish! There was a huge communion meal and those early to arrive were "pigging out." The slaves and others who had duties, came later to an empty table. A meal intended to bring people together was separating them! But there is far more meaning here! Those of us who hang on to gross sins like drunkenness, adultery and extreme anger and bitterness and then take communion, and say that we are all one in Christ, are lying! The Bible is clear. No such person has Christ's blood to cover their sins and cannot be part of His body!

Prayer: Lord, we see that when we do not judge our own sins, You will. For You desire our true devotion, spiritually and physically! May we be pleasing to You! In Jesus' name we pray. Amen!

December 4

"I have labored and toiled and have often gone without sleep; I have known hunger and thirst and have often gone without food; I have been cold and naked." 2 Corinthians 11:27

Paul's productive perseverance

Paul had an adventuresome spirit that carried him many places. He did not confine himself to the four walls of a church building. He was on the move. What was it that kept him going? This question needs to be asked because today we hear of many pastors and teachers who are frustrated that people in their church are not very hungry for the Word of God. Did Paul face these kinds of problems? What motivated Paul to go through so many sufferings, and still keep pressing on?

In our text we can see that Paul went without sleep, and at times without food and clothing. Paul even worked without receiving wages from those he ministered to, but still he kept going! Paul said, *"I have worked much harder, been in prison more frequently, been flogged more severely, and been exposed to death again and again. Five times I received from the Jews the forty lashes minus one. Three times I was beaten with rods, once I was stoned, three times I was shipwrecked, I spent a night and a day in the open sea,"* 2 Corinthians 11:23b-25. Paul continues for several more verses on how he suffered many hardships. But still he kept going. What was Paul's secret?

Paul kept going, not because he was looking for something, but because he had found something worth living and dying for, Jesus. Paul so dramatically changed that he was compelled to go into all the world to tell others about what he had found! Part of our problem is we want people to come to us. Jesus and Paul went to the people, searching prayerfully for those who needed God's grace! Paul just had to share with others his life-changing relationship he had with Jesus! What is in our heart that compels us to share?

Prayer: Lord, how desperately we all need what Paul had with Jesus. We need that close relationship with You that compels us to go into all the world and teach the Gospel. But Lord Jesus, You said, we cannot even seek You unless You draw us to Yourself. So Lord, draw us to Yourself we pray. Amen.

December 5

"Husbands, love your wives, just as Christ loved the church and gave Himself up for her to make her holy, cleansing her by the washing with water through the Word, and to present her to Himself as a radiant church, without stain or wrinkle or any other blemish, but holy and blameless." Ephesians 5:25-27

Husbands must be farmers at heart

When it comes to men in marriage, the words "husband" and "bridegroom" are God's words, loaded with meaning. See how God made the man and the responsibility he was given on day one! *"The Lord God took the man and put him in the Garden of Eden to work it and take care of it,"* Genesis 2:15. Adam's title was what we would call a farmer or gardener. In the Bible the word "husbandman" is often used. A husbandman's job description is exactly described in Genesis 2:15. A husbandman waters and cares for the plants and animals!

The day a husband gets married, he is called a "bridegroom." And the word means exactly what it suggests! It is the sacred duty of a man to groom his bride. He must care of her now, in addition to the plants and animals. The method is much the same! We farmers, know that if we neglect to care for our gardens or fields, we will have a huge mess! If those plants do not get water they get sick!

In our text, Paul borrows from this common knowledge, to instruct us in building a godly marriage. A husband is to wash his wife with the Word of God. He needs to read the Bible in the home! The Word of God enters the heart through the ear! When a husband is reading the Bible he is not only watering his wife's heart, he is pulling the weeds in his own garden! Sinful habits need to be pulled up like weeds! I can weed my garden in a good hour, if the weeds are scratched out when they first come up and are small. But if I wait a few weeks, it may take hours to clean out the weeds! If we regularly read the Bible and pray we get the sin out when it first sprouts!

Prayer: Lord, what simple and beautiful words You use in marriage to instruct us. If we just listen to You, we can profit so much. May we honor You in our marriages by respecting Your Holy Word that teaches us holiness. In Jesus' name we pray. Amen.

December 6

"Join with others in following my example, brothers, and take note of those who live according to the pattern we gave you." Philippians 3:17

Paul's parenting profile

If there is one thing we desperately need today, it is parents and leaders who set an example by how they live! Children and disciples may hear what we say, but they learn far more by what we do! In fact, if we say one thing and do another, we are a hypocrite. Children and disciples will imitate us. They will follow our example.

Paul set a good example, by following Jesus' example. Jesus lived what He preached! Jesus in turn followed His Father's example! Jesus said, *"I tell you the truth, the Son can do nothing by Himself; He can do only what He sees His Father doing, because whatever the Father does the Son also does. For the Father loves the Son and shows Him all He does,"* John 5:19b-20a. We are to model Christ also in all of our discipleship relationships! We would be wise to model three words that start with T: Tenderness; Transparency; and Touching.

We need to be tender! Paul said to the Thessalonian church, *"we were gentle among you, like a mother caring for her little children,"* 1 Thessalonians 2:7. If our boys are going to act like gentlemen and our daughters are going to act like ladies, then we need to show them what tenderness looks like!

We need to be transparent. Our children need to know why we do what we do. They need to learn from our successes and from our failures. We eagerly show them our successes, but we tend to hide our mistakes. If we are not open to what we do wrong, how will our children learn? How will they even know what confession is all about if our lips are sealed concerning our own sins? We need to be transparent!

We need to be touching. We need to show our affection and our emotions! Our children need to know by our hugs that we care for them!

Prayer: Lord, we are so thankful that You the Father set an example for Jesus, Your Son, and then Jesus set a perfect example for us, His disciples. May we model Your example and act like followers of Jesus Christ should act! In His name we pray. Amen.

December 7

"All the saints send you greetings, especially those who belong to Caesar's household." Philippians 4:22

Caesar's household, they believe!

We know from history that around 68 A.D. Nero Caesar destroyed Rome. From 54 to 68 A.D., he was the highest Roman official. As his reign progressed, so did his cruelty. He went after Christians with a vengeance to eliminate them. Jesus predicted it. Fleeing for their lives, Christians brought the Gospel to all parts of the world. God is building His church! Hitler, 1900 years later, followed Nero's example. But neither Nero nor Hitler could stop the Gospel!

When we search the Scriptures, Nero Caesar's name is in just one verse, which is our text. What we find, makes us jump for joy! Members of *"Caesar's household,"* have become church members through the ministry of the imprisoned Paul! That's right! <u>While the cruel Nero is going after Christians with a vengeance, members of his own household are coming to Christ</u>! Paul may be in prison but the Gospel isn't! Paul is older and is physically hurting, but spiritually he is productive for King Jesus! Paul shows us how to finish strong!

Our text ends Paul's letter to the Philippian church. He has not seen them for eleven years. He thanks them for sending an offering to him through the hand of Epaphroditus. What a beautiful gift this was to the needy Paul. Years before, Paul said, *"At my first defense, no one came to my support, but everyone deserted me. May it not be held against them,"* 2 Timothy 4:16. Then Paul testified in verse 17a, *"But the Lord stood at my side and gave me strength, so that through me the message might be fully proclaimed and all the Gentiles might hear it."*

If we think it's hard to live the Christian life, then remember Caesar's household! They were filled with joy in the midst of great persecution! Instead of feeling sorry for themselves, they send their greetings to the church that sent them a great minister in a very needy place!

Prayer: Lord, we pray for those who are Christians in pagan palaces. Feed them with Your Word. Help us all to keep our eyes on You in the midst of persecution. In Jesus' name we pray. Amen.

"But I do not want you to be ignorant, brethren, concerning those who have fallen asleep, lest you sorrow as others who have no hope. For if we believe that Jesus died and rose again, even so God will bring with Him those who sleep in Jesus." 1 Thessalonians 4:13-14 NKJV

The disciples' resurrection hope

To His disciples, Jesus was a great teacher and miracle worker! But when He came out of that grave, it proved to them clearly that He was truly the Messiah, fully God. His resurrection became their "Good News" cry! Jesus' Second Coming will be our resurrection day. Then, for the first time, <u>both in body and in soul</u>, we too will see Jesus. His coming will be <u>physical</u>, <u>visible</u> and it will be <u>triumphant</u>! In just six verses Paul tells us about the hope he has in his resurrection!

See two words clearly! When Jesus comes again, He will bring "<u>with Him</u>" those who had formerly died on earth. He will reunite their souls with their sleeping bodies! In Matthew, Jesus tells us just before His Second Coming that the sun, moon and stars will suddenly "*be shaken.*" No one will miss it! Then He says, "*At that time the sign of the Son of Man will appear in the sky, and all the nations of the earth will mourn. They will see the Son of Man coming on the clouds of the sky, with power and great glory. And He will send His angels with a loud trumpet call, and <u>they will gather His elect from the four winds, from one end of the Heavens to the other</u>,*" Matthew 24:30-31. The gathering of souls here in Matthew is the same event that Paul talks about in our text and what John sees in Revelation 20.

There are souls only in Heaven and Hell now. John said in Revelation 20:4 about those in Heaven, "*I saw the souls.*" Also, there are only souls in Hell for now. After The Judgment, there it will be both body and soul present in Heaven or in Hell. Unredeemed sinners must be punished in body and in soul, to fully experience the holy wrath of God. Those who have God's forgiveness will be rewarded, fully enjoying God's love in body and in soul!

Prayer: Lord, because You arose, we will also. Because You are glorified in Heaven, so will we who are Your children. We praise You for Your grace and mercy to us redeemed sinners! In Jesus' name we pray. Amen.

December 9

"For this we say to you by the Word of the Lord, that we who are alive and remain until the coming of the Lord will by no means precede those who are asleep. For the Lord Himself will descend from Heaven with a shout, with the voice of an archangel, and with the trumpet of God. And the dead in Christ will rise first." 1 Thessalonians 4:15-16 NKJV

Paul's personal resurrection hope

Paul did not believe in the kind of rapture many believe in today! His words to us are so clear in how Jesus' Second Coming will occur. What Paul tells us is, *"by the Word of the Lord"*!

Those of us who are still living on earth when Jesus returns, will not disappear with Jesus before the bodies of our dead forefathers come out of their graves! If Jesus were to come for living believers and take them to Heaven and then come back years later for the rest, that would be His Third Coming. Jesus is coming one more time. *"We who are alive and remain until the coming of the Lord will by no means precede those who are asleep."* We know the dead in Christ will rise first. What about the dead, not *"in Christ"*? When we see what happens to all the dead, we can more clearly see what will happen to all those who are living!

Jesus teaches us, *"Do not be amazed at this, for a time is coming when all who are in their graves will hear His voice and come out – those who have done good will rise to live, and those who have done evil will rise to be condemned,"* John 5:28-29. What the NIV here calls *"a time,"* the NKJV says *"the hour is coming."* So now, if all those who are dead rise at the same *"time"* or *"hour"*, and living believers after that, then will there be just living unbelievers left on earth?

Paul said about God, *"He has set a day when He will judge the world with justice by the Man He has appointed. He has given proof of this to all men by raising Him from the dead,"* Acts 17:31. Jesus taught in the parable of the Ten Virgins, that when He the Bridegroom comes, all must be ready to go into the marriage feast! Are we ready?

Prayer: Lord, make us ready to meet You. For the *"time"* is coming. The *"day"* is coming. The *"hour"* is coming. You tell us the day for salvation is now, for You are coming suddenly! We thank You for the warning! In Jesus' name we pray. Amen.

"Then we who are alive and remain shall be caught up together with them in the clouds to meet the Lord in the air. And thus we shall always be with the Lord. Therefore comfort one another with these words."
1 Thessalonians 4:17-18 NKJV

Paul's hope for a new Heaven and Earth

In the year 2013, the earth became 6017 years old. This is according to the genealogies in the Bible. Soon the created earth will be no more. The history of the earth is almost complete. Eternity awaits for everyone who ever lived. The only question is: Where will each one of us be living in the hereafter? Paul was sure of where he was going. He even tells us how Jesus will come. Paul says Jesus' Second Coming will be sudden and unexpected. Sudden, because; *"We who are alive and remain shall be caught up together with them in the clouds to meet the Lord in the air."*

In our text, Paul does not focus on The Judgment itself. He wants us to think of the endless time after that, as believers, *"we shall always be with the Lord."* We will *"always"* see God in all of His glory! We will *"always"* experience Him to the fullest. We will *"always"* see others in all of their glory! Our new Heaven and Earth will last forever! It will always exist. It is quite impossible for our finite minds to grasp that which is infinite! It would take an endless amount of words to describe the never ending beauty that awaits every believer!

Just think, everything we know now is so temporary. Everything, both the creation and the creature, is decaying and dying! In the Heaven and Earth that is coming, nothing will get old or rot. There will be no blemish in anything or in anyone! There will not be one argument in Heaven, no family problems, no lawyers, no courts. There will be no hunger, no shortage of clothes, no pollution of any kind! In fact, God tells us in Psalm 16:11, that there will be *"eternal pleasures"* at His right hand. No wonder Paul wanted to depart for Heaven!

Prayer: Lord, You have an eternity of joy that never ends for every believer! May we live for You today so we can live with You forever in the New Heavens and Earth. In Jesus' name we pray. Amen.

December 11

"Let no one deceive you by any means; for that Day will not come unless the falling away comes first, and the man of sin is revealed, the son of perdition, who opposes and exalts himself above all that is called God or that is worshiped, so that he sits as God in the temple of God, showing himself that he is God." 2 Thessalonians 2:3-4 NKJV

The son of perdition, the antichrist!

Paul writes this second letter to the Thessalonian church to clarify some things he wrote in the first letter. Some thought Jesus was coming again right away and had stopped working. Others were lazy and Paul told them to get busy! Then Paul goes on to tell them (and us) that a great apostasy in the church must happen before the end of the world comes. It is the corruption and falling away of the church that paves the way for a pretender to slip in and pollute the church. This *"son of perdition"* will be a real person. Paul tells us how it will happen in verses 9-12.

Satan will enter him and he will lead the world in one final rebellion against Christ and His church. Paul does not use the word "antichrist," although that is what this person is. He uses *"the son of perdition,"* and *"the lawless one"* to further describe this evil man. John, in Revelation 13, calls this evil man, *"the beast."*

True Christians will recognize this antichrist because of what he does! *"The coming of the lawless one is according to the working of Satan, with all power, signs, and lying wonders, and with all unrighteous deception among those who perish, because they did not receive the love of the truth, that they might be saved ,"* 2 Thessalonians 2:9-10 NKJV.

The *"son of perdition,"* in the end, will deceive those who are perishing, meaning those who are not Christian. He will use incredible powers to deceive them. John said by, *"great and miraculous signs, even causing fire to come down from Heaven,"* Revelation 13:13b. This evil man, *"the lawless one,"* will be so strong that no one will be able to stop him but God Himself. Only then will this world end!

Prayer: Lord, we are so grateful that You will destroy this *"son of perdition"* by the breath of Your mouth and the brightness of Your coming! In the meantime, help us to know the truth so we are guarded from being deceived. In Jesus' name we pray. Amen.

December 12

"Timothy, my son, I give you this instruction in keeping with the prophecies once made about you, so that by following them you may fight the good fight, holding on to faith and a good conscience. Some have rejected these and so have shipwrecked their faith. Among them are Hymenaeus and Alexander, whom I have handed over to Satan to be taught not to blaspheme." 1 Timothy 1:18-20

Hymenaeus and Alexander handed over to Satan

Paul here says, *"fight the good fight."* <u>Work diligently</u> for good, because Christianity is a war against sin, against Satan and his forces of evil. All it takes for evil to flourish, is for good people like Timothy and us to do nothing. The present church in this world is often referred to as "the church militant." In Heaven it will be "the church triumphant." The struggle will be over soon! This does not mean that Christians go around killing people but means that we are jealous for the truth of God to be known. We must seize the opportunity, praying for situations to present Christ!

Many discouragements, much opposition from various sources is the normal fare of a ministry worker. It is going to take a courageous and prayerful person to stand against evil and move forward for God! <u>The temptation to give up will be huge. So Paul tells Timothy, and us too, hold on to your calling.</u> Move with God and for God, with a good conscience. Confess our sins to God in detail and stay close to the Cross. Then our faith will not be *"shipwrecked"*!

Hymenaeus and Alexander were not on God's side in the war for truth. Even though they were inside the church, rather than using their voice for God, they used their mouth to blaspheme God and His church. They were an ugly example of an angry and bitter person in the church that lashed out at others. By definition, "blasphemy" is to curse God. It is to take the name of God in vain. God hands them over to Satan, to afflict them in the body, so their souls will cry to God for mercy and seek a serious and real relationship with God!

Prayer: Lord, what a serious warning for us to stay close to You, to stay humble! We have seen that two covenant breakers were actually handed over to Satan to be afflicted. Lord, we seek You! Fill us with Your presence! In Jesus' name we pray. Amen.

December 13

"I have been reminded of your sincere faith, which first lived in your grandmother Lois and in your mother Eunice and, I am persuaded, now lives in you also." 2 Timothy 1:5

Grandmother Lois passes on the faith

Grandmothers and grandfathers have a huge responsibility to pass on the faith. Grandparents have seen a lot. They have wisdom learned from living. They have heard and seen the promises of God. They generally have more time and more patience. They have seen what works in bringing up children and what does not. They have made many mistakes and hopefully have learned from them. Now they have, by the grace of God, grandchildren, flesh of their flesh. They have little lives so full of energy, eager to discover their world. It is the grandparents' God-given job to help the little ones see the world through the eyes of God. He is pleased and worshiped when we do our job!

Grandmother Lois is specifically commended here by God! She took to heart her job of helping to raise young Timothy. Undoubtedly, she prayed much for this little guy! She took serious, her sacred duty to love her grandchild! She knew what many other grandparents need to know! *"If anybody does not provide for his (or her) relatives, and especially for his immediate family, he has denied the faith and is worse than an unbeliever,"* 1 Timothy 5:8. This command by God is far more than just money or material needs! It includes the spiritual.

Look at grandma and grandpa from a "Timothy's" point of view today. They know what their parents are teaching them. They know what their school friends are telling them. They see what the T.V. is showing them. Which message will they believe? They have important questions that need to be answered. As children mature, they must be 100% sure of what they believe in, to go in the right direction! Faith must "live" in them. That takes grand parenting time, but it is time well spent for the children and for the kingdom of God!

Prayer: Lord, what a privilege for grandparents to share their love and faith. What a privilege for grandchildren to learn what love, faith, obedience is all about. We thank You for raising up many faithful grandparents like grandma Lois. In Jesus' name we pray. Amen.

December 14

"Just as Jannes and Jambres opposed Moses, so also these men oppose the truth – men of depraved minds, who, as far as the faith is concerned, are rejected." 2 Timothy 3:8

Jannes and Jambries, flee from them

Jannes and Jambries were magicians and sorcerers who worked for Pharoah. These men were considered *"wise men"* of the day! Yet they opposed Moses' efforts to free the Israelite people from bondage to sin, to the gods, and to the rulers of Egypt. Their worldview was basically an evil scheme by proud, powerful people trying to stay in power and to make lots of money and enjoy life at the expense of others!

Paul now warns Timothy and us. First, he tells Timothy that the actions of wicked people in "the last days" of the Jewish age, (Timothy's time), were just like what happened to Moses. Paul also warns us about this kind of wicked person in our last days, which is "the end of the Gentile age." See how carefully Paul describes what these evil people, these spiritual imposters will look like: *"But mark this: There will be terrible times in the last days. People will be lovers of themselves, lovers of money, boastful, proud, abusive, disobedient to their parents, ungrateful, unholy, without love, unforgiving, slanderous, without self-control, brutal, not lovers of the good, treacherous, rash, conceited, lovers of pleasure rather than lovers of God,"* 2 Timothy 3:1-4.

Today's "church" is now facing very difficult problems! Self-centeredness leads the way in many churches. Even Christian bookstores are filled with advice from supposed "Christian authors" who are telling us we need more self-love, self-esteem and self-worth to make it in this world. Nothing is more the opposite of the Gospel message! And who are these "wise men" of the current age. What profession offers even a master's degree in the doctrine of needing more self-worth? Dear friends, beware of psychology!

Prayer: Lord, we see Paul's warning to Timothy, *"Have nothing to do with them,"* (2 Timothy 3:5b). Lord, give us the wisdom to see our current evils so that we can flee from them and to You! Help us fully believe the wisdom of Jesus who said, *"deny yourself, take up your cross and follow Me."* In Jesus' name we pray. Amen.

December 15

"But as for you, continue in what you have learned and have become convinced of, because you know those from whom you learned it, and how from infancy you have known the holy Scriptures, which are able to make you wise for salvation through faith in Christ Jesus."
2 Timothy 3:14-15

Timothy, continues in the faith

Our text and the context, are the dying words of Paul to Timothy, his son in the faith. Paul knows that any day evil Nero will put him to death. Paul knows the world is falling apart, quickly going from bad to worse. Paul advises Timothy about problems in the *"last days."* Paul wants to be sure that his prized disciple responds well to what will soon happen. What great advice for those going off to college and to all of us!

"Continue in what you have learned and have become convinced of." As with Timothy, we too must hang on to how we have been brought up! We were taught the truth. Soon we will be blasted with competing voices trying to derail us from the truth! Non-stop noise on the T.V., radio and the Internet will pound us relentlessly to get our attention. People will dress, or be in a state of "undress," to catch our attention. Noise and distraction will assail us. Whom will we listen to?

We, along with Timothy, should listen to our godly mothers and grandmothers. Starting as a baby we were taught what was important! Never forget their advice. The Word of God guided them and they guided us in that same Word. Do not ignore that Word. The world will try to keep us so busy that we will not have the time to think about God. Satan will flood us with new and exciting electronic devices to try get our attention. Don't forget God! Listen to God. We all need clarity in the midst of confusion; peace in the midst of chaos. The world cannot give clarity or peace; only God can. Jesus said, *"I have told you these things, so that in Me you may have peace. In this world you will have trouble. But take heart! I have overcome the world,"* John 16:33.

Prayer: Lord, You are the Way, the Truth and the Life! In these times of confusion, fill us with Your presence! For You will never leave us, forsake us, or lead us astray. We are so thankful that You are our Good Shepherd. In Jesus' name we pray. Amen.

December 16

"Alexander the coppersmith did me much harm. May the Lord repay him according to his works. You also must be aware of him, for he has greatly resisted our words." 2 Timothy 4:14-15 NKJV

Alexander, the apostate coppersmith

This Alexander must have at some time wanted to follow Christ. He surely considered himself a Christian. He had some head knowledge about the Christian religion, but his actions showed that his heart was bitter! In the end, his energies were spent in trying to upstage Paul! This clearly shows that he was jealous of Paul's success as a speaker. He coveted this kind of praise for himself! He was there when Paul spoke. Alexander proudly criticized Paul, seeking attention and his own audience. <u>He feared the people would like Paul more than him</u>. The apostle Paul on the other hand wanted the people to love Jesus!

What kind of spirit is in a person like Alexander, who was so self-seeking? Was it the Spirit of God, or was it the spirit of another? By their fruit you will know them! Alexander's bitterness to Paul and to the Gospel Paul was preaching, pointed to his master! God had Paul write about Alexander to educate us, not only about others, but to examine our own personal motives for doing what we do!

Disciple James was not fooled by Alexander's behavior either! *"If you harbor bitter envy and selfish ambition in your hearts, do not boast about it or deny the truth. Such 'wisdom' does not come down from Heaven but is earthly, unspiritual, <u>of the devil</u>,"* James 3:14-15.

We need to be careful! If we should disagree with the preached Word, we should pray about it and search the Scriptures! If after a few days, we still think there is a serious error, we should say something to the speaker. Then, our words must be gentle, and in private. An argument in church, or right after a message, may be doctrinally right, but if we do it in a loud and angry way, we are still very wrong! Alexander was both doctrinally wrong and sinfully angry!

Prayer: Lord, how lovingly You warn us through the life of Alexander. This wicked man was in the church, trying to stop the church. He was like a Judas to Paul. May we never copy him. Forgive us when we have. In Jesus' name we pray. Amen.

December 17

"To the pure, all things are pure, but to those who are corrupted and do not believe, nothing is pure. In fact, both their minds and their consciences are corrupted. They claim to know God, but by their actions they deny Him. They are detestable, disobedient and unfit for doing anything good." Titus 1:15-16

Titus, the one who faced "church problems"

In Paul's day, there were too many bold and pushy "leaders," demanding to have their own way. When confronted, they get angry. Well, Paul here commissions Titus to confront this evil in the church. Paul knew, sound doctrine and good character go together! Paul knew both were necessary qualifications to hold any church office!

"Since an overseer (a minister who is a teaching elder) *is entrusted with God's work, he must be blameless — not overbearing, not quick-tempered,"* Titus 1:7a. A leader in the church who is "overbearing" or "quick-tempered" is unqualified, regardless of their education! These are not gracious responses to God for His saving grace. Nor is it gracious to others! In fact, they are the opposite. Paul says that a leader must be *"self-controlled, upright, holy and disciplined,"* Titus 1:8b.

Jesus was the model of grace! For a good reason, Paul's letters begin, *"Grace and peace from God the Father and Christ Jesus our Savior,"* Titus 1:4b. Grace must be visible and increasingly so in each of us! If the grace of God is really in us, then it must come out of us by how we live and treat others. Paul is saying that if we really believe in the beautiful doctrines of grace, then the grace of God will show!

Satan knows in his head everything about the grace of God, but it's never part of his character! God keeps pounding on this subject to make sure we get it! The loving grace of Jesus must show! Love is patient, love is kind, love does not envy, love does not boast, love is not proud, love is not rude. *"The grace of God that brings salvation... teaches us to say 'No' to ungodliness and worldly passions, and to live self-controlled, upright and godly lives in this present age,"* Titus 2:11-12.

Prayer: Lord, may we model Your grace in how we live! May Your beautiful grace govern in our homes and churches! May Your grace in us, lead others to You! In Jesus' name we pray. Amen.

December 18

"I appeal to you on the basis of love. I then, as Paul – an old man and now also a prisoner of Christ Jesus – I appeal to you for my son Onesimus, who became my son while I was in chains." Philemon 9-10

Onesimus, a slave who stole and ran

Some are in chains. Others are free. Paul, who is presently in chains, writes to a brother called Philemon. It seems he is a pastor type with a small house church. Paul's main concern is about a slave of Philemon, named Onesimus. He apparently stole something from Philemon and ran away. Onesimus has now become a disciple of Jesus Christ through the ministry of Paul, while Paul is in prison.

Paul is sending Onesimus back to Philemon. Paul is strongly requesting Philemon to forgive Onesimus, and more than that to receive him as a brother in Christ, not as a runaway slave. The law would allow Philemon to maim or kill Onesimus for stealing and running! Yet forgiveness (not law) is an act of love that God graciously gives to us through Jesus Christ. Forgiveness is also the number one act of love we are called to give to others, instead of giving them what they deserve! Forgiveness is the opposite of being angry and bitter! So Paul is pleading with Philemon to give Onesimus what he needs, not what he deserves!

Don't miss how Paul's letter to Philemon begins! *"Grace to you and peace from God our Father and the Lord Jesus Christ."* Don't miss how Paul ends his letter in verse 25, *"The grace of the Lord Jesus Christ be with your spirit."* This ending is a one verse summary for all of us! And in the middle of the letter, Paul is asking Philemon to forgive Onesimus on the basis of grace not law. What a huge point for us!

Philemon is being taught that grace specifically means not to ask Onesimus to do something before forgiving him! Because if we do, that is not forgiveness. That's why Paul adds, *"If he has done you any wrong or owes you anything, charge it to me."* Paul is showing Philemon, what Jesus did for him personally. May we also forgive Biblically!

Prayer: Lord, You tested Philemon's faith here in the area of forgiveness. You also test us! Help us on the basis of grace to be kind and compassionate to one another, forgiving each other, just as in Christ You forgave us. In Jesus' name we pray. Amen.

December 19

"Let us not give up meeting together, as some are in the habit of doing, but let us encourage one another - and all the more as you see the Day approaching." Hebrews 10:25

"Us" must go to church!

Sabbath observance was a problem in the Old Testament. Isaiah warned "*Us*" about doing our pleasure on the Sabbath instead of God's pleasure. Still today, so many of "*Us*" think we can be a healthy Christian without going to church regularly. We give the excuse, "There are so many hypocrites in church." True, but if we try that argument on God on Judgment Day, it will not matter how others lived! Some in protest change churches quite regularly. But what difference does it make which church we stay home from?

Someone once wrote a letter to the editor of a newspaper complaining, "It makes no sense to go to church every Sunday. I've gone for 30 years now. I've heard over 3000 sermons. But, I can't remember a single one of them. So, I think I'm wasting my time and the pastors are wasting theirs by giving sermons." This started a real controversy in the "Letters to the Editor," section in the newspaper. It went on for weeks until someone wrote these beautiful words:

"I've been married for 30 years now. In that time my wife has cooked 32,000 meals. But, I cannot recall the entire menu for a single one of those meals. But I do know this. They all nourished me and gave me the strength I needed to do my work. If my wife had not given me these meals, I would be physically dead today. Likewise, if I had not gone to church for nourishment, I would be spiritually dead today!"

Go to church! When we are DOWN to nothing, God is UP to something! Let us find out what it is! Our faith will see the invisible, believe the incredible and receive the impossible! Thank God for our physical and our spiritual nourishment! How He fills "*Us*."

Prayer: Lord, You clearly tell us not to forsake "*meeting together, as some are in the habit of doing.*" Lord, You put "*Us*" here on this Earth to worship You. May our spiritual engines also be recharged on Sunday and on every day for Your honor and for our good. In Jesus' name we pray. Amen.

December 20

"James, a servant of God and of the Lord Jesus Christ, to the twelve tribes scattered among the nations. Consider it pure joy, my brothers, whenever you face trials of many kinds, because you know that the testing of your faith develops perseverance. Perseverance must finish its perfect work so that you may be mature and complete, not lacking anything." James 1:2-4

James, teaches us practical Christianity

James is a son of Joseph and Mary, a brother of Jesus Christ. Can you imagine what he saw in his lifetime? He watched Jesus grow into manhood. More than anyone, he knew how Jesus lived and it left a lasting impression. Most of the other disciples, finally believed in Jesus when they witnessed His resurrection. Now that Jesus is gone and ascended into Heaven, James wants his brothers and sisters in Christ to be an effective witness about Him. So after a short greeting, James launches right into teaching practical Christianity.

James sees that the "scattered" brothers and sisters are going through serious trials for their Christian faith. He knows how important it is for believers to understand the purpose of their trials, so that they might have a "right attitude." So James begins, *"Consider it pure joy, my brothers, whenever you face trials of many kinds."* The attitude of Christians in their trials determines whether they will be good witnesses of the faith or poor ones! James encourages us in our time of *"testing"* to not give up and to learn patience from it.

Do you think James grew up being a bit impatient? Do you think James knew first hand that he had to go though some serious testing, for God to form a mature faith in him? I do believe it! That is exactly why James wants us not to be bitter and angry as a response to any trial, big or small. James knew that God had to test him a lot to refine him to act more like his older brother Jesus! And so will we be tested!

Prayer: Lord, we thank You for James, the brother of Jesus! What wisdom he learned as he watched Your Son grow up. He believed because of what he saw in Jesus. And now he encourages us to show others what a believer looks like to encourage them to follow Christ. Thank You Lord. In Jesus' name we pray. Amen.

December 21

"With the tongue we praise our Lord and Father, and with it we curse men, who have been made in God's likeness. Out of the same mouth come praise and cursing. My brothers, this should not be."
James 3:9-10

James teaches us to act like Jesus

We might think that James was related to Solomon as well as being Jesus little brother. He writes about living wisely. He also writes much about doing good works. So much so, that a reader might be tempted to think that James believed we could enter Heaven by our good works. But that is not what James believed. James knew that salvation was by grace alone, by Christ alone and by faith alone.

James had a passion for Christians to look like Christians. He saw too many hypocrites, who claimed to be followers of Christ, but openly lived for the devil. They copied Satan's way of living not Jesus' way. So James teaches that if we are a true believer we will have fruits. We will have many good works that show evidence of a changed heart! Let us look into the heart of James and see some concerns he had.

James said that a Christian's living faith changes them to be *"quick to listen, slow to speak and slow to become angry."* In other words those who have a wild tongue have a religion that is worthless. On the other hand, James says, *"Religion that God our Father accepts as pure and faultless is this: to look after orphans and widows in their distress and to keep oneself from being polluted by the world,"* James 1:27. We are to live a pure life in an impure world.

Another major point James makes is that a person who has a real faith will get rid of bitterness and replace it. *"Such wisdom* (he says) *does not come down from Heaven but is earthly, unspiritual, of the devil,"* James 3:15. Displaying forgiveness instead of bitterness was his big Brother's way of responding to people who tried to hurt Him. Jesus' response left a lasting impression on James. As we can easily see, a faith that saves produces works that show!

Prayer: Lord, we thank You for placing James in the same family as Jesus, to observe how He lived His whole life. Strengthen us to act like Your adopted children. In Jesus' name we pray. Amen.

December 22

"Peter, an apostle of Jesus Christ, to the pilgrims of the Dispersion in Pontus, Galatia, Cappadocia, Asia, and Bithynia, elect according to the foreknowledge of God the Father, in sanctification of the Spirit, for obedience and sprinkling of the blood of Jesus Christ: Grace to you and peace be multiplied." 1 Peter 1:1-2 NKJV

Pilgrims, visitors on Earth

Christians are pilgrims! We are both residents and foreigners at the same time. We are resident-aliens. We need to be reminded of this. For if we live like a resident alone we have a problem. If we live like an alien alone, we have a problem. Either extreme is not the Christian life.

A resident Christian lives like he or she will always be here on this earth. We build our castle and add so many other possessions. We act like they are permanent structures. We are in love with a world that perishes! An alien Christian lives with no care for this world, no care for others. They go into a cave to get holy. So heavenly-minded, they are no earthly good!

We are called to be a resident and an alien, which is a pilgrim. Abraham was a great pilgrim! He built altars and he pitched tents. One was permanent. One was temporary. A resident-alien understands balance, and lives that way. Abraham, *"was looking forward to the city with foundations, whose architect and builder is God,"* Hebrews 11:10. A pilgrim's permanent home is in Heaven!

We are called to be pilgrims! Paul said, we *"are the called according to His purpose,"* Romans 8:28b NKJV. That is what elect is. Not all are called! Those that are, have a destination and a God-given reason for living! Jesus said, *"You are not of the world, but I chose you out of the world, therefore the world hates you,"* John 15:19b NKJV. However, Jesus wants us in the world; He calls us to be salt and light. Salt makes things taste good. Be a good taste to others. Light penetrates the darkness. We must tell others about the Light of the world, which is Jesus.

Prayer: Lord, You give us a name of Christian, that others do not have. You give us a purpose that is eternally significant. You give us a future, a permanent home with You! May we live like Your children. In Jesus' name we pray. Amen.

December 23

"You are a chosen people, a royal priesthood, a holy nation, a people belonging to God, that you may declare the praises of Him who called you out of darkness into His wonderful light." 1 Peter 2:9

Peter's profound praises

Peter learned from his intimate relationship with the Lord. At first, Peter knew the Lord, but Peter didn't know the joy of the Lord which is a greater maturity! Peter did finally learned to rejoice!

Peter rejoiced in his new birth, a new living hope that was forever guaranteed. Listen to Peter's testimony! *"Praise be to the God and Father of our Lord Jesus Christ! In His great mercy He has given us new birth into a living hope through the resurrection of Jesus Christ from the dead, and into <u>an inheritance that can never perish, spoil or fade – kept in Heaven for you</u>, who through faith are <u>shielded by God's power</u> until the coming of the salvation that is ready to be revealed in the last time,"* 1 Peter 1:3-5. As Christians we can still focus on the wrong things! We can meditate on the things that we don't have, and try to find our joy in possessions and other people before finding it in God. Peter did this too, <u>until</u> Christ opened his eyes to the real truth, as underlined above! Peter finally learned to spend his time and energy on eternal things that lasted forever, instead of on earthly pleasures that quickly faded away!

Peter rejoiced when he learned that his present trials were actually a blessing. *"In this you greatly rejoice, though now for a little while you may have had to suffer grief in all kinds of trials. These have come so that your faith – of greater worth than gold, which perishes even though refined by fire – may be proved genuine and may result in praise, glory and honor when Jesus Christ is revealed,"* 1 Peter 1:6-7. Peter rejoiced that God was the author and perfector of his faith! He saw the gold that people worked for and thought, "If only you realized that your faith is worth a thousand times more than that gold!"

Peter rejoiced because he had the privilege of telling others the truth about life! We too are saved to serve, <u>with joy</u>!

Prayer: Lord, we have so little joy because we still serve self, more than we serve You and Your eternal kingdom. Change us Lord. Teach us real joy like You did to Peter! In Jesus' name we pray. Amen.

December 24

"You have spent enough time in the past doing what pagans choose to do – living in debauchery, lust, drunkenness, orgies, carousing and detestable idolatry." 1 Peter 4:3

Pagans choose drunkenness

In the past month, four drunken men near us in Chennai, suddenly died. They were still young! What a waste of a God-given life. A waste because our text shows they lived like pagans and died pagans. Some of these men even went to church, but none had God in their hearts. What any of them knew about Jesus and Bible will only add to their condemnation, for they did not repent! Paul says, *"I warn you, as I did before, that those who live like this will not inherit the kingdom of God,"* Galatians 5:21b. O that God would convict those with a drinking problem that *"drunkenness"* is a highway to Hell, not a road to paradise!

"Drunkenness" in the Bible is one of the ultimate examples of self-seeking, of doing what the flesh wants. Paul said, *"do not think about how to gratify the desires of the sinful nature,"* Romans 13:14b. You may say, "What is wrong with a few drinks?" <u>What a drinking person does is one thing. What they are not doing is quite another!</u> What are those so interested in drinking doing? *"They think it strange that you do not plunge with them into the same flood of dissipation, and they heap abuse on you,"* 1 Peter 4:4. Their "party spirit," their misdirected zeal, works overtime to pull others away to live like them. What they are not doing, is feeding their soul, their spiritual nature, or the spiritual nature of others! Where is their zeal for evangelism?

The four who just died thought they were having a good social time! They very likely ended up in Hell where there is no social life ever! After all, *"they will have to give account to Him who is ready to judge the living and the dead,"* 1 Peter 4:5. Drunkenness does work to push one out of life's frying pan! But the problem is, it is into the fire. God's concern is that we are prepared for eternity!

Prayer: Lord, in 1 Peter 4:7, You further warn us. *"The end of all things is near. Therefore be clear minded and self-controlled so that you can pray."* Lord, forgive us of our selfish sins! Draw us away from sin and to Yourself! In Jesus' name we pray. Amen.

December 25

"Each one should use whatever gift he has received to serve others, faithfully administering God's grace in its various forms." 1 Peter 4:10

Peter and Paul speaking on spiritual gifts

Peter is touching on a most important subject here! When a person becomes a Christian, *"each one"*... *"has received"* a spiritual gift from God. Our Lord now demands to use us in His service, in some way! God has designed us to be His ambassador to others! Peter says we *"should use whatever gift"* we have, to *"serve others, faithfully administering God's grace in its various forms."* In the next verse, Peter mentions the gifts of *"speaking"* and *"serving"* that God gives to believers.

Paul also writes on the same subject. *"Now about spiritual gifts, brothers, I do not want you to be ignorant,"* 1 Corinthians 12:1. Paul is more specific on the *"different kinds of gifts."* He lists service gifts, working gifts, speaking gifts, teaching gifts, tongues/language gifts. Notice, *"all these are the work of one and the same Spirit, and He gives them to each one, just as He determines,"* 1 Corinthians 12:11. God *"determines"* what gift/gifts we get! We don't go shopping for one! Our gift is given by the Holy Spirit, *"for the common good,"* says Paul. Or, *"to serve others,"* says Peter. There is way too much ignorance and bad teaching on these points! Our gift is not to build us up, it is to build others up! It is to build God's church!

What is our gift? If we do not know, then we must start serving others with our life! When we *"serve others"* in various ways, they will tell us how we are a blessing to them! We can look at our own physical body to understand this. We have eyes, ears, fingers and toes. They all exist to be a blessing to our body! If the members of our body do not serve us, our body will quickly die! So too, the body of the Lord needs us! It needs its members to serve one another and build each other up. *"Each one"* has a different gift to make it a healthy body! Serve, and God will bless His body and us too!

Prayer: Lord, You make it simple so we can understand. We thank You for using us to help build Your church. May Your kingdom come! In Jesus' name we pray. Amen.

December 26

"If we claim to be without sin, we deceive ourselves and the truth is not in us. If we confess our sins, He is faithful and just and will forgive us our sins and purify us from all unrighteousness." 1 John 1:8-9

John writes on assurance of salvation

Many people were not really sure if they had salvation, or they had lost the joy of their salvation. So John writes to all Christians to help us understand our problem. John wanted to make our joy complete. He tells us in verse five that he has a message for us from Jesus. First, we so quickly stray from the basics of Christianity, mainly the identification and confession of sin in our lives. Second, we need to stop listening to the many false teachers that are out there. What relevant topics these are for us yet today!

Jesus is both light and purity. He is the perfect solution for us who walk in darkness, with so little joy and so little assurance of salvation. We must all stop walking in darkness. We must all compare the life we are living to the Word of God, and then we will have a holy conviction of sin. Then when we confess our sin, we will be joyful and assured of our salvation! False teachers try to convince us that a certain life-style is not sinful! There are literally false teachers are among our friends, co-workers and on the T.V. They often try to tell us nothing is sin!

When I am able to help people who lack assurance of salvation and a closer walk with God, I ask them to look at the love chapter, in I Corinthians 13:4-8. I ask them, "How have you not been '*patient*' this past week? How have you not been '*kind*' to others. Who have you '*envied*'? What have you '*boasted*' about? In what ways have you been '*proud*'? When were you '*easily angered*'? Have you kept a '*record of wrongs*' that others have done to you?" According to God, these are the kinds of sins we must confess!

When we specifically confess these to God and ask for His forgiveness, we will be forgiven and will grow in grace! When we do, the Holy Spirit fills us with joy and assurance of salvation!

Prayer: Lord, how quickly we stray from the basics of Christianity and then wonder what is wrong! Lord, forgive us and heal us. We want to live for You. In Jesus' name we pray. Amen.

"Diotrephes, who loves to be first, will have nothing to do with us. So if I come, I will call attention to what he is doing, gossiping maliciously about us. Not satisfied with that, he refuses to welcome the brothers. He also stops those who want to do so and puts them out of the church."
3 John 9b-10

Diotrephes, the super selfish one

Diotrephes is not a hero of the faith! He is instead, a super selfish Gospel stopper! He was a bully leader in the church who greatly abused his power. He was a control freak. Things had to go his way or it was the highway for those who disagreed. This man did more to hurt the spread of the Gospel than to help it. Sad to say there are many in the church today like this man and they are unaware of their great faults.

Diotrephes did not allow others to speak or have any authority in the church. He was extremely jealous. He demanded to do "ministry" alone! If there was another "brother" that had a spiritual gift he would quickly recognize them, but only to push them out of his way and out of the church! Perhaps we can think of a person like this. If we look anything like Diotrephes, we need to change!

Do we know what Diotrephes' main failure was? Of course he failed at real Biblical love which is God first and others after that. He also failed at discipleship! And this is what the church is called to do! It is a main responsibility of a church leader to equip others for the work of ministry! Discipleship is also the job of every school teacher, every parent and every boss in the workplace. If we fail at discipleship, we fail at life itself! A pastor in Andra Pradesh came to me and said, "I have 4 churches and I am so busy that I am burned out from the stress!" I asked him, "Isn't there even one young man in the church that is gifted to help you teach?" To that he said, "Then what would I do?" This pastor had no idea what discipleship was. He loved to be first!

Prayer: Lord, what a serious problem we have. How we fail greatly when we fail in the discipleship process! Forgive us, Lord. May we teach others to follow the examples of the perfect Jesus, not us sinners! In Jesus' name we pray. Amen.

December 28

"Dreamers pollute their own bodies, reject authority and slander celestial beings." Jude 8b

Jude warns, don't pollute your body and soul

Jude is the brother of Jesus and James. He believed fully in Jesus after His resurrection! Jude admits he really wanted to write about salvation in Jesus, but pressing problems <u>inside the church</u> needed to be addressed quickly! Jude sounds an alarm to do what an alarm is supposed to do, wake us up. He brings a serious warning in just a few short verses. Jude saw *"dreamers,"* those who were trying to create their own reality. *"Dreamers"* because this is God's world, not ours. He has already established what is true. Jude says their problem is that they *"reject authority,"* they *"pollute their bodies"* and *"speak abusively against whatever they do not understand."*

We ***"reject authority"*** when we say, "I'm going to 'do life' my own way." That may sound like freedom to us, but it is a one way ticket to Hell. I don't even like to say that "H" word because it is so horrible! Hell is not just misery, it's misery forever, unrelenting misery! That's not freedom! And it's people in the church who Jude is talking to! *"Woe to them! They have taken the way of Cain,"* Jude 11a. God's rules don't rob us of life, they give us life! Hear Jude's smoke alarm that is going off. If this is not our problem, then we must lovingly warn those whom it fits.

We ***"pollute their bodies."*** Piercings, tattoos, eating too much, perverted or adulterous sexual activity, drinking too much, these all show a rejection of God's authority. We pollute our bodies when self-pleasure and peer-pressure is more important to us than God's wisdom! This shows we have so little fear of God. Our bodies are temples of God and as such they belong to Him. We can't desecrate the temple of God and then claim to worship Him! When we pollute our bodies, we have a major relationship problem with God! An emergency siren is going off, do we hear it? *"Do not be like Cain who belonged to the evil one,"* I John 3:12a.

Prayer: Lord, may we hear the warning siren going off for precious souls in the church body. Lord, save us from the storm that is threatening our life. In Jesus' name we pray. Amen.

December 29

"Dear friends, build yourselves up in your most holy faith and pray in the Holy Spirit. Keep yourselves in God's love as you wait for the mercy of our Lord Jesus Christ to bring you to eternal life." Jude 20-21

Jude encourages us to build up our faith

Jude understands the process of repentance, whereby we must put off the old habits, replace them by putting on God's way of living. For this reason Jude begins by teaching us that the habits that were "polluting" us, had to be put off. We have to see our sin as God does. We have to accept His worldview! We must confess our own way of living for what it is: sin. Then we will receive God's cleansing! For we must spiritually take a bath and remove the dirt, before we put new clean clothes on. Now to complete the change process, we must concentrate on what we are going to wear.

"Build yourselves up in your most holy faith." Plan how and when we will get more serious about learning the Word of God and doing His will. Study the Word of God privately and in groups. Make friends with those who are friends of God! Get involved in the life of the church.

"Pray in the Holy Spirit." Communicate with God! He delights to hear our prayers. *"Do not be anxious about anything, but in everything, by prayer and petition, with thanksgiving, present your requests to God. And the peace of God, which transcends all understanding, will guard your hearts and your minds in Christ Jesus,"* Philippians 4:6-7.

"Keep yourselves in God's love." We defeat Satan and his schemes by living close to God. May we never see how close we can get to sin but how close we can get to God! *"Wait for the mercy of our Lord Jesus Christ."* Stay hungry for the mercy of God! Never think we can earn the Christian life, or live it on our own. Stay dependent on God.

And finally, *"snatch others from the fire and save them,"* Jude 23a. People are hanging over a hot fire by a weak thread. Rescue them. Tell others about the mercy of God. It is amazing how God refreshes us when we do just that.

Prayer: Lord, we thank You for teaching us through the pen of Jude. Lord, we love You and want to love You more. May Your Spirit move us closer to You! In Jesus' name we pray. Amen.

December 30

"To Him who is able to keep you from falling and to present you before His glorious presence without fault and with great joy – to the only God our Savior be glory, majesty, power and authority, through Jesus Christ our Lord, before all ages, now and forevermore! Amen."
Jude 24-25

Jude's doxology and benediction

This doxology of Jude is a fitting way to end this book. Doxology in the Greek means, "glory to God." It is also a fitting ending to a time of worship. Paul ended every letter with a short doxology with a benediction added. Normally the pastor raises his hands at the end of worship and gives glory to God then blesses the people. This is God's blessing! Why do we do this? God told us to. Why? God wants to bless us! And God wants us to be reminded of that!

The first "blessing" is recorded by Moses. *"And the Lord spoke to Moses saying, 'Speak to Aaron and his sons, saying: "This is the way you shall bless the children of Israel. Say to them: 'The Lord bless you and keep you; the Lord make His face shine upon you, and be gracious to you; the Lord lift up His countenance upon you, and give you peace,'"''* Numbers 6:22-26 NKJV. This is a threefold, divinely inspired blessing! The words, *"The Lord..."* is repeated three times. God in Trinity is personally blessing us! And He will do it!

We must never say, "I didn't <u>get</u> much out of a worship service." We went to church to <u>give</u> glory to God. That is what worship is. So let us give glory to God and hear and see His sure blessing upon us. The benediction alone is a great blessing!

Do we not give a friendly good-bye and a wave when someone leaves our company? Where did this practice came from? Most likely, "God by" somehow became good-bye. It is fitting. We want our loved ones to be blessed and real blessings come from God. So, may the Lord bless you! "God by"!

Prayer: Lord, how gracious of You to bless us again and again. When we see the pastor's hands raised in blessing, may we be reminded that You want to bless us and will bless us. Lord, may Your name be glorified. In Jesus' name we pray. Amen.

December 31

"The revelation of Jesus Christ, which God gave Him to show His servants what must soon take place. He made it known by sending His angel to His servant John, who testifies to everything he saw — that is, the Word of God and the testimony of Jesus Christ. Blessed is the one who reads the words of this prophesy and blessed are those who hear it and take to heart what is written in it, because the time is near."
Revelation 1:1-3

John, to whom the end was revealed

John was Jesus' beloved disciple. At the end of John's life he was banned to the island of Patmos, a strip of land a few miles long and wide. This was a piece of rock with no trees, a nasty place. All who were sent there were not "politically correct." It was Rome's version of Siberia. Here John wrote the book of Revelation.

John had seen it all. He walked with Jesus, saw His miracles and witnessed His crucifixion. He outran Peter to see the empty tomb and was there for Jesus' ascension. John knew that Jesus was the Messiah and he wants us to know Him too. John begins his letter called "Revelation" with the words of our text.

The book of Revelation was not written to solve some puzzle about when Jesus will return! It is to remind us that <u>Jesus is coming again</u>! *"Behold, He is coming with clouds, and every eye will see Him,"* Revelation 1:7a NKJV. Jesus will not come this second time as a tender Shepherd. The leading of people to Himself will be finished! There will be no more opportunities to be saved by His blood! <u>Jesus is coming again as the Lion of Judah. He is coming to reward those who are His children and to punish those who are not</u>!

A small boy said the meaning of Revelation was, "Jesus wins, Satan loses!" Excellent! So then, may we follow Jesus who will lead us to Heaven, not Satan who will lead us to Hell. We must never forget, we are all born sinners and need to be transformed. We can't live like Hell and still go to Heaven! We must search for that closer walk with God and treasure it! His love is eternal! May God bless us all!

Prayer: Lord, in Your name, in the name of the Father, the Son and the Holy Spirit please bless us! We need You! In Jesus' name we pray. Amen.

A 1st yearly devotional, entitled
"Bind Them Upon Your Heart Forever,"
has been useful for many families.

A 2nd yearly devotional is titled,
"Guard Your Heart,
For it is the Wellspring of Life."
It has also been a favorite of many.